W9-ACL-470

CERVANTES
The Man and the Genius

CERVANTES

The Man and the Genius

by Francisco Navarro Ledesma

Translated and revised by
Don and Gabriela Bliss

CHARTERHOUSE New York

CERVANTES: THE MAN AND THE GENIUS

LIBRARY OF CONGRESS CATALOG CARD NUMBER: 72-84220

MANUFACTURED IN THE UNITED STATES OF AMERICA

Contents

Foreword

Between a nineteenth century dedicated to the study of Don Quixote by a chain of scholars and philologists and a twentieth century in which Cervantes' masterpiece is commented upon by another chain of writers more observant of its meaning than of its mere text, a young man leapt to fame by devoting a book not to the Knight of the Doleful Countenance but to his creator. No mean achievement. For his book was by no means the first life of Cervantes that saw the light; and he himself was no one in particular, just a "writer" who dispersed his powers over a varied field of subjects and who published his ephemeral work in newspapers and magazines of little more duration than autumn leaves.

His name was Francisco Navarro Ledesma, and he was born in Toledo, which amounts to saying that he was a countryman of Don Quixote and a next door neighbor of Cervantes himself; for Toledo is the gate of both Extremaduras, the better known as such, to the southwest where so many conquistadors came from, but also the southeastern one known as La Mancha, whence was to come in due time the greatest conquistador of all of them, who was to conquer the whole earth; while Cervantes was born in Alcalá de Henares, near Madrid, a small but illustrious city that "belonged" to the Archbishop of Toledo.

This old city, rising on a proud hill girded by a loop of the Tagus, has a soul of steel. The best steel of Spain used to be tempered there, and no treasure was more prized by a soldier who knew his job than a Toledo blade. The shape, the color, the design of the city seem all to have been dictated by the color, the elasticity, the curves and sharpness of steel blades; and it was there that the best blades of the intellect—Moorish, Jewish, Christian—used to meet in order to transfer to the West the knowledge and the wisdom of the Ancients and of the East.

All this tradition, two-edged, arms and letters, which one meets in Don Quixote's mind throughout Cervantes' book, as one does in the mind of Cortés, the Conqueror of Mexico, lived in the mind of the young man who, born in 1869, was before the end of the century a doctor of philosophy and letters and the head of the Toledo Gallery. A fall, an injury to a leg, a clot of blood, killed him in his thirty-sixth year. In this short life he had managed to enter into a regular correspondence with many of the best minds of Spain and of France, in particular with José Ortega and with Unamuno, the two most brilliant commentators on Don Quixote in our day, as well as with Maurice Barrès, the brilliant commentator on Toledo.

When his book came out, in the year of his death, it was an instant success, indeed a revelation. Navarro Ledesma had written a "Life" in a style no one had thought of before. Held, no doubt, by the inhibitions of strict scholarship, what is now often described (rather foolishly, I do believe) as *scientific history,* every biographer had endeavored to keep rigorously to the scope provided for, *proven,* established by his little slips of notes. The young Toledan had too much steel in his being and bones to confine himself to that. He saw to it that his protagonist was adequately surrounded by other "agonists," by their setting, their background, their seas, and their skies. If in the process it was necessary to appeal to one's imagination, well, why not?—provided one kept it well disciplined within an armor of facts.

The outcome of it all was a Cervantes who, for the first time, was truly alive. And that was the true reason of the book's success. This does not mean to say it was perfect. Ortega found some chapters obscure and profuse with ill-assorted facts, a defect due in part to the very wealth of the subject, in part to the usual hurry of the usual publisher. The translators have all but eliminated this aspect of the Spanish original by a judicious redistribution of the material at their disposal.

One could hardly reproach Navarro Ledesma for not having seen his model in a light other than of his day. We would not judge Charles V today quite as harshly as he does; nor would we be ready as he is to accept Cervantes as a Marian poet; and as to Cervantes' strictures against the Jews, we would be the more inclined to take them as camouflage for the fact that the case for considering Cervantes as a *converso* is very strong.

The chances are good that this translation may meet in the English-speaking world with as much success as the original did in Spain in 1905. Interest in Cervantes was always strong in the United States and in England, whose scholars were in fact pioneers in the study of Don Quixote; and as Navarro Ledesma pointed out, the first model for Don Quixote was Cervantes himself. But in this connection I should add yet another remark. For reasons it would take me too long to develop, I believe that while the Spanish-speaking world is fast becoming a land of Hamlets, there are a growing number of Don Quixotes in the Anglo-Saxon world where Sanchos used to wax prosperous.

SALVADOR DE MADARIAGA

Two Words to the Reader

Reader, if you are a Cervantist by trade or erudite by profession, I advise you not to read this work, in which there is nothing for you to learn, or almost nothing. But if it is enough for you to love Cervantes and your country deeply and without any compromising "isms," I invite you to read it, sure that the events will interest you though you may not like the way I have recounted them according to my humble capacities. The poem of the life of Cervantes demands to be sung by a great poet and not written by a poor journalist.

These narratives could be called "truth and poetry" if I have been able to bring out the poetry which emerges from the documents and shines brightly in the events uncovered by so many patient investigators who have in these latter times studied the life of Cervantes. But even though I have not achieved it, I trust that you, knowing that the truth is recounted in good faith, will garland it with the poetry that your love of Cervantes will inspire in you, which being your own, intimate, unspoken and free of literary flavor, will make you happy and satisfy your every desire.

The testimony on which this narrative is based, in which to my understanding there is nothing fanciful or even improbable, was published not so long ago by the distinguished man of letters Don Cristóbal Pérez Pastor, along with some very interesting material from the most praiseworthy Professor Don Julián Apraiz. Much of the information regarding the stay of Cervantes in Andalusia I owe to the remarkable generosity of my dear friend, the illustrious poet, critic and historian, Don Francisco Rodríguez Marín. May these famous names serve to validate the truth of the book, and I will hold myself as most happy if, by recounting it to you, I manage to bring to life in your spirit the love that all good Spaniards must feel for the Ingenious Hidalgo Miguel de Cervantes Saavedra.

F.N.L.

Editorial Note

Although incorporating research assembled over a considerable period, the text of this biography, originally entitled *El ingenioso hidalgo Miguel de Cervantes Saavedra,* was completed under pressure to meet a publishing deadline—the celebration in Madrid of the tercentenary on May 1, 1905 of the first appearance of the *Quixote* in print. In a letter to Navarro Ledesma, young José Ortega y Gasset, one of his fervent admirers, was therefore moved to combine his praise with friendly criticism to the effect that he found some chapters *touffus* (branched or bushy, i.e., in need of pruning). Navarro Ledesma's niece and her husband, in the course of producing this English language version of his work, have consequently ventured to do some of that pruning in the belief that he would have undertaken it himself if granted more time, but the deadline and his untimely death a few months later cut short any such possibility. On his behalf they have omitted passages not particularly relevant to the life story of Cervantes and have cleared up fortuitous inconsistencies and redundancies of the sort that often creep into work in progress and are completely eliminated only in a final draft.

Navarro Ledesma's work was not intended for the instruction of erudite "Cervantists," he tells us, and he did not plan it as a piece of formal scholarship. He cited no authorities, therefore, except for some general acknowledgments, although the working notes that have survived with his papers indicate that he consulted much of the available literature about Cervantes and sixteenth-century Spain and spent some time doing original research among the archives in Seville. He also felt no need to interlard his text with footnotes, since he was addressing a readership he took to be well versed in the history of Spain and its literature. For readers less familiar with that background we have provided our own informal footnotes designed to clarify allusions to matters that may be beyond the ken of any but specialists in sixteenth-century Spain.

In compiling these notes the translators have shrugged off the trappings of scholarship, as Navarro Ledesma did, and have endeavored only to answer the unspoken questions of American readers about the more important sixteenth-century Spaniards whose activities have some relevance to Cervantes' social, political and literary background. In the course of doing so they have satisfied themselves that Navarro Ledesma's account, imaginative as it is in some respects, has a solid basis in fact; he quotes or paraphrases the words of Cervantes himself; he writes only about real people, actual events recorded by history, and incidents documented in archives.

D.C.B.
G. de C. B.

Portrait

"He whom you see here of aquiline visage, of chestnut hair, of open and untroubled brow, of cheerful eyes and hooked though well-proportioned nose; his beard silver which only twenty years ago was gold, the moustaches big, the mouth small, the teeth not important, for he has but six and they are ill-conditioned and worse placed, having no correspondence one with another; the body between two extremes, neither large nor small; the color high, rather fair than dark; somewhat bent of shoulder and not very light of foot; . . . he is commonly called Miguel de Cervantes Saavedra; he was a soldier for many years, and for five and a half a captive, where he learned to have patience in adversity; in the naval battle of Lepanto he lost his left hand to a gunshot, a wound which, although it looks ugly, he holds as beautiful for having collected it on the most memorable and lofty occasion which past centuries have witnessed or those to come hope to see, fighting under the victorious banner of the son of the thunderbolt of war, Charles V of blessed memory."

[Prologue of *The Exemplary Novels*]

CHAPTER 1

State of the World—Christening—Father and Grandfather

IN the year 1547 it came to pass that the honest chirurgeon Rodrigo de Cervantes and his Christian lady Doña Leonor de Cortinas, residents of Alcalá de Henares[1] and dwellers in the Parish of Santa María, were blessed with a new offspring, thus repeating the blessings of 1544 and 1546. For the poor this fortuitous event, otherwise known as a divine blessing, consists mainly in bearing children without the means to rear and support them.

Autumn is a season of peace and calm everywhere, and more so in Alcalá, where the sun shines softly, the air is serene, and the many birds of the wheat country salute the sunrise and at sunset give a lovely concert in the poplars and acacias. The peasants rake the stubble, turn and cultivate the ploughed fields, never letting the rich soil rest. The market-gardeners of Alcalá break the crumbling earth, dressing the beds and clearing the ditches that water their garden-stuff. Along the smooth broad streets of the town go the creaking carts of the vintage, streaming Bacchic cheer from baskets dripping grape juice. The crack of the whip urges on the mules whose bells scandalize the academic gravity of the streets. From vineyard to winepress the sunburned grape-pickers are followed by a rout of rustic students dressed in earth-brown Aragonese kersey, some with swords, some without.

It is Sunday, and the scholastic crowd has spread over the country-side. Here one has climbed the hill of Los Santos de la Humosa, there another has pushed on to Anchuelo or Ajalvir where many of the poorer disciples of Minerva lodge, the paternal allowance being insufficient for living in the crowded and expensive university town. The dialecticians who study Aristotle's philosophy in the College of Santa Balbina have of course gone on a peripatetic expedition toward Camarna or Meco. The metaphysicians of the College of Santa Catalina make for the banks of the Jarama, there to try their patience, as all budding ontologists should, by casting their lines in hope of barbel or trout. The Thomists and Scholastics of the High College of Madre de Dios have put aside their quarrels and the shooting of theological cross-bows to spread nets together and trap the skylarks and groundlarks of the fields of Val. Finally the lighthearted humanists and grammarians of the College of San Ildefonso founded by Cardinal Cisneros,[2] having reached the famous vine country of Santorcas, return singing in chorus to the creaking of grape-laden carts the ancient hymn and macaronic salutation of the young university to that welcome and eternally youthful gift of wine:

Ave, color vini clari,
Ave, sapor sine pari
tua nos inebriari
digneris potencia[3]

or else another older and more popular refrain:

Gaudeamus igitur
juvenes dum sumus . . .[4]

the strophes of which resound simultaneously in Salamanca and Paris, in Heidelberg and Bologna.

In Alcalá de Henares that evening in 1547 is peaceful. There is no fear tonight of hearing the frightening cries of "Up the College" and "Up the City," as a result of which the streets of Alcalá were stained with blood not so long ago. The profound divisions that rent Spain during the *Comunidades* uprising[5] were reflected in the University by two parties: the *Cismontanos*, or dwellers on this side of the mountains, comprising students from Betica, Estremadura, Murcia, and La Mancha; and the *Ultramontanos*, enemies of the King, among whom were grouped those from Burgos, Valladolid, Avila, Toledo, and Segovia. Their quarrels have now ended. The heavy hand of Don Juan VIII Martínez Guijarro, Archbishop of Toledo, governs the city and keeps the University well within bounds. He is a sour and dogmatic man who spent a half-starved but vigorous and hard-working youth in the halls of the Sorbonne in Paris. A great theologian, a distinguished mathematician, and the first to hold the chair of Natural History at Salamanca, he later became tutor to Prince Philip, son of the Emperor Charles V, and well might such a dry and angular pupil come of this geometrical theologian and naturalist, one so full of pedantry withal that, his surname being Guijarro in plain language, he has to take on the Latin one of *Silíceo*.[6]

The city and University sense that the revolutionary times are over, the University has now mellowed, and with this mellowing faces are more cheerful, speech less angry. The eloquent words of the omniscient humanist Juan de Vergara of Toledo, who for many years instilled the wisdom of Solomon, of Jesus of Sirach and of Aristotle into Spanish minds, have been joined by the clear voice of Alfonso García Matamoros of Seville, for whom Latium had no secrets, a great writer and a great patriot, the first Spaniard to assert and demonstrate Spain's importance in all the arts and disciplines. The rotary press on which Arnoldo Guillermo de Brocar printed the *Polyglot Bible*[7] still rolls unceasingly day and night. Crossing the Calle de Libreros or the Calle de Escritorios there may perchance be seen a robust and sturdy personage, flowing of beard, with a great mane of hair and a sagacious eye; his name is Benito Arias Montano.[8]

After so many years of unbridled passion nations and rulers were longing for peace. Luther was dead. Charles V had enjoyed at Mühlberg[9] one of the greatest days to which a Caesar could aspire. The Diet had convened at Augusta, which today we call Augsburg. There the Roman theologians Sflug and Helding were working with the Protestant Agricola in search of a compromise, some decent arrangement by which to end the fratricidal struggle, at least temporarily. The Emperor also had gone to Augsburg, unbuckling his helmet with the red and white plumes, dropping his lance and alighting from the fleet trotter astride of which he was painted by Titian. His beard was already gray and his teeth yellowed; he has drawn on a semi-ecclesiastical bonnet and donned long doctoral robes. . . . But those who long to live in peace should never count on the Italians; the Fiesco conspiracy[10] had a tragic epilogue. The Dorias, Genoese protégés of the Emperor, in collusion with Fernando de Gonzaga, Viceroy of Sicily, had arranged for the murder of the Duke of Parma and Placenza, Pedro Luis de Farnese, son of Pope Paul III. The sovereign pontiff, Father of Christianity, burned with a desire for vengeance. Once more the Pope and Charles V were enemies. It would seem that the Most Christian Emperor had to spend his life at odds with the Vicar of Christ on Earth.

All this was soon known throughout Spain. In those days there were no newspapers but every man was a journalist—the merchant and the soldier, the vagabond of the underworld, the mendicant friar who roamed the countryside on foot. And with everything known in a form neither more nor less exaggerated than it is today, the ebb and flow of change and unexpected incident were no less sudden. Two great hidden treasures had just been disclosed to those seeking wider knowledge or hungering for action, two inexhaustible treasures undreamed of in the medieval imagination: the new world of free conscience revealed by the friar of Wittenberg, and the New World on the other side of the Atlantic discovered by the Genoese mariner. Neither Luther nor Columbus did more than open the door, but every day, then as now, it was given to all men to question the unknown.

Young but prematurely aged, Rodrigo de Cervantes walked through the Sabbath bustle of Alcalá on this Sunday in October, carrying a newborn child wrapped in a corner of his cloak. With head held high he wore the absentminded yet defiant look of the very deaf. He seemed to ignore the existence of half the things around him; he did not hear the jingle of the mule bells nor the clamor of the grape-pickers nor the singing of the students. He was accompanied by his friend Juan Pardo, godfather-to-be.

The sun glinted aslant the walls of the great mansions which form both sides of the Calle de Roma and lighted the door of the church toward which Rodrigo and Juan were walking. In those days the Church of Santa María la Mayor was not the redundant ogival embolism superimposed on another building that it is today. It was then the ancient hermitage of San Juan de los Caballeros, built in the middle of the thirteenth century and ornamented in the fourteenth and fifteenth centuries with elaborate works of stucco and stone, surely started by some skilled Moorish mason of Castile and carried on by who knows what German and Flemish decorators, disciples of the Copines or the Egas. Awaiting them there while being assisted into his robes by Sexton Baltasar Vázquez was the Reverend Bachelor Serrano,[11] priest of Santa María and a dear friend of Rodrigo de Cervantes, whose children Andrea and Luisa he had likewise baptized.

The ceremony was brief, as befitted a poor christening, but not so poor that a group of children were not waiting at the door of the church to stretch out begging hands. The religious ceremony over, Bachelor Serrano passed with the others to the sacristy, where Baltasar Vázquez wrote at his behest:

> Sunday nine days of the month of October in the Year of our Lord one thousand and five and forty and seven years was baptized miguel son of Rodrigo de cervantes and his wife doña leonor his godfathers juan pardo and he who baptized him the reverend serRano, priest of our Lady, attested by baltasar vazqz sexton and I who baptized him and sign my name
>
> The Bachelor
> serRano

The usual compliments were paid by the pastor to his parishioner, who accepted them with melancholy satisfaction like a man uncertain whether to thank Heaven for a favor or to demand compensation from the world. The crowd of children scattered, dissatisfied with the few small coins and a quartern of aniseeds preserved in sugar which Juan Pardo extracted from his pockets. According to custom, especially in the case of a parishioner who frequented the baptismal font so assiduously, the Reverend Serrano accompanied Rodrigo home to wish Doña Leonor joy.

The Cervantes family lived close to the church in a little low house[12] next to the orchard of the Capuchin friars, and there was certainly small comfort or luxury in the dwelling. The profession of chirurgeon has never yet made a man rich, and by reason of his deafness Rodrigo had not been able to study medicine, which, except for certain practical and experimental branches, was at that time taught almost entirely in terms of metaphysics. In all he had learned to bleed, to put a broken arm in splints, and to poultice and apply compresses under the direction of a physician. All the students and professors were cared for at the Hospital of San Lucas, outside the gate of Santiago and far from the intermittent agues emanating from the Henares. Rodrigo therefore had to live by bleeding, plastering, and poulticing the citizens of Alcalá, a sorry and far from lucrative employment in a healthy town where the only illnesses suffered were daily, tertian, and quartan agues, for which there is no need of even the best of surgeons.

The new Christian and those who accompanied him entered the humble home. Romping on the floor was a little girl of three, bright and of almost angelic beauty. She was called Andrea and was the eldest child of the married couple. The good lady Luisa de Contreras, her godmother and friend of the family, held in her arms another little girl not yet fourteen months old; this was Luisa, second of the Cervantes daughters. Licentiate Cristóbal Bermúdez, clergyman and godfather to little Luisa, displayed his reverend person in a monk's armchair. They all kissed the new baby and congratulated the mother in appropriate terms. The child soon fell asleep in the warmth of the maternal couch.

Now come to Cordova and to a low white house with a tiled doorway and a small shady patio where Licentiate Juan de Cervantes, on the eve of his sixties, works in his law office. It is a small whitewashed room with a barred window giving on the street. There is a blackened oak table with heavy legs joined by twisted iron crossbars. Parchment law folios are piled in two small cupboards whose ochre-painted doors seem to cry aloud, to be out of tune in the middle of the white wall. The room is exalted and semi-enriched by two or three ancient pictures painted on dark boards from which yellowing visages, an arm or a leg, emerge faintly from the surrounding patina. Between the pictures a small alcove lined in worn damask shelters a crucifix of antique fashion. The sunshine which enters through the bars illuminates nothing that is not austere and ponderous.

The Licentiate bends his aquiline countenance between two straw-colored pages of the Royal Statutes of Castile which he re-reads with the peevish attention of one following a daily routine. Later he takes the goose quill that rises from the inkstand of blue and white china, dips it and is about to pen something in his firm and aristocratic script.

Someone is calling at the door. The Licentiate hesitates. *"Deo gratias!"*[13] says a voice. "May they be rendered to God. Come in," the Licentiate replies. And there enters the carrier of Almodóvar, a man of La Mancha, round-faced, shaven, taciturn, with forelock clotted by dust and sweat, each eyebrow bearing a load of lint. "I bring," he says, "with Your Honor's permission, a letter for Your Honor. There is a real[14] due on it for porterage," he adds, seeing the perplexity of the Licentiate, who finally rises and rummages through the many small drawers of an old desk until he finds the money. "God guard Your Honor," the carrier takes his leave, repeating the compliment, for it would be unseemly to treat as merely "Sir" one who pays without saying a word, a rare thing to find in matters concerning the porterage of correspondence.

The Licentiate settles into his easy chair, looks at the envelope and recognizes the ostentatious yet somewhat wavering writing of his son Rodrigo. An involuntary, bitter smile appears on the thin lips of the old lawyer. From that poor son of his he can receive only unhappy news. His face is clouded further after reading the letter. Rodrigo tells how another son has been born, how business in Alcalá is daily worse and how he knows not what to do to find for his family. Perhaps he hints at the idea of soon going on a trip to the Court or to Andalusia. . . .

On the long thin face of the Licentiate an infinite compassion can be read, the saddest of all compassions, that of an intelligent, resolute father for a clumsy and irresolute son. He has a new grandson who has been named Miguel. The old man gives that most eloquent click of the tongue that so well denotes displeasure, he strokes his ear with the feather of his pen and then returns to writing in his handsome rectilinear script.[15]

CHAPTER 2

Alcalá—Valladolid—Madrid

STUMBLING and falling, by ups and downs, one day addressed as "thou" and the next as "Sir," thus did the family of chirurgeon Cervantes live in Alcalá around the year 1550. The number of students grew, the discomfort and paucity of inns and lodgings increased, but despite the growth in scholastic population there was no greater abundance in the city. To tell the truth, if Alcalá continued to enjoy credit in all of Europe because of its excellent studies it was above all because of its famous trilingual College of San Jerónimo, an industrious beehive of knowledge where every working day was spent in exercises of composition and translation in three languages—Greek, Latin and Hebrew. On Saturdays public *Sabatinas* or discussions were conducted and theses were defended.

But such refined and subtle knowledge did not attract the wealthy students of Spain. The nobles who owned the long purses could not move without a bevy of tutors, pages and squires, and they preferred Salamanca, where for centuries everything had been organized for leisure and the Muses opened their arms to followers of Venus rather than Apollo. It was there that the pithy saying *graecum est, non legitur*[1] was scholastically coined, by which the aristocratic students made it clear that from alpha to omega all that concerned the use of ink was a nuisance. Alcalá considered it a singular honor that no such denigrating phrase was heard in its halls.

Wealth and erudition have never gone together and therefore in Alcalá there was greater abundance of knowledge than ducats, and it was no rarer for students to suffer hunger and thirst than for muleteers to linger on the road. To lack of bread was added the discord sown in Alcalá by the harshness of Cardinal Martínez Silíceo, which on one occasion so roused the animus of the students that Alcalá rang with shouts of contention and rebellion. The mutinous rustics gathered in a hall of the main college where the arms the great Fray Francisco Ximénez bore at the conquest of Orán[2] and a culverin taken from the Moors were preserved as glorious trophies. The city consecrated to learning escaped an outbreak of civil war by a hair. Finally the discord died down, but the restlessness, the lack of funds, and the hardship continued.

As a crowning blow for poor chirurgeon Cervantes that year his wife Doña Leonor presented him with another son, baptized Rodrigo in Santa María la Mayor on June 23 of 1550 by Bachelor Juan García, successor to Bachelor Serrano. Doctor Gil Verte stood godfather to the child. It is no indication of greater prosperity that Rodrigo had a doctor for a godfather, for in Alcalá there were more doctors[3] than flies, and of those there was an abundance.

Life was becoming impossible there, nor was it any easier or more comfortable in the rest of Spain. A country recently patched together[4] was reduced to a state of uneasy futility and vague anxiety by the restless ambition of Charles V and the enormous costs of the many diplomatic and military enterprises upon which he embarked. The nation was always dreading reckless new adventures and ever hoping for riches from the Indies, although they brought no particular benefit to most people in view of the successive levies in preparation for war. The most useful young men disappeared from their homes never to return, or if they did it was with their consciences and their breeches slashed, addicted to a nomadic life and inclined to the arts of thievery. The monarchy did not even have a capital city and the country was governed only loosely by a wandering King and Prince.

A man who was half a professional, half a craftsman like Rodrigo de Cervantes was at his wit's end to know which way to turn to make a living. There was no Court, properly speaking, and the many activities that grow up around all Courts and support the mechanic, the artisan and those who profess the liberal arts did not yet exist. The nobility were dispersed and the ancient families had little in common, for the Palafoxes and Lanuzas of Aragón or the Moncadas and Cardonas of Catalonia barely knew the Pérez de Guzmáns or the Giróns of Andalusia. The land was exhausted, the industrious descendants of the Jews were persecuted, and those who were capable of developing fruitful ideas were in constant fear of the Inquisition.

In hope of something better Rodrigo de Cervantes moved his family to Valladolid sometime between 1550 and 1554. In Valladolid there were pestilential fevers of all the known species, carbuncles and pustules everywhere, and the intervention of the blood-letting and scarifying surgeon was constantly needed. And so Rodrigo de Cervantes went there with his bag of scalpels at his belt, and there his daughter Magdalena was born.

The inhabitants of Valladolid had high hopes that the capital would be established in their city, since the provisional character of that Kingdom without a Court could not last much longer. The Inquisition therefore functioned with great activity, hoping to cleanse the city of all Jewish and Lutheran filth so that the monarch could live there in peace, though it might not be free of the pestilential emanations of the river Esgueva. The important thing then was to cleanse the soul even though the body rotted, and if it did rot, so much the better, for in acquiring glory more souls came from putrid bodies than from the healthy ones.

It was surely in Valladolid that Miguel learned to read and know by heart the ballads displayed in bundles and sold on the pavement of San Francisco and by the massive walls of the Antigua. And was it not there that his ear acquired permanently the most deep-rooted and firmly established Castilian that is spoken in the world, if this may be said without offending Burgos or Toledo, simply by listening to those valiant townsfolk and gallant countryfolk of Castile, noble in both speech and gesture in those days as at present?

The fair arrived from Medina del Campo[5] and merchants from all over Spain and beyond traversed the city, but those who fascinated Miguel above all were the romancers and balladeers recounting the ancient epic poetry of Castile and chivalric cycles of the North and the Orient. Who can doubt that at the age of eight or ten the boy from Alcalá dreamed of King Arthur and Charlemagne, of the Twelve Peers of France and the Knights of the Round Table? Very soon he was familiar with the dense ranks of the ancient heroes and, to his delight, his own times were not too different from those in which knighthood flowered. Abhorred by all Spain in his youth, the Emperor had won his people over by his Homeric gallantry. Here and there new paladins came forth, as valiant as those of the *Romancero*,[6] and new knights-errant filled the world with the glory of Spain. The knights of America, those of Italy, those of Flanders. . . . Hernán Cortés, the Duke of Alba, Sieur Antonio de Leiva, Don García de Toledo, Pescara, Navarro, were the Amadises and Esplandians, the Rolands and Cids[7] of the new era, and there echoed in Valladolid before anywhere else the cries of glory with which the starving Spanish people daily breakfasted, lunched and dined. So that nothing would be lacking in the great book of knighthood the hero Emperor retired to Yuste when still in his prime and behind him there trailed a wake of poetic fables that enlarged his image as it faded away in the shadow of the forest and the sackcloth of a monk's coarse gown.[8] The Emperor died and his throne was occupied by his enigmatic son, never loved by the Flemish people, rejected by the Germans, and held in little esteem by the English after they had caused him the greatest displeasure by making him marry the truly ugly Queen Mary. New Iliads were appearing over the rim of the Atlantic Ocean with the enmity between Philip and the Virgin Queen Elizabeth I of Great Britain, while in the Mediterranean there was an intolerable increase in the boldness of the Algerian corsairs.

But Philip II, the austere pupil of the lean Cardinal Guijarro, was no warrior King. The exuberance, partly Homeric, partly Rabelaisian, of his father, the Caesar, was followed by the remoteness and subtlety of this pale blond man, who had no eyebrows and consequently was bothered by the light, of this man who loved women very much in secret, admitting it only in the confessional, of this man who delighted in being mysterious in an age when all men lived in public, of this man who dressed in black velvet and knew how to be silent, presenting the same countenance to what was favorable or inauspicious.

One day in the year 1561, without any previous warning, the gentlemen who had custody of the royal seal, the courtiers, and the whole Palace establishment left Toledo from the Alcázar, in whose roomy stables the horses of Charles V were still stamping, and, stopping off to sleep at Illescas, after another day's journey they arrived at a large town of some twenty-five to thirty thousand souls that reared its walled precincts among parched olive trees, dried-up live oaks, and evergreens. The Court had been transferred to Madrid, and in that year or the next the Cervantes family arrived.

In Madrid there was a Latin School maintained by the Corporation of the City. Both Latin and Castilian grammar were taught there, and it was divided into three sections according to the age of the pupils. Between 1561 and 1562 Miguel must have joined the juveniles or grammar school students of syntax. He may have listened to the lectures and explanations of Licentiate Vallés, who retired from the class in October of 1562, "leprosy having attacked him,"[9] as is set down in the Corporation records.

Vallés was replaced by Licentiate Jerónimo Ramirez, a witty and elegant poet who instructed young Miguel in knowledge of the Latin classics. Of these he remembered not a few verses and odd passages, but not so faithfully, though his memory was a good one, that he did not ascribe to Cato the couplet *Donec eris felix multos numerabis amicos*, etc., which is from Ovid in the Sixth Elegy, Book I of the *Tristes*, as well as confusing the nymph Calypso of Homer with the Circe of Virgil, and he will forget when he quotes *Non bene pro toto libertas venditur auro* that it is from the Aesopian fable *Canis et Lupus*, which he attributes to Horace or to "whoever it was who said it."[10]

It has been demonstrated, however, that Miguel understood the Latin language very well and if he did not compose verses in it he was perfectly capable of doing so. Very soon he was familiar with the serene face of Horace, the handsome visage of Virgil darkened by war and following the plough, the somber face of Ovid the lover. Who can state categorically how these men and their works were mixed up in Miguel's mind with the men and the works of the heroic legend of knights-errant and the *Romancero*, and with the men and the works of his own epic century?

The revelation that classicism is for all young minds was like bringing wealth to the affluent in the case of Miguel. At times he spent hours and hours wrestling with the adventures and misadventures of pious Aeneas, whereupon he would turn exhausted to his beloved *Amadís de Gaula,*[11] the incomparable, the one and only awakener of great Spanish energies, and without knowing that Ignatius and Teresa[12] had likewise devoured *Amadís* when they were young he felt himself as great and capable as both Ignatius and Teresa put together. The blurred images of the Latin and Greek heroes fled and the romantic figure of the Squire of the Sea[13] grew gigantically as he dreamed of glory.

Miguel was fifteen years old.

CHAPTER 3

Madrid to Seville—The Jesuit College—Friend Mateo

LIFE in Madrid was difficult in the years 1561 to 1564. The expansion of the city necessitated by the establishment of the Court was undertaken without order or planning. The walls were not all torn down, but instead the bulk of the flimsy new housing leaned against them and these houses were so badly constructed that they looked old almost before they were finished. As winter drew near the fields surrounding the city were to see, first the branches, then the stumps of the oaks and olive trees disappear to provide firewood for the courtiers in the freezing winters of Madrid. The poplar, elm, and pine groves that followed the course of the river and impinged on the inhabited precincts also fell to the construction needs of new palaces and houses, but since no one believed that Madrid was to be definitely the capital there was no attempt to provide residences with luxury or even comfort. The tendency to vacillate characteristic of Philip II, as it is of all subtle spirits, seemed to pervade all around him, and only when the great walls of the Escorial[1] were to rise prodigiously was there any certainty that something solid and lasting had been built.

For these and other reasons living in Madrid was expensive. Rodrigo de Cervantes, to whom another child, Juan, had been born, was again to find himself in new and serious difficulties and it became necessary for the family to separate. Doña Leonor returned to Alcalá to live under the protection of Licentiate Cristóbal Bermúdez, the godfather of Luisa, who by then was sixteen or seventeen years old. It would seem most probable that Luisa did not accompany the family in its wanderings but remained in Alcalá where Licentiate Bermúdez, a pious man who had little faith in the talents or enterprise of chirurgeon Cervantes, inclined the child toward the cloister, seeing to it that she frequented convents and contracted spiritual and holy friendships. This must all have been discussed thoroughly in the family and Doña Leonor, a prudent lady of very different temperament from her husband, decided to take advantage of such a good opportunity to provide for her second daughter whatever peace was obtainable in this world. Meanwhile, in agreement with Doña Leonor, Rodrigo and his children, Andrea, Magdalena, Miguel, Rodrigo and Juan, moved to Seville.

He who has never noted the fires of curiosity and burning restlessness that light up the eyes of the young members of a family which wanders from city to city without ever settling down cannot imagine the exalted state in which Miguel found himself when he started out on the road to Seville sometime between the years 1563 and 1564. A long trip on foot or horseback and four to six nights at wayside inns or taverns broaden the understanding more than seven academic courses. Step by step the family caravan crossed the vast cruel plain of La Mancha. It was there that Cervantes for the first time saw the sun break forth from the earth as if it were its fruit, and sink into it as if beyond the horizon there was no further known world, for on the plain the sun does not send out messengers and forerunners of its birth in the regiments of clouds that string their golden frills on the summits of the hills. There are no hills, the world seems to be flat and to end at twenty leagues in every direction, which is as far as the eye can reach, and when night falls the emptiness of a desolate world is overpowering. Here there is no fear of ambuscades or of being waylaid, as in broken country or wooded hills. Here the stoutness of the heart and the strength of the arm can triumph without any artifice! O land of poetry, O land of knight-errantry! And upon crossing it Miguel called to mind, not the Latinate leaders of the classical poems, but rather the rude companions of the *Romancero*.

With the Sierra Morena left behind, strange new sights appeared before him. The sun's rays were now a caress, the wind's breath was perfumed, the women's smiles, streaks of white across their golden faces, lent gaiety to life, and their slow, lisping speech was music to the ear.

Interminable rows of squat prickly pears divided the cultivated fields. In solemn procession the olives displayed their weighty overgrown heads. Orange trees grew in undisciplined platoons decorating the highlands, their golden promise peeping out through their thick foliage. The pointed agaves, as graceful as gypsies, loosened and let the frills of their charming garments fall to the ground in green and yellow stripes. A few days later that monarch of rivers appeared, turning and twisting through the landscape, the clear, elegant, noble Guadalquivir, in whose placid current the willows and orange trees were mirrored. Miguel felt a triumphant virility, he was a grown man, and he capered with joy, jesting with his sister Andrea, a young woman of twenty and of exceeding good looks.

At last one fine morning, when the sun shone kindly from the sky on all things and all beings, Miguel saw a large white stain far away across a wide plain and close to the great river. As he approached more closely something strange and without doubt beautiful could be seen dominating the city, something that from afar seemed to be a golden tree and from nearer at hand a glorious naked giantess flaunting her rosy flesh, something that could finally be recognized as the Giralda, the laughing tower.[2] Looking to the left Miguel saw what seemed to be a furrow in the prairie, but which in truth was the river hidden amid the greenery, from which emerged exceedingly tall poles with pure white linen streamers flapping gently in the wind. These were the galleons, brigantines and feluccas moored in the Guadalquivir. Seville lay before him.

The Fathers and Brothers of the Company of Jesus[3] had started upon the conquest of Seville eleven or twelve years previously. Begging from door to door they penetrated house after house, lodged themselves in conscience after conscience, and when the converted Marquis of Lombay, now worshiped on the altar as Saint Francis Borgia,[4] arrived in Seville in 1554, he felt bound to praise their zeal. The Fathers had started by collecting ten maravedis and four pieces of bread on their rounds, and lo and behold, four years later they owned a spacious residence and school, so well stocked that Saint Francis ordered them to move to a more humble abode.

But Lombay was not congratulating his brothers in religion for their material success. Thanks to their skill and cunning they had confounded the heretical depravity of Doctor Constantino Pérez de la Fuente,[5] prebendary of La Santa Iglesia Metropolitana, who had seduced and subverted souls from all over Seville, alienating them from the only true religion. There came a day when Father Benito of the Company mounted an attack on the doctrine that the Doctor enunciated, refuting his argument and achieving an immense victory.

The Jesuits battled from their small house in San Miguel and from the other bank of the river they received powerful aid from the Castle of the Inquisition of Triana and their friend the Inquisitor Carpio. The partisans of Doctor Constantino abandoned him and the Chapter sold him out. He died in the prison of Triana, not by cutting his veins like Seneca or tearing open his wounds like Cato the Censor, but by smashing a glass tumbler to bits and swallowing them so that they lacerated his entrails, a horrible act very proper to such an intransigent and contumacious man.

Triumphant in their struggle against the Lutheran heresy, the Jesuits also burned to ashes in the fires of Tablada many of his public followers, among them the noble Don Juan Ponce de León, a man so led astray by the wicked ideas of Doctor Constantino that he wasted the greater part of his fortune on absurd charities for the poor and on founding an asylum for the innumerable lost children who wandered about in Seville.

The College of the Company was soon to see itself filled with students from the most noble families of Seville, and with some eight thousand ducats the good Fathers in 1556 bought a large house near to the Church of San Salvador where they started to read grammar in two large halls. It was a sight to see—as Cervantes was to say many years later in the *Dialogue of Scipio and Berganza*[6]—"the love, the solicitude, and the industry with which those blessed Fathers and teachers taught those children, straightening the tender shoots of their youth so that they should not be twisted or take a wrong turning in the path of virtue, which they taught them together with their letters." It was worth considering "how they scolded them gently, punished them with leniency, encouraged them with examples, stimulated them with prizes and condoned their failures: and finally they completed their upbringing by depicting for them the horrid ugliness of vices and delineating the beauty of virtues so that they would abhor the one and love the other."

He who declared this with such persuasive reasons was not only an eyewitness, he was almost certainly one of the pupils who received the benefit of the Fathers' instruction. Miguel probably attended classes in one of the great halls; only by having learned in them what it was possible to learn, and being moved by a sense of gratitude without thought of reward or exercise of pressure, could the dog Scipio say: "There are none so prudent in the whole world as those blessed people who are devoted to the welfare of those who inhabit it, and as guides and leaders on the road to Heaven few can touch them. They are the mirrors in which are reflected honesty, Catholic doctrine, most singular prudence, and finally profound humility, bases on which the whole edifice of blessed happiness is built." A reflection which loses nothing by its author having placed it in the mouth of a talkative dog.

The meekness and gentleness with which the Fathers directed youth, as shown here, and possibly the simplicity of their studies, which were limited to reading grammar by the text of Antonio (such was the name of the teacher Nebrija),[7] matched the soft and gentle climate of Seville so well that it could not fail to win over its people. So much benevolence was in sharp contrast with the didactic dryness and doctrinal severity of studies in the former College of Master Rodrigo,[8] the embryo of the University of Seville, which, enclosed in marble joined by chains, enriched by a charming chapel and gaily sunlit by its open patios, was close to the Puerta de Jerez. Perhaps Miguel attended the College of Master Rodrigo for a time; perhaps he found the studies there harsh and tasteless and returned to the grammar and counsel of the Ignatian Fathers, in whose College were found the sons of the most opulent families of the city, together with poor lads like himself, in an entertaining confusion.

Among them he met a certain Matihuelo, or Mateo, who was one of the bright lads of the class, a wide-awake boy, inventive and most prolific in plotting. He told of himself that he had been born in captivity in Algiers, his mother having been imprisoned there by the Barbary pirates, and how, upon the good lady being liberated, she never again had any news of her husband, who had been last heard of from the island of Corsica. Out of this he built a thousand ingenious and fabulous stories, to the great delight of his listeners, for in the graceful indulgence of Seville truth and fiction have pretty much the same value. Among the other boys it was whispered that Mateo, whose surname was Vázquez, was the son of a high ecclesiastical magnate called Diego de Espinosa.

Mateo and Miguel often met on the way to school. The two friends would walk together, one the son of a humble chirurgeon, the other not even knowing who his father was, and they soon found themselves bound together by that close friendship in which one believes fanatically before the age of twenty. Miguel would recite to Mateo the immortal poems of Garcilaso[9] and Mateo to Miguel those of Fernando de Herrera.[10] Just about then there was talk that the lovely Doña Leonor de Milán, adored by the Sevillian poet, had been affianced to the Count of Gelves, Don Alvaro de Portugal. The great, the much-admired bard must perforce renounce the only love of his life, relapse into poverty, and never again think of the woman he idolized, for the poor wretch had no other possession than his divine inspiration.

"He who rose by never before trodden paths"[11] fell into profound despair while the adolescent Miguel learned then those lines of his that were being circulated all over Seville:

And what condemns me most
is the gift of memory,
for he who has known glory
knows best how to feel sorrow.

CHAPTER 4

The Steps of Seville—Lope de Rueda

THE Steps of the Cathedral of Seville in those days were what the Steps of San Felipe in Madrid were to become later, but to an even greater degree. A mass of humanity congregated close to the stone walls on the wide pavement that surrounds the cathedral, engaged in selling and bargaining for all the innumerable products of a large city. There were the vendors of fruits and vegetables, their stalls leaning against the thick walls, the mercers, the lace or ribbon-makers who worked in the open air, the filigree or hammered-silver workers, who in less time than it takes to cross oneself could put graceful initials of wire on buckle, ring, or medallion, or could take a small disc of silver or gold and cover it with Moorish designs in relief. These semi-artisans, semi-vagabonds shared the workbenches with the makers of bonnets and woollen hose, and with the banks, money-changers, and financiers in miniature with their trimmings of usury and fringes of thievery. Leaning against the short pillars which, joined together by a heavy iron chain, closed off the pavement, and scattered on the four or five steps rising above the street level, the hucksters launched their strange unearthly cries. The occupation of huckster peculiar to Seville constitutes a real art in which there is much of Arab music to modulate the voices of the criers, all the more suggestive and inciting when least intelligible.

Some days, in the very same place where the criers announced sales or promised generous rewards for the recovery of lost jewels, a pilgrim from Rome or Santiago, or perhaps a friar coming from the Lord knew where, would establish himself and preach against all ostentatious, vainglorious and devilish luxury, which to his mind was represented by those displays of venality. The curious and idle would press around to listen to him and in the crowd there were always certain venerable old men clothed in black baize and equipped with spectacles or green eye-shades, under the protection of which they could cast scrutinizing eyes toward pockets which were soon visited by the agile fingers or clever scissors of the pickpockets who swarmed there. The friar's or the pilgrim's sermon ended, a blind man would grope forward, his dog on a cord, singing remnants of old ballads blended into pious salads, or posing enigmas and riddles that always ended up in praising the Holy Sacrament.

The blind man, the friar, the pilgrim, the auctioneer were surrounded by idly curious soldiers in search of a company, their waxed mustachios reaching to the edge of their wide-brimmed hats—the braggarts, swashbucklers or bullies who were called *hombres* [he-men] in Seville. To be an *hombre* was to be a well-known bravo, mutinous and quarrelsome, one part ruffian, two parts drunkard, and always a thief. It was a pleasure to mingle and talk with these *hombres*, as it is nowadays to associate with bullfighters and folksingers, gentlemen of that ancient nobility in which the title of *hombre* seems more worthy of merit than inherited blazons.

Thievery reigned and dominated Seville by day and by night. The great thieves came from Italy on the scent of the galleys arriving from the Indies, and they lived in fine offices on the Calle de Genoa. These were the Florentines and Genoese into whose hands came to rest for a time all the moneys that formerly had found their way into Jewish purses. The common thieves frequented the Steps, along with those assembled at the secondhand market near the Arenal, the boy and girl orphans of the Compás,[1] the fishermen of the Costanilla and the butchers of the Meat District with their retinue.

Such were the people who made up the verminous breeding-ground around the great church. The clergy grumbled at seeing the House of the Lord encircled by merchants worse than those of the Temple of Jerusalem, but not one of them was virtuous enough or sufficiently free from sin to raise a hue and cry against them. For its part the Municipality, that great house of corruption which flaunted itself proudly in the Plaza de San Francisco, defying its eternal enemy the Audience Chamber,[2] charged a high rental for the benches of the Steps and had no desire to give it up. Also many of the thieves were in the service of the Municipal Chapter, which protected and made use of them.

Paid by the Municipality, when night fell the criers for the souls of the dead wandered through the dark and deserted streets, ringing a mournful little bell to remind the restless sleeper or pampered diner of the souls in purgatory and their sufferings. At the same time the good savers of souls peered through this barred window or into that patio, felt the hinges of a door, pressed a ball of wax against a lock, took note of a pair of breeches or a shirt hung out to dry or forgotten, and thus smelled out "business" everywhere.

Young Miguel learned all this and much more besides, and the gaiety, style and ways of the picaresque appealed to him greatly, for what we have just described, that today seems so sad and even horrible, was considered by the valiant spirits of those days as both festive and pleasurable. The fires in the field of Tablada for those persecuted by the Inquisition and the gallows in the Plaza de San Francisco for those condemned by civil justice were two spectacles highly prized by the young, two open-air classrooms where death gave almost daily lessons and where it was held in neither more nor less esteem than life. The grimaces of the hanged, the faces of those wearing the *sambenito*,[3] the patient resignation of the bawd smeared with honey and feathers were considered as tasty a dish as the merry farces and playlets of the great Lope de Rueda,[4] which in those days helped to relieve the yellow complexions and circles under the eyes of sufferers from tertian fevers in all Spain. As exciting as watching Lope play the dunce, the negro, or the man from Biscay, youths like Miguel, engaged to the hilt in that intense and abundant life of which the weaklings of today can have no idea, enjoyed going to the outskirts of the city, to Brenes or toward Castilleja or Algaba, to see rotting in the implacable sun the hanging limbs and caged heads of those who had been quartered, which for fun the lads or passing muleteers would use as targets for their slings, emptying the eye sockets with well-aimed stones. Or else, next door to the wealth with which the holds of the galleys were pregnant and the bales in which Italy, the Orient and the Indies sent their richest gifts, to observe how, corroded by misery, consumed by cancer, or simply starved to death, so many perished whose bodies were almost daily collected off the streets, the sixty or seventy hospitals and almshouses being unable to receive them for lack of space.

Daily want was no secret to Miguel when he lived in Seville, but it was only there that he could contrast great opulence with extreme misery, it was only there that he was in daily contact with the harshness of life and death, and he turned eagerly toward whatever of this there might be to see. Those of us who have never seen a corpse until we were thirty, we who flee from hospitals and gibbets and from the slums where misery swarms, cannot boast that we have seen life or pretend that we know what humanity is like. Here the greatest genius that Spain has begotten was already from his seventeenth year steeped in reality, seeing all its wretchedness, feeling its wounds, smelling its pestilence, listening to its laments, tasting its bitterness.

He was a slender blond youth with an open face, a confident manner, his cap cocked, his rapier ready as he wandered aimlessly through the narrow streets of Seville like one who knew that wherever he went he was bound to find something to enchant him. As when he saw going toward the Church of San Miguel a brilliant company preceded and followed by an escort of shrieking children. It was a christening with pomp and ceremony. The middle of the crowd was overtopped by the tall staff, the slouch hat, the white ruff and the bearded corpulence of Don Sancho, High Constable of the city, who marched sweating on foot, encumbered by a velvet cowl, most vexatious furnishings for such a day, one of the really hot ones of the summer, the eighteenth of July of 1564. Accompanying Don Sancho were his chief lieutenant Alonso Pérez and the usual patrol of liveried constables and catchpolls. Some wore hats, others caps, this one bore a staff and that one a sword, some sported curved daggers at their belts and others carried them in their hands. Beside Don Sancho walked the rich Sevillian Don Pedro de Pineda, known to Miguel through being his neighbor, and the respectable judge of the Supreme Court, Hernando de Medina, both people of distinction and wealth. Miguel was naturally surprised by so much ostentation for a christening but his surprise changed to deep admiration on seeing that the protagonist of all that procession, believe it or not, was the great Lope de Rueda, "a notable man in understanding and dramatic poetry, an excellent and famous man." Yes, yes, it was Lope de Rueda! Those were his malicious bright little eyes, that his close and already grizzled beard, that was his lively countenance. Miguel then remembered that the joy of the witty playwright upon the discovery that he was to be a father was a matter for comment in the neighborhood.

Lope de Rueda was the most popular man in Seville, he who entertained his fellow citizens best and to whom they owed their most relished hours of pleasure. "He was admirable in pastoral poetry and in this form from then to the present day no one has surpassed him." What diversion for the people who filled the city and led vigorous and complicated lives could equal those simple amorous colloquies of Cilena and Menandro and their gallant phrases of exquisitely artful simplicity?

> Go forth my horned flock
> by the leafy bank,
> do not go so turbulently
> follow toward the gentle slope
> of this so pleasant meadow.
> Enjoy the fresh morning,
> filled with a thousand perfumes,
> pasture upon the flowering blooms,
> by the groves of Diana,
> by the hills and uplands . . .[5]

Miguel, all ears and eyes, watched the childish farces in which lie the essence and embryo of all our theater, reflections of Italy with light Spanish touches, and even more importantly he was captivated by the immortal *pasos*[6] of this first Lope on the eve of the appearance of the other Lope who was an ancestor of Molière. Amidst the stiffness and starchiness that strangled the poetry of the Castilians and Sevillians, between the imitations of Latin and Greek classics and sacred recollections of the Bible with which they paved their verses and obscured their flashes of inspiration, in the course of this made-to-order official literature extolled as something scholastic and consecrated to a church, the frank, the human, the explosive peal of laughter of Lope de Rueda rang in the ears as a first fresh voice of the real genius of Spain.

Lope de Rueda, the creator of theatrical dialogue as a technique, was the John the Baptist of Spanish humor, as Cervantes was to be its Messiah. The clear, smiling and generous concept of life that the fortunate goldbeater presented to the public in his *pasos* was the positive, the true, the healthy one; it was the concept that Miguel followed in his *entremeses,*[7] refined in his novels, and rendered sublime in the *Quixote*. Lope de Rueda was an inspiration for Miguel, and especially so in Seville, where the sky and the earth, the air and the speech rejoiced the spirit, where death and misery were an excuse for jest and nothing was absolutely irreparable; in Seville where the aging Lope could devote his many different skills to surprise and delight his countrymen, they who had known him as a poor artisan beating out sheets of gold. It was surely there that Miguel came to admire and appreciate that peerless man who "with four white hides adorned with gilded trimming, and with four beards and wigs carried in a bag, and with four shepherd's crooks and an old mantle drawn by cords to serve as curtain" had by virtue of his peals of laughter aroused the Spanish spirit that lay somnolent, dreaming of warrior knights-errant and mystical adventures. Years of misfortune and calamity were to pass over the head of Cervantes when, still sound though maimed, he discussed theatrical comedies with a group of friends and as the oldest man among them recalled with pleasure the impression watching the works of Lope de Rueda had made on him as a boy. It is very clear that from then on there remained forever lodged in his breast the highest literary quality, which only genius can attain, loyalty and devotion to Our Mother and Lady of Irony, which saves men from oblivion.

CHAPTER 5

Miguel's Sisters

IN Alcalá the Convent of the Conception of the Unshod Carmelites, popularly known as the Convent of the Images, was an edifice comprising several large houses put together at different times. Situated close to the Palace of the Archbishop, the Convent of the Images was splattered with architectural-sculptural refinements in the plateresque style. This courtly architecture impinged on the chaste severity of the convent, climbing up a palatial stairway that connected the whitewashed arcades below with the plastered cloisters of the main floor.

On the eleventh day of February of 1565 the beautiful balustrade of rose-tinted stone was caressed by ten, by twenty, by thirty white hands lighting upon it as they descended the stairway like a flock of restless doves. The nuns were dressed in habits cut on simple circular lines and unpleated, the scapulary four fingers above the habit, their veils made of thick linen or flax tow, also unpleated and allowed to fall freely, their shoes open sandals of hemp so that as they walked two rosy heels could be seen below their gowns playing at hide-and-seek with the serge or sackcloth of the skirt. Over the gowns they wore great choir capes of white serge.

A cold wind blew through the bare cloisters and the nuns shivered as they formed up and moved in procession to the choir. A novice sneezed and the others raised a chorus beseeching Jesus, Mary and Joseph to aid her. The mistress gently reprimanded them, because what they were doing came close to playing and right clearly the very wise Rule of the Doctoress of Avila[1] lays it down that "play is in no manner permitted, for the Lord will give grace to some so that they may entertain others," and she adds, "Let words and jests always be discreet."

The day was a happy one for the community. A most comely and worthy young woman, the goddaughter of the devout Licentiate Cristóbal Bermúdez, was going to be received as a religious. She was an amiable and gentle creature and by her conversation appeared to be endowed with just the degree of wit that is becoming to a nun and so spiritedly seasons the long convent hours, and particularly those postprandial chats in which, according to the Rule, "all together may speak of what most pleases them as long as it not be of things outside the conduct of a good religious," because, it also says, "experience shows that in gossip there cannot help but be sin."

The young neophyte was called Luisa de Cervantes, and the prioress knew from respectable and trustworthy sources that she was one who wished to serve the Lord with joy and understanding and who had a talent for reading the divine office, which had been scrupulously taught her. The nuns of the convent, and especially the novices, received her with loving and gracious words, though always with the distant coolness and religious courtesy that the Rule contemplates. "No sister will embrace another nor will touch her face or her hands nor have any particular friendship."

Despite the frequency of such solemnities, the best people of Alcalá flocked to be present when Luisa took the veil. The curious and idle, persons of notorious and ostentatious piety, clergy, bigots, and friars filled the small church and the whitewashed porch, together with students eager to see if the novice were good-looking. In the corners of the altars, leaning against the confessionals and pilasters in doleful attitudes, the devoted gallants of nuns, who abounded in Alcalá as in Toledo and Seville, cast looks as of men condemned to purgatory toward what they thought to perceive behind the veils. Some were ardent fetishists in love with a pair of hands, and the hands sensed it, and without interrupting the murmured prayers they moved provocatively over the scapulary or perhaps rose audaciously to arrange the veil, the obscurity of which augmented their beauty, and by this they fired a thousand red-hot coals in the hearts of the suffering lovers, adorers of the impossible, great-great-grandsons of Plato, whom they had most certainly never read.

The solemn moment of pronouncing the vows arrived. The priest was a young man new to such ceremonies. He approached the iron grille of the choir, a heavy one of black bars at the intersections of which menacing sharp spikes of twisted iron were placed. The church was in almost complete darkness; in contrast the cold wintry light shone down from the large window of the choir, passed quickly over the veils and lingered on the line of gold formed by the wax tapers that the nuns held in their hands. All the light seemed to concentrate on the face of the novice. The priest had not committed the ritual formulas to memory and a gentleman who deemed it an honor to act as acolyte, perhaps to see more closely the eyes or the hands that were his torment, lighted the book with a small wax candle. The priest read slowly, penetrating word by word the mystery of the Rule given to Brocardo and the hermits of Mount Carmel in the thirteenth century.[2] He was tremendously moved and his voice trembled as the wide-open blue eyes of Luisa de Cervantes were fixed avidly upon him. When the reading was finished the priest realized and his companion observed that the book was stained with blood, blood flowed on the sacred vestments, blood was dripping on the floor from the iron of the grille. Absorbed in what he was reading, the priest had pierced his forehead on one of the spikes.

A great tumult broke out in the church; everyone pressed forward and absurd rumors circulated, instantly believed by men and women hoping fervently for something supernatural to happen. The nuns felt that some great profanation must have taken place outside the grille and with a gesture the superior ordered the curtain to be drawn. Invisible hands closed it, and in the center of the choir inundated with light, curious, frightened, amid the glow of the candles, the great blue eyes of Luisa de Cervantes Saavedra looked upon the world for the last time. Her mother, Doña Leonor, wept, half in sorrow, half in rejoicing, oblivious to the tumult that had broken out in the church.

Well into the month of March the news that Luisa had taken the veil reached Seville. Meanwhile the fortunes of the Cervantes family had nowise improved. Neither the excellent intentions of chirurgeon Rodrigo nor the good offices of his brother Andrés, who had been living in Seville for a long time, could secure comfort and ease for the unfortunate family. The belongings of Rodrigo had even been sequestered at the demand of one Francisco de Chaves, doubtless due to that common daily tragedy which in modern parlance is called "money troubles".

Still living with Rodrigo was his daughter Andrea, who appeared as a party to the litigation, alleging that among the goods attached as belonging to her father were certain rights and shares that belonged to her. In view of this she demanded that a custodian *ad litem* [for the duration of the litigation] be appointed for her; this may well have been a legal technicality contrived by her attorney or perhaps by herself, for she was always extraordinarily shrewd in conducting lawsuits. The noteworthy signature of Doña Andrea de Cervantes S. (Saavedra) appears on this document, traced in a bold script that seems masculine in the decisiveness of its strokes but feminine in its emotional inclination. And it is here that the commentator examining this piece of writing—now looking at its content, now at the handwriting of the signature—begins to understand what the older sister of Miguel must have been like.

Doña Andrea was actually the head of the family, showing from the first great perspicacity and an unusual knowledge of life, for both of which her brother always admired her as teacher and leader. There was no mother at hand, for Doña Leonor lived in Alcalá or in Arganda taking care of her own ailing mother. The father was usually away following his practice as chirurgeon. The lads Miguel and Rodrigo spent most of their time out of the house, Miguel following his studies and roaming the streets, Rodrigo loitering on the barbicans of the Guadalquivir, listening to the sailors cursing as they fought among themselves, watching the ships unload their merchandise and embark soldiers for Italy or adventurers for the Indies. The house was unguarded, the gate open, as was the rule in Seville where everything was organized for an easy and pleasant life—from the air one breathed under the warm sun to the arrangement of the streets and houses and to the manners and customs of high society and low. A young woman like Andrea and a girl like Magdalena, both endowed with beauty as it was later demonstrated, inevitably had assiduous courtiers, generous with gifts and lavish with promises, escorting them by day and serenading them by night.

There was no great harm in it, nor had consciences then become as tender and fearful as they were, or pretended to be, sixty years later when the theologian Calderón de la Barca[3] elaborated an inhuman and anti-Christian concept of family honor, illustrating it with his dramas, examples, theorems, and postulates of a metaphysic which was high-sounding and addled rather than based on what goes on in the world. It was already being developed, but it had not yet put consciences in irons nor stultified customs. To that end this same concept had to be distilled in the Escorial, consecrated in the confessional of Father Aliaga,[4] applauded by adulterous royal hands and given its final polish in the malls of the Buen Retiro.[5] The comedy of comings and goings, of noise and confusion, of cloak and sword, already existed; the tragic drama of jealousy and vengeance was not yet clearly portrayed.

Such a comedy of comings and goings, of gallants and ladies in love, of amorous promises and obligations, must obviously have existed in Miguel's house, since in later days it did so exist, and neither Doña Andrea nor Doña Magdalena was so dull that in such a game they would end up with any loss of reputation, nor did they fail to take advantage of the promises of their suitors. From that time on, and perhaps from some time before, the patio in Seville served as a charming stage for those entanglements of which the lady need have no fear if she be discreet. Of this comedy Miguel saw only occasional scenes, fragments of talk, charming phrases and gay gallantries. Seville the indulgent, good-natured and forgiving Seville, asks of such things only that they be graceful and delicate, and in the Cervantes house they doubtless were.

CHAPTER 6

Return to Madrid—La Mancha—Getino de Guzmán

AT the end of 1565 or beginning of 1566 the restless and unhappy family was again taking the road to the capital. To return to Madrid from Seville, even at the age of nineteen when hope swells the heart as air swells young lungs, is always a step backward. For Miguel it meant leaving behind the rich and stimulating life where his eyes beheld new sights every day and his energies responded to unexpected sensations at every moment and returning to the grim monotony and narrow-mindedness of the nascent Court. His sister Luisa was cloistered forever, renouncing the world to live in the solitude where, as the King of Spain once said, "one teaches without speaking and learns without listening," and his sister Andrea was taking her first courses under the faculty of love, in whose schoolroom we are born and during whose apprenticeship not a few perish, while Miguel had already passed the greater part of his novitiate in the school of life.

It does not seem credible that at nineteen years of age, even though two of them had been spent in Seville, Miguel could have a clear notion of most of the things he had seen, but certainly he had assembled a store of impressions a hundred times greater than those of any youth of his age today. He had also thought deeply, as do the sons of incompetent fathers and the brothers of marriageable sisters. A cheap second-hand psychology maintains that nineteen is not an age for deep thought. Experience proves the contrary. At that age the mind is fresh, is thirsty and has time to think. Action comes later and thought must then be quick, concise, with no room for indecision or reflection. Finally come the indispositions and failing memory of old age and then good-bye to deep thought.

And so Miguel returned to Madrid with his family. He had no luggage, but in the pockets of his coat he carried all he needed, an *Amadís de Gaula* and a *Diana*[1] by Montemayor. He once more followed the course of the olive-bordered Betis,[2] perhaps he passed through Cordova, he certainly felt his heart swell at the sight of the mysterious Sierra Morena, the jagged peaks of which cut the spiritual life of Spain into two distinct and even hostile sections. The plain of La Mancha again stretched before him, furrowed by the tracks of the muleteers and their teams, tilled by the yoked animals, made musical by the tinkle of the mule bells and the songs of the peasants who break the sod and plough their fields for the second and third time. The song of the ploughman, a long-drawn-out chant with Moorish cadences, is an old ballad from this side of the olive trees, in which one senses a touch of resentment against Andalusia the corruptor.

> The young girl
> who came from Seville
> and brought with her
> a fine apron
> and now
> because the apron is torn
> the young girl weeps.

Beyond the lands plowed for wheat and barley are those where the golden saffron is gathered. In the middle of the plain, standing dauntless or climbing the slope of a narrow pass in a menacing line, the windmills appear, short and squat of body with the rebellious and restless arms of a madman; the mouth, which is the door, wide open; the eyes, which are the windows, watchful and insolent. Toward them plod teams of mules; peasant lads and lasses journey in couples, the man walking, the girl sitting sideways on the haunches of a donkey who, if he arrives black, will return silver gray with the powdering of flour that will also bleach the hair of the girl. The windmill sings too, not with the grave deep tones of the peasants' chant but rather with a light and lively dance tune of facile rhymes spiced by lascivious fancies referring to the hopper, the grinding of the millstones, and other words and usages of wheat milling in which metaphors with coarse meanings abound. The chorus of a baker's song rends the air with the lewd rhythm of the wheat sifting:

> Four bakers
> enter your house,
> one of them sifts it,
> another then kneads it,
> another does take it,
> and in the stove puts it,
> another out brings it . . .
> and it's I that does eat it,
> my love. . . .

The great steppe that to Miguel had once seemed deserted, and because it was deserted very fitting for a battle between giants and poetry-inspired champions, is now peopled by a vulgar, malicious and piquant life shining in the little eyes of the flour-covered millers, emanating from the sweating farmhands, the wayward country lasses and the cunning muleteers, and showing even in the gracefully feminine movement of the mule's haunches and the comic erectness of the donkey's ears. Miguel contemplated the windmills, which looked to him like giants, and after some uncertainty he burst into a spontaneous shout of laughter, first cousin of those evoked in Seville by Lope de Rueda when he was acting the cowardly bully and allowing his goodwife to administer some brisk swipes on his nose.

That laughter of Miguel's when confronted with the windmills on the way back from Seville was his first creation, perhaps the greatest of all, young as he was: his eyes, brimming with merriment, were already seeing clearly. He has taught all of us that the whole world is a windmill which many people take for a giant, and they only become real men when they correct their error.

Miguel then surveys the broad desert of La Mancha, sees the peacefulness of the land, and goes into the villages within their earthen walls thatched with thorn and thistle turning from green to purple under the sun. Leaning against the houses, gaunt hidalgos bask in the sun while their hounds, no leaner than their masters, crouch yawning at their feet. There is scarcely a village without its convent or religious house; there is scarcely a large dwelling without four or six or twenty volumes that treat of unseen things, of wonderful and fantastic adventures. In the sacristy two hungry students argue aimlessly, like two dogs over a dry and marrowless shinbone; they hope to compete for a chaplaincy or benefice of some ten maravedis a day. In the plaza the lads spend all day aiming sticks at the sky to bring down swifts and kestrels. On the steps of the pillory the village idiot calmly lets flies wander at will over his face smirched with snot and spittle, waiting for someone to pass by who may give him a crust of bread in exchange for some cruel and amusing silliness. The barber keeps open house all day, at times excoriating his neighbors or pulling their teeth or opening up their ulcers from which inherited or acquired putrefaction may issue, at times playing on his guitar, at others commenting on the raids of the Turks, that inexhaustible topic of all chatterboxes. At the barber's club there was always an old soldier who, according to him, lost his hand at Cerinola, according to others at a tavern in Alcocer, as well as a young soldier who poked his nose out at Cartagena, saw the galleys laden with men-at-arms, and, deciding that his help was not of great importance when such good troops were available, returned to the village, sporting gallant plumes, spouting blasphemies and dispensing tall tales.

Miguel saw all this, noted, collected, and stored it up, without any thought that the pleasure and curiosity thus inspired would serve him well one day much later. The road teaches, the road indoctrinates, and the road sharpens the mind. God bless the road!

The family reached Madrid. Doña Elvira de Cortinas, the mother of Doña Leonor and grandmother of Miguel, who had been dangerously ill, finally died. We know nothing of this lady save that she left an inheritance to be collected, but in those days anything was called an inheritance. As the last will and testament was made more for the sake of the soul than for worldly goods, everyone inherited and everyone continued to be poor. This happened to the Cervantes family who, on their arrival at Madrid, had to sell one of their few meager properties: a small vineyard of some five hundred sad grape vines in the district of Arganda, for which their neighbor Andrés Rendero gave them seven thousand five hundred maravedis. With these moneys the family established themselves in Madrid.

In two or three years Madrid had changed greatly. The natives of the city and residents at the Court were becoming accustomed to the idea that the royal sojourn was to be permanent. The Civic Council, in view of the increase in population and the little or no care taken to improve public facilities, at times found itself in funds and could be liberal in the luxury and ostentation of fiestas and entertainments rather than anything useful. But what had changed the character of the city most was the moral atmosphere created by the slanders and whisperings coming out from the Royal Palace or the halls of the Council of Castile or confessionals and monastery parlors. Disseminated by the talk of street-idlers and corner-loungers, they spread into the patios of the inns and insinuated themselves into private homes.

The concern that Prince Don Carlos caused his father was soon known in the streets. The people, who did not love the Prince, said of him "he is marked, he cannot be good," since he was weak and his forehead was covered by the scars of the operation he had to undergo in Alcalá when he fell and rolled down the staircase of Tenorio[3] as he was chasing young Mariana de Garcetas, who was later made to enter the Convent of San Juan de la Penitencia as a nun. One day the actor Alonso Cisneros boasted before a large company that he had been the cause of the Prince threatening the President of the Council with a dagger. It was said on another occasion that Don Carlos and his uncle, Don Juan de Austria, had both laid hands to their swords in an apartment of the Palace and that the courtiers had to disarm them. It was also whispered that the beautiful Queen Doña Isabel of France was disgusted and unhappy over the lovesick condition of her husband, a situation passed over in silence by historians but well known to the people.

During this period Miguel's house was frequented by a certain

Alonso Getino de Guzmán, a municipal constable and a man of some thirty years or more, of good appearance and subtle talent, who was charged by the gentlemen of the Municipal Government with responsibility for all the machinery and organization of arches, hangings, illuminations, and other demonstrations of public rejoicing that were being undertaken on any pretext.

Getino de Guzmán was a good friend of the family and he doubtless held in high esteem Miguel's talent for amusing repartee and for turning out a verse with facility. In those days the raising of an arch or placing of a hanging was not merely a matter for carpenter and tapestry-maker but required someone endowed with oratorical talent, a knowledge of pagan mythology and everything else involved in creating symbolical and allegorical placards and figures. It is probable that Miguel composed some of the verses that adorned the arches raised in 1567 for the happy childbirth of the Queen; almost certainly he accompanied his good friend Getino de Guzmán in all the organizing of the official diversions and festivities with which he was always busy.

From day to day Miguel grew in talent and fecundity of thought and speech. He attended the city Latin School, where at first he received instruction from Licentiate Francisco del Bayo, who read grammar for twenty-five thousand maravedis of salary and two reals a month paid him by the wealthier students. The school had a competitor in the Theatin monks,[4] who tried to get the twenty-five thousand maravedis and give free instruction, but the city decided to have an open competition for the place and after four days of lessons and arguments it was granted to schoolmaster Juan López de Hoyos, a man of great wisdom and learning and a protégé of the omnipotent Don Diego de Espinosa.

The memoirs of the Court written by López de Hoyos[5] do not enable us to imagine his face or figure as really any different from what teachers of grammar were like at that time, but we are inspired to praise his memory because he was the first, after the constable Getino de Guzmán, to recognize what might be expected of Miguel. Amid the ingratitude and indifference with which many apparently illustrious men have overwhelmed Cervantes, the gentle and moving words of the venerable cleric of San Andrés when referring to Miguel echo in our ears: "my dear and beloved pupil." He who does not feel a twinge of gratitude to the schoolmaster on recalling those two eloquent adjectives "dear" and "beloved" must have little regard for Cervantes.

In those days the class in grammar in all grades of the school was what was later to be called "composition." The pupils did not just go to listen to a reading and then repeat the lesson in a mechanical sing-song. They all composed, some in prose, some in verse, on subjects assigned them by the teacher. And at that time no one did it better than Cervantes. Listening to his words, reading his first verses, Juan López de Hoyos felt the blessed satisfaction of the teacher whose pupil does him honor in life and promises him fame after death.

Little by little, at that disturbing age of twenty, Miguel acquired what a man most needs, the consciousness of his own value, which from then on was never to abandon him, not even amid the greatest adversities. Thus from early youth he developed serenity, a high standard of thought, a clear and precise use of words, that were to save his life and make him the admiration of centuries.

CHAPTER 7

Locadelo—Deaths of Don Carlos and Queen Isabel—First Poem

AFTER Madrid became the capital and the great families congregated there with the wealth that had previously been dispersed over the country or kept hidden for fear of the inconsiderate demands of the Caesar, a cloud of Italians had alighted on the city. Not a century had passed since the Moors were flung out of Spain, and in that uneasy land, where the roads and even the streets were unsafe, where the grandees were engaged in constant warfare or made an occupation out of idleness, where the wretched population lived miserably, there was no active and diligent middle class concerned with the great volume of business that a powerful and vigorous nation develops. The money industry had just then begun to supersede all other industries. With the expulsion of the Jews all the good and bad arts of finance they had taken with them were lost. Soon they were replaced by the clever, astute, amoral merchants and bankers who came from the plutocratic states and opulent duchies of Italy, more particularly from Genoa, Florence and Milan. Italy was an Argus with its eyes fixed on Spain; it penetrated all kinds of business, sucked out money, intervened in politics, smelled out domestic secrets, and, distorting them for its own ends, spread them in rumor over all of Europe.

Meanwhile the ambassadors accredited to the Court and the secret representatives and agents maintained there by the States of Italy wormed their way in everywhere. The astute and flexible character of the Italians, the facility of their speech and their dexterity in all activities calling for worldly and social adroitness—and even in all the arts requiring manual skill—opened doors for them, and when one of them saw an open door he was very soon master of the house, or at least of that part of it which could be exploited. In exchange for this kind of pervasive control the Italians brought a little literature, of which they had a surplus, and some crumbs from their pictorial and sculptural wealth with which to adorn the vast cold walls of the Escorial. Men capable of staggering activity and incredible endurance, they could be hangers-on today and tomorrow court secretaries to some prince whose chin they had scraped only the day before. The solemn hidalgos of Madrid looked down on them, the grandees of Spain apparently did not even suspect their existence, and so they lived, multiplied, enriched themselves, and one fine morning they packed up and left, their venture having come to a successful end, and they were never to be seen again.

The Cervantes family knew many of this kind of Italian through the occupation of chirurgeon Rodrigo. Frequent visitors to the house were a certain Pierro Boqui from Rome, a Francisco Musaquí from Florence or Milan, and a Santes Ambrosi from Florence who always looked desirously on the beauty of Doña Andrea.

One day in 1567, or perhaps in the following year, another Italian, a certain Juan Francisco Locadelo, presented himself at the insistence of these friends. He was a wealthy merchant who had fallen ill, possibly due to the changeable climate of Madrid, or perhaps he needed to be cured of a wound, pustule or ulcer such as people were liable to in those days in view of the insecurity of life and the general lack of cleanliness. It seems likely that it was the last of these from which he suffered and that Locadelo needed lint, plasters, or bandages calling for the delicacy of feminine hands. The ailing Italian had already tried several remedies, including the famous specifics of Pinterete, the Moor from Valencia who claimed to cure all the ulcers and abscesses in the world with a white "repercussive" salve and another hot black one, but what Locadelo needed most was what neither doctors nor medicines can provide—affectionate companionship, care and attention. Doña Andrea de Cervantes was, for Locadelo, a Sister of Charity, nurse, friend, and comforter in affliction.

With Italian nobility Locadelo declares over his signature:

> I being away from my native land in this country, she and her father have cared for me and cured me of certain illnesses I have had and have done for me and for my benefit many other things that I consider it my obligation to remunerate and reward. . . . for the above reasons

and for many other good works that I have received from her and so that she will be better able to marry honorably and for assistance toward her said marriage in which no other person may intervene, neither her parents nor her brothers, nor can any one of them have or hold anything against the will of the said Doná Andrea, who will hold and possess them, enjoy and use them as she so desires and considers good, and spend or distribute them according to her will. . . .

This gift from the grateful Italian was more than a wedding present: writing desks, tables, sideboards, chairs, carpets,

36 pieces of red and yellow taffeta
1 dress skirt of embroidered black satin
4 upper petticoats of taffeta and velvet
1 robe of taffeta and velvet
3 jackets
6 coifs of gold and silver
2 veils of Canton silk crêpe
10 bolts of Flanders linen
8 Rouen linen mattresses,

household linen and cutlery, braziers, candlesticks, mirrors, a rosary, a guitar, and three hundred gold escudos in gold. It is obvious that Locadelo, cured and happy, was returning to his homeland and wished to leave to Doña Andrea everything he had in his house, adding to the gift whatever a woman might most appreciate—costly clothes in the latest fashion and material from which to cut many more, a holy rosary, and a guitar to banish care.

Locadelo also settled his account with Rodrigo de Cervantes, the largest that the humble chirurgeon had ever collected in his life: eight hundred ducats. Rodrigo made the mistake of lending them to his friend Licentiate Sánchez de Córdoba, from whom he never collected anything after many years of litigation.

Locadelo's generosity ameliorated the lot of the Cervantes family and engendered in Miguel the enthusiastic sympathy he later felt for Italy and the Italians. His traffic with them polished and refined his talent, contributing an agility and lightness that Spaniards lacked in their conversation and behavior. It is possible also that through conversing with the Italians he met at his house he may have learned enough of the Tuscan tongue to regale his ears with the martial octaves of Ariosto,[1] whom he worshiped all his life. Ariosto was the last great poet of knight-errantry, as Lucan[2] had been the first.

Dark tales about the Court had begun to circulate. Since the month of January the disobedient and foolhardy Prince Don Carlos had been imprisoned in the Palace. The King, who was compared by many of his faithful vassals to the patriarch Abraham, compelled by the Lord to sacrifice his son, had informed all the courts of Europe and all his own realms. After announcing the terrible news the King desired the world to keep silent; but not even Philip II could ensure that tongues would abandon their function.

It was known that Prince Don Carlos, relapsing into his madness, had committed new follies that threatened his life and destroyed his already greatly impaired health. The people said, which the King and his courtiers would never admit, that the Prince was mad because of his fall down the stairs at Alcalá. Everybody knew that the injury to his head was so serious that it had been necessary to trepan his skull, and even with this some matter had remained inside, as the doctors Chacón, Colmenares and Gutiérrez attested before the eminent Andrés Vesalio. It was no surprise, then, that the emaciated and feeble Prince, who had suffered from quartan agues since childhood, died on the twenty-fourth of July of 1568 in the Palace of Madrid. Only a lack of diligence on the part of Spanish historians could have allowed to develop the stupid legend of Prince Don Carlos, which no one believed in the year 1568.[3] For not declaring that his son was mad, Philip II has been burdened with maledictions and execrations he perhaps deserved for other reasons.

Two and a half months after the death of the Prince, the young Queen Isabel of France, wife of Philip II, also died; she whom he had received in his arms when she was but a child and whom he returned to Heaven when she had not reached her twentieth year.

Both sad events not only gave the populace much to talk about but also not a little to do for the worthy Maestro Juan López de Hoyos, who was commissioned by his protector, Cardinal Don Diego de Espinosa, to prepare a *Memoir on the death and funeral honors of H. H. Prince Don Carlos, son of His Majesty the Catholic King Don Philip II, Our Lord and Master*, on which the Maestro labored all that summer. Maestro López de Hoyos declares that he composed the epitaphs, emblems, and verses "in the little time that my ordinary lessons and studies left me, with great haste (which I wish the pious reader to take very much into consideration)," and he further declares that "in addition to all the above, the students in our Latin School composed many funeral Orations, Elegies, Stanzas, very good sonnets with which they displayed their talents." The verses of the pupils were not published and because of this we have no knowledge of Cervantes' first works to be read in public, but indubitably they must have given great pleasure to those who heard them, and it was especially so for Maestro López de Hoyos when shortly afterward, on the sad occasion of the death of the Queen, the teacher and the whole school (for in those days nothing was done in class without reckoning with the pupils) agreed that Miguel should be the one to write the Castilian verses lamenting the royal tragedy. These are included in *The History and True Memoir of the illness, most graceful passing and sumptuous funeral obsequies of the Most Serene Queen of Spain Dona Isabel de Valois, our lady. With Sermons, Poetical Compositions and Epitaphs on her tomb, etcetera,* printed in the most noble and royal city of Madrid in the house of Pierre Cosin, year 1569. Fray Diego de Chaves, in approving the book, says: "Maestro López has done well in including some of the sermons preached for this purpose, because they are very good doctrine and since they are writ in the vulgar tongue people will never avail themselves of them to get academic degrees, as sometimes happens with similar things."

From this very first moment when Miguel's poems reached the world we must undertake to study them, consider the youth of their author, and take into account their nature as commissioned works on an imposed theme . . . and then compare them with all that was being written in his day, for example with the elegy on the death of Prince Don Carlos that Maestro Fray Luis de León composed at the same time:

> Whoever saw the sumptuous
> tomb raised up to the high Heaven. . . .

and his famous epitaph:

> Here lie the remains of Don Carlos. . . .

which, because it has been quoted so often and repeated in all the booklets on rhetoric, is familiar and sounds well to ears that have become inured to it. The verses of Cervantes in his twentieth year are neither better nor worse than those of Maestro León, the prince of lyric poetry, a man of forty in all the vigor of his flowering years. And I would even declare that Homer himself, if he had been required in the same circumstances to compose a sonnet, a roundelay, or two stanzas in the old style, four double stanzas, and an elegy in *terza rima* dedicated in the name of the whole school to Cardinal Don Diego de Espinosa, could not have done any better than Miguel, who started with these three lines of great poetry:

> To whom will my sad song go,
> In whose ear will its voice resound
> That will not melt the heart to tears. . . .

Doubtless Miguel's triumph was very great, as much as it could be on such a famous occasion. The pride of Maestro López de Hoyos was already justified. His dear and beloved pupil took a firm and sure first step, treating of "very original things with delicate conceits" and "making use of rhetorical figures." At that time no elegy or song could be considered good if the author did not put in it "conceits" and "rhetorical figures." Glance through the best works, the most famous and popular of Fray Luis de León, set aside the strophes in which you feel the mysterious flame burning, and in what remains you will find conceits and still more conceits.

Thus the teacher López de Hoyos was not mistaken nor were his praises exaggerated. Miguel de Cervantes was already a poet at twenty years of age.

CHAPTER 8

Song of the Dead Queen—Monsignor Julio Aquaviva—First Sally Abroad

HAVING reached the summit of civil power as President of the Royal Council, of ecclesiastical power upon his investiture as Cardinal of the Holy Roman Church with the title of San Esteban de Monte Celio, and of the darkest and most terrible power of those days as the Apostolic Inquisitor General for the Kingdom and Dominions of Spain against all heretical perversity and apostasy, the Very Illustrious and Most Reverend Gentleman Don Diego de Espinosa was highly regarded by Philip II for his prudence and moderation.[1] At the same time the King very much liked those who served him to have something that they must keep secret, and it occurred to the Cardinal, recalling the days of his youth in Seville, how very useful it would be for him to gather unto himself young Mateo Vázquez, with whom he had certain ties. He therefore had him brought to the Court and was well pleased with his appearance and behavior. As half-page, half-secretary to the President, Mateo, who had wandered freely around Seville in former days, could now enter royal palaces with the same freedom. From the very first he kept all his Sevillian sharpness and levity locked deep in his breast and, submerged as he was in the black mass of billowing velvet robes, cloaks, and gowns that commonly surrounded his protector, he adopted a posture of modesty and gravity remarkable in one of his tender years.

In the street one day, Mateo Vázquez came upon a familiar face and a pair of arms opened wide in greeting. It was his friend Miguel, that is to say, youthful frankness and gaiety personified. The courtier held out his arms with measured condescension. But after the first moment of confused reserve that opens all conversations in which the fortunes and social conditions of one of the participants have changed, the colloquy broke out buoyantly. Miguel spoke of poetry and Mateo responded. He had a liking for certain odes and songs of an Augustinian friar called Luis de León which circulated in manuscript copies[2] among the ladies and old people, but he well knew that the said friar was not looked upon with much favor by the Supreme Council of the Inquisition.[3]

Mateo had also heard President Espinosa breathe something about the priest Don Gonzalo Pérez, the translator of *Ulysses*, who entered the Court one day leading a boy by the hand and, without saying he was his son or any kin to him, arranged to leave the child there in the Royal Secretariat. The lad, Antonio Pérez, who turned out to be smart and wide-awake, was already so spoiled and pampered in the Palace that he did not remove his cap even for the Duke of Alba, and it was also said that, contrary to every known precept of etiquette, he had been known to rise from the royal table before anyone else had done so.

Miguel mentioned to his friend the verses he was shaping in the name of the Latin School, and more particularly the song in tercets mourning the dead Queen. He recited some of the lines:

> Fair spirit, deserving of Heaven,
> see how the hapless earth darkens
> without the sight of you to light it. . . .
> . . . .
> The vain trusting and the beauty. . . .
> That firm hope, holy and constant. . . .

Mateo was all ears. Those conceits had the gracious sobriety, the lordly and human style of Seville. In his delight Mateo offered to serve his friend in any way he could. But with President Espinosa counting on the mystery in Mateo's life to ensure a good place for him at the Court, the road was already mapped out for him and the Muses could lie fallow.

For the first time it occurred to Miguel that poetry alone was not the only path by which to get ahead and in this doubt lay the great vacillation that was to rule his life. There were two roads to follow, one that of learning and literature, the other that of bearing arms.[4]

He discussed this quandary with one of the Italians who frequented his house. For the Italian there was no doubt. Little or nothing could be gained in this harsh, ungrateful land, whether in arms or letters. Flanders could offer only military glory. On the other hand, for lads like him, Italy, tumultuous Italy, lovingly opened her arms like a woman who is never satiated by youth. Italy welcomed valiant swords and ready pens with the same love and favored them with equal enthusiasm.

Miguel was already dreaming of Italy when very soon he had an opportunity to realize his hopes. Monsignor Julio Aquaviva arrived in Madrid on an official mission. This chamberlain and secretary to Pope Pius V, "a very virtuous and well-lettered youth," as reported by Don Juan Zúñiga, Spanish Ambassador in Rome, was a young man belonging to the old Neapolitan nobility. He was one of those aristocratic Italian youths who was not attracted by the hurly-burly of arms and who, because of his wealth and noble demeanor, seemed born to ornament the Court of Rome. It was such young men who were the heirs of the Maecenases, the Messalas and the Agrippas of the Empire, and as the outward difference between the pontiffs and the ancient Caesars was not very great, so was it also with their respective courtiers. The Pope esteemed him, confident that he would be one of the cleverest of the young cardinals to serve him. It was doubtless to try him out that he confided to him an extremely delicate diplomatic mission, that of presenting his condolences to Philip II on the death of his son and discussing privately with the King and the gentlemen of the Royal Council the differences that had developed between the ecclesiastical jurisdiction and the civil authority represented by the King's ministers in Milan, Naples, and Sicily.

Monsignor Aquaviva's official mission to Madrid was not a success. On arriving at the Court he was met by the news that the Queen was dead. No one, and perhaps least of all Philip II, remembered Prince Don Carlos. By contrast there was general mourning for the exquisite, timid young woman who had occupied the throne quietly and without fanfare. The mood of the monarch was thus not the most suitable for solving conflicts of jurisdiction. Aquaviva soon understood that his embassy was to prove useless, and wishing like a good Italian to employ his time to best advantage with pleasant things he took to conferring with the most talented gentlemen of the Court, seeking the company of the poets. He entertained them as often as he could, lingering with them over delightful postprandial dialogues and perfecting his knowledge of the Castilian tongue.

In these colloquies, in pauses during his official interviews with Don

Diego Espinosa, the President of the Royal Council, the conversation must have turned at times to the poetic crown woven by the talents of the Court in honor of the unfortunate Queen. It is almost certain that Don Diego, urged to do so by his Mateo Vázquez, spoke to Monsignor Aquaviva of the youth who had written the song and the roundelays offered by the Latin School. Either spontaneously or in response to the wishes of Espinosa, Aquaviva promised to take such a mature talent with him to Italy. He already had Italian poets in his service and to the monsignor it seemed no bad thing to add to their company a Spanish chamberlain who could versify so sweetly.

Since Aquaviva's trip to Spain turned out to be a calamity and there was very little in the Spanish Court to interest a resident of the Vatican he lost no time in preparing to leave. As the cold began to bite in Madrid, Monsignor Julio, somewhat discomfited, therefore gathered up his baggage and his attendants and departed toward the Kingdom of Valencia before the end of the year 1568.

Behind him, with his sword at his side, not too well outfitted as to clothes but with his *Amadís* and *Diana* in his pockets, together with a quantity of paper covered with scrawled verses, Miguel set out gay and happy. It was his first sally as a man, seeking adventure, testing the world. Little he cared that he went as a servant, for such service was not considered dishonorable then, when there was a very different concept of dignity than there is today.

Nothing can be said of Miguel's leave-taking from his family, for we know nothing of it. For a lad to go to a foreign land was a commonplace in those days. People traveled a great deal and for months and years there was no news of them, but their intimates were not worried.

There are few journeys as lovely or instructive as that first trip by Miguel. Valencia the beautiful was the first great city they came to, and according to what he says in the *Persiles*[5] he was full of admiration for the "grandeur of its setting, the superiority of its inhabitants, the amenities of its environs, and finally for everything that makes it beautiful and rich above all cities, not only of Spain but of Europe, above all for the beauty of its women and their extreme cleanliness and agreeable way of speaking, with which only the Portuguese can compete in sweetness and grace." It was of the city of Valencia that Miguel was always to preserve memories free from bitterness: the place where there first appeared before his eyes the immense green prospect of the Mediterranean; the window from which he looked out on the world's greatest beauties; the basket of living flowers in which each and every woman seemed to him lovely and desirable; and finally the pleasant harborage in the tranquility and comfort of which he enjoyed the first delightful days of liberty after his grievous captivity.

Whoever has traveled along the Mediterranean coast from Valencia to Nice can have a good idea of how Miguel's soul was filled with happiness and the joy of living. As they approached active and powerful Barcelona he beheld "the festive sea, the jocund land, the clear air, the multitude of galleys crowding the beach, the incessant traffic of the port, the cannonades of Monjuich," and he was full of admiration for the city, regarding it as "flower of the handsome cities of the world, honor of Spain, terror and dread of its enemies far and near, gratification and delight of its inhabitants, asylum of foreigners, school of knight-errantry, example of devotion and satisfaction of everything which a discreet and enquiring desire could ask of a famous, rich and well-established city."

Leaving Barcelona behind Cervantes trod the delightful land of Provence, so similar to Andalusia because of its olive and orange trees that he felt perfectly at home; but it was not then or ever the landscape that immediately took possession of Miguel's spirit, but rather living, moving humanity, alive and in action. In an inn of Perpignan he learned how freedom can be lost through a cast of the dice, and in another inn, not many leagues from there in Languedoc, he learned of the caprice of the Duc de Nemours, who sent messengers to scour France for a woman beautiful enough for him to marry, and his only requirement was that she be beautiful. He was able to confirm that in France there was not a man or woman who did not learn the Castilian language, and he felt patriotic pride. One cold January morning he was astounded by the imposing white grandeur of the Alps, the peaks of which displayed in the sun their ancient whiteness, eternally renewed.[6]

CHAPTER 9

The Free Life of Italy—Milan—Rome

IF one of the modern psychologists who cavil so much over the cult of the ego and self-discipline could have thought out a plan for the efficient ordering of his youthful impressions it is very likely that it would have differed very little from the one traced by the itinerary of Cervantes in Italy.

What was then beginning to dawn in other nations had long since been firmly established in that blessed country. For things of the spirit Italy is the perfect mistress of the house, an alert early riser who wakens the rest of the European family when she has already done most of the work. Other countries follow or imitate her until they develop a creative power rooted in native sentiment which produces genuine literary or artistic orginality. But Italy begins to develop before anyone else, Italy points the way.

When Cervantes arrived in Italy, for the very reason that his artistic temperament had not yet been definitely shaped, he got the most benefit from the impressions that the country, the cities and the people made on him. He had no preconceptions as to how things should be, nor had the prolix lectures and wearisome commentaries of pedants blurred his vision or colored it in advance. Miguel was a lad with some book learning but he was not erudite. He was full of curiosity, but what interested him was whatever lived, whatever throbbed, whatever could be admired without any desire to imitate it or put it into the literary still and extract its spirit as if distilling an essence. More than cathedrals and monuments the things that appealed to him in Italy, as they did to his beloved and almost inseparable Licentiate, were "the country festivals of Palermo, the abundance of Milan, the feasts of Lombardy, the splendid meals of the inns, the *aconcha patrón, pasa acá manigoldo, venga la macarela, li polastri e li macarroni* . . .[1] the free life . . . the liberty of Italy!" You can see here the greatest words of praise that have ever been written about Italy. Modern writers have never and will never arrive at this, and here is where we must recognize the finest development of the spirit of Cervantes. "The free life of Italy," that is to say, the tranquility of the sky and the ambient air, the graciousness of the language, the benevolence and courtesy of behavior, the ease and good humor of manners, as of a country that has no master to tyrannize it or has only temporary masters who can be dismissed out of hand amid shouts of laughter and cruelly witty taunts.

Now consider this youth of twenty-one whose heart had been refreshed by the immortal gaiety of Seville for only two years and who had spent the rest of his life in the miserable austerity of the capital of Philip II, where he saw a companion of his boyhood like Mateo Vàzquez already becoming scornful, reserved and stiff, muffling his youth in the black livery of the Palace, and where in literature the odious rule of "conceits" and cloying rhetoric was beginning to destroy every spark of talent and every trace of spontaneity. Imagine then the eagerness of Miguel, happy and bursting with life, when he irrupted into Italy to enjoy himself to the full.

There life was free, and nothing truer or more eloquent can be said of it. One spoke as one wished with no fear of a sideways glance or cocked ear belonging to some pious soul who might note the words and denounce them in a black chamber. Italian women cajole and their speech caresses the ear; it was from them that Miguel learned the most pleasing part of his vocabulary. If you study it you will see that it contains some martial and maritime expressions of Italianate usage, but the Italianisms are more plentiful in all the passages about love. Before Miguel did so, Maestro Fray Luis, in order to temper the harshness of the Castilian language, had already turned to the honeyed love tales of Petrarch. But Miguel did more and better, since he imbibed the sweetness of Petrarchan speech from feminine voices and discovered tender words flowing tremulously from sensual scarlet lips at an age when marauding looks wander, melting with delight.

It is our misfortune that Miguel discreetly said nothing about the amorous adventures of his twenty-one years. But in the burning passion with which he depicts young loves in his novels it is obvious that he did not waste his opportunities, frequent enough in the free school of Italy, to stammer, spell out, and finally to speak that delightful language.

The Milanese countryside, where the bees hum, wandering from the mulberries to the grape vines, displayed its floral dress and, lest the fertility and abundance of the earth appear vulgar and monotonous, the evening light illuminated the gigantic white crests of the Alps, like a row of enormous stationary clouds, to quote the simile of Taine. Along the roads were quiet well-stocked inns where Miguel, as did the Glass Licentiate, tasted the most exciting diversity of wines,

> the blandness of the Treviano, the full body of the Montefiascone, the tang of the Asperino, the generosity of the two Greeks, Candia and Soma, the nobility of the wine of the Five Vineyards, the sweetness and charm of the Lady Vernaccia, the roughness of the Centola, while common Roman wines did not dare to appear among such gentry. And the innkeeper, having described so many different kinds of wine, offered to produce, not by sleight of hand but really and truly and without exaggeration, Madrigal, Coca, Alaejos, and the Imperial, greater than Royal City, abode of the god of laughter; he offered Esquivias, Alanís, Cazalla, Guadalcanal and Membrilla, not forgetting Rivadavia and Descargamaría.

This enthusiastic paragraph is one of the few in which Spanish genius takes a frankly Rabelaisian view of the world, tearing asunder the black veils of mysticism and asceticism in which it commonly enwraps itself. Those, Miguel thought, were the true humanities, learned with gusto, pleasant to experience, and perhaps he foresaw how in his old age he would recall the potions of Italy with delight.

He therefore came to Milan, the great and very rich "workshop of

Vulcan, envy of the Kingdom of France," that home of pleasure and gracious frankness where work and solemn fault-finding (so says Beyle)[2] were considered a penance which must be lightened as much as possible, and where the essential thing was to laugh, enjoy oneself, go forth to lunch or on a country outing and, young or old, always be in love, not in the languishing and sighing manner of the Spaniards, but in the delightful and diverting way of pagans.

It was significant that Miguel's first experience of Italian life was in Milan, generous and lighthearted Milan, where the women were beautiful and walked gaily through the streets, listening to the language of love as though accustomed to it, a language well suited for endearments, quick gallantries and witty repartee, and he watched as they paraded the city, their sleek heads under black hoods fastened to the hair by a rosary of silver pins like a diadem.

In contrast to their silvery voices he heard the clang of hammers in the forges from which came the arms favored the world over, brilliant as the jewels of a bride, embossed and encrusted with gold, dressed with plumes, and fastened by creaking leather straps: Burgundy helmets, basinets, cuirasses, greaves, thigh-pieces, and also the strong steel blades that strove to compete with those of the immortal Julián del Rey, of Alfonso de Sahagún, father, son and grandson, of Domingo the cutler, and the whole illustrious throng of sword makers.

Milan appeared to Miguel as one great sputtering forge, and similarly the complicated and confusing flower ornaments, spires, cantilevers, canopies, pinnacles, reversed pyramids and gargoyles of the Cathedral seemed to have the ebullience of an active subterranean furnace where marble instead of steel was being forged.

Perhaps he did not have time to mark how the tireless burning spirit of Leonardo, the great sage and the great artist, still lived in the churches and palaces of Milan. It is unlikely that he took the opportunity to see the *Last Supper* in the refectory of Santa María delle Grazie, the colors of which had even then begun to fade. On the other hand is it not almost certain that on rounding a corner his glance would light on disturbing eyes behind the curtain of a window, on an ironically ambiguous mouth, on sensual cheeks that contrasted with the candor of a forehead shaded by a light veil? Think in an Italian context of the women in the *Persiles* and some of the novels and plays, a contexture which in those theatrical works reminds us of Shakespeare, who likewise drew on Italian genius, and tell me if those delicate profiles are not copies of the women of Leonardo, of La Gioconda, of Lucrecia Crivelli, or his other models and their daughters and granddaughters.

With these images stored away in his memory Cervantes continued on his way. He crossed the marble mountains of Carrara and tarried in

Lucca, "a small city but beauteous and free, which, under the wing of the Empire and of Spain, looks down from a privileged position on the cities of the princes who have long coveted it. There more than anywhere else Spaniards are well received and highly regarded, and the reason for it all is that in the city they do not command but rather request, and as they never stay for more than a day they have no occasion to display their quality which is held to be arrogant."[3] In the environs of this city a first testimony to the ancient grandeur of Rome was the amphitheater whose marble seats the centuries had corroded and crumbled, while the fields were taking on the austere and solemn aspect of the marshes. As Miguel says at the beginning of Book IV of the *Persiles*: "Now the breezes of Rome blow in our faces, now the hopes which sustain us glow in our souls, now, now I realize that I find myself possessed of what I have longed for."

He entered Rome by the Porto del Populo and, if he did not kiss them, he wanted "to kiss again and again the lintels and verges of the entrance to the Holy City." It was then that Miguel could write that sonnet, neither better nor worse than those he had written before:

O great, O powerful, O sacred
soul city of Rome! Before you I bow,
a devout, humble, newly arrived pilgrim
who marvels to see so much beauty. . . .

Then he conceived that magnificent eulogy of Rome, queen city of the world:

> He visited its temples, worshiped its saintly relics and admired its grandeur; and as through the claws of the lion one comes to know its power and savage cruelty, that of Rome is revealed by its broken marbles, whole and half statues, broken arches and ruined baths, by its magnificent porticos and great amphitheaters, by its famous holy river that always fills its verges with water and beatifies them with the many relics of the martyrs buried on its banks, by its bridges which seem to mirror each other, and by its streets whose names alone claim authority over those of all the other cities of the world: the Via Appia, the Flaminia, the Julia, with others of the same quality. He was no less full of admiration at the arrangement of the hills: the Caelian, the Quirinal and the Vatican, with the other four whose names attest the greatness and majesty of Rome. He also noted the authority of the College of Cardinals, the dignity of the Supreme Pontiff, the crowds of varied people and nations. All this he gazed at, noted and stored in the back of his mind.

And we should note here how feelings about the imperial grandeur of Rome entered Miguel's spirit, not by reading Titus Livius or Tacitus, as other poets did, but by seeing it with his own eyes, so that even before coming to Rome but much more so after wandering through its streets and temples, his was a Renaissance spirit, offspring of the gentle, melancholy soul of Tasso,[4] whose praises were then on everyone's lips.

The retinue of Aquaviva entered the Vatican, where Miguel was to see everything at close hand, note everything, and appraise everything. Remember that another who entered the Vatican to shape and mature his spirit was our great humorist of the Middle Ages, the satirist Juan Ruiz, Archpriest of Hita,[5] who, shades of history! had also been born in the enlightenment of Alcalá de Henares.

Cervantes got to know the Vatican from the inside, from the servants dining room and the chamber of Aquaviva, and his heart was a little chilled among its marbles. The fresh laughter with which he saluted the vigorous grace and sensual gaiety of Milan faltered before the thin laughter of old men, the pursing of tightly folded lips like those of some of Raphael's cardinals. After a few months he concluded that he had learned everything he needed to know and was tired of the servants' dining room and ecclesiastical service. He heard that his master was to be named cardinal and the thought of being chamberlain to a great seigneur dedicated to an orderly and suavely intriguing life did not attract him. He knew that war with the Turks or someone or other was imminent, and Miguel, who had now seen Rome, demanded his sword and enlisted as a soldier.

CHAPTER 10

Moncada's Tercio[1]—*Venice—The Gaiety of Italy*

M*aestre de Campo*[2] Don Miguel de Moncada was a noble gentleman descended from one of the most illustrious families of Catalonia. He was brave and sound of judgment, which is the highest praise that can be given a military man. Wise in council, decisive in action, strong and courageous, he served the King from his earliest youth to his extreme old age. We must not think of him as one of those military braggarts with scarlet cheeks painted by Velásquez when Mars had become a drunken soldier, but rather as one of the great men with pale faces, black sleeveless jackets, sharp and willful chins we encounter every day in the pictures of El Greco.

And so that you can imagine Cervantes' military life and the appearance and character of the people who surrounded him in those years, you might well recall that proud and arrogant figure of the centurion in the picture of *The Spoliation of Christ* (in the sacristy of the Cathedral of Toledo), whose burnished cuirass reflects like a scarlet flame the Venetian tunic of the Redeemer; and later the heavy-armored body of the Count of Orgaz (in the Church of San Tomé in Toledo); and finally the somewhat imaginary throng of soldiers who surround the Centurion Maurice in the picture in the Escorial.

These soldiers were thin-faced, all bone and muscle, with legs strong as steel, broad chests, and athletic biceps, the soldiers that Cervantes knew, those men who had been victorious at St. Quentin[3] with Pescara and Leiva, the men who took the summits of the Alpujarras[4] in bloody fighting; and Don Miguel de Moncada, who was in command of one of the four *tercios* on a war footing in Naples, was a gentleman of that splendid strong race that lasted for so short a time. In the war in Granada[5] he won his promotion to *Maestre de Campo* on the battlefield and from there crossed to Italy with his *tercio* of veterans, greater in quality than in numbers. It was necessary to reinforce it with two companies of raw recruits, and Miguel had no difficulty in enlisting among many others.

Moncada's *tercio* was made up of ten companies whose captains were men with surnames suggesting that most of them were Catalans, Valencians, and Aragonese, indomitable commanders for whom the fatigues of battle were recreation and the bustle and tumult of the camp were repose. Miguel's company commander was the Alcarreño Don Diego de Urbina, "a famous captain from Guadalajara," as his immortal soldier says. The people of Guadalajara and those of Alcalá consider themselves closer kin than those of Alcalá and Madrid. It is therefore not surprising that from the first Captain Diego de Urbina should know the spirited young man personally and have an affection for him almost as though he were his fellow countryman.[6]

And now that we have Cervantes doffing the habit of a cardinal's chamberlain for the bright colors and plumes of the military, let us think of what it must have been for him to find himself introduced to the life of a soldier, crossing Italy from coast to coast, as he doubtless must have done, tasting freely all the delights that before had barely reached his lips. It was then that he perhaps traversed the heart of Italy, from Rome to Ancona, and embarking there passed by Ferrara to Venice, of which he wrote:

> It seemed to him that its riches were infinite, its government prudent, its site impregnable, its opulence great, its surroundings pleasant, and

> finally, all of it, in itself and in its every part worthy of a fame which reaches all parts of the terrestrial globe, this truth being supported further by the organization of its famous arsenal, which is the place where galleys are built as well as other vessels without number.

It would be an error to think that Cervantes at his age could absorb what Venice offered the tourist of a later day in search of exquisite and almost morbid emotions, but it would be an even greater error to think that the sensation of the color and light of Venice did not stay with him and to doubt that if he had been a painter he would have belonged to the Venetian school. The courtly parts of his works are full of Venetian scenes of delicate fragmented light falling upon lordly scarlet velvets and damasks, and his noble ladies are ladies of Tintoretto and Titian, lovely ladies with curly golden hair.

Venice also perplexed him and he did not know how to take that home and refuge of perfidy, more to be feared than Florence despite Machiavelli, because in Florence there was only one and in Venice every citizen was a minor or major Machiavelli. At that time one had to count or did not count on the Venetians for everything, and more particularly for maritime enterprises; it was never possible to leave them out of consideration, whether for or against. Note that Cervantes speaks of Venice with admiration, but not with the enthusiasm that pours from him when he mentions kindly Milan. This was a common reaction in his day. Venice was consulted but distrusted.

Miguel as a Spaniard also liked to visit religious houses, pious relics and monuments, and being in Ancona he did not fail to make the short journey to Loreto to visit the Holy House. When old and devout he would recall with pleasure for himself and others how

> in that holy temple I saw no walls or partitions because they were entirely covered with crutches, shrouds, chains, fetters, manacles, locks of hair, wax sculptures, paintings and effigies that testified to the innumerable mercies many had received from the hand of God through the intercession of His Divine Mother whose sacred image He sought to exalt and authenticate with a multitude of miracles in recompense for the devotion of those who adorned the walls of her house with offerings such as these. He saw the very apartment and bedchamber where was delivered the highest and most important message that all the heavens and all the angels and all the dwellers in the eternal abode had ever seen beyond comprehension.

This fragment of a sermon interlarded by Miguel among the apothegms set forth in his exemplary novel *The Glass Licentiate* reflects the state of his mind on visiting the Holy House of the Virgin preserved in

Loreto. It gave him a pleasant feeling and perhaps reminded him of his own faraway home, from which he received news most infrequently.

We must not think that Miguel busied himself only in exploring cities and visiting churches. His military duties took him from one place to another and being far from restrictive in peacetime permitted him at times to wander at will among the many hostelries and entertaining country establishments with which a pagan Providence sowed the Italian land to make life in it both pleasant and expensive.

As always happened the soldiers' pay was so much in arrears that they went through terrible alternating periods of scarcity and plenty. At one moment the needy soldier shivered from cold and hunger within his doublet, slashed not for ostentation but by wear and tear, and the next moment would see him strutting proudly around the streets, mustachios bristling, pockets open wide, all because he had received several wage payments at once. Urbino's company being made up of hard-bitten veteran soldiers, Miguel soon learned all the tricks of the trade that they employed to help one another through these perpetual ups and downs of fortune. And here we must admire something we have already noted in Seville, and that is how our hidalgo touched the fringes of the underworld and of knavery a hundred times and always maintained his dignity, without any stain on his character, which is all the more creditable since difficulties were great, license unlimited, and the fear in which soldiers were held sufficient to ensure their impunity in any case. Read the lives of soldiers, leaving out novelistic fiction and imaginative trappings, that we still have around: that of Alonso de Contreras, for example, or Miguel de Castro, and you will find in them a thousand details that will surely disgust you even if you are above morality and profess the religion of the strong. Miguel witnessed things like this daily among the soldiery, but he knew when to stand timely aside although he never shut his eyes to them. And do you know why? Because he possessed what the others lacked, the ideal that inspires men of genius and so often lifts them from the mire.

This ideal harbored by Miguel, who was not yet reconciled to the weight of the pike or the arquebus on his shoulder, led him to penetrate the enchanted garden of Italian poetry, which he now regarded as his own orchard. Here and there he came up against his faithful friends the giants and the knights-errant speaking in fine Tuscan endecasyllables, at times in the interminable hundred cantos of the *Amadís de Gaula* where old Bernardo Tasso[7] placed his needy inspiration, badly paid by the French, at the service and in praise of the Spaniards, at times in the *Morgante* of Pulci,[8] who was then beginning to stir Italy with his lusty bellowings. Circulating everywhere, not only in books but in clubs, in the talk of the *trattoria* [tavern] and the guardroom, were the hundred thousand little anecdotes of the *novelieri*, the amusing and innocent narratives of Masuccio Salernitano, the recondite and graceful stories of the great Boccaccio.[9]

Miguel was absorbed in pleasant contemplation of his surroundings when more loudly than ever the oft-repeated cry resounded through Italy—The Turks are on us! The Turks are on us!—and all Italy looked toward Venice, knowing that the Venetians held the key to the future. Pope Pius V, a most saintly man who today is venerated on the altar, was in torment; Philip II shared the fear and apprehension of all Christianity. Both of them made ready whatever galleys and armaments they could. The Pope appointed Marco Antonio Colonna[10] to lead his forces; Philip II appointed Juan Andrea Doria,[11] with Don Álvaro de Bazán under his command. In the last days of May of 1571 it was known everywhere that a League against the Turk had been formed. The shrewd Venetian merchants had weighed their interests and joined their forces to those of the Pope and the Spaniards. At the head of all came, not a Doria and not a Colonna, but the brother of the King himself, he whom the soldiers, with filial and affectionate confidence, called "Señor Don Juan."[12]

Between May and June the *tercio* of Don Miguel de Moncada was brought to its full strength. Rumors of war were everywhere, accompanied by cold shivers of delight. The sea and the earth prepared for combat; the heavens seemed to listen, casting an azure blessing on the clatter of muskets and the beat of oars. Miguel felt his soul possessed by a heroic impatience. The long-awaited door opened wide.

CHAPTER 11

Don Juan in Genoa—The Fleet in Messina

Do you know what Don Juan de Austria looked like? In the Prado there is an admirable portrait of him, painted by an Italian hand but sometimes wrongly attributed to Sánchez Coello. Don Juan is a handsome young man, fair of skin, his leg long and slim, his womanish foot imprisoned in laced buskins. The hands are slender and tapering; on the first finger of the left hand is a woman's ring with a ruby, a diamond and an emerald carved in the shape of a heart, proclaiming what the

Sieur de Brantôme[1] said, "that Don Juan was greatly loved and on good terms with the ladies." The scarlet armlet that encircles the right sleeve confirms this. It is further corroborated by the bold gray eyes, the quivering nostrils, and the eager expression—infinitely more alive than that of Philip II—and Don Juan's hair is chestnut, not the cold blondness that makes his brother's face seem inhuman. There is also something martial in the stance and other aspects of the figure that prevails over the intangible amorous quality emanating from his person.

Don Juan was not only loved by the ladies; his soldiers loved him, because the soldiery, like every grouping of men joined in a common purpose, and especially so when life and comfort have to be sacrificed to that purpose, always recognize the man to be venerated and followed. At the same time there were military leaders with greater reputations than Don Juan's. Among the men who were themselves generals but were prepared to serve under him was Juan Andrea Doria, upon whose brow the laurels won in Tripoli were still unfaded, and with other divisions of the League came Marco Antonio Colonna, Don Álvaro de Bazán, a Venier and a Barbáriga, Venetians, men of war and of the sea, strong and capable. Who doubted that the enterprise was to be difficult and arduous? Who was there who did not realize that Philip II, when he gave his brother the command, was reasoning coldly and dispassionately that if Don Juan came out of it well it would be a great boon to Christianity, while if he failed it would be a salutary lesson for the proud and spirited young man?

Because of this we must think of Don Juan as being fully aware of how formidable a mission he had to accomplish, but with no lack of confidence in his own power. Under the arched delicacy of his eyebrows the sparse but untamed little moustache bristled and the jutting jaw of the Austrian dynasty, strong and willful, showed indominable determination.

Don Juan arrived in Genoa on the twenty-sixth of June of 1571, at the head of forty-seven galleys in which were the *tercios* of Don Lope de Figueroa and Don Miguel de Moncada. Moncada's *tercio* had been reinforced in Naples with two companies. Miguel was there when they joined up, at which time he could observe "the arbitrary power of the quartermasters, the obnoxiousness of some captains, the importunities of landlords, the careful accounting of paymasters, the complaints of the population, the traffic in billets, the cheekiness of the recruits, the disputes with lodgers, the demands for more military stores than necessary." Then, dressed like a parrot, as he says, he roamed the wide streets of Naples, enjoying its mild climate and the splendor of its sky to such an extent that he took a fancy to it that lasted for the rest of his life, and this love affair, intensified soon after, was lodged in his soul so firmly that when old and with few illusions left he will always cherish the most alluring one of returning once again, and in his middle and old age he considered himself an exile from Naples.

When the *tercio* left Naples, Miguel had already undertaken short excursions, but only on the passage to Genoa, when he found himself crowded in with many hundreds of men in the holds and cockpits of the galleys, was he amazed by the "strange life of those maritime dwellings where most of the time one is tortured by bedbugs, robbed by the galley slaves, insulted by the sailors, harassed by rats and sickened by the motion of the sea." Heeling to the wind and running before the squalls the galley sailed along the Tyrrhenian Sea. Since the passage was short, as many men as could be packed in were loaded on board, so that "having sat up all night, wet and heavy-eyed, they arrived at the lovely and most beautiful city of Genoa and, debarking at its sheltered Mandrache,[2] after visiting a church he went with all his comrades to a hostelry where they drowned their recent trials in the present *gaudeamus. . . .*" Genoa offered herself at that time of early autumn, "full of ornamental gardens, white houses and resplendent spires that, irradiated by the sun, reflect such flaming rays that they can scarcely be looked upon."

Genoa was for Miguel a vision of golden glory. It is one of those cities like Lisbon, like Oporto, like Naples, built as an amphitheater facing the west and courted by the sun with its most generous caresses. Our Miguel arrived in Genoa, now a soldier, with all the liveliness and ardor of the recruit but without the wiliness of the veteran. He had a glimpse, though he still knew little about it, "of the cold of the sentinels, the danger of the assaults, the horror of battles, the hunger of sieges, the destruction of mines." And Genoa was then as now a point of departure for perilous undertakings. Then as now the ships tied up to the quays opened their gullets, unconscious fatal bearers of illusion to the unknown future. You can imagine what that first setting-forth toward glory or death meant to Miguel.

They waited in Genoa more than a month for Don Miguel de Moncada to return with the supplies provided by the dilatory Venetians, and on his arrival all the troops went off to Messina in the heat of August. The vineyards, pomegranate trees and olive groves of Sicily welcomed them with luxuriant foliage. The boiling waters of the Strait sang a hymn of war. The spacious port swallowed galleys and more galleys whose mouths vomited men and more men. Don Juan came and went, his face flushed by fatigue and heat, sharp of sight, quick of tongue, his ear as attentive to the complaint of the officer as to the grumble of the most insignificant soldier.

Around the middle of August the galleys from Spain arrived under command of the Genoese Juan Andrea Doria. Grave, haughty, and silent, Juan Andrea looked like one of those wise and venerable paladins who, satiated with war and loves, retired to shady woods or enchanted palaces in the books of knight-errantry. In his galleys Doria brought with him two veteran companies he himself had organized, which today we would call marines or landing troops: rough bearded men, old heroes of Tripoli, skilled in the business of war. Miguel gazed at those leathery faces, at those grizzled beards, those calm and contemptuous looks: some were Italians, other Germans, a few Portuguese and many Spaniards from the Levantine coast, but they all seemed to belong to the same race as glimpsed in ancient parchments, in the exaggerations of the *Romancero* and in the vague accounts of an America greater than life, the progeny of which appeared in the books of chivalry with all their kindred and their pretension of verity. But it was the robustness of their shoulders, the imposing fierceness of their moustaches, the swarthiness of their skins, the scars on their faces and hands that made them kinsmen of the Amadises and Esplandians, of Hector and Ulysses.

As the troops that were to embark arrived they were distributed to each vessel. Miguel was posted to the *Marquesa* galley, which was under the command of an Italian, Francisco de Sancto Pietro. He soon found himself mingling with those heroes whose appearance filled him with admiration, but in association with them he soon learned what heroes were like as seen at close quarters. They all complained of their way of life and, between blasphemies and execrations, swore they would quit after this naval action, which promised to be a fine thing to see. They showed by their talk that they were dominated by gross instincts that found expression in habitual cheating at cards, stupid quarrels, unrestrained love of drunkenness, and intolerable cruelty. There was not much difference between these real bravos and the bullies, braggarts and *hombres* of the underworld of Seville.

On the twenty-fifth of August Don Juan wrote to Don García de Toledo,[3] telling him that he had seen Marco Antonio Colonna with the twelve galleys of His Holiness, "which are in good shape." But while the galleys of Doria promised thunder and fury those of the Pope commanded by Colonna represented ease and riches, being provided with everything, amply supplied with arms and munitions, the troops well paid and commanded by a prince of the most illustrious house in Italy.

A little later the armada of the Venetians arrived under the command of Sebastián Venier with forty-eight galleys, six galleases and two sailing ships. "These," Don Juan said, "are not as well found as I would like. . . . The said general," he added, "has assured me that very shortly he expects another sixty galleys that are in Cyprus."

Once more the rebellious and insubordinate spirit of Venice, its scarcely disguised independence, the duplicity and ill-will with which it supported the League, were made clear to the eyes of all. On August 30 Don Juan, already somewhat exasperated, wrote:

> Yesterday I started to inspect the galleys of the Venetians and was with their captain. Your Honor would not believe how badly off they are for fighting-men and sailors. They have arms and artillery, but as one cannot fight without men I am dismayed that the world expects me to accomplish anything important when galleys are counted by number and not by quality. In spite of all this I shall try not to overlook any opportunity to show that for my part I have performed my duty.

After dictating this, Don Juan continued in his own hand:

> I wish to add to the poor condition in which the Venetians are another even worse which is that they have no kind of discipline whatever; rather each galley takes whatever course it wishes. Your Honor will judge what a fine situation we will be fighting in.

The haughty and impertinent Venetians, like men without lord or master, did not allow themselves to be ordered about nor did they accept the authority of Don Juan. They also resisted taking Spanish soldiers into their galleys, saying that they had agreed to fight with their vessels, not to have them serve for the transport of troops. Among the Venetian galleys there were possibly many merchant ships that a mass of soldiers could damage or ruin completely. Finally, after councils and lobbying between their chiefs, "these Venetian gentlemen," Don Juan wrote with a touch of irony on September 9, "at last have decided to take into their galleys four thousand of His Majesty's infantry, two thousand five hundred Spaniards and one thousand five hundred Italians." Previously the sixty Venetian galleys had arrived from Crete.

The spacious port of Messina was a forest of masts and a Babel of peoples of all races and languages. Miguel was excited, wildly exhilarated. Don Juan felt in very much the same mood, seeing that his difficulties were being amicably resolved. On September 15 the fleet put to sea, having been divided into three combat armadas, a scouting force and one in reserve. The galley *Marquesa* sailed in the third combat armada on the left under the command of the Purveyor General of Venice, Agustín Barbárigo.

CHAPTER 12

The Island of Ulysses—The Day of Lepanto

THE breeze from the Gran Sirte blew hot, swelling the sails toward the Adriatic, where the Venetian galleys approached the Strait of Otranto as one would open the door of his house to enter. The Turk had rounded the coast of Morea; he had been seen from Cephalonia and from Zante. The Venetians advised Don Juan to take a rest before attacking and the fleet made for Corfu, where the great bay of Govino would shelter it.

Winding their way between the islands the ships soon reached Corfu. In the *Marquesa* galley, one of scant tonnage, there were hundreds of galley slaves, sailors and men-at-arms. Miguel was seasick, suffocated, eaten by fleas and lice, disgusted by the grossness of the crew and the slaves of the row galley, full of every kind of apprehension except fear.

He longed to leap ashore, to stretch his arms and legs and wash his face and hands, an impossible luxury in those narrow quarters. Corfu seemed to him a terrestrial paradise, and as they approached its shores a classical memory leaped to Miguel's mind: the arrival of Ulysses in the land of the Phaeacians, in Canto V of the *Odyssey*.

And with his stomach heaving and his head spinning, he recalled the hardships of the Greek hero and like him he looked on the beach of Corfu as a providential asylum. Later he thought back and recalled that his imaginings were not idle. That beach was the very Phaeacian beach that welcomed the wandering Ulysses.[1] That river was the river in which Nausicaa, the virgin of snowy arms, washed the clothing. . . . There on a slope was to be seen the sacred wood of white poplars that the forebears of King Alcinous dedicated to Minerva, the goddess of wisdom. Soon the crew and soldiers leaped to earth and Miguel feasted his ears on hearing the language of Homer spoken, as at the banquet of Alcinous it was sung and declaimed by Demodocus, the bard of the ancient poem. The mild Ionic clime bathed Miguel's spirit and the waters of the river dear to Nausicaa bathed his body.

The island of the Phaeacians, Corfu in the modern idiom, is a beautiful island where one is forever liable to quartan agues. Miguel fell ill with fever and was transferred back to the galley. There he curled up in a corner, shivered, burned, became delirious, and found himself alone in the midst of a horde of soldiers who swore, shouted, drank, and cared not that there were one or two or a hundred sick men among them, for they were completely insensitive to the misery of others as well as their own. There was only one human and compassionate man in that hard-eyed crew. He was Mateo de Santistéban, a generous man with a brave heart who came from Tudela in the Kingdom of Navarre and was an ensign in a company that joined Moncada's *tercio* in Naples. From time to time Santistéban took care of Miguel and he may have alerted his captain, Diego de Urbina. This valiant soul from Alcarria tried to comfort his fellow countryman from Alcalá de Henares, whose face was not unknown to him among the two hundred soldiers under his command, but both Urbina and Santistéban were officers with a thousand cares and responsibilities. Cervantes passed the most severe attack of his fever alone and forsaken in his corner, poorly wrapped in a blanket in which bedbugs flourished, defending himself against the rats that came to gnaw his boots at night and even in daytime in the darkness of the hold.

Every day he heard news of the movements of the armada but the old soldiers did not discuss it and most of their talk had to do with quarrels over drink. The recruits talked wild nonsense and concealed poorly the fear that invaded them as they felt the time of action approach. Drowsy and weak, Miguel did not know what day it was or what time of day.

One morning, the seventh of November, a tremendous outcry was heard on deck. As usual the soldiers had left Miguel alone in his corner, but they now returned hastily, some pale, others flushed, their eyes alight, their footsteps stumbling, their hands clumsy. "To arms, to arms!" they were shouting. The attack had begun. Suddenly the frame of the boat creaked, all the timbers trembled, and a rosary of crashes announced that the *Marquesa* had just fired its first broadside. Miguel flung aside his blanket, clapped on his steel morion and looked for his arquebus. His legs were shaky, his face yellow as that of a corpse.

On deck he encountered his captain with Ensign Santistéban and another ensign, a highlander named Gabriel de Castañeda. All of them, when they saw the heavy-eyed soldier, his face yellow and his eyes bleary, told him to take cover below deck since he was not fit to fight. But Miguel had already glimpsed the fire, had smelled the powder, had breathed the smoke. The dead and wounded fell on every side as cannon shots coming out of the blue stunned the ears. The galley slaves on their benches shouted in unison "For-ward! Ro-ow!" Miguel would not return to his corner. In his own words: "What would they say of him if he did not do his duty?" Excited by fever and danger he addressed his chiefs in a short speech which has been conveyed to us by Ensign Gabriel de Castañeda with the calm precision of the highlander: "Gentlemen," said the hidalgo from Alcalá, "on every occasion when His Majesty has been at war up to now and I have been sent to it I have served as a good soldier, and thus today I will not do less though I am ill and fevered; it is better to fight and die in the service of God and His Majesty than to go below. Señor Captain, put me in the most dangerous place and there I will take my stand and die fighting."[2] With those noble words Miguel showed an attitude and bearing worthy of the ancient heroes, one that brooked no contradiction. His fellow countryman and captain, Diego de Urbina, shook his head in sorrow and as one who abandons to destruction a precious object that could still be of service he ordered Miguel to station himself with twelve men in the place where the longboat was carried on deck.[3] What was there in the eyes, the words, the personality, and bearing of this soldier that he was entrusted with a command post, however small, in the midst of battle?

Promptly carrying out Urbina's orders, Miguel occupied his post, from which the scene of battle unrolled before his eyes. Between breaks in the clouds of smoke appeared the knifing prows, the menacing rams, the iron hooks and the prongs with which galleys tried to grapple others in order to board them.[4] A handsome youth in a silver helmet flew over the waters through fire and smoke, like the Archangel Saint Michael who adorns Gothic altar paintings in a flame of gold, blood, and silver. It was Don Juan in a light skiff, in his right hand a naked sword with gold quillons shining in the sun and in his left a crucifix of ivory and ebony. Shouting imprecations and exhortations he passed unharmed, dauntless, his breast bared to the bullets that laced the air and burst on ships' sides or whizzed into the deep green waters of the Gulf. "Long live Don Juan!" the proud Spaniards shouted hoarsely. The war-hardened Venetians looked on in silent amazement. Never had they seen such audacity in one so young.

Soon the sea spawned more and more Turkish galliots coming up in close formation. The howling of the Christians rowing in them could already be heard. They were Greeks, Italians, Spaniards who rowed furiously without any need for the cruel floggings of the boatswains. Perhaps more closely than the Turks desired, their ships approached those of the Christians. Anguished voices rose from the hidden benches, supplicating the fleet of the League, "Here we are, we are Christians. Free us from captivity. For Christ's sake! For the Virgin Mary! For the Holy Madonna!"—and keeping time with such cries their chests heaved with exertion.

Miguel then saw

> two galleys attack each other head on in the midst of the open water; and as they grappled and were locked together he finds himself on only two feet of the flat top of the ram, and despite the fact that at the first false step he would be exploring the depths of Neptune's bosom, nevertheless with intrepid heart, carried away by the exaltation that inspired him, he offers himself as a target to all the archery and makes his way over the narrow space onto the other vessel.[5] And what is most admirable is that no sooner would he have fallen never to rise again when another would take his place; and if this one were also to fall in the sea which awaited like an enemy, another and yet another would follow him without faltering in the face of death: the greatest valor and daring that can be met with in all the crises of war.

"How fortunate were they," Miguel continues reflectively, in this crisis he described as having happened to himself,

> how fortunate were those blessed centuries that were spared the terrifying fury of those devilish instruments of the artillery . . . that allowed an infamous and cowardly weapon to take the life of a valiant gentleman without his knowing how or whence, although he may display the courage and mettle which fires and animates courageous breasts, with a stray bullet, perhaps fired by one who fled terrified at the flash of fire when he let off the cursed machine that cuts off and in an instant wipes out consciousness and the life of one who deserves to enjoy it for many long years.[6]

And this, as he himself relates, and no one else can do it better than he, followed step by step. With the strange lucidity that a high fever and danger and the proximity of death communicates to all spirits, Cervantes on that high and memorable occasion, the greatest that the centuries have seen, reviewed all that he had planned, imagined, or dreamed of in his short life; passing through his mind were his illusions of glory, the flattery of poetic fame, perhaps he recalled the school in Madrid, perhaps the delicate image of Queen Doña Isabel, together with the kindly face of his teacher López de Hoyos, the lovely seductive form of his sister Andrea and the monastic profile of his sister Luisa. In the midst of such imaginings a violent blow and most intense cold paralyzed his left hand. He looked down and saw blood gushing from it, but gave it little heed. Without a quiver of lip or lid he stood the pain of the wound. Fever and pride sustained him, no less than curiosity and a desire to see how it would all end.

Doubtless he did not notice that, facing him in the Turkish galley which had attacked the *Marquesa*, two pairs of hostile eyes were peering at that soldier with a wounded hand who was holding his ground so dauntlessly. Two bullets fired at the same time from two muskets sought Miguel's breast and almost flung him to the deck. . . . A red cloud covered his sight and for a time he lost consciousness.

Hear how he himself tells it:

> . . . on that lucky day when sinister
> as was the fate of the enemy fleet
> so to ours was it right and favorable,
> by fear and courage companioned,
> in person was I present at the action,
> armed more by hope than steel.
> I saw the ranked squadron broken and destroyed
> and with barbarous folk and Christians
> was Neptune's bed reddened in a thousand places.
> Wrathful death in its insane fury
> racing urgently to and fro,
> showed itself early to some, to others late.
> The confused sounds, the terrifying clamor,
> the faces of the miserable wretches
> who were dying between fire and water.
> The deep mournful sighs
> that wounded breasts breathed forth
> cursing their hideous fate.
> The blood froze in their veins
> when by the sound of our trumpets
> they learned of their loss and of our glory.
> The high victorious voice signalling,
> piercing the air, clear as day, showed that
> the Christian right had prevailed.
> At that happy time I stood melancholy,
> one hand gripping a sword
> and the other dripping blood.
> By a deep hurt I felt my breast
> wounded, and the left hand
> was broken in a thousand pieces.
> But my happiness was so great, to see
> the rude infidel defeated by the Christian,
> that it pervaded my soul,
> So that I scarcely noted I was hurt,
> although so mortal was my pain
> that at times it took from me all my senses. . . .[7]

The *Marquesa* galley had suffered heavily in the battle. The master, Francisco de Sancto Pietro, fell dead and with him many members of the crew and not a few soldiers, both veterans and recruits. The wounded Cervantes saw swarthy men falling who had seemed towers of strength, and he himself could scarce believe that he was alive. Deafened by the thunder of the artillery and half blinded by the smoke and fire, he half consciously saw the huge bulks of the galleys pass like fantastic shadows, and the outlines of the fighting soldiers seemed tiny, like the little figures on an altar piece.

Miguel was brought out of his stupor and nervous shock by the triumphant echoes of the clarion trumpets proclaiming that victory was won and by the outcry of the five or six thousand galley slaves who rowed in the Turkish galleys and broke into shouts of jubilation and of praise to the saints and the Virgin when they were boarded by Christians. Topping all rose, hoarse, deep, vibrant, the Spanish cry uttered by Spaniards and Italians: "Long live Señor Don Juan! Long live Señor Don Juan!"

Two inspired friars who were on board repeated the holy words, strangely prophetic, that later all Europe from the Pontiff Pius V to the least village priest was to remember: *Fuit homo missus á Deo cui nomen erat Joannes*. . . . There was a man sent by God whose name was John. . . .

CHAPTER 13

The Flavor of Glory—Hollow Victory—Messina—Hospital

THE flavor of glory is neither sweet nor salt, neither bitter nor sour, nor can it be appreciated straightaway. Its aims and the extent to which they are attained must be savored. What can we say of the flavor of a glory as great as that of Lepanto, that battle in which all the enemy ships were captured or destroyed save for a few belonging to the King of Algiers which managed to escape; in which the Turkish admiral was killed and his sons taken prisoner; in which, finally, when the action was over the battered fleet of the Christians was replenished with the best of the Turkish armada? No one could remember such a complete triumph, and for years and years there was no need to refer to Lepanto by name but to say only "the naval battle" to be instantly understood. Cervantes proudly and delightedly savored that flavor of triumph for many years, and when already near death he was proud to have played a role in it, to have had, "however humble, a part in the victory." The glorious day of Lepanto was the greatest in his life. That is how he regarded it and that is what he sought a hundred times to establish for the ages, and there is no other reason for his repeated claims for the superiority of arms over letters.

Cervantes was first and foremost a soldier, and he regarded the military profession, as was customary at that period, as the most honorable human occupation. Thus he loved action more than thought, and his thinking had to do with action, whether in the dungeons of Algiers, in the inns and roadhouses of the Sierra Morena, or in the prison of Seville. He was not tainted in any respect with the passive and pacific attitude that engendered ecstatic mysticism and through it the decadence of Spain. If he had taken to mysticism he would have done so actively, tirelessly, like Saint Teresa, a mystic of the road and wayside inn as interested in works of masonry as in the construction of his inner castle;[1] or like Saint Ignatius, mystic and general, conqueror of souls, organizer and leader of the most feared militia that has ever been known. Cervantes was a soldier who wrote verses when young, as did many soldiers, composing them out of high spirits and a desire to show off. He preferred to dedicate the rest of his vigorous life to action, and only when his physical powers began to decline did he take refuge exclusively in literature as the last resort of an old man incapable of grasping a sword. The doubts that had been in his soul before Lepanto completely disappeared after it.

With his hand shattered, with his chest pierced by two bullets, thrust into a corner, on emerging gradually from his heroic delirium Miguel began to understand what he had done and what had happened around him. The hero does not know that he is a hero until afterward when others tell him so. Consciousness of his heroism had not yet entered Miguel's confused and shocked mind, and as always happens the sounds of battle still rang in his ears and behind his closed lids terrible flames exploded. He knew then that the battle had been a great one. Perhaps he did not suspect, as he later affirmed repeatedly, that it had been the greatest that past centuries had ever seen or future ones would see. He could not guess that the resounding name of Lepanto would ever become as it did the great balm of his life and that, poor and unappreciated, beset by poverty and by a blind and stupid justice, ignored by his contemporaries or sent to prison and harried from pillar to post, he would take refuge in the name of Lepanto as the highest pinnacle of life and, scorning any other cause for pride, he would assuage his trials and tribulations by saying with head held high: "Poor and old I may be, those who do not know me esteem me but little, I live precariously and sordidly, but—I was at Lepanto!" Lepanto was high noon for Miguel, following a short and splendid morning.

On the night of the seventh to the eighth of October, mustered and half put in order, the victorious fleet was coasting through the Gulf of Patras, while the *Marquesa* and some other galleys anchored at the island of Petala which rises from the sea near the coast of Acarnania. The agonies and sweats of Miguel that night not even he has been able to depict. With the ships sailing and surgeons far from plentiful, he got only summary first aid, possibly a simple bandage, which increased rather than alleviated his anguish. On the morning of the eighth Miguel found himself faint and suffering, shivering and weak, when, like a figure from a Flemish tapestry he saw before his eyes the hero of the expedition, ever blond and flushed, an audacious smile on his lips, at his belt the sword with the golden quillons, his agile legs steady, his arms relaxed and eloquent. It was Don Juan de Austria, who was visiting the sick and wounded, distributing kind words and just rewards. He called his soldiers "sons," nearly all of them being older than he was, and, by God, it seemed a guarantee of fresh victories and of certain immortality to hear oneself called "son" by such a young father and one of such goodly elegance.

With Don Juan came another personage, in his forties, with pointed beard and great grayish moustache, dark cheeks, stern brow; over his cuirass he wore the lizard of the Knights of Santiago. If Don Juan seemed the Archangel of battles that other personage, who also carried a general's baton, was the exact image of the God of War, with something of Mars and something of Neptune. He was the first Marquis of Santa Cruz, Don Álvaro de Bazán, the hero of Muros, of La Gomera, of Malta, "the father of soldiers."[2]

With admiring eyes Miguel saw them approach; with complete surprise and inexpressible joy he saw them stop before his couch. There in a few gruff words Diego de Urbina, the captain from Alcarria, told the generals what Cervantes had done the previous day. The gray eyes of Don Juan and the blue eyes of Don Álvaro looked with interest at the wounded soldier. Miguel did not clearly understand what those eyes and those tongues were saying. It could be that they asked him for his name and country. Miguel was never to know. He only heard clearly that Don Juan, turning his head toward someone who followed him bearing a case with ink and paper on which to make notes, said to him: "Let this soldier have three escudos over and above his ordinary pay, and let him be given every care and attention, informing me of his recovery." The Marquis of Santa Cruz also said some words of cheer and encouragement, sincere and of value as coming from a man who had often visited the sick and wounded. The generals turned their armored bodies and moved on, hands on the pommels of their swords.

On the day after the victory it was impossible for Don Juan to imagine that he was to get no advantage from it. What he had achieved constituted the most important part of the plan, but not by any means all of it. With the fleet scattered among the islands along the coast he thought he could rally it in a few days, traverse the archipelago, go up the Dardanelles, and there blockade the Turks while he wintered in the comfortable shelter of Corfu. But when he inspected the ships, which seemed more like floating hospitals, he soon realized the great difficulties created by the enormous number of sick and wounded. At the same time the Venetians, knowing that they had contributed powerfully to the victory and to the destruction of the Turkish fleet, were beginning to fear future reprisals, or possibly to calculate what the triumph had cost them in money.

Don Juan had shown great ability for his age, but he was baffled, like a man who has just demolished a wall which took all his strength, only to find an even more solid one blocking his way. This did not grieve his brother, who perhaps controlled these events secretly from the frozen slopes of the Guadarrama. As it turned out Don Juan did not follow through after Lepanto and the today turned into yesterday without yielding any of its fruits.

In the last days of October the galleys separated. The Venetians sailed up the Adriatic, Marco Antonio Colonna headed for Civitavecchia and Don Álvaro de Bazán for Naples. Don Juan's galleys left for Messina and the *Marquesa* departed Petala to join them. Forging ahead, the ships rounded Taranto, entered the Straits, raised the lighthouse of Messina, the citadel and the arm of San Reniero. Messina is an amphitheater like Genoa, a city with wide-open arms.

From the galleys the great buildings which embellish the city could be made out, the black and white marble of Santa María la Nueva, the horseshoe arches of the Anunziata. From terraces and roofs, from arches and galleries, pennants, curtains and hangings of all colors fluttered in the wind. Don Juan ordered his galley also to be decked with streamers and pennants. In tow, stern foremost as a greater indignity, the captured Turkish galleys came lashed together. The rich standards of the Prophet, embroidered with the once victorious crescent moon of the coat of arms of the Great Lord and re-embroidered with gold and silver in relief, were hung upside down, sweeping the dirty waters of the port. Cannonades resounded from the citadel, the trumpets of the fleet shattered the air, the people shouted, joyously taking part in the triumph without having done anything to achieve it.

At last the ships came alongside and all eyes were fixed on the royal galley, where the handsome symbol of victory appeared, Señor Don Juan, gay and eager. The nobles of the city received him and paid homage. They agreed to raise a bronze statue to him and meantime they presented him with a gift of thirty thousand crowns, which Don

Juan accepted and allotted to his wounded soldiers. The man with the ink and paper made a note of this and everything else.

After the clamor of triumph the wounded were brought ashore and Miguel entered the hospital of Messina with many other wounded. His badly treated wounds, the cold and privation had brought him to a piteous state.

During the next few days Don Juan was busy reviewing and counting his troops, determining how many soldiers he needed for the forces that had to be maintained in Naples, and aranging to provide them from the *tercio* of Don Miguel de Moncada. The rest of the winter he spent in reorganizing and rehabilitating his forces.

He visited the hospitals often after presenting the sick men with his thirty thousand ducats and was greatly interested in seeing that all his wounded were cured quickly. More than once Don Juan saw Cervantes, remembered his face, asked after his wounds. Miguel's left hand was gangrened and in danger of being lost. Don Juan charged Doctor Gregorio López, his personal physician, especially to visit and assist that wounded man as being a hidalgo from whom His Majesty could expect much.

One day Doctor López arrived in his black gown and his flat doctoral cap without plumes. He was followed by servants carrying boxes of unguents and topical applications, and another with an operation bag. Miguel looked askance at all this bag and baggage. Hand wounds are always extremely painful. The doctor undid the bandages, washed the wound, examined it closely through his spectacles. Miguel bit his lips, shattered by the pain. The doctor observed his pale face and said: "Fear not. These hands which tend you, do you know whom they have tended? May God keep him in his holy glory! Our beloved lord, the Emperor Charles V."

CHAPTER 14

Maimed but Well Again—Don Lope de Figueroa—Navarino

AFTER the road and the ship, the barracks and the field of battle, the hospital is another rewarding school. Miguel was to pursue all the courses and disciplines in living and he was not to be spared an apprenticeship in hospital and jail.

Those who visit hospitals today and see them clean, tidy, well provisioned and governed by kind doctors and virtuous women in white coifs have no conception of the hospital at Messina in which Miguel spent six months, from the thirty-first of October of 1571 until near the end of April 1572, in being cured, or rather in deciding whether or not he would die. As a privileged soldier he enjoyed some advantages in medical attention, but in everything else he was one of many. In the hospital of Messina, as in all hospitals at that time, there were some who died of hunger for lack of resources of their own or the charity of others, and there were malingerers who pretended to be sick and spent two or three or fifteen days in bed on the look-out for whatever might go astray from the really sick. Robbing the living, the moribund, and the dead was established practice and tacitly accepted. There was none of that beatific peace which today takes possession of the man who goes to hospital with only his own recovery to think of.

For those who did not have plenty of money the hospital was the gateway to the graveyard and not a sanctuary of hope. Fortunately there was no lack of money for Cervantes, who was remembered very often and with rare appreciation by Don Juan or someone near him. On January 15 Cervantes was given twenty ducats to help meet expenses and complete his recovery, in the form of a bank draft provided from special secret disbursements by Don Juan. On March 7 he was given another twenty ducats for account of the paymaster Juan Morales de Torres, and on March 17, among other bank drafts drawn in favor of persons deserving rewards for the battle of October 7, there figures one of twenty-two escudos in Miguel's name.

Most probably, therefore, he did not lack what he needed for his maintenance. The chest wounds must have healed soon, since no serious wound in such a place can last long without finishing the patient or being finished itself. He suffered much more pain and worry from his hand. Once the gangrene had been cleared up it was certain to remain dry, stiff, and useless.

The loss of his hand, since it was his left, must not have been too great an affliction for Cervantes, who began to recover new strength and spirit with the approach of spring, and he did not give up his intention of gaining fame in the military profession. He must have left the hospital around April 20, recovered, happy, and with his young soul tempered by what he had seen in that abode of pain and want. It is not known that Cervantes was ever again in his life to enter a hospital; it is certain that from this one he came out well versed in the greatest and most terrible miseries of humanity.

Once again the Spaniards took fire, with Don Juan anxious to continue the task he had begun and to fling down the new wall that barred his path. But the Venetians were standing much less than firm and he received letters from the Court at Madrid and from secret agents in Paris and Constantinople with intelligence that caused him to fear active intervention by the French in favor of the Turks, not directly but by diverting the attention, the forces and the money of the Spaniards toward Flanders and Italy to give the Turks time to recover. Besides, the pontiff was gravely ill, there was no certainty that the forces of His Holiness would move from Civitavecchia, and the Pope's death would create further difficulties.

Consequently Don Juan hastened to get his forces ready, but first he decided to disband Moncada's *tercio* and with it complete the garrison of four thousand soldiers stationed in Naples. When Cervantes came out of hospital, therefore, he was assigned to the *tercio* of Don Lope de Figueroa, in the company of Don Manuel de León, and on April 29 the fleet officials were ordered to enter in their books three escudos of additional pay per month to Miguel de Cervantes.

The *tercio* comprised fourteen companies with captains famous for their deeds, and among them Don Manuel ranked high by reason of his long service, valor, and practical experience. He was so called by the purveyors and commissaries in their accounts, doubtless because his popularity and reputation in the army were so great that upon saying "Don Manuel" it was understood that one was speaking of Ponce de León. He may have been related to that famous knight Don Manuel de León, so greatly admired by Don Quixote for his memorable deed of retrieving from the claws of a fierce lion the glove flung there purposely by his lady to prove the valor of her paladin.[1]

But above all the leaders the great Don Lope de Figueroa y Pérez de Barradas, famous among the famous, brave among the brave, stood out as the cedar over the live oaks. In Don Lope de Figueroa and his honorable military record Miguel found what encouraged him to persevere in the profession of arms. Figueroa had been born in Guadix of a noble but not wealthy family. In Lombardy he served as a soldier in the ranks and achieved command by merit and services rendered. He was taken prisoner in the disaster of Los Gelves[2] and for three years rowed as a slave in the galleys of Constantinople. Ransomed in 1564, he served in various military expeditions and went on to Flanders. In Friesland near the River Jama he won glory by taking seven pieces of Nassau artillery with only three hundred arquebusiers; no one can explain how this could be done but that is the legend. As *Maestre de Campo* in Granada he received a bullet in his side from which he limped and suffered pain the rest of his life. He was at the battle of Lepanto in the royal galley with Don Juan, who esteemed him highly.

Don Lope de Figueroa was thus the most prestigious commander in

Don Juan's army, his life a bright mirror in which young soldiers saw themselves, hoping to emulate him, and it was also an example of what valor can accomplish by itself. He was in his forties when Cervantes knew him; his head was already grizzled, his temper sour, his words few. Careless of life and suffering his pains in silence, he was also very devout when occasion offered and he held holy relics in high esteem, divine miracles seeming perfectly natural to one who had achieved the human miracle of taking cannon with only arquebuses.

In Miguel's imagination Don Lope de Figueroa was one of the ancient heroes or knights-errant reduced to human proportions and contemporary terms. He now saw his heroes as they really were, in their true size and with their true value. The six months of hospital had cleared his vision. But heroism, like love, has its quarter of an hour. With the fever of victory over there was no way to revive spirits. Don Juan was the only person to keep up his enthusiasm but he did not receive the order to sail for Corfu until well into August. In the meantime Marco Antonio Colonna had arrived in Messina in June with the papal galleys and Don Juan loaned him the thirty-six galleys of Don Álvaro de Bazán, in which Moncada's *tercio* and two of Figueroa's companies sailed. Cervantes again plowed the waters of the Ionian Sea and arrived in Corfu, where the troops were reviewed and a pretense made of pursuing some Turkish galleys that refused to fight. When Don Juan arrived he found none of Colonna's galleys; they had reached Zante in pursuit of the Turks. The two squadrons met at Cephalonia, but all their efforts were in vain. Let the captive[3] tell the tale.

> In the following year, which was '72, I found myself in Navarino, rowing in the flagship with three lanterns on the poop. I saw and noted there how the opportunity was lost for catching the whole Turkish fleet in the port, because all the Levantines and Janizaries that were in it were quite certain that they were about to be boarded in the port itself, and they had their clothes and *pasamaques*, which are shoes, all ready to flee overland without staying to fight, such was their fear of our fleet. But Heaven ordained otherwise, not through any fault or carelessness on the part of the general who led us but because of the sins of the whole of Christianity and because it is God's will and with His consent that we always carry within us the seeds of our punishment. In fact El Uchalí (who was the ex-King of Algiers, a hero of Lepanto) withdrew to Modón, which is an island near Navarino, and landing his people he fortified the mouth of the port and lay low until Señor Don Juan turned back.

The attack on Navarino was thus a failure. Miguel took part in it with the disembarked infantry and artillery, which had to retire under cover of night to the protection of fire from the fleet. It was then that he saw at close hand a general as young as Don Juan and brave to such an extreme that, according to what the soldiers recounted, not a day or night passed when he did not engage in sword or dagger play with someone in the streets of Madrid on the slightest pretext. This impetuous gentleman, whose courage Cervantes held in all the more esteem since it was obvious that it served no useful purpose, was the Prince of Parma, Alexander Farnese.[4]

Miguel continues to narrate through the mouth of the captive:

> On this voyage the galley named *Presa* was captured, whose captain was a son (some historians say a grandson) of that famous corsair Barbarossa. It was taken by the Neapolitan flagship named *Loba*, commanded by that thunderbolt of war, by the father to his soldiers, by the fortunate and never-conquered captain Don Álvaro de Bazán, Marquis of Santa Cruz. And I do not want to leave untold the story of what took place in the capture of the *Presa*. The son of Barbarossa was so cruel and treated his captives so badly that when those who were at the oars saw that the galley *Loba* was bearing down and catching up with them they all dropped their oars at the same time and seized their captain, who was standing on the gangway urging them to row faster, and passing him from bench to bench, from the poop to the prow, they tore at him so savagely with their teeth that shortly after passing the mast his soul had already gone to Hell. Such, as I have said, was the cruelty with which he treated them and the hatred they bore him.

Now tell me, you who have never seen a man bitten to death by his slaves, who have never known generals who in their youth would engage in daily sword fights for pleasure and as a sport, how without such a background can we appreciate the mind and spirit of Cervantes or understand other aspects of his life, for we would only be talking nonsense if we judged his as if it were like ours, the tidy bourgeois life of people who settle their moral and financial accounts punctually and tremble as they read stock market quotations.

To capture a galley and kill one more corsair was a small thing for such a great armada. With everyone bored and peevish from having accomplished nothing, the ships of the League separated and Don Juan returned to Sicily gloomy and restless. It was then that Miguel came to know the tiresomeness and procrastinations of war, the burdens of routine service, the prosaic daily round inseparable from the glory of warfare, and the workaday aspect of even the most inspiring professions. He could also see at close hand how the spirit that drives men to fight bravely falters after victory is won, when heroes fold their arms and lose all initiative.

He spent the whole winter in Sicily enjoying its pleasant climate, its Arcadian landscapes, the gentle manners of its inhabitants; he may have written some pastoral verses. Perhaps many of those in the *Galatea*[5] date from this idle time in the life of our soldier.

Meanwhile Philip II, Don Juan, and the new pontiff Gregory XIII prepared an expedition for the following year, planning for three hundred galleys and sixty thousand soldiers. Strange rumors coursed through Italy, and around March it was known that as a result of negotiations in which the Bishop of Aix and the French Ambassador Noailles participated the Venetians had signed a peace treaty with the Turks, paying them three hundred thousand ducats annually. It was indeed remarkable for a Catholic cleric to come to an agreement with the Grand Turk in opposition to the Holy See.

On hearing of it Don Juan in a passion of rage removed the standard of the League from the royal galley and ran up his own.[6] The League was another great illusion destroyed.

CHAPTER 15

Glory and Hunger—The Portocarreros—Tunis—Sardinia

In the first months of 1573 the victorious Don Juan and his humble soldier Miguel found themselves covered with glory but living from hand to mouth, as the saying goes. Miguel was not getting his pay and lived precariously; the same thing was happening to the rest of the troops. Don Juan appealed to Spain almost daily for emergency relief for his hungry army; he also turned to Naples for the same purpose, but Cardinal Granvelle remained cautiously silent. Neither Madrid nor Naples would give him a penny. Consequently the soldiers had of necessity been let loose to live an undisciplined life as best they could. The captains winked at a great deal and the troops scattered among the villages, living off the country. This perennial transition from the heights to the depths, these continued reversals of fortune in Spanish life, were what engendered the *Quixote*.

But necessitude, which for a poor soldier means only a temporary setback, for a general like Don Juan de Austria arouses urgencies in which it would be silly not to see the beginning of protest, if not of rebellion. His role as paladin of Christianity was no longer very flattering when the Very Christian King of France was trafficking with the Turks. Shorn of means with which to pursue the overthrow of the Ottoman power on its own seas, and approaching thirty, an age at which every man looks out for himself, Don Juan was tempted by the Kingdom of Tunis.

With the profound discernment of a confessor who penetrates to the core of one's intentions, Philip II understood the purposes and vehement desires of his brother and intended to divert them for the benefit of himself and his monarchy. For the moment it was enough, he told him, to dethrone the terrible Uluch Alí and put Muley Mohamut in his place, without undertaking anything more on the Barbary Coast. Thus the suspicious mind of Philip, far too subtle to rule an empire as vast as his, an empire that needed at its head someone with the Pantagruelian brutality of Charles V, proceeded to undermine the results of the victory of Lepanto. And not content with trying to distract Don Juan from his so firm determination, Don Philip took great care to place faithful and watchful eyewitnesses close to his brother to advise and direct him.

Of these the chief was the Duke of Sessa,[1] Don Gonzalo Fernández de Córdoba, grandson of the Great Captain, most valiant gentleman, wise Governor of the State of Milan, hero of the Alpujarras, and with all this a delicate poet, a singer of the disillusionment that, perhaps prematurely, was taking possession of even the stoutest Spanish spirits. The hot blood of the Great Captain had cooled in the veins of his grandson, not to such an extent that he did not discharge his duties very well, and always as a gentleman, but sufficiently so that he lacked the touch of madness that inspires real heroes and makes a people great. Don Juan wisely held his peace, obedient to his brother's orders, which in any case did not run counter to his own designs.

Meantime in Madrid the Court was slowly becoming a Court, discarding the black pall that the sorrows of the monarch had cast over its life. Fine gentlemen from all the rich Spanish families were arriving in Madrid, many of them accustomed to nocturnal gallantries common in the towns where they lived, while others had perhaps known the free life of Italy and tasted the pleasures of amorous delirium. The type of the professional Don Juan appeared at Court and started to fill the streets of Madrid with gallant adventures that were to provide endless plots for comic and dramatic authors. Whole families of loose-living young men gave themselves over to contracting debts, pursuing veiled women, making false promises of marriage, quarreling and stirring up trouble, in short playing the fool, although not as coarsely as the bravos and bullies of Seville nor as courtly as the Petrarchian gallants of Italy.

In this pattern were the brothers Portocarrero, sons of the respectable Don Pedro Portocarrero, who was a general in the army in Italy and belonged to an ancient and distinguished family with lands in Estremadura. The eldest of these dissolute youths, Don Alonso Pacheco de Portocarrero, on August 27 of 1571 undertook to pay Doña Andrea de Cervantes five hundred ducats, the price of a necklace of heavy gold, jeweled with fine pearls, rubies, emeralds and diamonds, an *agnusdéi*[2] of gold, and a crystal rosary. At the same time another of the brothers was in debt to Juan Martínez, capmaker, to Master Pedro, the tailor to the staff of His Majesty's stables, and to Jácome Trezo, the famous lapidary, who had entered a claim against him with the Council for Military Affairs. Finally, the youngest of them was Don Pedro Portocarrero, of whom nothing more need be said than that he was condemned to the galleys despite the nobility of his surname. The type of young man of noble family dedicated to merrymaking and a ruffianly life is not so rare today that we cannot, with their example before us, reconstruct the behavior of these characters with whom the Cervantes sisters were in constant contact for many years, first Doña Andrea, later Doña Magdalena, or perhaps both at the same time.

They were the kind of young gentlemen who start by making love to every women they meet; later they become involved in unsavory monetary affairs, cadging on members of their families; and then they resort to banks and moneylenders and end up, when their credit is exhausted and their name besmirched, by committing outrages that land them in jail or even in the galleys. Then the family is in a turmoil, all who bear the name feel dishonored, they descend to petitions and bribes, but by then nothing can be done to avoid scandal.

At the beginning of the year 1573, when the Cervantes girls were taking legal action against Don Alonso to make him meet his obligations, presumably things were not going too well with the family of Rodrigo. The good chirurgeon on one occasion had to borrow money urgently; the small amount and short term of the repayment show most clearly that his credit was not good and his need pressing.

The fortunes of Don Juan and his soldier Miguel had up to now run parallel. Both were in need of money and neither could see how to get it. The news they both received from Spain was not encouraging. At last Don Juan, without money but never lacking in resolution, put together as best he could a fleet and an army that included a rabble of miscellaneous adventurers. He departed Messina on September 24 with a hundred and four galleys and many ships and frigates in which were the regular troops and the contingents recruited in Italy, altogether a total of twenty thousand men.

The fleet approached the African shore, ever coveted by Spain, and very soon they made out the golden coast where Carthage once stood. On October 8 they reached the Gulf, where the waves are stilled behind the protection of prodigious rocks towering to heaven. Here was La Goleta, a strong position that dominated the Gulf and defended the approaches to Tunis. They captured it quickly and Don Juan detached twenty-five hundred veterans, among them four companies of Figueroa's *tercio*, "who used to make the earth tremble with their muskets," according to the oft-repeated exaggerations of Van der Hámen.[3] Miguel went with them, his arquebus on his shoulder, his left hand hanging down, presumably not so useless that it prevented him from holding and firing the weapon. The march turned out to be a pleasant military stroll and Don Juan's spirits swelled when he traversed the fields where his illustrious father covered himself with glory.[4] Upon reaching Tunis they found the gates wide open and the Moorish governor yielded up the Alcazaba in the name of Muley Mohamet. Everything was there, including forty-four pieces of artillery, munitions and victuals. The army was happy to find abundant supplies, but the veterans thought, and with them Miguel and perhaps Don Juan also, that it might not be easy to hold a place that yielded so readily. The surrender of the Moors augured no good and Don Juan commissioned the Milanese engineer Gabrio Cervellón to build a fort next to the lagoon for the defense of the city.

Finding himself in possession created a tremendous struggle in Don Juan's mind; it was a unique opportunity to have himself crowned King of Tunis. He hesitated for only a week, however. A good soldier and above all an obedient general, he limited himself to carrying out the orders of his brother and so he returned to La Goleta with his troops once the foundations of the fort had been started. As governor of this Spanish outpost he appointed Don Pedro Portocarrero, the father of Don Alonso Portocarrero and a worthy gentleman, but not much of a soldier to leave behind with a small garrison in such a dangerous situation.

On October 24 the navy and the troops were back in Palermo and at the beginning of November the fourteen companies of Figueroa's *tercio* were transferred on Don Juan's orders to the island of Sardinia, so that pending the arrival of a permanent garrison for the island they might be available to help out in Africa if need be.

Consequently Miguel spent that winter in Sardinia. Perhaps there he made the acquaintance of the absurd poet Antonio de Lofraso, whose extravagances he commented on amusingly on several occasions.

Lofraso was a soldier with an itch to write, who would be called silly today, and his *Ten Books of the Fortune of Love* is praised by the priest in the *Quixote* as a unique book and the best of "this kind" that has ever seen the light of day.[5] But if Miguel did not meet the original Lofraso there he got to know the strange Arcadian customs of the island, where he could and certainly did take notes for the *Galatea* and for the lovely pastoral scenes which it pleased him to insert in the *Quixote*.

Miguel's sojourn of six months in Sardinia explains something that we observe in the bucolic parts of his works. Sardinia is an island of simple rustic customs, of lovely landscapes, of shady woods confined between rocky mountains. Until the seventeenth century and even later Sardinia preserved the simplicity of its customs. The Catholic religion had difficulty in penetrating its dense forests, or if it did manage to get in it failed to cast out a multitude of pagan ceremonies celebrated by peasants and shepherds even in Cervantes' time. The worship of Hermes or Mercury, combined with the terrible cult of Pan, was preserved by those simple country people, as cruel and revengeful in spirit as the Corsicans, but perhaps for that very reason innocent in their brutality. In the *Galatea* we are surprised, and at times it strikes us as having a strangely theatrical effect, to see a priest of we do not know quite what religion or cult conducting strange poetic ceremonies attended by shepherds who speak of the Tagus and the Henares and who have been in Toledo and Alcalá. It is not enough to say that Cervantes was copying other pastoral works. In his descriptions there is much more the feeling of something actually experienced and it is certain furthermore that in the *Quixote*, particularly in the second half, Miguel would not have interpolated pastoral scenes if he had believed them to be only poetical fiction.

What he had first read in Virgil and later in Montemayor and in Sannazaro,[6] he saw in the lovely land of Sicily and even more on the mysterious island of Sardinia, or something very like. For him that respite from the fatigues and clamor of war was a period of peace and reflection. He was already beginning to savor country life. He tasted with delight the aromatic and generous malmseys of Quarta and of Bosa, the *giro*, the *bernacho*, the *murago* of Galler, honeyed wines which seem to have been made by bees. From that time onward the drop of honey in pastoral poetry never failed to delight his lips.

CHAPTER 16

Don Juan Waits—Loss of La Goleta—Return to Naples

THE life of a soldier has two aspects which can be taken as of equal importance: one is that of action, brief periods during which opportunism and the sudden surprise attack count for much; the other is that of waiting, the length of which tries the spirit. His soldier Miguel followed Don Juan in action and in his humble way he also followed him in waiting. Each of them, without lapsing into self-interest or covetousness, also thought that he should be recompensed in some way for his past deeds and promising future. Miguel was given three escudos a month on top of his pay, which he collected late, in part, or never. Don Juan was perhaps promised something and continued to have faith in those promises.

His secretary, Juan de Escobedo, proceeded to negotiate actively in Rome for a grant of the title of Infante to Don Juan and permission for him to assume the title of Tunisian monarch. The Pope, of course mindful of the interests of Christianity but fearing the reaction of Philip II, could not decide anything. Don Juan moved to Gaeta with the intention of going to Spain, but in Gaeta he received letters from the King ordering him to Lombardy to deal with disturbances that had broken out in Genoa and at the same time discover the intentions of France. At the beginning of May Figueroa's *tercio* was brought back from Sardinia and Miguel returned to Genoa rested and ready for new adventures.

Don Juan, involved in a diplomatic and investigative mission alien to his nature, wrote to the King from Begeben on the sixteenth of May:

> I, Sir, am so deeply concerned with the matters for which I am responsible that I would very much prefer to be busy at sea than to have no more to do than I now have, and I think the time would not be ill spent, seeing as I do that the preparation of the fleet is going forward slowly and that it would be advisable to have it in very good order as a deterrent to our enemies . . . and though I have done my duty in that respect it is not enough to relieve me of very great anxiety

> about the difficulties that might have arisen had it not been done. I await with much interest the decision about Tunis, and I thus beg most earnestly that if it has not been sent when this is received it be done, if you are so disposed, and I shall be particularly happy to undertake anything else that can be done in the service of Your Majesty.

All the warnings of Don Juan proved useless and in the first days of summer he was in despair when he heard that the valiant and greatly feared Turkish mariner Uluch Alí had sallied forth from Constantinople with two hundred and thirty galleys, thirty galliots, forty cargo vessels and forty thousand soldiers. The worried Governor of La Goleta, Don Pedro Portocarrero, reported that a great deal of restless movement had been observed among the tribes all over Barbary. The Turk was supplementing sea action by action on land to stir up the ferocious Berber tribes, nomads avid for booty.

All of Miguel's hopes hung on the resistance of La Goleta and the valor of its defenders. If Don Juan arrived in time and could again defeat the Turks, acquiring new glory and perhaps being crowned King of Tunis, which his soldiers hoped for as much as he did, Miguel would surely have an opportunity to distinguish himself in the fighting, even at the cost of his right hand, to wear again the laurels of victory, and to achieve, of the two glories in the world, the one most to his taste.

Don Juan tried to help La Goleta, but could get no support from either Naples or Sicily, and the stronghold, attacked by land and sea, had to surrender. In the *Quixote* the captive Rui Pérez de Viedma tells in simple words and with ideas reflecting military and political perspicacity what Cervantes afterward thought about that occasion:

> Finally La Goleta was lost, the fort was lost, besieged by seventy-five thousand regular Turkish soldiers and more than four hundred thousand Moors and Arabs from all over Africa. Together with this great number of men there were so many munitions and engines of war and so many sappers that with their bare hands they could have buried La Goleta and the fort with fistfuls of earth. La Goleta, previously regarded as impregnable, was the first to fall. It was not lost by any fault of its defenders, who did all that they should and could do in its defense, but rather because they had happened on water at a depth of two handbreadths while the Turks did not encounter any at a depth of two yards and in the event found it easy to raise earthworks in that desert sand.

And at this point do you not recognize the old Spanish improvidence? Did those men not rely on an inadequate test and therefore considered an attack impossible of success? Do you not perceive the irony with which Miguel speaks of the matter, his deep awareness of the stupidity which had prevailed in all this?

> And thus with many sacks of sand they raised earthworks so high that they overlooked the ramparts and by attacking them from above (that is to say, from an altitude greater than that of the ramparts) no one could man or defend them. . . . It was the common view that our people should not have shut themselves up in La Goleta but should have awaited the disembarkation in the field. Those who say this do so from afar and with little experience of similar situations, for since there were scarcely seven thousand soldiers in La Goleta and the fort how could such a small number, however more valiant they might be, go into the field against forces as great as were those of the enemy? And how is it possible to allow forces to be lost without coming to their support, all the more so when they are encircled by stubborn and resolute enemies fighting in their own land?

Those who directed the campaign were blind to commonsense truths such as these that a simple young soldier proclaimed, possibly sitting on a box on the pier at Trápani surrounded by soldiers and sailors waiting for the storm to subside so that they could go to the aid of La Goleta while meantime the desolating news was on its way to them. Now one sees what a grave error it would be to speak of Cervantes as a common soldier or to depict the events of his military life in the manner of Stendahl, as if Miguel, in the ranks of the *tercio* of Figueroa, had been one of so many irresponsible soldiers praiseworthy only for courage on occasion.

> The fort was also lost, but the Turks took it inch by inch, for the soldiers who defended it fought so valiantly and effectively that more than twenty-five thousand of the enemy were killed in the twenty-two general assaults that were launched. Of the three hundred they captured alive there was not one who had not been wounded, a sure and clear sign of their courage and fortitude and of how well they had done their duty in defending their positions. . . . Don Pedro Portocarrero, the commander of La Goleta, was taken prisoner. He had done all he could to defend the fortress and he felt its loss so keenly that he died of grief on the way to Constantinople, where he was being taken as a captive. . . . La Goleta and the fort having surrendered, then, the Turks ordered the dismantling of La Goleta, for the fort ended up in such a condition that there was nothing left to demolish, and to do so more easily and quickly they mined three quarters of it, but nothing could destroy what seemed least strong, namely the ancient ramparts. . . .

All this that Cervantes reasoned out with the wisdom of a man of fifty he had felt some twenty-five or thirty years before. He was not the kind of soldier who does not realize what is happening or who is not affected by it. Furious and enraged, he listened to the tales about La Goleta and in desperation he embarked with Don Juan and the best soldiers of the *tercio* in the ships that were at hand.

Many men were lost in that useless sally. With horrified eyes Miguel watched the sea swallow them and he himself suffered the countless afflictions of a storm aboard ship. Several times he saw the fleet dispersed and ships lost in the turbulent sea, but at last they managed to reassemble at Trápani, at the tip of Sicily, but by then La Goleta had already surrendered. By the grief and melancholy of the captive we can infer Miguel's disillusionment, a reflection of Don Juan's disappointment. Spirit and determination are not always enough.

With their forces expended to no useful purpose the fleet returned to Naples on September 29 of 1574, there to suffer further afflictions. According to a report from Paymaster Sancho de Zorroza fifty thousand escudos were owing to the fourteen companies of Figueroa. The eternal Spanish figure of the soldier, needy, ragged, barefoot, and hungry, who haunts the streets "tired of the trade of the pike, but not of the practice of the picaresque" was to be seen more frequently than ever all over Naples and Sicily.

Miguel, however, was not a man to be intimidated by the ups and downs of military fortune, and unhappiness over the abortive expedition cannot have upset him for very long. Don Juan returned to Spain to discuss his nomination as Infante and perhaps also to discover the real reasons for the difficulties which had confronted him and might do so again. Don Lope de Figueroa also departed. The army remained under the command of the Duke of Sessa and Figueroa's *tercio* was billeted in Sicily and Naples.

As rich in freedom as short of money, Miguel gave himself over to the gay life of the splendid and carefree city of Naples, where he spent the happiest time of his life, "his refreshing early morning hours," in the city

> . . . . where friendly Nature
> combined its every attribute
> with much else to form a whole.
> The gentle melancholy of lovely Parthenope[1]
> is seen seated there
> on the shore of the sea which laps her feet.
> With castles and towers crowned,
> for strength and beauty in equal measure

feared, known and esteemed. . . .
glory of Italy and splendor of the world,
for all the cities on this earth
it inspires as none other can,
gentle in peace, terrible in war,
mother of abundance and generosity,
of Elysian fields and pleasant hills. . . .[2]

Miguel's spirit expanded in Naples and in that abundance of life which draws its inhabitants at all hours from their homes into the streets, from the streets into the fields, good-humoredly mocking and wrangling, enjoying today and careless of the morrow. He recovered the serenity that he had acquired as a child in Seville, the Naples of Spain. Even more than the streets of Seville those of Naples and its docks and environs were a perpetual carnival: songs, dances, love affairs, salty conversations, interesting tales, notable arguments, memorable excursions into the country to rest or in search of entertainment, generosity in both rich and poor, splendor in the benevolent sky and in the friendly air that favors the needy, letting him sleep under the dew and dream all night. In the morning the Neapolitan sky is blue as a turquoise, sapphire blue in the evening. Thousands and thousands of men and women arise every day, determined only to live without knowing how or on what. There Nature is a mother, and even more than a mother, a grandmother who indulges and pets her grandchildren and forgives them their childish mischief.

Dressed up and sprightly, Miguel roamed those streets and fields, at times in pursuit of a red-haired Nisida "who greatly enjoyed his boldness," at times getting to know and studying the cunning stratagems of the Jews who swarmed through the city, perhaps having friendly intercourse with the already famous Calabrian bandits like Pirro of *Persiles*, "a quarrelsome man, impatient and wicked, whose estate lay in the edges of his sword, in the dexterity of his hands, in the lures of his Hipólita (his concubine), and in his fleetness of foot, which he considered more useful than his hands . . . for these tame pigeons are always pursued by kites and torn to bits by sparrows," at times in courtship and pursuit of others like Hipólita, "an obliging lady who in adornments might compare with the ancient Flora and in manners with good breeding itself."

The social relationships and friendships of Miguel with persons of whom we know nothing must have been so intimate and continuous that in his sixties, when he would refresh his dejected spirits with sweet memories of Naples, he could still imagine a meeting on the street with a young soldier and . . .

My friend embraced me tenderly
and, holding me in his arms, said
that he could scarce believe I was there.
He called me father and I called him son,
I agreed with him it was the very truth,
and he could certainly bear that name.
Promontorio said to me: I surmise,
father, that some accident to your gray hairs
brings you so far and but half alive.
—Son, in my refreshing early morning hours
I lived in this land, I said to him,
in vigorous and splendid strength,
but the will which governs all of us,
the will of Heaven, I say, has brought me
to a place which cheers more than it troubles me . . .

What carefully kept secret do the verses in italics conceal? Who was this young soldier who could call Miguel "father" with such assurance? Had he anything to do with the blonde Nisida of the *Galatea*? Nothing is known. But certainly it was not only the inns, the pigeons and the sausages that delighted the soul of Miguel. Without a doubt Naples was for him the site of happy and felicitous loves. He dreamed of it often, even in his old age, "half alive" as he says calmly and without rancor, making fun of his own gray hair. In Naples he became a complete man. Perhaps it was there that the mysterious hour of a fertile love first sounded for him.

CHAPTER 17

The Duke of Sessa—Farewell to Naples—Cervantes Captive

In those times there was frequent communication and a constant exchange of news between Spain and Naples. Hardly a week or ten days passed when the inns of Pozzuoli or Portici did not know and comment on what was being said in the Calle Mayor of Madrid. Curious and always anxious to know everything, Miguel did not miss a day without visiting the waterfront, particularly when a Spanish ship was discharging, and usually there was one. Every Spaniard who landed was a living gazeteer, pregnant with truth and falsehood. The doings of the King and Court were discussed endlessly, as also those of Flanders and France. One day Miguel learned that Antonio Pérez,[1] that undisciplined lad, had been named Secretary to His Majesty and had acquired considerable influence over the monarch, being privy to his secrets and perhaps feared just a little by the Man of the Escorial, who, upon choosing a motto for the tokens that served him as gambling counters, ordered engraved around his escutcheon this inscription: *Nec spe, nec metu*, that is to say, neither by hope nor by fear. Nevertheless Philip II had found in Antonio Pérez the corrective that the intimate companionship of a pliant and ingratiating personality brings to all arrogant and inflexible characters.

Shortly after learning that his acquaintance Antonio Pérez had the ear of the King, Cervantes also learned that his intimate friend Mateo Vázquez de Leca,[2] the alert lad of Seville, son of a slave and God only knew who else, had likewise been named Secretary to His Majesty. From what he already knew Miguel could easily surmise that the appointment of Antonio Pérez was not a matter of chance and was well merited, while that of Mateo was the product of influence. In any event the knowledge that these two men whom he had known from childhood were so successful and highly placed made him examine his own situation, which was certainly far from prosperous. As in the case of the rest of the soldiers, several wage payments were owing him in November, and hopes for payment dwindled rather than increased. Miguel, like so many other soldiers, continued to lounge in the streets and tramp the roads, assuaging his poverty and hunger with love and gaiety. His spirit being in no way inclined to hypochondria, he needed little to be happy and to show a smiling face to the world, but his amusements were never so intensive and absorbing that they prevented him from understanding clearly the facts of life.

He was nearly twenty-seven years old and meanwhile the young men of his age had fitted into places in the Palace and were already enjoying royal favor in that dark precinct where benefits were gained or lost as if they were the wounds of battle. Miguel was only a poor soldier who made the earth shake with his musket and the vine-clad walls of the inns of Naples with his laughter, but most of the time without a penny or the slightest hope of a brighter future. Miguel was not envious, but rather he was making a careful assessment of his situation and his future prospects. He had already tasted the grandeur of the epic poem, the piquant thrill of the novel of adventure, the salt of the picaresque, and the sweetness of the pastoral. The time had come to stop telling tales and listening to the tales of others, to get out of the anonymous chorus and begin to play a role in the drama of life.

Don Juan also had much to think about. A campaign that fails teaches more than a successful one. His soul had been tanned and pickled in the futile marches and countermarches of the year 1572, and he had received a disastrous blow with the defection of the Venetians. In 1573 he had exausted himself in vain, worn out by the struggle against tempestuous wind and wave and against the enmities or spiritless wills of men.

He finally realized that it was essential for him to seek out the furnace where the thunderbolt was forged. It was for this that he had gone to Court, anxious to talk with his brother and more than that to meet him face to face and interrogate his cold enigmatic eyes. He also wanted to talk with the people around Philip and smell out from the gossip of the Court what were the monarch's present attitudes and the secret influences that swayed his vacillating mind.

Without anyone knowing how or why, Spanish life had gone through a great transcendental change, one of those that history is very careful not to record, because history is interested only in prattle and not in the quietly immutable developments of which no one speaks, just as the old painters had not divined, until Velásquez taught them, that it is not as important to paint the precise outlines of figures as it is to depict the intangible atmosphere around them.

Before Philip II the Court not only had little influence on Spanish life but there was no Court. Whole regions of the peninsula lived by themselves, and in many towns even the name of the King was unknown. Philip II established the Court permanently in Madrid and this altered the whole face of things. Unity was not created, an impossible thing in so vast an empire, but rather a central power, irresponsible and subject to paltry influences, that governed badly but nevertheless infiltrated the life of the nation quietly and effectively, very much in the manner of the Jesuits. The first effect of this mysterious something, the source of which lay somewhere between Madrid and the Escorial, was experienced by Don Juan de Austria when he discovered that for the dwellers in the Escorial and in the Alcázar of Madrid the great day of Lepanto had no more meaning than the futile expeditions of Modón and Navarino.

The Court controlled events from its monk's chair, piously telling the beads of its rosary. With the attack of the Turks on La Goleta, which was their retaliation for Lepanto, Don Juan burned with impatience, soldiers like Miguel raged, seeing such a good opportunity lost, and the Court, remote from everything, repeated a pious phrase, or one that sounded like one, so that it could be said aloud when occasion for it arose: "It was God's will. I sent the galleys to fight the Turks, not tempests." Transcending success or failure, remote from human influences, Philip II contemplated the panorama of the tremendous struggle developing around him, and from very far away he saw the galleys of Don Juan move like pieces on a chessboard. They won? He gave thanks to the Lord. They lost? He thanked Him anyway. Life was for him an eternal game of chance; whether he lost or won, for him who had no wish to do either, it was simply a matter of paying or collecting. On the counters in his pocket he had written the terrible motto, the motto his spirit had chosen: "neither by hope nor by fear."

After the departure of Don Juan little by little Miguel began to understand the situation in terms of the campaign that he had observed and of what could be inferred from the reports of newly arrived Spaniards. Even the victorious general had found it necessary to present himself at Court so that they could legalize him and put the stamp of approval on his heroism. It was therefore essential to resort to the Court to achieve anything.

Miguel's younger brother, Rodrigo de Cervantes, was then in Italy, also as a soldier, though it is not known when he arrived. Perhaps through him Miguel had been able to confirm the sad news regarding the situation at home, where the father of the family continued to practice his profession but gained little from it. His sister Andrea was prosecuting her lawsuit against the Portocarreros, in which her sister Magdalena was in some way involved, but Don Alonso was struggling with all his might against meeting his obligations, perhaps because he was negotiating his marriage with an Andalusian lady.

In those days family feelings, particularly in a home where the sons were in military service, were not as close and demanding as they became later, but Miguel nevertheless felt a desire to return home.

He therefore managed to approach the Duke of Sessa, who was then in command of the troops in both Naples and Palermo. We do not know what the general said to Cervantes but he certainly remembered him even after the passage of years and recalled his exploits at Lepanto, renowned in the army and attested by his broken hand. Perhaps Miguel could talk to him of poetry and that he likewise said to him:

> I also am a poet and I value the title
> more than a new judge his robe.

This worldly-wise philosopher was doubtless another of those who recognized in Cervantes that something which set him apart from other men in his position. He pointed out that the heroic times were now beginning to fade and that nothing of importance could be accomplished without the approval of the Court. The Duke then addressed letters to the King and to some influential courtiers in which he recommended Miguel as a very good soldier and he possibly advised him to await the return of Don Juan in order to obtain letters from him also.

The spring passed quickly and Don Juan returned to Naples around the middle of June. He had come from the Court and was beginning to appreciate how things were changing since the days of Lepanto. He was now thirty years old, at that bright summit of life which affords a view of the high peaks and wide valleys, but with less emotion and less ambition than before, without as much composure and as much skepticism as later. Either through the Duke or addressing himself directly, Cervantes managed to see him. Like every great leader Don Juan had a good memory and recalled very well the faces of his veterans, especially those he had recognized through the smoke of battle.

He approved Miguel's decision and gave him a letter for his brother, the King, so generous and flattering that later it was to be a passport to slavery. In it he said that Miguel could well be given the command of a company, being a man fully qualified for it. It was not rare, although it did not happen often, for a soldier with extra pay (a first-class soldier, or what we now call corporal) to jump to captain. Miguel was never an ensign, as some have believed because of what is said in the tale of the captive Rui Pérez de Viedma, or else he was one for a very short time, since it is certain that he was a soldier and nothing more on the fifteenth of November of 1574.

The letters filled Miguel's breast with hope, perhaps that of the Duke more than Don Juan's, for he was sufficiently perceptive to observe how, while it could not yet be said that things were going badly for Don Juan nor that his brother was losing interest in him, the enthusiasm for the recent victory had somewhat abated. If it had been difficult for Don Juan to obtain at Court the means with which to pursue a profitable and glorious campaign, it did not seem a very easy matter to get attention for his recommendation in favor of an obscure soldier. On the other hand the sympathy of the Duke of Sessa, a perceptive poet and a man experienced in the ways of life, surely impressed Miguel much more than the purely military appreciation that Don Juan gave of him. Arms and letters, the two great loves of his life, once more appeared before him in the commander at Lepanto and the poet of Naples. And in the existing state of his spirit perhaps letters were again recovering their primacy.

Having received his furlough and the letters, Miguel had an interview with the master of the galley *Sol* which was to weigh anchor and lay a course for Spain around the middle of September. The galley left Naples on the eighteenth or twentieth of that month. Miguel, full of hope as he leaned on the rail, looked his farewell on that broad bay, the immense white city, the massive cone of Vesuvius with its plume of smoke, and the friendly fields where grapes ripened in the golden sun. Many times in his long life he recalled the light and the colors in which the eternal beauty of the city seemed to clothe itself that morning.

Traveling in the galley *Sol* were people as important as General Pero

Diez Carrillo de Quesada, an old soldier and expert artilleryman, Don Juan Bautista Ruiz de Vergara of the Military Order of St. John, and many other respected gentlemen. The galley was coasting along in the Gulf of Lions near Marseilles, in sight of the little port of Las Tres Marías in the Camargue where the Rhône debouches, when it was pursued by a swift flotilla under command of the Albanian renegade Arnaut Mamí, Captain General of the Turkish galleys of Algiers. Faster than the others, a galley of twenty-two benches overtook the *Sol.* It was commanded by Dalí Mamí, a Greek renegade, whom they called the "Lame One" because he was so and because it was the custom among the Turks to refer to the defects of their captains (whereby they named Uluch Alí the "Fartax," which meant he had scurvy).

It would be foolish to tell of the encounter when Miguel himself does so in the *Galatea* and in *The Anglo-Spanish Lady* and refers to it in the captive's narrative in the *Quixote*:

> It so happened that when the wind started to freshen the diligent sailors hoisted all the sails further. . . . One of them who was seated in the prow discovered by the faint light of the moon that four rowing vessels were making for the ship with long strokes of the oars and at great speed, and as soon as he recognized them as enemies he began to shout in a loud voice: "To arms, to arms, Turkish ships in sight." This sudden outcry inspired such dread in all those in the ship that, unable to contrive anything before the imminent peril, they only looked at each other, but the captain (who had at times found himself in similar circumstances), coming to the bow, tried to make out the size of the vessels and how many there were. . . . and he recognized them as galliots rowed by slaves, which must have caused him considerable apprehension, but concealing it as best he could he ordered the artillery to be got ready and as much sail as possible be made toward the enemy vessels, with a view to passing between them and letting go broadsides of artillery. Everyone rushed to arms and taking up their posts they awaited the enemy attack as best they could. . . . I ran to find out what the captain ordered, as he with prudent care was preparing beforehand everything required by the situation, and . . . putting me in command of the poop castle he with some soldiers and passengers hurried back and forth the length of the ship. The enemy was not long in arriving, and the wind even less in dropping, which was the real cause of our ruination. The enemy did not risk boarding us, for they saw that the breeze had dropped and they thought it better to wait for daylight before attacking us. That is what they did, and at daybreak . . . the fear in our hearts that we were indeed lost was then confirmed. Despite all this the brave captain and some of those who stood by him were not dismayed, and he waited to see what the enemy would do. As soon as morning came they sent a small boat from their

> admiral's ship and through a renegade they called on our captain to surrender, for he could see that it was impossible to defend himself against so many ships, the more since they were the best in Algiers, threatening him on behalf of his commander Arnaut Mamí that if the ship fired a single cannon he would hang him from a yard when he was captured, and adding other threats the renegade tried to persuade him to surrender. But the captain being unwilling to do so he replied to the renegade that he stand away from the ship, for if he did not he would send him to the bottom with his artillery. Arnaut heard this reply and immediately, surrounding the ship on all sides, he began to let go his artillery at long range with marvelous speed, fury, and clamor. Our ship began to do the same, with such good luck that it sent to the bottom one of the vessels that was attacking the poop, for it hit the mark with a cannon ball right in the strakes, so that in the absence of succor the seas quickly swallowed it. Seeing this the Turks pressed the fight and in four hours they attacked us four times, and as many times retired with great damage to themselves and not a little to us. But so as not to fatigue you . . . I will only say that having battled us for sixteen hours and after our captain and all the other members of the ship's crew had been killed, at the end of nine assaults on us they finally boarded the ship furiously. . . .

It is easy to see what is true and what is poetry in this description, the one nearest the event and therefore the most detailed and credible. Cervantes fought in the poop castle with no less courage than at Lepanto. The artillery was commanded by a man as expert as General Carrillo de Quesada. They had bad luck and were outnumbered.

In the short space of time from morning to evening Cervantes found himself loaded with chains, in a grievous state. His brother Rodrigo was also a prisoner. The worst that Miguel could imagine had happened.

CHAPTER 18

Arrival in Algiers—First Attempts to Escape

"IN Africa there are only two safe havens, which are June and July." These words of the old mariner Andrea Doria to the Emperor were confirmed for Miguel by his complete misery in body and soul during the futile maritime ventures undertaken by Don Juan to save La Goleta, and he now confirmed them anew while the pitching and tossing of the galliot commanded by the Greek Dalí Mamí drove his painful thoughts out of his mind.

The seas on the coast of Algiers, always turbulent and threatening storm, were then the best defense of the city. In order to make port it was necessary to survive their constant buffeting, as the Greek captain and his chief, Admiral Arnaut Mamí, were now doing. Cervantes knew something of the latter, for he had a great reputation in the Mediterranean as a mariner, a cruel man and a bold leader. The fact that Arnaut Mamí was an Albanian renegade is the best indication of his fierceness and inhumanity. When Arab Amat governed Algiers in the name of the Grand Turk in 1572 or 1573 Arnaut was named admiral because of his skill as a navigator, but the two fell out and Arnaut was dismissed. This required him to use all his influence in Constantinople to get Arab Amat deposed and himself reinstated in his position. Arnaut had been at La Goleta with Uluch Alí, for which he was highly regarded officially, and in addition he was greatly esteemed by the corsairs whom he led because he did not stint in dividing up the captured booty and slaves, in which he had a right to one part in fifteen by virtue of his position. Arnaut Mamí, while always getting his share, knew that it would not be wise to demand more than that from the greedy captains and corsairs under his command.

While the galliots were sailing along the loot had been divided and it was Miguel's lot to fall into the hands of the lame Dalí Mamí. Expert hands searched him and soon came across the letters of Don Juan de Austria and the Duke of Sessa. The signature of Don Juan was so well known that when Dalí Mamí saw it he was delighted. It was not every day that a gentleman of whom Don Juan would say over his signature what he said of this one fell into the hands of the Algerian corsairs. And see how the parallelism of the two heroic lives was to persist in adversity as in success. From then on the shadow of Don Juan was disastrous to Miguel, without his realizing it until many years had passed. Had the letters been lost he would perhaps not have suffered as he did; certainly his ransom would have been arranged more easily and quickly.

In any case the covetous eyes of the Greek surveyed his slave from head to foot, judging him valuable as soon as he saw him. Without doubt this captive, as shown by his demeanor and a valor attested by his withered hand, must be an eminent gentleman and worth a great ransom, whom it was advisable to hold in tight security. Consequently two iron rings soon handcuffed his wrists and iron shackles his ankles; it is possible that the odious and humiliating *pie de amigo*[1] constricted his throat and forced him to look skyward when he most longed to cast his eyes to earth, begging it in pity to swallow him up.

Miguel now watched the turbulent sea with mournful eyes, while the Christian galley slaves at the oars looked at him sullenly and resentfully, for they reckoned Miguel to be an important gentleman who would shortly be ransomed and returned to his homeland. As had already happened to him at Lepanto, and as might happen to any imaginative spirit in such a sudden and terrible turn of fortune, no less terrible because it was a commonplace in those days, Miguel recalled much of his former life. The jingle of a certain ballad of the road in far-off La Mancha haunted his ears, at first confused and fragmented and then clear and complete. It was the refrain of "The Laurel Branch," which is still sung between the swaths and windrows and when the wheat is being bagged and taken to the gristmill:

> The branch is of laurel
> of green laurel,
> of laurel, ever green
> as is my love,
> the laurel branch;
> imprisoned is
> my lover in Algiers,
> Jesus, what anguish!
> Imprisoned,
> captive is my love. . . .

The soft and languid music of the song dominated his thoughts for a moment and he looked at the sea as if he were trying to see beyond it the vast plain of La Mancha, furrowed by patient mules and stout, soft-eyed donkeys. He then turned to look at the coast now drawing near. As evening fell the black undulations of the land were stained by the white, white, white of a great city. Open terraces could soon be distinguished, then the great bulk of the Alcazaba, the Acropolis, palace and fortress of the Turks, the minaret of the old mosque of Sidi Abderrahman, slender and elegant as a great white palm tree banded with shining green and yellow glazed tiles, and in the background toward Sidi Ferrux a ridge of red mountains like the highlands of Alcaén which occasionally cut the horizon of La Mancha. Against the red-brick color of the mountains the leafy crowns of palms showed green, and blue were the copses of fragrant aloes.

That was "the city of Algiers, terror and whore of all the shores of the Mediterranean Sea, the port for all the corsairs and the shelter and refuge of the robbers who sallied forth in their ships from this small harbor to upset the whole world, for they dared to go through the *plus ultra* of the Pillars of Hercules and to attack and rob distant islands that, because they are surrounded by the immensity of the ocean, thought they were safe, at least from Turkish vessels." And upon writing this in the *Persiles* many years later Miguel revealed his secret admiration for those audacious seafarers, as much heroes as they were robbers, who were masters of the sea, linked only very slightly with any organized power or force, obeying almost no law, a threat to the most powerful nations and the bugbear of all authorities, from the spiritual of the Pope to the commercial of the Venetians and Genoese, without excluding the immense and irresistible Spanish power that embraced the whole world.

Dalí Mamí, Arnaut, and all the other corsairs, a blend of adventurous knights and bandit chiefs, constituted the lawless revolutionary force that turned the normal and universally established and accepted order of things upside down, destroying property, threatening peaceful merchants, and upsetting the middle-class families of those days, for in Spain alone at that time there were thirty thousand homes that mourned as many sons, brothers, or husbands held captive in Algiers, and there was no town or village in which some weeping young girl did not repeat the sad refrain:

Imprisoned is
my lover in Algiers,
Jesus, what anguish!

Such people, battling against all Christendom, were most certainly not ordinary men. It was told of the grandson of Barbarossa (in the memorable attack by Don Álvaro de Bazan's *Loba*) that with one blow he cut off at the shoulder the right arm of a man who was marking time with his oar in the stern, and grasping the bloody and still warm arm as if it were a rope's end, started to flog the backs of the other galley slaves with it. Miguel, who had already observed similar acts of incredible ferocity, understood that from now on he was entering an inferno of primitive passions carried to the point of barbarism, in a world new to him in which pity was unknown. If life everywhere was of little value, as he had learned in battle, in that kingdom of brutality and injustice he had best hold it as worth nothing from the beginning and be prepared to lose it for the most trivial reason. With freedom lost for God only knew how long, nothing was left in the game but the stake of existence.

The disembarkation was carried out with curses and blows from the captain and his boatswains amid the babble of the spectators. Always when the hunting galliots returned, and especially if they were those of the admiral, all the idle folk in Algiers came down to watch them unload.

Though accustomed to the cosmopolitan life of the port of Naples, Miguel had never seen so many different kinds of people nor heard such diverse and confusing voices as he saw and heard there. There were slaves, soldiers, sailors, and merchants of all races, traders in all commodities, renegades from all religions, male and female panders to all the pleasures and vices. There were ragged Jews, dirty and pompous Turks, gay and vulgar Greeks, Knights of Malta, friars of the Orders of Mercy and of the Trinity, rich and lavishly dressed bankers from Florence, Barcelona, and Valencia, and a miscellaneous crowd of the curious who came to see the captives as they would a parade or procession. Everyone looked to see who was carrying the most chains, since it was the custom to inflict the greater indignities on those who were supposed to be persons of high rank. All eyes were therefore turned on Cervantes, who, forced to hold his head up by the *pie de amigo* that constricted his neck, could not avoid them. Among them were the coldly calculating looks of those who appraised the value of each prisoner and regarded him covetously; others were inquiring, those of men who thought to recognize a friend or relative; others were insolent and licentious, those of Armenian, Egyptian and Turkish prostitutes, their faces bare, their lips painted with vermilion and their cheeks with henna. There were other looks, the majority, indifferent and inspired only momentarily by a passing curiosity.

The first name that Miguel heard on Algerian soil was that of Don Juan. They shouted it, making hideous faces and horrible gestures, planting themselves before the helpless captive, spitting in his face, pulling at his chains, flinging gobs of mud at him, a flock of Moorish boys from seven to twelve years old, black, dirty, ragged, insolent and meddlesome as monkeys who, in a chorus with a strangely melancholy tone, chanted to all the captives they saw the same pitiless words:

> Don Juan no come,
> Don Juan no come,
> No escape, no ransom.
> Die here, dog, die here,
> Don Juan no come.[2]

To crown his misfortune, he turned his head with difficulty and saw behind him, also in chains, his brother Rodrigo, to whom hardship had come without his having tasted glory. This was the greatest calamity Miguel had ever encountered. At Lepanto he had learned the first lesson in courage; in Algiers he was to learn the first lesson in patience, his spirit tempered in that furnace, as he went to prison reconciled to martyrdom like a Christian in the early days of the Church.

In that first period of captivity Cervantes must have suffered so much that his master, fearing that so valuable a slave might pine away and die, made him more comfortable and gave him more liberty. From what he tells us it can be deduced that his close imprisonment did not last long, and this is easily explained, not only for the reasons given but also because of the limited facilities for keeping captives provided by Algerian residences. Dalí Mamí was not a man to spend much money on feeding his slaves, nor did he have a palace for a home. It was only a miserable building where he barely had room for his hoard of arms, carpets, and other bulky objects stolen from the hulls of Christian galleys. Perhaps Miguel could also take advantage of the frequent absences of the corsair, who was always at sea, eager to win one of the three posts of admiral held by Arnaut Mamí and two other renegades. He must soon have found himself, like the other captives, wandering through the steep, tortuous lanes of Algiers seeking alms.

By natural law the commonest attitude among the captives was to chafe and threaten violence in the first days of adversity, and when those reactions were over, to fall into a state of deep despondency, fretting, getting ready to recant, and in the end submitting to the yoke and chain with the passive resignation of habit. It was not unusual to see men who fought like lions when captured and whose breasts were decorated with stars and crosses become dispirited, once their initial passion of rage abated, and after four or six months of slavery come to terms with their misfortune, turned into submissive dogs and renegades from their faith. This created great difficulties for the owners of slaves: the renegade slave, having abandoned any idea that he might be ransomed, was a feckless being, without energy for work or anything useful; he usually became timid, lazy, sluggish, and idle, and there was a surplus of idle folk in Algiers.

Captivity completely wiped out all social differences; in the face of a common misfortune there were no gentlemen and no plebeians. Rather there was on the one hand a confused mass of unstable weak characters from which emerged many a perjurer and renegade, and on the other a group of honest and noble souls of whatever origin.

Among the company of the good and brave men Cervantes soon distinguished himself, for in such a situation it was not enough to be resolute and determined if one were not also clever and careful. They had confidence in him as an able man and very soon came to depend on his discretion and resourcefulness. Included in this group were gentlemen as noble and of as ancient lineage as two Knights of St. John: Don Antonio de Toledo, a brother of the Duke of Alba, and Don Francisco de Valencia, a nobleman from Zamora who had served under that great general, as well as a young captain from Talavera, Don Francisco de Meneses, a hero of La Goleta and a very good friend of Cervantes.

In fact all of the men waiting to be ransomed were influenced by the attraction that Miguel exercised, be it by his artful words, his careful reasoning, or his commanding voice and presence. Very soon he stood out conspicuously among the thirty thousand men who were in the same situation. The fact is that the captive Cervantes was a unique captive, just as the soldier Cervantes was a soldier recognized by Don Juan himself.

In Algiers, naturally, people were ransomed or made their escape every day, and every day a few slaves gained freedom by daring or clever means or perished in the attempt. Cervantes never lost sight for a moment of his intention to be ransomed or to escape, and according to witnesses worthy of credence "a book could be written" just out of the escapes he organized and carried out. Those are the words of Padre Haedo, on whom the works of Miguel, if he knew any of them, can have made little impression.

According to one report, "wishing to do something useful and free some Christians [Cervantes] sought out a Moor to guide them by land to Orán and after they had traveled for some days with the said Moor he deserted them and so they were forced to return to Algiers where the said Miguel de Cervantes was greatly maltreated by his master and from then on was confined with more chains and was more strictly guarded."

He perhaps tried again to escape to Orán, alone or with some comrade of the chain, and he depicted the misadventures of the road in admirable strophes that do not seem to be about something heard but rather about something suffered, which he puts into the mouth of the captive in *Life in Algiers*:

> This endless road
> through wilderness and mountains
> amid the constant howling
> of wild beasts
> has brought me to such a pass
> that I think of ending it all by death.
> My food is spoiled,
> my clothes in shreds,
> my shoes broken,
> and my energy spent,
> so that I cannot move either foot
> another inch.

Now hunger afflicts me
and thirst torments me;
now my strength fails me
and my only hope of escaping
this agony is to give myself up
to whoever will capture me again.
Now I have lost my sense of direction;
I know not what is the way to Orán;
it is my unhappy lot that
nor road nor path is revealed,
and if I were to find it, alas,
so weary am I, I could not move a step. . . .
Blessed and lovely Virgin,
protector of the human race,
be you here the star
that in this insane sea
guides my poor bark
and averts so many perils!
Virgin of Monserrat,
who makes a heaven of its rude crags,
send me redemption,
lead me out of this affliction,
for your noble gesture is
to stretch out your hand to the fallen. . . .
In this thicket I yearn
to hide myself, for the day is come.
Here I hope to die,
most saintly Mary.
In this bitter peril
I yield my body and soul to your care.

In the first months of the year 1576 Ensign Gabriel de Cástañeda managed to escape to Orán and he bore with him a letter from Miguel to his parents telling them about how things stood with him and Rodrigo. The letter must have reached Madrid about the middle of the year. In the house of the poor chirurgeon there was not a penny to spare and the unfortunate man was at his wit's end. He remembered the debt owed him by Licentiate Sánchez de Córdoba and tried unsuccessfully to collect it. He also petitioned the King to grant him the grace of some money to ransom his sons from their captivity, again without success.

Fortunately the ingenious constable and good friend of the family Alonso Getino de Guzmán, a man fertile in expedients, continued to frequent the house. Inspired by a desire to do something about this situation, he thought up a theatrical scheme he had read about in an old booklet of Ciceronian rhetoric. He made Doña Leonor de Cortinas put on widow's weeds and in that garb she began to solicit assistance in the capital to relieve the sad condition in which her sons, the sole support of the family, found themselves as captives in Algiers. Thus that resolute and spirited woman, not being a mother for nothing, and the mother of such a son, wrapped herself in her weeds and metaphorically slew her husband. Getino de Guzmán, delighted with his invention, laughed in anticipation at the thought of how his friend Miguel would also laugh when he found himself freed by the arts of the theater and the work of a dramatist.

CHAPTER 19

Inside Algiers—Mulay Maluc—Juan the Gardener

ALL the animation and hubbub of the waterfront and harbor of Algiers turned to deathly silence in the city. There time passed slowly, lacking the sound of bells that marks the hours in Christian towns. The little donkeys bringing water to thirsty neighborhoods clambered slowly up narrow, twisting lanes. The few women to be seen moved slowly on foot, "the face hidden by a veil, a small brocaded cap on the head, wearing a long robe that covers them from shoulder to foot." Morning and evening the voices of the muezzins rang out as they intoned the mournful Mohammedan calls to prayer echoing from minaret to minaret.

The city was short of water and inhabited by a multitude of miserable slaves, battalions of diseased beggars, herds of swine and packs of vagabond dogs. There was always white plague or black plague in the city, as well as tumors, dysentery, mange, and every variety of infectious disease bred by filth and negligence. Corpses abandoned in the streets and rotting in the gutters were a feast for the dogs and for the vultures and crows that flocked in from the neighboring hills.

Algiers seemed a city organized for death, and the houses with their tall whitewashed walls, without windows or openings on the street, and with only one narrow closed door, looked like great sepulchres waiting to receive their dead and keep them eternally.

As in all Mohammedan cities, and even more than in those of the

Orient, the inhabitants lived indoors; they fled the noxious streets and plunged into their houses, defending themselves with strong perfumes against the torture afflicting their nostrils. The pestiferous odor of Algiers in the summer was so pervasive that at times it attracted wild beasts from afar. The sentinels at the Babazón Gate, at the Ramdán Gate and at the Fort of Twenty-four Hours had heard the whine and shriek of hyenas on many summer nights and some asserted that they had also heard the hoarse roar of a lion break the silence.

The opulence and ostentation of the houses of leading Moors and renegades contrasted with the misery of the streets. Among them were rich landowners belonging to the old families of Algiers who were extremely annoyed by the predominating influence attained in the city by seafarers, corsair captains, and officials sent from Constantinople, nearly all fugitives from Italy, Greece, and Illyria. They were despicable and lawless folk who bought their posts and lived by exploitation and bribery and who always died in an unseemly manner. The powerful Moors and the leading renegades had nothing to do with such rabble, typical of that which corrupt governments have always sent to exploit their colonies.

Among the rich renegades were cultured people of refined feeling, men who had lost their faith through the disappointments or exigencies of life but were very intelligent and fond of intellectual pastimes. Outstanding among them was the Slavonian Agi Morato, whose house was the most sumptuous in the city. He married his daughter Zorayda to Mulay Maluc, whom various authors of those days call a famous Moor, intelligent and very well educated. He had admirable judgment and a gentlemanly disposition, was a skillful penman and tracer of the curves and lines which constitute all the graphic art of the Moors, and with all this he was a great singer and dancer and player on the lute, monochord, and guitar.

Mulay Maluc was one of those urbane men, those delicate artists, whom decadence breeds. He was dethroned as Viceroy of Fez by one of his brothers who was more warlike than lettered, but his elegance and culture when he presented himself to the Grand Turk were such that Ramadán Pasha, King of Algiers, was ordered to organize a military expedition and replace Mulay Maluc on his unsteady throne. In 1576 he was in the house of his father-in-law Agi Morato, and Cervantes met him there:

> Mulay Maluco. . . .
> He who claims to be King
> of Fez, a very famous Moor
> and in his doctrine and perverse law

well versed and diligent.
He knows the Turkish language,
the Spanish and the German,
the Italian and the French,
he sleeps on high and eats at a table,
seated in Christian style.
Above all he is a great soldier,
liberal, wise, composed,
adorned by a thousand graces. . . .[1]

Perhaps Mulay Maluc knew that among the Christian captives there was one who recited poetry, and Miguel doubtless profited by the occasion to get to know from the inside the life and customs of those palaces whose white walls seemed identical from the outside with those of the most miserable huts. He was very much impressed by what any impartial person would agree were the courtesy and gentlemanliness of the Moors, the beauty of the Moorish women, their circumspect way of life, and the ingenuousness of those feminine minds that their shut-in life rendered forever childlike. It is possible that for some of them the gallantry of the captive Spaniard, the vivacity of his gestures and the somewhat extravagant gaiety of his chatter made him a favorite.

It is undeniable that in Cervantes' novels and plays about Algiers there is much that was imaginary, circulated in those days by word of mouth and later in books, but there is also much of reality, of things seen and felt. The descriptions by Cervantes coincide with those of Padre Haedo,[2] Padre Zuñiga and other contemporaries, and they do not differ essentially from the very careful accounts written in manuscript a century later by the Trinitarian friar Bartolemé Serrano, a discerning, devout and cheerful man whose book merits being printed. It is clear that in those works there could not be a more faithful description, lacking only the genius that enlivens Miguel's. Compare them with the accounts of La Goleta by the captive in the *Quixote*, or with the narratives of the talented Cristóbal de Villalón[3] and let these true descriptions testify to how little Cervantes was dreaming when many years later he recounted what he saw among the Moors.

To imagine that Cervantes spent his life in captivity moaning and weeping is not to know his character. Without losing sight for a moment of his intention to escape or be ransomed he used his time to advantage, and with an activity proper to his twenty-eight or twenty-nine years he mixed with all kinds of people, knew and associated with rich and poor Moors, renegades of high and low degree, and carefully hidden Moorish women. The women were not at all circumspect with the Christians, and many of them even had a good time with them while forever calling them dogs, as the vicious courtesans of Alexandria sometimes sought the lubricious caresses of their stinking black slaves, and even those of dogs and monkeys.

For the Moorish women Christians were dogs because they generally smelled bad. They reeked of the street, with that stench of Oriental cities so familiar to those who have traveled in China or India, while they, the Moorish women, with their bodies bathed and anointed daily, their hair drenched with essences, spread intoxicating heady perfumes throughout the house. Those sensitive to odors can detect something of this in the more sensuous pages where Cervantes speaks fondly of Moorish women, with a gentle longing easy to understand in one who spent most of his life among inn servants and country wenches whose proximity only a muleteer could stand.

It is also worthy of note that Cervantes rarely expressed antipathy or hatred toward Moors in general, while the acerbities of his pen were reserved for Jews and renegades. He distinguished clearly between the cruel corsairs, ferocious and greedy, and the gentlemanly and gallant Moors, courtly and generous, such as Agi Murato and Mulay Maluc, who died fighting as a good man should against the ill-fated King Sebastián at Alcázarquivir. From the moment he found himself captive, Miguel not only started his apprenticeship in patience under adversity, but also in tolerance at all times, and perhaps he acquired this tolerance in his relations with the skeptical spirits of the renegades or from the sweet lips of Moorish women. In any case he wandered freely everywhere, scoured the city in all directions, and established friendly relations with all sorts of people. He was not too hopeful of succor from Spain, for he understood all too well the difficult situation of the family. Nevertheless he thought that Don Juan and the Duke of Sessa would answer for him if they were asked, and he took advantage of every opportunity to write and transmit letters, appeals and petitions.

While he was writing, his mother and sisters, with tearful diligence, sought favor at the Court and used all their connections to get His Majesty's help with the ransom. With some difficulty they succeeded in obtaining an order from the King that they be given fifty escudos from the funds of the *Cruzada*,[4] which were delivered to Doña Leonor after some delay. This was a case of a heroic soldier of Lepanto, it is true, but there were many others in the same situation and money was short.

Seeking help elsewhere, Doña Leonor found out that Fray Francisco Maldonado had been chosen General of the Order of Mercy, and that he, as a newcomer to the post and desirous of acquiring prestige, intended to undertake the ransoming of captives with great diligence. He assigned this task to Fray Jorge de Olivar, prelate of Valencia, Fray Jorge de Ongay, prelate of Pamplona, and Fray Jerónimo Antich of Mallorca, while efforts to collect funds were intensified with a view to making the ransom program an extensive and brilliant performance. The Order of Mercy took great pride in its praiseworthy competition with the Order of the Trinity.

In order to achieve their ends, members of the Order of Mercy invaded the Royal Palace and all houses great and small, soliciting charity equally from King and Queen and simple soldiers, particularly from those who had spent some time as captives and knew the hardships of Algiers. The three friars chosen to arrange ransoms were three saintly men, wise, prudent and astute; as men of the world and versed in its ways they knew all the wiles as well as the weaknesses of pirates and slave owners.

Miguel's mother and sisters visited these good Friars of Mercy frequently in their convent near the Casa de la Latina; they confessed their troubles to them and managed to interest them in freeing those two captive soldiers, the only hope of the family. They presented themselves as forsaken widow and orphans, and in fact Doña Andrea was a widow, her first husband, Nicolás de Ovando, having died only recently, leaving her a daughter, Doña Constanza de Figueroa. The three women with their long black veils were the image of grief and despair and the soft heart of Fray Jorge del Olivar was moved by seeing them day after day with their petitions and complaints of hardship. The whole winter of 1576 and the first months of 1577 were spent in such activities.

Meanwhile Miguel waited in vain for an answer to his memorials and importunities. He was unaware of the situation of his idol, Don Juan, and could not persuade himself that his services had been completely forgotten; he still cherished poetically grandiose concepts and could not believe that it is nearly always prose that governs the lives of men and peoples. But while he still held to these poetical illusions he did not abandon practical plans for escape.

Passing one day along the seashore east of Algiers he saw a large, well-cared-for garden, apparently belonging to some rich Moor. From behind the low walls came a fine high tenor voice singing in a Moorish singsong, breaking off the cadences rapidly, the very ancient Spanish ballad of Aben Jot;

> Were my mother a Moor
> and I born in Algiers,
> I would renounce Mohamed
> only to see you once more,
> lovely snow-white dove. . . .

Miguel approached the Christian who was singing. He was from Navarre, a captive of the Greek renegade Hassan and a very skillful gardener. On a generous impulse he invited Miguel to visit the grounds. At the back, above a declivity, there was a cave[5] among the rocks, half hidden by the undergrowth, apparently an ancient refuge for shepherds or bandits with room for a good many people. Miguel quickly conceived a plan for escape and went in search of his recently acquired friend, Doctor Antonio Sosa.

This is what was experienced and borne with Christian patience by Cervantes' greatest friend in Algiers, that is, by the clergyman Doctor Antonio de Sosa who, while sailing from Malta in the galley *San Pablo*, was captured near the coast of Sardinia by Mahamet, the Jewish governor. As always when a priest fell into the hands of corsairs, Doctor Sosa had barely set foot in Algiers when several renegade Christians, out of spite or to ingratiate themselves with Mahamet, began saying that the priest was a man of great importance and worth a high ransom. Some made him out to be a secret chamberlain of His Holiness, some a Cardinal Archbishop; for some he was the Warden of Castilnuovo in Naples, for others the confessor of the Queen of Spain. In any case, as happened with Miguel, the great spirit of Doctor Sosa created a serious prejudice against him. He spent the first days of his captivity starving, naked, spread-eagled on a rough slab, imprisoned in the deepest dungeon, a cellar three or four stories below ground where moisture oozed from walls and floor. Three times they took him out for dead and finally transferred him to an upper dungeon in company with villainous Moors and highwaymen.

We do not know when or how Doctor Sosa got out of his prison, nor when and how Cervantes came to know him, but the fact is that he was the most cultured man of Miguel's acquaintance and the captive who most appreciated him. They may have met through a girl from Alcalá de Henares named Mariana Ramírez, also a captive in Algiers, whose ransom the Doctor paid in 1581. What is certain is that Sosa and Cervantes talked together often, exchanged their literary works, and alleviated their captivity by reading to each other.

But Doctor Sosa was not the only man of letters with whom Cervantes conversed in those days. About then he met the Piedmontese soldier and writer Bartolomé Rufino Chambery, who occupied himself during his captivity in writing an account *Sopra la desolazione della Goleta e Forte de Tunisi*, which is preceded by two laudatory sonnets written by Miguel in captivity. A little later he established relations with Doctor Domingo de Becerra, a priest from Seville, who had spent not a little time at the Court in Madrid and at that of Rome. The mystical gravity and ascetic sufferings of Doctor Sosa were in marked contrast with the gaiety of the courtier Doctor Becerra, who spent the most distressing days of his imprisonment in translating a certain Italian pamphlet entitled *Galatea* in which the urbanity and courtliness of Italy are compared with the clumsiness and rusticity of the Turkish rabble. Calliope sang about this learned doctor in the *Galatea*:

> That wise man who with knowledge
> arms and enriches his pure heart
> does not disdain to look upon the fount
> which gushes waters of wisdom upon our hill;
> rather in that incomparably clear current
> he so quenches his thirst that by it
> the bright name of Don Domingo de Becerra
> flourishes here upon this earth.

Miguel discussed his plan of escape with both of them and later conferred with Captain Meneses, Don Antonio de Toledo, Don Francisco de Valencia, and other leading captives from whose fortitude and courage he expected much. But the way of life and moral environment in Algiers were so deleterious that they bred the greatest degradation and it was impossible for even the most acute intelligence to distinguish with complete certainty between good men and bad. Among fourteen men there was bound to be a Judas and in the end there was: a native of Melilla whose nickname was the "Gilder" and who was one of the captives to whom Miguel confided his plans.

From the month of February or March these noble gentlemen who risked their lives for liberty began to hide in the cave by agreement with the gardener Juan. Poor and with no resources, for his master was so mean that he did not even give him any food or clothing, Miguel was able to arrange matters so as to live himself and to keep alive those who had hidden in the cave, at times using the "Gilder" to provision those shut up in the cave and keep them informed.

How this miracle was accomplished in that hostile city, where for those who had nothing there were not even windows giving on the street from which alms might be thrown, nor scarcely a door at which to knock, no historian has been able to explain, nor did Cervantes himself say anything about it.

In this part of Miguel's life there are steps that left no footprints, like those of supernatural beings. He went everywhere, intrigued, begged, solicited, salvaged, and if there was no time for these he thieved for his friends in the cave. If he did steal for them what theft more saintly and more praiseworthy could there be? In that constant search for ways and means he frequented the waterfront and public squares, consorted with the worst conceivable rogues, learned how to deal with Moors and Jews, exploiting their weaknesses and cheating them when he could, and each and every day he risked his life. And seeing and feeling the perils of his existence he saw and felt them with the intensity of the artist.

It was because of this that later he had no need to torment himself, as Flaubert and other modern artists have done, to achieve a synthetic view of world events and a placid indifference in transcribing them. His conception of a full life was broadening, humanity was revealing its secrets, and each one of them cost Miguel blood, suffering, humiliation, hunger, and deprivations of every kind, but—the saint had already said it—the purest suffering brings the purest understanding. On attaining thirty years of age the tortured Miguel understood the language of life, the words of which are so often learned in the dictionary of pain and poverty.

CHAPTER 20

Rodrigo Ransomed—Plan of Escape—Betrayal—Capture

EARLY in 1577 Fray Jorge del Olivar, Fray Jerónimo Antich and Fray Jorge de Ongay arrived in Algiers, determined to arrange for a memorable redemption that the Trinitarians would envy. Miguel soon got in touch with the good fathers and through them had news of home.

Fray Jorge del Olivar told him how he had seen Doña Leonor and Doña Andrea in widow's weeds, which cause Miguel much sorrow, not only through natural grief at learning that his father and brother-in-law Ovando were dead, but also through knowing for certain that his family, as always, continued to be in straitened circumstances. This belief was confirmed by the meager sum that the distressed women had been able to give Fray Jorge for ransom money.

But Miguel was not one to be disheartened by the thought of those distant griefs and he immediately sought to discuss his ransom with his master, but Dalí Mamí was not in Algiers. Cervantes knew very well that in any case Dalí Mamí would not be easily satisfied with the paltry sum the Order of Mercy could offer. Freedom was within his grasp and once again it eluded him. However, he was determined to use the money to ransom his brother Rodrigo, and this was accomplished at the beginning of summer.

The Friars of Mercy knew that very soon Hassan Pasha, the new King of Algiers, was due to arrive from Constantinople. He was a Venetian renegade whose cruelty and greed, it was rumored, far exceeded that of all his predecessors in the post. They made as much haste as they could, fearful that ransom demands would be increased upon the arrival of Hassan Pasha when it became known that among the liberated captives were men as eminent as Don Miguel de Villanueva, the canon of Valencia, and Don Juan de Lanuza, son of the Chief Justice of Aragón. They were ready to return to Spain with their liberated captives when Hassan Pasha arrived with his galleys, bringing Dalí Mamí with him as his admiral.

No one could remember a time in Constantinople when two such posts had been filled by any means other than selling them to the highest bidders, and of late they might be only traders, merchants, or usurers like Hassan Pasha, for whom to rule in Algiers meant a short-term business of considerable risk to be exploited without wasting time or squandering compassion. In committing his notorious cruelties he was not playing the role of a governor like the Duke of Alba,[1] who considered strictness necessary to maintain discipline, but rather that of a trafficker in slaves to whom it was important to keep his merchandise in order.

Hassan Pasha saw the first fruits of his business miscarry with the ransoms previously arranged by the Order of Mercy, and as he may have perhaps counted on their product to pay for the bribes to which he owed his appointment, he flew into a rage and demanded that Canon Villanueva and the noble Zamora be delivered to him so that he could wreak vengeance on them for alleged insults to certain Moors, but the good Fathers managed to abate his demands by giving him more money, although he had sworn that those two gentlemen would row in his galleys and then be burned alive. The friars had wisely got both gentlemen out of Algiers, but upon finding this out the other captives awaiting ransom rebelled, considering that in captivity they were all equal and that there were no differences between a gentleman and the lowliest peasant. As was their habit, they threatened to become renegades in order to move the friars to pity and get them to spend their last maravedi and pledge the credit of the Order to arrange more and more ransoms.

Then everyone saw an unparalleled act of sublime Christian love when the good religious, Fray Jorge del Olivar, presented himself before the King and offered to remain in captivity as hostage for those Christians. Hassan Pasha accepted the exchange, confident that the powerful Order would not leave one of its prelates and a man of such worth in slavery for very long. Fray Jorge del Olivar, burdened with chains, went to the King's bagnio. Meanwhile, on August 24, Fray Jorge de Ongay left for Spain with a hundred and twelve liberated captives.

Among them was Rodrigo de Cervantes, who carried an order from his brother Miguel to charter an armed frigate in Mallorca or Ibiza which could sail into Algerian waters and in which the refugees in the cave could escape. He also carried letters from Don Antonio de Toledo and Don Francisco de Valencia for the Viceroys of Valencia and the Balearic Islands seeking their help in making the vessel ready. The best hopes of his brother went with the ship that carried Rodrigo away.

Watching her white wake from the seashore, Miguel sang within himself:

On the shores of the sea
which laps the walls of odious Algiers
with its thrusting tide,
at times gently, at times furiously,
with longing eyes
four miserable captives
gaze toward their country
as they rest from their labors,
and to the sound of the coming and going
of the waves on the beach,
their voices faint,
this their lament and this their song
How dear art thou held!
Oh sweet Spain!

Heaven has conspired
with our adverse fate
to keep our bodies in chains
and our souls in great peril.
Would that the Heavens now
might open their secret springs
and instead of water let there rain down
pitch, resin, brimstone and live coals!
Would that the earth open up
and in its bowels be concealed
many a Datán and many a Birón,
many a wizard and many a witch. . . .
How dear art thou held!
Oh sweet Spain![2]

At last Miguel decided that he too would wait for the arrival of the liberating vessel with his comrades in the cave, some of whom had already been there for six months. He went to visit his friend Doctor Sosa, but the poor priest was full of aches and pains and almost crippled by the rheumatism he had acquired in the dampness of the dungeon and he refused to go lest he endanger the success of the venture by his clumsiness. The two friends took tender leave of each other and

Miguel escaped from his master's house on September 20 of 1577, taking refuge in the cave.

Emaciated, sick, and sad, some of the Christians in that mountain den thought that with the summer over and the rainy season approaching it was going to be difficult for them to stay on in such an asylum. Miguel entertained them by his conversation and comforted them with an eloquent account of the example set by Fray Jorge del Olivar. To them, it is not idle to repeat, he was a semidivine leader, patient, brave, provident, diligent, and benign.

After Miguel had been with them for eight days they observed out to sea the masts of a frigate tacking some distance from the coast. At night, with ears on the alert and eyes watchful, they sensed the bark approaching the coast; perhaps they could make out a black bulk. Unfortunately some Moors had gone out to fish in the moonlight and seeing the stealthy ship trying to come silently to land, inclined as they always were to raise a hue and cry, they began to shout loudly and the frigate fled.

On the following day some thirty men commanded by a captain entered the orchard and approached the cave, some on foot and others on horseback bearing lances, guns, and cutlasses. They were accompanied by the "Gilder," who, it was now clear, had denounced and betrayed his friends.

Miguel, alone and serene, advanced toward the soldiers, declaring in a loud and firm voice that he was the author of everything and that he alone was guilty. They manacled Miguel, they manacled all the others, and they sent a messenger on horseback to give Hassan Pasha the news. The unhappy procession set out, surrounded by Turkish soldiers of the King's guard dressed in their white cotton trousers, shod with crimson buskins and armed with ornate muskets.

CHAPTER 21

Miguel Before Hassan Pasha—Miguel Writes a Letter

THE news that many Christians had been surprised on the point of escaping in a phantom ship that had fled into the night had reached Algiers with the mounted messenger and soon spread through the city. The numerous idlers and the mob of street urchins licked their lips in anticipation as they did then in any Spanish town when there was a thief to be hanged, a witch to be impaled or an *auto-de-fé* to be turned over to the secular arm. In those days cruelty was as natural for the Christians as for the Moors and the sight of another's blood being spilled wiped out fear of shedding one's own. For people living in sordid misery, also, there was no dread of contagion nor fear of promiscuities such as we would feel today. Out of blood and the miseries of the flesh a contempt for life was perhaps born. Cruelty was, if not the mother, certainly the nurse of asceticism and mysticism.

His hands tied but his brow serene, Miguel de Cervantes walked erect between the bloodthirsty executioners of Hassan Pasha. The way to the Alcazaba was a stony tortuous climb, sometimes so narrow that the guards had to squeeze against Miguel's body to get through. Doors never opened for charity were flung wide out of hostile curiosity and a deep perfumed coolness emanated from them, along with sounds of feminine laughter and singing. It was the last day of September, pleasantly mild. The palm trees showing their heads of vivid green above the tops of the mud walls let their golden clusters of fruit hang down or give way to the dark fig trees tucked away in patios and small orchards that allured the captive's eyes with their foliage and released to his nostrils the aroma of the black figs on the ink-colored skins of which drops of fragrant honey trembled. Life was pleasant, even in captivity; to lose it was a great pity and a monstrous absurdity.

The way was long and as painful as it was long. In imploring tones the other captives begged Cervantes not to abandon them to the cruel vengeance of the Turks. Miguel tried to encourage them, assuring them that he would remain steadfast under torture and lose his life to save them. At last, more dead than alive, they arrived before the King.

Hassan Pasha looked them over with the expert eye of a merchant appraising a bargain. Thanks to the many months spent in the cave without any means to care for themselves, they were all long of beard and nails, dirty and ragged, but the astute trader knew by various signs, by the vestiges of good breeding and deportment they retained under their rags, that they were a good catch, and he immediately marked them for his own. The captain of the guards pointed out Miguel to his master as the gentleman who had declared himself the sole author and principal organizer of the escape plot.

Upon this Hassan interrogated Miguel in the lingua franca spoken in the Mediterranean ports, a mixture of Greek, Venetian, Neapolitan, Provençal and Mallorcan patois, along with a medley of other languages and dialects.

Miguel's appearance persuaded him that the captive was a man of great importance and of strong and noble spirit, and even though he already suspected that the fear of dying would make no impression on him, he threatened him with a most cruel and pitiless death. Miguel cast his eyes to Heaven and gave the tyrant to understand that he was indifferent to the loss of his life since he was certain to save his soul. Hassan then wondered if this man were perhaps a mystic or an inspired martyr such as he had seen at times seeking martyrdom and dying gladly, as is said to have happened in Nero's time, but he soon dismissed any such notion.

The interrogation continued and Miguel saw in Hassan Pasha's tortuous insinuations and involved arguments the twistings and turnings of Venetian perfidy. Miguel as a prisoner was of interest to Hassan, but the more distant end he was pursuing promised to be more lucrative, for he intended to involve Fray Jorge del Olivar in it. He thought correctly that by imprisoning the poor friar closely as being guilty of an attempt to escape he could double and even triple the ransom, putting the Order of Mercy in the position of having to pay whatever he demanded.

The eternally dramatic scene of the struggle between the serpent and the lion was then enacted. Hassan Pasha gave himself away between threatening words and pretense of indulgence, while Cervantes argued roundly, erecting strong verbal barricades in defense of his own interest and that of the other catpives.

In this game in which life itself was at stake Hassan realized, even more than the Christians themselves, what kind of man he had to deal with, and because of this someone has wisely suggested that Hassan Pasha above all should be included among the great admirers of Cervantes, for he understood from their very first encounter that Miguel was not a man whose life could be thoughtlessly contemned and delivered to the gallows without further consideration.

Mindful of his own interests certainly, but also taking the value of Miguel into consideration, Hassan Pasha passed judgment, taking all the Christians as captives for himself and ordering Miguel to be kept in his own bagnio, secured by many chains and irons. Miguel breathed freely again and the rest of the Christians expressed their gratitude.

Let it be said now whether or not it is an exaggeration for a devoted biographer to declare that in this case Miguel matched some of the great heroes of history. It is true that necessity forced him into it, compelling him to defend himself and his comrades, but who would not have been confused and have lost all his eloquence upon finding himself in such a tight corner?

At thirty years of age Miguel was a complete man and the extraordinary new tests in which he had been put to the proof enabled him to recover the confidence and strengthen the faith that he always had in himself, inspiring and nourishing ever greater illusions. He was a student who had learned much of life, although from it he was still to receive many severe lessons.

Confined in Hassan Pasha's dungeon he went over by himself the reasons why his well-contrived plot had failed, but instead of losing faith because one of the fourteen Christians he had sought to save had turned out to be a Judas, his confidence in his own salvation did not waver. The "Gilder's" accusations had achieved nothing, since Miguel was alive and his indomitable spirit continued at work to weave the fabric of his eventual liberation.

After three days in prison Miguel was taken to witness a barbarous and bloody torture, that of the poor gardener Juan, whom his owner, that other Hassan, the Greek renegade, perhaps to ingratiate himself with the King of Algiers, undertook to punish for his participation in the frustrated escape. In order to shock and impress Miguel's mind with such great brutality they took him to the garden of Hassan the Greek and there he saw, still alive but already blind and unconscious, the unfortunate man from Navarre who in days past had sung in his open-hearted and untutored voice the old couplet of Aben Jot:

> If my mother were a Moor
> and I had been born in Algiers. . . .

His master had hung him with his own hands, stringing him up by one foot from the trunk of a palm tree and then amusing himself by playing at tightening and loosening a cord around his neck so that the suffering and the agony should last longer. The poor gardener's face was black and blue, his bloody tongue hung out from his mouth; threads of blood ran from his nose to the ground and rimmed his purple eyelids, between which the white globes of his already dulled eyes projected from their sockets. Every now and again black slaves shook the palm tree and the corpse danced in macabre contortions as the ripe dates fell and bounced upon it.

It is not likely that the ferocious spectacle crushed Miguel. He returned to his prison and to his meditations and his hopes. He soon learned that King Hassan had paid his master Dalí Mamí a goodly sum for him, and the news did not displease him, for he preferred to contend with a man of perspicacity and intelligence like Hassan Pasha than to be dependent on a simple usurer like Dalí Mamí. The drama of life was getting complicated before his eyes, but the confusion of events did not obscure his poetic vision of reality, a vision that today seems romantic to us because we do not realize that in those days events compelled men to behave romantically.

Miguel could not convince himself that poetry did not play as great a part in the lives of others as in his. About that time he learned that his old comrade Mateo Vázquez de Leca had risen to being *Archisecretario*, that is to say, he who handled the greater part of Philip II's correspondence and reports, while Antonio Pérez reserved for himself the important secret part and perhaps was already sensing the storm about to break upon him.[1] Knowing something of this, Miguel sent Mateo Vázquez a letter written in tercets.

This letter to Mateo Vázquez[2] was given much thought and written unhurriedly and carefully polished. Miguel must have spent months in thinking out and composing it in order to convert his own personal troubles into patriotic afflictions. He started by singing the praises of his old friend and then told the tale of his misfortune:

> In the galley *Sol*, whose light
> my ill luck darkened, to my sorrow,
> causing the loss of others and myself.
> At first we showed strength and valor
> but later by bitter experience
> we learned that it was all useless.
> I felt the heavy burden of a foreign yoke
> and in accursed sacrilegious hands
> my anguish has lasted for two years.
> I know well that my infinite sins
> and the small repentance I have felt
> keep me among these treacherous Israelites.
> When I arrived defeated and saw the land
> so famous in the world, which in its bosom
> hides, protects and shelters countless pirates,
> I could not stay my weeping,
> which to my shame, feeling my face stained
> by I knew not what, found they were tears.
> Before my eyes there lay the shore
> and hills where the great Charles
> lifted his standard high in the air
> And the sea which could not tolerate such vigor
> then moved to envy of his glory
> became angrier than ever before.
> These things recurring to my mind
> brought tears to eyes
> moved by such flagrant misfortune.
> But if High Heaven in hurting me
> is not conspiring with my future
> and death does not leave my body here,
> When it sees me in a more happy state,
> if by your intercession, Sir, you aid me

to see myself kneeling before Philip,
My tongue stammering and almost mute
I imagine moving in the Royal presence,
in adulation and stripped of lies,
Saying: "High Lord, whose power
subjects a thousand barbarian nations
to the harsh yoke of obedience,
To whom the dusky Indians by their gifts
recognize their just vassalage,
bringing gold here from their secret stores;
Let there awaken in your Royal breast a mighty rage
at the great presumption with which such paltry folk
continually aspire to outrage you.
The people are many but their strength is small,
naked, ill-armed, who have not
fort, wall or cliff for their defence.
Each of them looks to see if your armada comes
to take over the burden and remedy
of preserving a life which endures.
It has the key to the lock
of the bitter prisons, dark and dismal
in which twenty thousand Christians are dying.
All of them (as myself) from here, with hands raised
and kneeling on the ground, sobbing,
surrounded by inhuman torments.
Brave Sir, they pray to you
to turn the eyes of mercy
toward theirs, which weep forever.
And now that you are free of the discord
which hitherto oppressed and wearied you
and you can enjoy a peaceful harmony;
Act, good King, that you may complete
that which so bravely and audaciously
was undertaken by your beloved father.
Just the thought that you come will spread
terror among the enemy people who can foresee
already from here their downfall and destruction."
Who doubts that the benign Royal breast
will be responsive to the sorrow
in which these miserable beings remain? . . . .

This letter arrived in Madrid at a very bad time. Every day there passed through the hands of Mateo Vázquez hundreds of letters, memoirs, plans, and projects for bringing Flanders and other problems to a happy conclusion. Usually the King paid no attention to such flights of the Spanish imagination, nor to secret accusations against Secretary

Antonio Pérez, against the Princess Eboli, against Escobedo, the secretary of Don Juan, against Don Juan himself, who was fighting in Flanders.

In the midst of this confusion Mateo Vázquez one day received the letter of his old friend and he recalled the happy days when he enjoyed poetry. The impressive rounded fullness of the tercets gave him to pause for a moment, and though he had little time to spare he read and re-read it, reckoning its author a great poet.

As he was savoring the verses an usher informed the secretary that His Majesty was waiting for him. Mateo quickly collected his papers, doors opened, curtains were raised, and he found himself in the presence of the sovereign. Standing by a writing table, beside which serving as equerry there was a large table laden with a mass of papers, the monarch, black save for his face and hands, replied to the salutation, asked questions, concisely and authoritatively. Mateo turned over his papers. The monarch set some aside, rejected others. Mateo left Cervantes' letter to the last.

The King took the paper from the hands of the secretary and, looking at the unequal lines, asked if it were verse. Mateo turned red and realized that he had committed a small folly, while the King said nothing and returned the paper with a disdainful gesture. When, both of them were thinking, were serious matters of state dealt with in verse? If attention were paid to all the ideas that passed through the pate of every poetaster His Majesty's Kingdom would be in a pretty state. The letter therefore remained unanswered.

CHAPTER 22

Miguel Writes Another Letter—From Mercy to Trinity

As he was aware of so many other things, Miguel then remembered that the general in command at Orán at that time was Don Martín de Córdoba, later Marquis of Cortes. It was related of this illustrious gentleman that when he was a captive in Algiers with sixteen thousand other Spanish prisoners taken in the expedition of Mostagán,[1] he proposed that all the slaves rise in rebellion (for they were much more numerous than the Turkish garrison) and take possession of the city, presenting it as a gift to the Spanish King. The conspiracy having been discovered through the treachery of a Valencian named Morallón, Don Martín de Córdoba was locked up in a remote tower and his ransom cost his family twenty-three thousand gold escudos.

In the stories about this ill-starred venture, which had happened nineteen or twenty years previously, there was much that was fantastic legend, but not in its essentials, the truth and soundness of which Miguel deduced, calculating and weighing all the difficulties such a plan might entail from the practical point of view. At the same time he imagined how happy a gentleman as famous for his valor as Don Martín de Córdoba might be if, with the forces that he then disposed, he could realize in his mature years the enterprise he had dreamed of in his youth. Very calmly and carefully Miguel considered the possibilities of the project, and with the eloquent and well-chosen words we must infer he used, judging by the skill and precision with which he always spoke when giving his opinion on military matters, he wrote what he was thinking about.

He must have spent more time in finding a way to get the letter to Don Martín than in its writing. Historians are silent about how Miguel managed to suborn a Moor into taking the letter, along with others directed to gentlemen and military leaders resident in Orán whom he knew and who must have known him, perhaps because they had been at Navarino and Lepanto. But if Miguel, accused of various crimes and a prisoner in the bagnio of Hassan Pasha, would be unlikely to have the means to bribe the messenger, would it be madness to suppose that some amorous feminine intrigue played a part in this plan, like those that figure in all his works when they deal with such matters? It is not a hypothesis out of a cheap novel, but rather an opinion made respectable by a hundred similar cases recorded by history, that in this matter of the Moor feminine hands did intervene, furnishing the money or giving orders that could not be disobeyed.

Miguel was the "gallant Spaniard"[2] of Hassan Pasha's bagnio. All who knew him at close hand praised his talent and cheerfulness; he was an interesting and sympathetic figure; recent events and his old mutilation proclaimed his courage. How authentic was the protection of Christian captives by those lovely and intriguing Moorish women in the plays of Cervantes perhaps we cannot tell, but doubtless there is some truth in it since all the rest is a faithful picture of reality.

The Moor left bearing Miguel's letters, but so ill-starred was he that other Moors, spies or soldiers, waylaid him on the road, searched him, found the papers, and took him before Hassan Pasha. The fury and indignation of the crafty Venetian upon seeing the signature of Cervantes at the foot of those seditious compositions can be imagined.

It was evident that the captive of the crippled hand was the most dangerous and stubborn man in Algiers. Hassan had to find out how far the plan had progressed and how serious it might be. For this he began by torturing the Moor; later he had him impaled; but the man died on the stake without saying a word that could compromise Miguel directly, possibly because he was only carrying out orders blindly.

Once again Miguel found himself face to face with Hassan Pasha, who knew by now that with this captive threats were of no avail. Nevertheless he ordered him to be shackled hand and foot with a rope around his throat and given two thousand bastinados on the belly and the soles of his feet, as was the custom when disobedient captives were to be killed slowly. In the end the cruel sentence was never carried out and not a hand was raised against Miguel.

However that might be, once the moment had passed in which heroism exalted Miguel's soul, he lived in a state of constant frustration, as he complained to Mateo Vázquez in the memorable tercets of his letter:

> I who have walked the worst and roughest
> road through a cold dark night,
> have fallen deep in mire.
> And in the cruel prison corner
> where I now am I mourn
> my brief unhappy venture.
> I importune heaven and earth,
> obscure the air with sighs,
> make the sea swell with tears.
> In this state, Sir, I am dying
> among barbarous people, unbelievers,
> losing my ill-rewarded youth.
> The reason for my being here
> was not that I had roamed the world,
> lost to dignity and principle.
> For ten years I marched and countermarched
> in the service of our great Philip,
> now at rest, now exhausted and weary. . . .

Thus did the unhappy Miguel bemoan himself when his attempts to gain freedom were once again dashed. Still intent on this end, however, he learned that Don Francisco de Meneses, the captain from Talavera, had managed to persuade the master in whose power he was captive to let him leave for Spain, pledging his word to pay his ransom of a thousand gold ducats. Two Portuguese gentlemen had previously made a similar agreement with good results.

How Miguel communicated with Meneses from his prison we do not know, but it is a fact that this noble Talaverian, his word having been accepted in exchange for his freedom, was in touch with Miguel and promised to visit his family in Madrid. He left Algiers at the beginning of the year 1578, having signed a contract with two merchants from Valencia who were doing business in Algiers, according to which they would pay the stipulated ransom after a certain time and be reimbursed by Don Francisco in Spain. When he arrived in Madrid he confirmed this obligation on February 27.

In the meantime the distrustful Hassan Pasha held the erudite Doctor Becerra of Seville as guarantee and hostage for the thousand ducats. We do not know what means this ingenious Doctor employed to get Meneses to pay his own ransom also, in an amount of only two hundred and forty ducats for a poor writer, but we do know that later both ransoms were paid, the remittances being confirmed by Baltasar de Torres, brother and partner of Hernando.

Like others who had opened offices in Algiers and were in constant trade relations with their other branches in Valencia, Barcelona and Mallorca, these Torres brothers were successful bankers who had organized an active business in merchandise and money by way of ransoms. Many captives were freed through their handiwork without participation by the Fathers of Mercy or the Trinity, and both Orders would seek their help in case of need or when, due to the brutal exigencies of the Turks, they could not come to terms with them. These merchant bankers also carried on business which came to them marginally through the grant of licenses to export "licit merchandise" (according to the official formula) with Algiers as its destination, licenses which the King granted, without its costing him a cent, to assist the wives of captives or needy widows like Doña Leonor who came begging His Majesty to ransom their sons.

Upon arriving in Madrid Captain Meneses saw the family of Cervantes and, doubtless stirred by Miguel's letters and the pathetic picture of his situation that Meneses drew for them, the chirurgeon Rodrigo, Doña Leonor and her daughters started again on their diligent quest.

Rodrigo de Cervantes asked for a new judicial inquiry into the merits of Miguel's case before Licentiate Ximénez Ortiz on March 17 of 1578. At the suggestion of Captain Meneses and at the request of Miguel himself his old comrades of Lepanto appeared as witnesses. The good Mateo de Santistéban from Navarre and the precise Gabriel de Castañeda from Santander told of the glorious deeds of Miguel in the naval battle. Sergeant Antonio Godínez de Monsalve, one of the veterans of Tunis who made the earth tremble with their muskets, also testified. Don Beltrán del Salto y de Castilla, who along with Godínez had seen Miguel in captivity and who knew how the soldier of Lepanto had been prejudiced by the discovery of the letters from the Duke of Sessa and Don Juan, bore witness on his behalf.

Not content with the inquiry, the result of which was not in the least doubt, Rodrigo de Cervantes again recalled the old debt owed him by Licentiate Pedro Sánchez de Córdoba. In the Cervantes family this debt was one of those false hopes on which guileless souls or those who have no regular means of support are wont to depend. They hope to collect the debt as one hopes to win a prize in the lottery, inherit from some distant relative, or acquire any other imaginary or ephemeral resources which never appear. It is known that in the year 1578 Sánchez de Córdoba was in Madrid, but apparently the family never even saw their insolvent debtor. Rodrigo de Cervantes was so unfortunate in all things that none of the methods he used ever had even a shadow of success.

Meanwhile his wife and daughters hastened as much as possible to put into effect every available means of advancing their purpose. In May Doña Magdalena gave a power of attorney to a certain Alfonso de Córdoba to go to the city of Jerez de los Caballeros, where Don Alonso Pacheco de Portocarrero resided—by now married and come into his patrimony—to demand, claim, and require from him payment of the five hundred ducats, by now almost as illusory as the eight hundred of Licentiate Sánchez de Córdoba. For her part Doña Andrea, who must still have had funds from her defunct husband Nicolás de Ovando and who was perhaps married for a second time or preparing for her nuptials with the Florentine, Santes Ambrosi, undertook to contribute two hundred ducats from her own pocket.

All the women of the house repeated their visits to the Convent of Mercy without the good fathers being able to give them any hope with regard to ransoms, for the saintly Fray Jorge del Olivar, old, sick and almost at the point of death, was still in Algiers due to the Order's lack of funds. Nevertheless a friar of the Convent in Madrid, Fray Jerónimo de Villalobos, moved to pity by the supplications of the weeping women, devised a plan that gave them some hope of raising the money to ransom Miguel.

With Father Villalobos serving as intermediary, the Cervantes women got in touch with Hernando de Torres, the Valencian merchant of whom Captain Meneses had doubtless already spoken to them, and through Fray Jerónimo they handed over one thousand and seventy-seven reals to be passed to Torres. In addition to this they had the promise of two hundred ducats already offered by Doña Andrea, and to top it all, on June 29 the whole family obligated itself to pay Torres at some future date the balance of the sum needed to effect Miguel's ransom, as yet undetermined.

Note how in this document Doña Magdalena has assumed a personality, and although unmarried she engaged her signature and her possessions. See also how great was the unity of the whole family and how absence had not dampened the affection they bore their son and brother. They were making a supreme effort to save him, and believing that it would be appropriate to add the moral support of another testimonial to bear witness to Miguel's merits they decided to approach the Duke of Sessa, who was in Madrid at the time. The Cervantes women must have had great difficulty in getting into the home of the grandee but they finally achieved it, and on July 25 of 1578 the Duke signed another certificate.

If any proof were needed of the strange fascination exercised by Cervantes upon those around him we would have it in the precise and eloquent words of the Duke of Sessa. Almost seven years had passed when suddenly some women clad in deep mourning presented themselves before him, questioning him about one soldier among the many who did memorable feats of valor in the naval battle. . . . When the Duke remembered so particularly those of Miguel, how can it not be attributed to the deep impression that seeing, knowing and later in Naples conversing with that simple soldier made upon him?

The Duke tells in concise terms, with no kind of eulogy, what he had seen Miguel do and what he can remember about him. The certificate is all the more impressive in that no line in it reveals the smallest spark of affection. Ask the knights of the *Spoliation* or the soldiers of the *Saint Maurice* of El Greco for affection or graciousness; ask it of those men of the black surtouts and slender fingers. It was no time for softness. "He fought very well and discharged his duty as he should" were carefully considered words of high praise from a general speaking of a simple archer.

Doña Leonor and her daughters spent the whole summer knocking at various doors, often accompanied by their faithful friend Getino de Guzmán, who helped to get them into government offices where, between yawns of boredom or hunger, clerks received hundreds of similar appeals every day. The women had made little progress until in December they obtained a royal decree authorizing Doña Leonor to export two thousand ducats' worth of "licit merchandise" from Valencia to Algiers, the profit on which would go toward meeting the cost of the ransom. These licenses were given out freely, more to close the mouths of petitioners than really to satisfy them, and it took much hard work to re-sell them to merchants who could use them. The one granted to Doña Leonor expired in six months and it was not until March that she found a merchant willing to give her as much as sixty ducats for it.

Ostensibly generous as the monarch was in making these worthless concessions, he and his clerical employees, the treasurers and accountants of the *Cruzada*, were exigent in requiring justification for any money that might be released for ransoms. Repeatedly they demanded of Doña Leonor that she justify the expenditure of the money given her for her son's ransom without the good lady's answers appearing to satisfy the clerks. In February of 1579 she finally received a paper in which the Treasurer of the *Cruzada* ordered her to return the fifty ducats granted her two years before and threatened to act against the bondsman, who was the constable Getino de Guzmán.

Guzmán was able to parry the blow by telling the secretary Juanes, who told the other gentlemen of the Crusade Council, that he had actually seen the ransomed Rodrigo. They accepted the word of Juanes, since he was one of them, and they stopped the order, paying more attention to recommendations and influence than anything else, however valid, as always happened and still happens in Spain.

It became known in the first months of 1579 that the Order of Trinity was preparing a new redemption that would be long remembered and would overshadow the one lately achieved by the Order of Mercy. The Cervantes women now directed their steps and repeated appeals to the Convent in the Calle de Atocha.

Late in the year they met a saintly man of transcendent quality who listened to the women in mourning with kindly interest. Getting confidential with him, Doña Leonor ended by confessing the innocent deception into which she had fallen in order to inspire pity by saying she was a widow. Fray Juan Gil, besides being a friar, was also a wise man of the world who was prepared to take all circumstances into account. In the best terms he knew, and he knew some excellent ones, he tried to lighten the heavy burden overwhelming the poor woman. The friar was a cheerful, animated, and optimistic man whose round shining countenance inspired confidence, and Doña Leonor felt that at last her affairs might be on the right track.

Meanwhile Miguel, who had again managed to obtain more ease and less severity in the prison, was once more in touch with the more important captives in Algiers. Walking the streets or visiting the bagnios he recognized such old friends as his fellow countryman Captain Jerónimo Ramírez, a native of Alcalá de Henares, whom he had known in Italy, as well as Don Antonio González de Torres, a Knight of St. John, and Don Jerónimo de Palafox, a nobleman from Aragón, held by Hassan Pasha as the captive worth the highest ransom among all those he owned. Perhaps Miguel also visited the ailing old man Fray Jorge del Olivar, who was chronically ill and lay stretched on a pallet peacefully awaiting death.

Slowly the days and months went by without a gleam of hope appearing. Throughout the summer and beginning of autumn there was no news to be heard in Algiers save that a formidable army had arrived in Africa commanded by the King of Portugal himself, Don Sebastián "the Brave." The captives thought an action equal in importance to that of Lepanto would be repeated on land and it was known that Don Sebastián was a knight-errant king who dreamed of mastering the whole of Africa, speeding on to Arabia and reaching India. The audacity of the Portuguese navigators was to be rounded out and confirmed by the intrepid courage of Portuguese soldiers. From that small kingdom perhaps European dominion over the whole world might emerge eventually. The design of Don Sebastián was the commencement of a poem such as Tasso's *Gerusalemme* or a book of knight-errantry like *Orlando*.

At the beginning of August the news that the army of Don Sebastián had been annihilated at Alcázarquivir ran sudden and terrible through Algiers. The rout had been greater than that of the Turks at Lepanto. Nothing was known of the King. The poem had been broken off in the first canto, the book on knight-errantry drowned in blood in the first chapter.

In November even sadder news came to chill Miguel's heart. Christians arriving from Spain told that Don Juan de Austria had died in Flanders at the beginning of October, not on the field of battle but on the bed of an inn like any common soldier. Miguel contemplated the broken images of the two valiant paladins and wept for the death of the general in whom he had placed all his hopes. As he walked through the streets the Moors repeated in their lugubrious singsong:

Don Juan no come,
Don Juan no come,
Die here,
Die here.

CHAPTER 23

The King's Bagnio—Two Spanish Renegades—
Cervantes, a Marian Poet—The Trials of a Trader

THE great bagnio of King Hassan was a spacious barrack seventy feet long and forty wide in which at times hundreds, at times thousands of captives were crowded together. It had two stories and was surrounded by rooms for captives who achieved the felicity of being alone. In the center of the lower floor there was a cistern of clear water. At one end there was a small improvised altar without altarpiece or images, so that priests could say Mass with whatever vessels they might have saved from disaster and with their own or a borrowed crucifix. At times Mass was celebrated with no image save that stamped on a scapulary, a page from a missal, a Virgin painted on a playing card, or a Christ taken from a rosary. Some of the captives told others of the days when Mass was said, and there were many, and those from other bagnios came to take part in the devotions.

One can only imagine how starved those men were for conversation and thirsty for news, and how they took advantage of these occasions to get together and exchange the endless speculations with which they nourished their failing hopes. How can we possibly appreciate the state of mind of almost all the captives unless we recall that many of them had forgotten what happened before their captivity and some even their surnames? It is because of this that there were so many called Juan the Biscayan, José from Cuenca, Antonio from Santander. Also perhaps some concealed their real names, ashamed of the miserable life they were dragging out.

Despite all this, as always happens with a group of men suffering a common misfortune, it was not unusual for the King's bagnio to be swept by gales of laughter. It is known that comedies were acted out on the premises. Who can say that Miguel was not one of the actors or directors of dialogues and passages from Lope de Rueda that were certainly presented there? His spirits could not be long depressed, for we know that the greatest tribulations did not rob him of his good humor. Furthermore the ordering of such an entertainment would be for him a way of capturing the admiration of the other captives, of stirring up that amorphous long-suffering mass, perhaps to recruit from it the men he needed to carry out his never-abandoned projects of escape.

For their part Hassan Pasha and the Turks who owned the captives did not object to these festivities, which kept the slaves happy for a few days. And since there were many men of talent and fluent and facetious wit among the Spanish and Italian captives, people other than slaves would flock to the performances: free Christians, rich Algerian traders, distinguished renegades, Moors and at times even Moorish women who, if their faces were well veiled, had no objection to rubbing elbows with Christian dogs since, according to their law and custom, they did not regard them as men. In the performances there might be a Venetian who could sing pretty roundelays and *fiorini* in the voice of a man and the high tones of a woman, a Frenchman who had trained his dog to leap for the King of France, two Neapolitan or Greek wrestlers and a Spaniard who intoned wonderful long ballads to the sound of guitar and castanets.

Who knows if this Spaniard who recited with a smooth and melodious voice and much amusing play of the eyes was not Miguel de Cervantes? And if it were he, who can doubt that as soon as he opened his mouth he commanded the attention, not only of the captives but also of the renegades and Turks who understood Castilian and could appreciate the talent of one who was to entertain the centuries to come so delightfully?

Among the renegades whom Miguel knew and associated with there were two men who soon won his confidence. One of them was called Abderramán and, according to what he told Miguel from the first, his real name was Licentiate Girón, a man from Granada, son of a nobleman of Osuna. The other was a cheerful and likable chap from Murcia whom the Moors called Morato and the Christians by the nickname "Maltrapillo" [Sloven], a reckless and venturesome man who had lived a dissolute life and who had been captain of a galliot.

These two very different types were soon great friends of Miguel. The man from Granada was reserved and taciturn but Cervantes soon guessed that a deep inner struggle troubled his heart. The Levantine was gay and carefree, and Miguel's talents appealed to his character and won the complete sympathy of his lighthearted spirit.

If a Cordovan is always dogmatic and a Sevillian almost always skeptical, a man from Granada is always a man of deep though uneasy faith, a man of troubled conscience. Licentiate Girón, although we do not know for what reason he had apostatized, repented it deeply. Miguel was able by skillful converse to bring the perturbed spirit of his friend to the surface. "Understanding," Cervantes says, "that the said renegade repented for what he had done in becoming a Moor, and his desire to return to Spain, many a time I exhorted and urged him to return to the faith of our Lord Jesus Christ."

But it would be wrong to believe that Miguel assumed the role of preacher or catechist only to get assistance in freeing himself. No. This year of 1579 in particular was to be a decisive one for the soul of Cervantes. His conversations and religious dialogues with Doctor Sosa, Doctor Becerra and the suffering martyr Fray Jorge del Olivar and the impulsive gestures of self-abnegation that took possession of him from time to time doubtless had an influence on his mind and created in him a manly and robust devotion, a firm adherence to the Christian faith. He had had no occasion to show this during his wanderings as a soldier save in his visit to Loreto, although an unannotated Garcilaso and an "Hours of Our Lady" had accompanied him through Italy as books for his intimate devotions.[1] So that everything in his spiritual makeup be purely Spanish, perhaps no saint or member of the Holy Trinity inspired as much faith in him as the Virgin Mary. Cervantes is not usually counted among the Marian poets, for he could not be at ease amid so much insipid nonsense circulating under that heading, but possibly after Petrarch and Fray Luis de León there is no poet comparable to Miguel in fervency toward the Virgin, and of his youthful poems the best are Marian verses. If he did not compose them in Algiers, it was in Algiers that he felt and thought of the admirable strophes spoken by the fugitive to Orán in *Life in Algiers*:

Blessed and lovely Virgin
redeemer of the human race . . .

and the others which Aurelio, the protagonist of the work, that is to say, Miguel himself, recites:

To you, most holy Virgin Mary
intervening between God and man . . .
to you, Mother and Virgin, I entrust
my soul which without you has no hope . . .
I know that I do not deserve
your eternal memory of my pain,
for in my soul I have fresh and green
the sweet fruit of a marvellous love:
but your great clemency, which never fails
the chance to do good, will repair
my evil state, for now I am almost lost
threatened by Scylla and Charybdis. . . .

and finally the magnificent sonnet in the play *The Link*, which those men of execrable taste for whom Cervantes was not a poet have never read:

For you, lovely Virgin, the peasant poor,
despite the danger of threatening skies,
cheerfully sows the rich seed
between the furrows of the ploughland.
For you the trader cleaves the ancient seas
in his frail sail-borne bark,
and in extremes of sun and ice
the soldier strides o'er hill and dale.
Through you so many times, when he
who seeks and prays loses heart,
it revives and victory is assured.
Through you, firm staff of life,

it is sometimes possible to aspire
and long for the gates of glory.
 Oh, hope perceived,
the comfort of a fainting heart
even when buried deep in misery!

The piety of Cervantes was a poetic flight of fancy proper to an unhappy youth, but neither in these verses nor in the others that he dedicated to the Virgin in his early years as a poet is there any rhetorical argument or lyrical artifice. The sentiment which inspired them was deep-rooted and remained with him even after the years of adversity. He was able to communicate it to Licentiate Girón and to convince him that his inner struggle should and could have no other end than a return to the land and faith of his forebears.

When at last he was persuaded, Miguel and Licentiate Girón talked with a certain Valencian merchant among those resident in Algiers called Onofre Exarque, a friend or relative of the Torreses and Juan Fortuny. Like the other merchants who did business at the expense of slavery, he was a cheerful and kindly man but not particularly scrupulous, accustomed as he was to dealing with both Moors and Christians and living among them. Nevertheless the passionate arguments of Girón and the persuasive eloquence of Miguel together convinced him that it might be a good thing to advance more than thirteen hundred doblas to buy an armed frigate, "persuading him," Cervantes declares, "that nothing could be more honorable or acceptable in the service of God and His Majesty. So this he did, and the said renegade bought a frigate of twelve benches and made it ready, being governed in everything by the advice and precept of Miguel de Cervantes." The persuasion of Exarque to put out thirteen hundred doblas for such a preposterous adventure, similar to so many others that had failed, is one of Cervantes' masterpieces.

It is not said ironically or as a joke, but seriously after close examination, that it seems even more admirable than writing the *Galatea* to be able to convince a thick-skinned trader that he would be carrying out a magnificent exploit by putting out his money and turning it over to a renegade and a number of captives who were no more accountable than the poor soldier Miguel, simply to provide them with a means of escape.

It is also remarkable that Miguel never could conceive a paltry project. If he had only used all the talent and industry devoted to this and previous attempts to escape in organizing his own he could have succeeded a hundred times, but he was not satisfied with his own liberation if his good friends could not participate. Thus news of the projected escape circulated secretly among a select number of the captive population and up to sixty gentlemen and captives of lesser quality knew about it and were ready to take part.

The month of September was passing and autumn approaching. The fruitfulness of autumn for Cervantes should be noted. From his adolescence to his old age it was always between September and October that he conceived and carried out his great exploits. Spring was usually adverse to him, autumn propitious. He was not a simple soul, the kind of man who has confidence in spring; he was a man of experience, one of those who believes in autumn, and thus it was in the autumn of his life that he produced his ripest fruits.

Miguel's confidence, his inextinguishable faith, must also inspire admiration. We are amazed that Don Quixote should attack windmills and provoke lions because we forget that Miguel attacked renegades and Moors and repeatedly provoked Hassan Pasha, a man he knew to be as fierce as a tiger. We are surprised to see Don Quixote being beaten so often and fail to bear in mind that within a year of his being betrayed by the "Gilder" Miguel put an identical secret, not just in the hands of fourteen or fifteen men hidden in a cave but of sixty captives scattered all over Algiers. Like Don Quixote, his creator did not learn by experience and the worse his situation the more reckless he became. If we know the psychology of Cervantes is it difficult to explain the psychology of Don Quixote?

Two or three days before the one chosen for the escape Cervantes learned that the episode of the "Gilder" had been repeated. The Judas this time was a Dominican monk from Estremadura, a native of Montemolín near Llerena, who gave his name as Doctor Juan Blanco de Paz and said he was an agent and familiar of the Holy Office. This despicable man, who is already sufficiently punished in that his name is recorded by history, betrayed Miguel's plan, confiding it to a Florentine renegade called Caibán, who told King Hassan. Aware of Miguel's activities and knowing about the purchase of the frigate, Hassan kept silent in order to catch the fugitives *in flagrante delicto*, punish them appropriately, seize their accomplices, and above all lay hands on Onofre Exarque, whose wealth he coveted.

Miguel was indignant with himself for having made his project known to an impious man and perverse priest like Blanco de Paz, but he had considered that for an escape from Algiers it was not feasible to expect only archangels and seraphim to accompany him, but rather men of every description. Pondering on how to remedy the disaster he fled the King's bagnio and took refuge in a hideaway arranged by his friend Corporal Diego Castellano, who was one of those preparing to escape. Through Corporal Castellano Cervantes made the news of the treachery known to the other conspirators. Onofre Exarque heard about it and was overcome by the fear of the capitalist who sees his moneys, his liberty, and perhaps his head in danger.

The fears of Onofre Exarque, a connoisseur of human frailty by virtue of his business and way of life, were fully justified. Once the plot was discovered, if any of those involved in it revealed under torture the participation of the Valencian trader he could consider himself lost. Meanwhile King Hassan ordered a search for Miguel, put a price on his head by public proclamation, and decreed the death sentence for anyone who had hidden him. Full of anguish, Exarque went in search of Miguel and told him of his fears.

Miguel thought it all over and told Exarque that he was going to present himself to Hassan Pasha and take upon himself the whole responsibility for everything that had been planned. He swore with his hand on his heart that neither threats nor torture would make him denounce his friend the generous merchant. It is difficult for us to imagine how Miguel could give his word, but we do know that Onofre Exarque believed him and did not even think of fleeing himself. Is further proof needed of the charm that Miguel exercised upon those who spoke with him and the confidence which his words inspired in them?

Miguel left his hiding place, taking leave of the worthy Corporal Castellano, and went in search of his friend, the ship's captain Morato Maltrapillo. He told him the whole story and about his resolution to present himself to the King for him to work his will on him. Amazed, Maltrapillo could scarcely believe that such a series of colossal blunders could have been committed by a man he had regarded as worldly-wise. Nevertheless he promised to use all his influence with Hassan Pasha lest the punishment be irreparable, though he very much doubted that so much recidivism would discover any pity in so cruel a man.

For the third time Miguel was brought before Hassan Pasha and the familiar court of bailiffs, soldiers, and executioners. The King ordered a rope placed around his neck and his hands tied behind his back. He questioned him closely, but all his Venetian astuteness failed to get any other answer than that he, Miguel alone, had authored and carried out that plot, in which four gentlemen who were already free had also participated while the other folk who were to have gone in the vessel did not yet know about it.

Hassan Pasha watched the inconceivable audacity and matchless serenity of Miguel, rather enjoying the spectacle. Though many slaves and fugitives had appeared before him, their faces pinched with terror, he was impressed by the tranquil visage of this captive of his against whom threats were of no avail. Miguel also was aware that his life depended on the indifferent calm of his face and the firmness and determination of his words. It may be that other renegades besides Maltrapillo, who was one of Miguel's great admirers, and even some Moors who knew him for a resolute man or as an amusing reciter of verses, may also have spoken to Hassan Pasha. In any event he could not persuade himself that this was not a man of mysterious origin, definitely superior to the other captives, and he therefore decided to spare his life again, though with horrendous threats.

Miguel returned to his prison, dragging his chains and shackles, but again without anyone venturing to touch a hair of his head.

Do you believe for a moment that Hassan Pasha's clemency toward Miguel meant that he had given up his cruelties? Know then that two months after Cervantes was pardoned one of his acquaintances, a certain Juan from Biscay, was caught trying to escape to Orán and was brought before Hassan Pasha. It was Christmas Eve of 1579 and the Christians of the great bagnio were celebrating the Feast of the Nativity as best they could when bailiffs entered the prison and ordered the captives up to the courtyard of the Alcazaba where they saw the King and his executioners bastinado the unfortunate Biscayan to death. On a mild day at the end of May the captives were again ordered to attend the execution of a Spaniard, a robust mountaineer named Lorenzo, a Hercules of a man who would not give up his life although Hassan Pasha and the executioners exhausted themselves with beating him.

As the captives quit the Alcazaba to return to the bagnio they heard cries of jubilation shouted through the streets: "The Trinity is coming! The Trinity is coming!" The redeemers Fray Juan Gil and Fray Antonio de la Bella had arrived in Algiers.

CHAPTER 24

The Knight of the Doleful Countenance—Fray Juan Gil—The Day of Freedom

THE spring of 1580, a happy time for many of the captives in Algiers, was sad and painful for Cervantes. With an iron ring on his ankle and dragging his chains, he listened day in and day out to news of the ransoms arranged by the Trinitarians. He heard exaggerated accounts of the amount of money they had brought with them and of the many pious bequests and donations that had swelled the total of what families had raked together and the King had contributed. To believe some of the captives the bagnios of Algiers were going to be deserted. It was not so, but nevertheless when any captives were ransomed it seemed to the others an augury that they all would be freed.

Miguel saw one captive after another go free, and he began to despair. Slowly fading away were the illusions of the *Romancero*, the dreams of warlike adventures, the book of chivalry he had forged when he thought it possible to escape from Algiers, as Don Quixote thought of conquering islands and winning empires with nothing more than the boldness of his heart and the strength of his arm.

His shackle on his ankle, trailing his chains in the bagnio of Hassan Pasha, Miguel did not hear of the esteem in which he was held by some good souls, and he could see only the evil passions surrounding him. Finally realizing that his dreams of chivalry were impossible, and sensing how humanity had an urge to live, well or badly, but above all to live, he recalled the mysterious death of Don Juan de Austria, about which many strange tales were heard; he thought also of the many captives, some of them illustrious gentlemen of ancient lineage, who had been as brothers to him in captivity but who, when they were free, never again remembered Miguel. . . .

All this was something to brood over at length, and Miguel was thinking about it one day when, perhaps in a bit of broken mirror, perhaps in a basin of clear water, he caught sight of his face, long, yellow and with circles under the eyes, his expression melancholy and disenchanted, and breaking into a wonderful, heroic and Homeric shout of laughter, it occurred to him to call himself the "Knight of the Doleful Countenance" in memory of the "Knight of the Burning Sword" and the other high-sounding appellations of the sons and descendants of Amadís.

This second laugh of Miguel, an outgrowth and an echo of that great peal of laughter which burst out before the windmills on his return from Seville, was another leap toward immortality. Laughter after tears or sorrow saves men from oblivion and makes their names eternal. Homer might be dead, in spite of all the great deeds of Achilles, if he had not, in the bloodiest and most savage of his strophes, included a little of that which with divine simplicity he put on the lips of Andromeda[1] upon seeing Astianax frightened by his father Hector, that *dakruóen guelásasa* (between tears and laughter), which is the secret of the great ones. The creative plains of La Mancha and the fruitful bagnio of Algiers placed on Cervantes' lips the redeeming laughter that is born of tears.

And having laughed at himself, by which he showed the greatness of his soul, Miguel tried to meet with the Reverend Father Juan Gil in order to be liberated in the most vulgar and least quixotic manner, in exchange for cash like any other Juan, Pedro, and Diego who groaned in the bagnios of Algiers. But the most serious difficulty of all was that Miguel was locked up and surrounded by guards and sentinels, especially since the Trinitarian Fathers had arrived in Algiers, for it was then that Hassan Pasha became stricter with the captives whom he regarded as particularly valuable, with a view to raising the toll by inspiring the redeemers with compassion and inducing them to pay large sums in ransoms. That was the case with Cervantes as well as with Don Jerónimo de Palafox, the Aragonese nobleman who was Hassan's most important captive.

On the other hand the Trinitarians did not busy themselves with difficult and costly ransoms while they could be arranging the easier ones. The months of June and July were spent in effecting these, and in the first days of August Fray Antonio de la Bella left Algiers with a hundred and eight ransomed captives who arrived in Valencia on the fifth after encountering a great storm.

Fray Juan Gil was thereupon left alone in Algiers to carry out the most difficult part of the mission. He was a man of long experience, great perspicacity and skill in dealing with the Moors, and so habituated to running risks and taking chances that he had often seen his head in danger, which in part contributed to ensuring its safety as he grew older.

Although he had never seen or spoken to Miguel the fame of his heroic virtues and his Christian chivalry had come to the ears of Fray Juan Gil from the first. Consulting his papers he confirmed that this captive was the one on behalf of whom an old lady and three beautiful women in mourning had come to beg at various times at the Convent in Madrid. He also recalled the innocent deception by which Doña Leonor had declared she was a widow in order to arouse greater sympathy among ransom donors. He remembered all this and linking it with the good reports about him he had heard from other captives he became extremely interested in doing all he could to liberate Miguel.

Perhaps these motives of Christian compassion were supplemented by others adduced by Doctor Antonio de Sosa, with whom Fray Juan Gil was in frequent communication. Doctor Sosa showed the good Trinitarian some of the devout poems composed by Miguel and read to him on various occasions, which the Doctor had been pleased to copy, and through them Fray Juan Gil learned that this captive, besides being a brave man, was a very accomplished poet. This could not influence him too much as a man of action but did appeal to him as being rather rare among the Algerian captives.

Fray Juan Gil had already decided to make every effort to arrange the ransom as soon as possible when Doctor Juan Blanco de Paz, pretending to be a commissary of the Holy Office, came to see him, showing him a false document accrediting him as such, to demand his assistance in testifying against certain people and in particular against Miguel de Cervantes. This unexpected development perplexed Fray Juan Gil greatly. Blanco de Paz was an unctuous man of smooth and insinuating speech; the credentials he presented appeared to be in order. The machination against Cervantes inspired by this evil man was carefully contrived solely in order to invalidate Miguel's testimony when, once he was free, he might attempt to expose the treachery of the pitiless Dominican friar.

Unfortunately for himself Blanco de Paz was too clever for his own good, having the audacity to present himself to Doctor Sosa with the same request. That wise man spurned the insinuations of the malevolent friar and told Fray Juan Gil all about it. The Trinitarians had never gotten on too well with the Dominicans, and possibly that contributed to dissipating the storm raised against Miguel and to increasing the esteem in which he was held by Fray Juan Gil without his ever having seen him.

The negotiations to ransom Cervantes, the noble Palafox, and various other important people were then initiated. Hassan Pasha was now somewhat impatient, anxious to collect the greatest possible sum in ransoms because these were the last days of his governance in Algiers; he had been ordered to leave for Constantinople whence Jafer Pasha would very soon be coming to replace him. In discussing Miguel's ransom, therefore, he greatly exaggerated what Fray Juan Gil already knew in order to increase the toll and finally demanded a thousand Spanish escudos in gold.

The Trinitarian had long known that both Moors and renegades loved to bargain and he knew that on top of this Hassan was a Venetian, a trader to his fingertips. He had in hand the sum he had received in Madrid for Miguel's ransom, which amounted to only three hundred ducats, and he added all that the Order could donate on behalf of such a deserving captive, but found he could contribute only fifty doblas. He took another fifty from the legacy of Francisco de Caramanchel, which was one of the pious bequests frequently donated to the redeeming Orders to provide dowries for maidens or to ransom captives. But even with hard bargaining he was short of a great deal of money, since he needed almost three times as much as he had in hand to make up a thousand escudos.

This ransom appeared to be as difficult to negotiate as that of Don Jerónimo de Palafox. Fray Juan Gil tried in vain to convince the Venetian that he had made a mistake and that Cervantes was just a poor gentleman, great only in spirit and rich only in courage.

It is very probable that Hassan Pasha permitted the friar to speak to the captive of the maimed hand, but not often, for he always suspected Cervantes of concocting a new plot. One or two years previously he had said that as long as he kept the crippled Spaniard well guarded he considered the city, the slaves, and the ships to be safe.[2]

Fray Juan Gil observed the Knight of the Doleful Countenance carefully, and though his heart had been hardened by daily contact with misery he felt great pity for him. Miguel did not waste time in talk about fantastic projects but rather he told the friar who were his good friends in Algiers and from which of them he could ask for help; in particular he mentioned the Valencian merchants who had always been good to him and whose liberality could be counted on. But even if every source were tapped it would still be difficult to raise a thousand Castilian escudos. Miguel was in the painful situation of a man who needs money with which to save his life and can find no way to obtain it.

Hassan Pasha then took a decision that aggravated Miguel's black despair and almost destroyed his last hope. One day he, the noble Palafox, and others from their bagnio found themselves in a galley, dragging chains attached to both feet, their hands shackled, flung on a bench before a long oar. The news was that the ships were to weigh anchor immediately after their holds were filled, for Hassan had no intention of leaving anything of value behind. No Christian would ever get out of that alive. What heart, even if made of steel, would not have broken before this terrible trial? Laughter, that good friend, was perhaps about to abandon the lips of Miguel forever.

On the morning of September 19 the movement of seamen, the shoutings, blasphemings, and floggings of the boatswains, the final loading operations and many other signs gave them to understand that the moment of departure had arrived. The galley slaves, with Miguel and Palafox among them, sat their benches, their jackets loosened, their caps pulled down, their sleeves rolled up and their feet secured to the traverse. All that was needed was the ritual cry of "Forward! Row!" when, like a holy figure with golden nimbus, Fray Juan Gil appeared before Miguel's eyes, portentous, exhilarated, and smiling, with his trailing habit and the blue and red cross on his breast. Following behind him, black-robed, grave and respectable, came the notary Pedro de Ribera with his inkwell full of ink and his well-worn papers.

Fray Juan Gil stretched out his arms to the astonished Miguel, who at that moment thought that the gates of Heaven had been opened to him by some saintly monk like those one sees on the altarpieces of Italy, having been chosen for such high office by their painters. In a few words the friar and the notary described how they had raised two hundred and twenty ducats among the traders and how Hassan Pasha, after much bargaining, had agreed to accept half of what he had demanded, contenting himself with five hundred gold escudos as Miguel's ransom. This he demanded in Spanish coin, which in those days was readily accepted and honored in the entire world from the westernmost of the Indies to the distant lands of Cathay, but it had been difficult to get it together in that currency from the Moors, Christians, and Jews of Algiers, and only at the last moment had the whole amount been collected.[3]

Fray Juan Gil kept inviolate the tragic secret which Miguel was not to know until some time later. That very day, when the friar was negotiating the ransoms of the two captives in a final meeting, Hassan Pasha agreed to release Cervantes for five hundred escudos, but he would not reduce by an *aspero*[4] the toll of one thousand escudos for which he held Don Jerónimo. With skill and fervor the friar drew on every argument he could muster to save the high-born nobleman from Aragón, who would have been the greatest ornament of such a celebrated ransom mission. Bargaining as he had seen the gypsies of the Souk in Algiers and the slums of Seville do, he flung five hundred shining gold pieces down on the carpet before the greedy eyes of the corsair, but Hassan would not play, and the redeemer had to be satisfied with ransoming Miguel and leaving the unfortunate nobleman in captivity.

What Miguel felt upon walking the earth as a free man could be depicted here only by quoting the many paragraphs in which he speaks of this delight, the greatest of any the world can offer.[5] If Lepanto had been the day of supreme glory Miguel counted the nineteenth of September of 1580 as the one of greatest happiness and deepest significance of all his life. If he had always been cheerfully witty, what sparkling nonsense must have occurred to him then! Miguel felt himself all over, stretched his arms, embraced all and sundry about him, and above all he laughed, laughed, laughed. . . . And all who heard him laughed with him, and at that moment was engendered the healthy and redeeming laughter that follows the works of Cervantes across the centuries without ever fatiguing or satiating laughing humanity.

When they saw Miguel free, many and many a captive who owed him favors, conversation, advice or attention gathered around him. They all bore witness and praised Miguel highly in the statement regarding his conduct during his captivity that he asked Fray Juan Gil to make, in order to thwart the calumnies of Juan Blanco de Paz. In their verbal declarations and in the one written out by Doctor Sosa, as in the one signed by Fray Juan Gil confirming all the other depositions, there is much more than conscientiously bearing witness to something well known; there is an admiration, a respect, and a love for Cervantes that we will have difficulty in finding again among his contemporaries. Hardly any of those people of good faith, soldiers, workingmen and priests, knew that Cervantes was or would be a writer. Nevertheless they all loved him unreservedly *as a man* and maintained that it was a great honor to acknowledge that *man* as the greatest they had known.

This is a document of tremendously moving power in which there is no room for misunderstanding. It is impossible to read it without feeling one's soul filled with the human satisfaction it gives us to see confirmed that the man we already took for a genius was also a very fine man.

Once the statement had been completed, signed and dated October 22, Cervantes had nothing more to do in Algiers. All those ransomed were going home, and on October 24 six captives sailed for Spain on the ship of Master Antón Francés, among them Miguel de Cervantes Saavedra. Fray Juan Gil paid fifteen doblas for their passage.

The voyage was not long. One morning the sun, beating on the backs of the travelers, first flushed and then reddened the green shores of the Kingdom of Valencia. The beautiful city of Denia opened her loving arms to them.

CHAPTER 25

Miguel in Valencia and Madrid—Conquest of Portugal—Lisbon

WHILE Miguel was happily walking the streets of Valencia he knew that the time had come to reconstruct a life truncated by captivity. But first he had business to do with some of those bankers, traders, and commission merchants from Algiers, with the Torreses, with Juan Fortuny and with the very grateful Onofre Exarque, discussing with them arrangements for selling the merchandise licensed to Doña Leonor and payment for what he had left owing in Algiers for the balance of his ransom. Busy with these affairs and enjoying the blessings of liberty in a city so apt for it as Valencia, where the sky, the earth and the air proclaim freedom, he spent the latter part of October there, the whole month of November and the beginning of December of 1581, whereupon he set out on his return to Madrid.

Miguel had now come to realize that youth was over for him, or at least the best part of it, and that the serious age had arrived when every moment must be devoted to creating and ensuring security for the future. As we have seen, ever since he embarked on the hapless galley *Sol* Cervantes had acquired more unhappy and painful experiences than in all the rest of his life, and his youth had turned into a premature old age. Captivity in Algiers affected many men in that situation by endowing them at the age of thirty with all the apprehension and hopelessness peculiar to seventy and constraining them to fashion for themselves a second artificial youth as though they were coming to life again. Miguel's own struggle in this situation did not last long nor was his mind greatly troubled.

Before he left Valencia, knowing that his friend and comrade in captivity, the Valencian Juan Estéfano, was proceeding to the capital, he gave him letters to be delivered at his home and asked him to see his father and point out to him that it was extremely urgent to have a report on his services and captivity drawn up as a basis for claiming remuneration for them. Like anything entrusted to the simple Rodrigo the report was brief and badly done, and nothing happened.

Miguel, particularly since his need was pressing, did not hesitate at all to ask for compensation for his services. He may have thought quixotically that the Court must already have received flattering accounts of them. He was sure, like Don Quixote, that the exploits by which knights prove the ardor of their hearts and the strength of their arms are rewarded by crowns and empires; he was sure, like Sancho, that the laborer is worthy of his hire and that the dog dances for his dinner. It would be years before he could convince himself that in Spain a Don Quixote expecting crowns is as illusory as a Sancho hoping for islands and it would be years before he would be satisfied with a barber's basin, with the saddle bags of a monk, with a madman's forgotten satchel, as all that he would garner from his exploits in the world.

This haste of his to solicit reports and to get credit for his services, rather than demeaning him as is hinted by some, shows all the more clearly the ingenuous candor of his mind. He had just emerged from a black world in which injustice and prejudice combined with cruelty and inhumanity to govern everything, and because he found himself in Valencia, where sky and earth and air smiled on him and the women seemed to him patterned on the celestial multitude of a Flemish altarpiece, he was already building up new illusions and thought that he had entered into the kingdom and sanctuary of justice and equity, where merit was rewarded and disastrous misfortunes suffered for the common weal were compensated by a good life. Miguel's soul was a fertile, ever-blooming field; no sooner had green illusions dried up and faded than others were born, fresher and gayer, red, blue or parti-colored. Perhaps his greatest merit was his capacity for maintaining the uniformly cheerful attitude that lies behind all he says and does.

Light of heart and lighter still in pocket, he reached Madrid and early in December was at his home, where time had not stood still. The poor chirurgeon Rodrigo de Cervantes was more useless and sickly every day, only occasionally able to find very precarious means for helping to maintain his family. Many were the days when no one dreamed of calling on him for bleeding and plastering and next to the window grilles giving on the street a dozen leeches were dying of boredom in their bottle.

Doña Leonor de Cortinas was old, tired of so much struggling, scheming and getting nowhere. Doña Andrea and her daughter lived away from the paternal home but were its sole consolation and support. Doña Magdalena, the girl whose high spirits had been captivating ten years ago, was losing her freshness and was in the terrible position of becoming an old maid. She was having a love affair with an employee of the Palace called Juan Pérez de Alcega and she already knew how difficult it was going to be to hold him and how much more to find another if she lost this one.

The house presented a perfect image of the wishful thinking that was already beginning to be observable in almost all the homes in the capital and still persists as a chronic and incurable malady. Shortages were covered by debts which led to greater debts, and people hoped that the creditor would die or give up, or they awaited the happy moment when he returned to his own country. What today we call "going to the English" in those days could have been called "going to the Florentines or Genoese." The malady is the same and the means of dealing with it identical. One day clothes are pawned, on another a piece of furniture. Lunch or dinner may be suppressed, invitations are eagerly accepted, and always one praises God, who allows so many people to live without knowing how or whence.

Miguel, accustomed to living through much worse tribulations, observed what was happening in his home and recognized the urgency of doing something to remedy matters. He may have had long conferences with his sister Andrea, a past master in money matters and the successful management of life, but they could only agree to carry on as best they could. When did two Spaniards ever meet to solve an economic problem, or even approach it, without concluding that continued temporary expedients were the only solution?

Meanwhile young Rodrigo had rejoined his old regiment and was with Don Lope de Figueroa in Portugal, which now belonged to the Castilians. The King had been at Badajoz for months, waiting to enter the country won for him by the Duke of Alba with his troops and Don Cristóbal de Moura[1] by the fruitful application of his diplomacy and the wonderful arts of corruption. He was going to be crowned in Lisbon as soon as the plague which decimated the city was over.

Cervantes realized that Lisbon was going to be the place where he had to seek a way of life for himself, and with this in view he asked for another report to replace the feeble one drafted on December 1 on his father's initiative. This one was drawn up on the eighteenth of the same month and in it his great friends and comrades in hardship Rodrigo de Chaves and Francisco de Aguilar testified, describing what had been Cervantes' situation and the obligations he had incurred toward the Trinitarians and the merchants who had advanced money for his ransom.

Wandering about the capital, Miguel managed to talk with some famous writers who were curious about him and delighted by the exploits of the soldier as recounted by his own eloquent lips. Among them, outstanding in his appreciation of Cervantes, was a fastidious bard from Guadalajara who was composing a new *Diana* and a second *Arcadia* that would cut Jorge de Montemayor and Sannazaro down to size. This cultured and talented gentleman was Luis Gálvez de Montalvo,[2] a great admirer of Italian poetry and translator of Tansilo. To his uneven *quintillas*,[3] some of which were too strong and others weak and swooning, Cervantes replied with the devotional poetic works and fragments of verse he had composed in Algiers and from which he later drew the speeches in his plays.

Gálvez de Montalvo encouraged him and urged him strongly to publicize himself as a poet. In those days it was common for an author to be well known without having published any work in print, inasmuch as a poem which had been recited and liked was copied in great numbers and soon became familiar to persons interested in such things. Not very long before this the poetical works of Garcilaso and Luis de León were passed from hand to hand and from manuscript to manuscript without anyone having seen them in print. Praise of Cervantes' poetry therefore traveled from the lips of Gálvez de Montalvo to those of other poets and lovers of poetry, mingled with panegyrics about his prowess as a soldier. They reached the ears of another writer who had known Cervantes in Italy, had been at Lepanto and perhaps had some contact in Naples with the soldier who was known as a *protégé* of the Duke of Sessa and Don Juan. As Homer was the poet of Achilles and Ulysses, Juan Rufo Gutiérrez[4] was the poet of Don Juan, but his poem *La*

Austriada is to be esteemed more for good intentions than admired for the excellence of its execution.

It was known as such by Miguel, who was no stranger to the difficulties of meter and rhyme inasmuch as he frequently struggled with them and rarely conquered them, any more than did other poets of his day. Neither Garcilaso nor Fray Luis nor Herrera had mastered the endecasyllable[5] completely. They controlled it with bit and bridle and at times made it walk sedately at the Castilian gait, but if they wanted it to rear or curvet or take off at a full gallop the Italian charger rebelled and responded poorly to curb and spur. Those poets did not understand that to produce polished endecasyllables it was necessary to Italianize the language. Miguel understood this and Italianized as much as he could, but not to such an extent that he abandoned the system of bridle and spur, believing that the endecasyllable was an ordinary beast of burden and not really a winged horse like the Pegasus of the poets. Nearly all Spanish poets have failed to let him spread his wings because the language born and brought up close to the earth of Castile did not permit. Instead they traveled with the gait of the horse loaded with jangling armor on which the paladins of the *Romancero* rode.

Cervantes and Don Juan's poet came to know each other very quickly and they esteemed each other all their lives. Juan Rufo told him that to present oneself at Court as an old friend of Don Juan de Austria was not propitious. In no time all the courtiers, following the example of the King, were pleased to forget the son of the "thunderbolt of war," while to have been present at the naval battle was scarcely a recommendation. Juan Rufo himself, after devoting a great deal of time and effort to singing the praises of Don Juan, found that it would not be advisable to dedicate the poem to the King, his brother, and he had to be satisfied with naming his sister, the Empress of the Romans.

In the capital Miguel also discovered how Mateo Vázquez now enjoyed the King's favor, having been granted prebendaries and canonries that required nothing of him save that he dress himself in the robes appropriate to them. Warned by experience, Miguel did not count much on Mateo, who had not even replied to his famous epistle, but felt it would be advisable to approach him eventually, see how matters stood, and seek to throw down by some means or other the wall that constantly looms before anyone who tries to get ahead in Spain. That wall is called procrastination, the great Spanish characteristic.

As his destiny ordained, Cervantes departed for Portugal early in 1581 in the company of his friend Rodrigo de Chaves, who was returning to his native city of Badajoz, but Philip II and the Court had already left that city for Yelves, which today we call Elvas, and in December he had convened the Cortes at Thomar since the plague continued to ravage Lisbon. When Miguel arrived at the temporary seat of the Court in Thomar he took good care to disavow the sponsorship of Don Juan de Austria, and he soon managed to see Mateo Vázquez, who continued to enjoy the confidence of the King, but the cold atmosphere very soon made clear what he had failed to understand in the burning heat of Algiers. He did, however, see his old comrade and friend in captivity, Don Antonio de Toledo, brother of the Duke of Alba and a very important figure at Court. The Duke himself was of course there, a haughty, dry and aged figure, his eyes sunken, his brows drooping, pale of face and white of beard, altogether an ancient and terrible presence.

On July 29 of 1581 Philip II made a solemn entry into Lisbon and with him came the Spanish courtiers who had followed him in the campaign and those who had joined him at Thomar, as well as the Portuguese aristocrats indoctrinated by Don Cristóbel de Moura.

Miguel's spirits began to revive when he entered Portugal, following the course of Father Tagus. There he saw the banks of the beautiful river covered by flowering orchards and beheld the satisfaction of the Portuguese at the happy ending of the conflicts and bloody mishaps of war, although the war itself was less terrible for them than the outrages of all kinds committed before and after the pacification proclamations by the troops of the Duke of Alba and Sancho Dávila, who found themselves short of rope not only for hanging rebellious Portuguese but also for punishing their own undisciplined captains and wantonly cruel soldiers. Taking the conquered kingdom as their own they had continued to sack and plunder incessantly.

When Miguel arrived all this was over. The time for apologies and compensation had come. Philip himself presented a pleasant and cheerful visage to his new courtiers, the Portuguese grandees. The great city throbbed with joy, not so much over the arrival of the new master as over the termination of the war and of the pestilence, plagues with which the people had been required to contend simultaneously. The Court seemed to have changed completely and a mood of unaccustomed frivolity prevailed. It was also springtime and from the immense garden which forms the banks of the Tagus up to Lisbon pleasing scents perfumed the air while a retinue of beautiful women and aristocratic poets followed and surrounded the King. Love worked its ways, inspired by this delightful gaiety. Cervantes himself has said it: "'Milan for gallantry, Lusitania for love."

On the eighteenth or twentieth day of May he was sent on a secret official mission as a courier taking some papers and tax collections to Orán and bringing back letters from the Governor of Mostagán. He was provided with a hundred ducats for his expenses and in the last days of July he was back with the letters. Perhaps in that short time he came upon a friend of his who today is one of ours, as hapless as he is amusing: Corporal Campuzano, on whose sayings he based the exemplary novel of the *Dialogue of the Dogs*.

CHAPTER 26

The Poem of the Tagus—La Galatea

EVEN for someone who, like Cervantes, had entered Genoa from the sea and was familiar with the Neapolitan waterfront, Lisbon is a noble and beautiful city, her arms opened wide and her eyes fixed on the Occident, a city gilded by the sun and by the wealth brought to her from the Indies in galleons loaded to capacity. Rúa do Ouro [Street of Gold] and Rúa da Prata [Street of Silver] were the names of the two principal thoroughfares.

But if Miguel found in Lisbon the beauty and grandeur of the cities he had loved in Italy that also face the West, and if he recognized in it the slightly artificial and ephemeral gaiety appropriate to a royal visit, what traced the deepest impression on his mind was not so much the city itself as its surroundings and what he had seen before reaching it.

He was well aware that the demonstration of joy was a thing of the moment and that normally the Portuguese character is grave and melancholy; he did not fail to notice the difference between Italian flirtations and Portuguese love affairs. In Italy love was an occasion for jests, chaste or otherwise. Platonic seriousness was a thing of the past, while Petrarch and his idealism had given way, first to Ariosto, the high-living enjoyer of good things, later to Tasso the decadent. In Portugal, on the other hand, love was the delicate ardor of the early troubadours who found peace and took delight in pastoral poetry. The greatest pastoral poet of all, Jorge de Montemayor, was a Portuguese, and his book is a book born of the gardens of Lisbon and the banks of the Tagus.

This great river, maker of music and history, which recounts to the centuries a poorly attended and worse interpreted history, was the father of the Spanish pastoral novel. Garcilaso had imitated its song, had clothed the white bodies of his nymphs in its shadows, the crowns of the poplars were mirrored in its waters. Miguel tried to harmonize with his own inspiration the rhymes that the singing river presented to him.

> He who has seen, as I have, the broad banks of the renowned Betis and those that deck and adorn the famous Ebro and the well-known Pisuerga, and who in distant lands have passed by those of the sacred Tiber, the delightful Po, famous for the fall of the daring boy, not neglecting to wander in the coolness of the peaceful Sebeto,[1] being moved to marvel at the sight of other waters would indeed be a great occasion. . . . Above most of these river-banks a clear and luminous sky appears, the wide sweep and bright splendor of which seem to invite the most alien heart to rejoice and find pleasure: and if it is true, as some say, that the stars and sun are nourished by the waters here below, I firmly believe that those of this river are responsible in great part for creating the beauty of the sky that lies above it, or I shall think that God, for the very reason that they say He lives in the skies, dwells mostly here in this part of them. The land which embraces it, clad in a thousand green ornaments, seems to be celebrating and is happy to have in it such a rare and agreeable gift, and the golden river, as if in exchange, gently intertwining itself in her embrace, designedly forms a thousand entries and outlets which fill the soul of whoever looks on them with pleasure; from which it follows that though the eyes may return many times to look at it they never fail to find things which give them renewed pleasure and cause for admiration. . . .

And it cannot be doubted that the idea of *La Galatea* was born in such a delightful place as a first fruit of Miguel's talent, in which a thousand memories of Italy are preserved, as is manifest in the inspiration and the language. There are reminiscences of the valleys of Sardinia, the grottos of Naples, and the gardens of Corfu, but much more is derived from the great creator called the Tagus.

In possession of some ducats and several friendships, some renewed and some new, Miguel stayed on at the Court, at that Court which, by the miraculous virtue and unimaginable power of the Tagus and its green banks, had been transformed from lugubrious and gloomy to gay and laughing, like an Italian Court. The peace and happiness of the environment and of the land had cheered even the melancholy spirit of the monarch. Always a man of refined taste, Philip II understood that his black clothing, so proper to the Escorial, the Palace of Madrid, the live-oak austerity of the Pardo and the solemn blue of the Guadarrama did not comport well with the rose trees, laurels, and myrtles of the banks of the Tagus. He doffed his black clothes and the austere ruff he had worn for so many years, and dressed himself splendidly in rich stuffs in the gay colors of the Portuguese style. On that excursion, the happiest time of his life, he enjoyed himself, laughed, joked as he had never done as a youth. When Philip II himself dressed in bright colors Cervantes could stay on at the Spanish Court with a happy heart.

In Lisbon was where the melancholy King showed himself at his most human in other ways; he also may have managed to taste the sweetness of love at the same time that Cervantes was sipping it. It must not be forgotten that the King had at least as amorous a disposition as his vassal. Neither does it need much audacity to suppose that before leaving Lisbon Miguel sang of his loves in the little-known ballad he recalled[2] when old, the *Filena* of which he said:

> Also the equal of *Filis*, my *Filena*
> echoed through the forests which heard
> more than one or another cheerful chorus:
> and in varied sweet rhymes the gentle breezes
> bore away my hopes which were strewn
> in the forests and on the sand. . . .

Those forests and those sands were the poplar groves and golden banks of the Tagus.

Possibly through his friend Don Antonio de Toledo, or through Mateo Vázquez or through other courtiers, Cervantes learned of an amorous intrigue between a lady of the Court and a gentleman who wooed her in vain, in part because of a disdain for him that ill concealed her true affections, in part for family considerations, or due to the opposition of the monarch himself, as is made clear in the course of the novel. From this he drew the inspiration for the *Galatea*, in which we must not see Doña Catalina, later his wife, as Galatea, nor Miguel as her lover Elicio, even though other shepherds represent his friends and companions Gálvez de Montalvo, Francisco de Figueroa, Pedro Láynez, Ray de Artieda and others. The artificial bucolic style surely conceals a real story about highly placed personages under guise of a pastoral fable, and if there is any doubt about this Miguel says so himself in the Prologue. The same thing happened in the *Arcadia* of Lope, who recounted in it the loves of his master the Duke of Alba.

Furthermore, if the Prologue is read carefully there cannot be the slightest doubt that most of it was composed at a period long before Miguel had any connections with Doña Catalina. Parts of the *Galatea*, more especially the poetical compositions, antedate the rest of the work and, it is almost certain, were written long before Miguel returned to Spain. The principal components of the book he already had in his memory or had written down, but arranging and bringing them together was not to be realized until Miguel found himself once more in a bucolic and pastoral environment like that of Lisbon and in a courtly society where conflicts resembling the one in *Galatea* frequently occurred.

He must have kept it to himself for a long time, as he himself declares, and he decided to publish it "because my mind conceived it as for something else besides my own pleasure. . . ." As he explained it, his effort to enrich the language was

> for the loftier and more important purpose of showing the way so that the narrow minds which seek to confine the abundance of the Castilian language within the brevity of the ancient tongue can understand by imitating it that there is open country, spacious and easy of access, over which they can run freely with pleasure and facility, with gravity and eloquence, discovering the diversity of acute, subtle, serious and lofty concepts of which Heaven's favoring influence on the fertility of Spanish talent in many different senses has bestowed and each hour bestows the benefit in this our fortunate generation: of which I can be a sure witness. . . .

Miguel thus gives us to understand that he intended something with a very different and much higher aim than merely entertaining.

He was now regarding it as his mission to renovate the language, reinforce it and rejuvenate it with what he had learned in the school of Italy, from the halls of the Vatican to the *trattorias* of Genoa and the suburbs of Naples, with what the military and naval life had taught him and what captivity and its trials left encrusted on his soul. By now he regarded his talent as being fluent and significant, unique, free, unafraid, but he was not to begin with the final result, rather with what was easiest, with what was likeliest to lead to what he hoped to achieve. Finding himself at a Court where the pastoral style was in vogue and permitting himself a certain Arcadian predilection we have already noted in him and which prevailed in his spirit at times, whether in youth or old age, he did not hesitate to gather together everything he had written, felt and thought, and with it to form that first youthful work, seeking by it to win favor at the Court and earn the approval of other writers and poets.

If the prologue and dedication are carefully examined one can detect a certain slight touch of disdain that Cervantes reveals in his attitude toward this work of his. Those are his *juvenilia*, his rehearsals, little more than a rhetorical school exercise "to get his hand in," even though he knows that he is destined for better things and will soon be putting them out. They are also things composed with one eye on the Court: let us carefully observe here that, upon letting himself go with his natural bucolic inclination in the *Quixote* and other works, he does so to please himself at the time but also to amuse the powerful gentleman to whom the work is dedicated and from whom he expects protection, and we note that he spends the last years of his life offering the Second Part of the *Galatea* to the Count of Lemos as a work proper for a courtier and a man of his taste, that Second Part he never did manage to write.

Those who have written about Cervantes have paid very little attention to this period of his life when he must have followed the Court. It is absolutely certain that at this time he was in contact with the most highly placed people, that he learned their way of speech and that at close quarters he watched them walk, speak, move and act as they always walk, speak, move and act when they appear in his works. That highly ceremonious courtliness of Don Quixote when visiting dukes and his whole behavior when with high-ranking people is not something that can be invented or imitated, nor could Cervantes have learned it in the barracks, nor in the Algerian dungeon nor in the galleys nor in the hospital nor during his short stay in the Vatican. There is no doubt that he associated and conversed with those elegant and spirited gentlemen whose portraits El Greco painted. He knew their tastes, weighed their intelligence, looked into their hearts, and it did not take him long to be convinced of what he later was to say rather bitterly—that "he was not made for the Court."

How could he maintain this with the firmness and conviction he does if he had not been at Court and involved in its activities? And if he had been in any Court it was that of Lisbon, access to which was readier than to the awe-inspiring Alcázar of Madrid or the terrifying Escorial.

In 1583 Cervantes returned to Madrid, where his heart was saddened by the everlasting afflictions of his family. They continued to have too much business with the Florentine and Genoese moneylenders, and in September Miguel himself pawned some bolts of cloth with Napoleón Lomelino, who had a moneylending establishment in Madrid. It is obvious that Doña Andrea, though she did not live with her parents and her sister, continued to be a mainstay of the family. They were always turning to her for help and on this occasion, not having any money at hand, she gave Miguel the rich stuffs that Locadelo had donated for upholstering her drawing room, and he pawned them. It can also be conjectured that neither Miguel's friends at Court nor the reputation he was gaining with his poetry provided him with any hard cash.

Nevertheless at this time Miguel was in touch with many writers and poets. Through Juan Rufo he met another Cordovan, Don Luis de Góngora,[3] a noble youth of good family who had just come from studying in Salamanca and of whose poems much was expected. At the same time he may also have encountered a lively young soldier who was returning from Terceira[4] spewing out endless boastings, all in verses of unprecedented fluency. His name was Lope Félix de Vega Carpio[5] and he spent most of his time in amorous intrigues and in concocting plans for poems, comedies and all categories of poetical works. He was an orphan and nephew of Inquisitor Carpio, about whom Miguel will hear much talk in Madrid.

A greater friend of Miguel's than these was a Bachelor of Arts born in Linares who was called Pedro de Padilla,[6] a man with a rare and happy facility in amplifying and improving on the verses of ballads. His was the famous amplification of the ballad of Don Manuel:

> Who will be the gentleman,
> the most esteemed of all I have,
> who will bring me the head
> of that celebrated Moor. . . .

copies of which were found in all the bookstalls at all the fairs in Spain. Padilla was at that time getting together collections of his own poems of several kinds. One, to be included in the *Romancero*, was praised by Cervantes in a sonnet at the beginning of the edition; others were used to make up a book of pastoral *Eclogues*, and finally others to pad out new editions of his already well-known *Thesaurus of Various Poems*.

Accompanying his friend Padilla in these editorial adventures, Miguel established relations with the bookseller Blas de Robles, who recognized him as a fellow countryman, remembering his family and the days when they lived in Alcalá de Henares. Padilla, Láynez, López Maldonado and other friends encouraged Miguel to publish the *Galatea*, parts of which they had read. Perhaps Blas de Robles suggested that if Miguel could get a license he might buy it for a decent sum. These were all hopes long overdue.

This same year, upon Miguel's return from Lisbon, his heart bursting with thoughts of love and his lips with sweet conceits, he met Ana Franca and knew with her the happiest love of his life. The love affair was of brief duration, but she bore his only daughter, later known as Doña Isabel de Saavedra, while Miguel went on to marry Doña Catalina de Palacios.[7]

CHAPTER 27

First Plays—Miguel a Forerunner of Lope—Poet Friends

In Madrid there was no lack of writers who had been soldiers and of writers who had been captives, but none of them could tell of so many spirited incidents of the soldier's life and of captivity as Cervantes could. Taking his personal characteristics into account it would be logical to suppose that whenever the occasion arose Miguel recounted with great wit and animation what he afterward put in writing, not so much to give importance to his own merits, although with some justice he always liked to boast of his military qualities, but in order to persuade those who heard him and as many other people as possible of how mistaken they were with respect to military matters and of the criminal indifference with which they regarded everything that had to do with Algiers and the Algerian pirates.

It is indubitable that in recounting these events and giving tongue to these opinions Miguel was eloquent, effective, occasionally moving, sometimes visionary, and as he knew how to vary his tales and dress them up each time with new witty sayings and salty and piquant turns of thought and word he very soon won over his audience, whether it was made up of ignorant folk or of lettered and worldly people.

Thinking over what he had been through and observing the emotions aroused by his recitals, he could not fail to realize that from those experiences (as perhaps it had already occurred to him in Algiers) he might put together and dress up many a pretty tale. His friends encouraged him to do so and he himself saw the eagerness with which the public, in general indifferent to books of fiction or of poetry, thronged to the recently opened playhouses of Madrid. It was not enough for one to be opened; very soon there had to be two, *La Cruz* and *La Pacheca.*

More and more people delighted in seeing events enacted on the stage. This was a change resulting from and explained by the national character. While a nation is giving its life and soul to action, as had been happening in Spain under the Catholic Kings and Charles V, and while Don Juan, its last man of successful and glorious activity, is still alive, there is no need to have represented on the boards what is taking place daily in the great theater of reality. When the continuity of real and positive action on the seas, on battlefields, in ports and markets and in diplomatic and political cabinets begins to languish there is a marked increase in the gratification and delight with which the public takes to looking at dramatic renditions of fictional events, at first famous and grandiose, later refined and aristocratic, finally vulgar imitations of contemporary life. That is what happened after Lepanto.

Actually Miguel had the honor of being present and taking part in the last act of the great political and military drama and of getting to the heart of the causes that put an end to the play, dispersed the company, and killed the leading actor.

We cannot suppose that what we can now see *a posteriori* was appreciated by Cervantes and later by Lope de Vega; rather they were obeying those blind impulses that guide peoples and great writers, with writers taking the lead at times and peoples following, while at other times the reverse may be the case, thus creating the revolutions and evolutions of thought and feeling engendered by events which are at the same time pregnant with other developments.

The mother lode from which Spanish dramatic ore was to be mined was already not unknown to Miguel. Lope was not yet off the ground with his overlordship of the theatrical field, but it cannot be denied or doubted that if Lope was the Messenger, Cervantes was the Precursor. In all of Lope's theater there is not one kind of dramatic work which did not exist in embryo and already sketched out in that of Cervantes. If Lope in his innumerable adaptations was able to draw on the Spanish epic tradition contained in the ancient sagas converted to prose in the *Crónica General,*[1] and on the whole historic theater as well, Cervantes had done so before him. It is a great pity that only two of the Cervantes plays performed at the same time or shortly after the appearance of the *Galatea* have been preserved, but these two works enable us to imagine what the others must have been like.

The *Numantia*[2] of Cervantes is the best and might almost be termed the only Spanish patriotic tragedy. Taking it from an old ballad, Miguel exalted and enlarged upon its subject in such a manner that nothing as vigorous and grandiose can be found in the very rich theater of Spain. Everything in it is spacious, everything conceived with breadth of vision: the ideas, the manners, the tragic atmosphere in which the characters move, the introduction of allegorical figures like Spain and the River Douro. . . . This beloved imaginary figure that was called Spain, no one before Cervantes had dared to make walk and talk. A work without a protagonist, *Numantia* conveys a sense of a whole people inspired, fighting, and dying. Cervantes was the first Spanish dramatist who knew how to handle crowds in the theater.

Going beyond Spanish epic tradition in his search for themes, the drama of his triumph and the tale of his captivity were there in his heart and in his head, the blood of his wounds still fresh, and from them he drew two works, first *The Naval Battle*, which we do not know but which by its title alone gives us to understand Miguel's theatrical audacity, unsurpassed by even the greatly daring Lope. In it he tried to present the great and glorious day of Lepanto; how he did it we cannot say. That the play was appreciated is indubitable.

On the other hand we can enjoy the best drama of the four he wrote on his captivity and the first one to be acted, *Life in Algiers*, the largely autobiographical character of which cannot be doubted. There are later works more carefully composed, but none more interesting than this vivid picture of the life of the Christian captives, and it won the highest praise in various popular books of the period.

Miguel went on to compose other plays, but this first dramatic outbreak of his is of inestimable value to literary history for it proves the sure instinct, the superb confidence with which, having recently arrived in Spain after so many years of turbulent life, he divined the public taste and was able to satisfy it. It would be a gross error to suppose that he reasoned all this out, but it would be worse to deny that when he did, whether consciously or not, he was drawn into it by the subtle force of popular feeling and tastes foreseen by him even before Lope himself.

When or how these plays were produced we do not know for sure, but it seems almost certain that many of them were staged between 1583 and 1584, at times by Pedro de Morales, at others by Jerónimo Velázquez or one of his companies, and that they were successful, as was *The Perplexed Lady*, which "appeared admirable in the theaters," according to a line in the *Parnassus*. This and *The High-Spirited Arsinda* must have been acted on many different occasions and were cited with considerable pride by their author and praised by others. "In the theaters of Madrid," Cervantes says,[3] "I ventured to reduce plays to three acts from the five which they had before; I showed, or rather I was the first to present on the stage, the imaginings and secret thoughts of the soul, bringing moral figures into the theater to the universally pleased applause of listeners. At this time I composed up to twenty or thirty plays which were all performed without attracting offerings of cucumbers or other missiles; they ran their course free of whistlings, shouts and tumult."

Having definitely abandoned the Court, where there was no place for him, and perhaps disappointed for always in Mateo Vázquez and the other courtiers, of whom he never spoke again until very much later, Miguel was already well known to nearly all the literary men of his age.

Those he was most intimate with were López Maldonado from Toledo, Pedro Láynez,[4] a native of León or whose family came from León but who was brought up in Madrid, the already mentioned Pedro de Padilla, and a most amusing man from Ronda called Vicente Espinel,[5] who was four years younger than Cervantes. He was a most famous musician, and just as López Maldonado, singing the songs he composed himself, would enchant by the sweetness and harmony of his voice, the great Espinel was unrivaled at playing the guitar, to which he added the fifth string so very necessary for melodic transition from high-pitched to deep bass strings.

Espinel, born in the highlands of Andalusia and brought up in Ronda, the semi-Arab city where the most melancholy and suggestive ballad of all Andalusian music was created, came to Madrid to solicit an ecclesiastical benefice, equipped more with guitar, gay ballads, and dissolute jokes than with theological lore. In him was reflected the Spain of that time and of all times, in which a man who plays the guitar well and sings songs from Ronda with wit and charm is made a canon while the greatest poet in the country is ignored. Espinel's wit and originality must have greatly pleased Cervantes, who was to retain all his life a happy memory of that extravagant mocking person in whose company he spent delightful hours. But if he owes him anything, Espinel owes Cervantes much more, and it cannot be denied that later he tried to emulate his friend by creating a Sancho Panza in *Squire Marcus of Obregón*, who stands on tiptoe trying vainly to reach up to Don Quixote.

Thus did Cervantes, at thirty-seven years of age, have his moment of popularity. He was counted among the established poets of Spain, his poems were sought after to put in new books, he was applauded at the theater. The actor and playwright Pedro de Morales was his great friend, and remained so all his life. Let us pay tribute to the memory of this worthy actor, of whom we know almost nothing, but it was he who acted in Miguel's plays, who had faith in a vocation and theatrical talent so bravely shown, who lent assistance never to be forgotten by *his* author, ever needy and in want. Speaking of Pedro de Morales the aged Cervantes was so moved in the *Parnassus* that two tears of gratitude rolled down from eyes which had seemed forever dry:

> He who is the delight of the Muses,
> who bears off the trophy for discretion
> with grace and wit and judgment.
> He is Pedro de Morales, a very model
> of courtly taste and he is the *asylum*
> *on which my fortunes depend. . . .*

And in that work, at the same time that the memory of Morales appears, so also does that of Espinel, friend of both of them, who is recalled in these lines:

> This one, though he has something of Zoilus,[6]
> is the great Espinel, who on the guitar
> comes first, in a rare, uncommon style.

The prose and poetry of *Galatea* having been read to nearly all these authors and praised by them, and the royal patent for its publication having been obtained on February 22 of 1584, some months went by before Miguel was able to take advantage of the terms offered by his fellow countryman Blas de Robles, who bought the book from him on the fourteenth of June of that year for one thousand three hundred and thirty-six reals. Those who regard the sale as a bad piece of business know nothing of publishers. It was not a sum to be despised in those days, as anyone can learn who examines similar contracts of the period, and even today it is well known that some budding novelists, in order to get their first work published, have had to make a present of it, or even pay to have it printed.

With the publication of the *Galatea* Miguel had now realized the first dreams of his life, and since he was a man who could never completely forget reality he decided that he had better marry and settle down, the knight-errantries of the soldier-adventurer being done with, on the assumption that it would not be difficult for a writer to find employment with which to eke out the flimsy and uncertain earnings of literature. He never even considered marriage with a lady of the Court.

Family discussions turned up the name of some relatives, well-to-do hidalgos of Esquivias in the Sagra of Toledo. The Cervanteses were close relatives of the Salazars, and in Seville and other parts the two surnames are often found linked together. Cervantes de Salazar and Francisco of the same name had been eloquent philosophers and delicate poets, as was also Juan, presumably a cousin of Miguel with whom he was acquainted in Seville.

There were two hidalgos in Esquivias, one Don Francisco de Salazar and the other his brother Hernando de Salazar Vozmediano. The latter had a daughter named Catalina. There was also talk of an uncle or cousin whose mother had been a Salazar; he was known as Alonso Quijada.

CHAPTER 28

Esquivias—Salazars and Palacios—Miguel Finds a Bride—His Father Dies—Lope de Vega

THE banks of the Tagus, as soon as it leaves Aranjuez in the direction of Toledo, lose the adornment and protection of trees to cool and shade the waters of the river. Those waters, forever steaming in summer and freezing in winter, flow between dismal fields where nothing pleases the eye or invites one to pause. The soil close to the river and for a broad strip back from it is deep and very friable. Almost the whole year round the creaking of waterwheels sounds on the banks as they spill foaming water from their top buckets and distribute it among the garden plots where the irrigator, hoe in hand, lets the earth drink and then diverts the flow. Here the best melons and watermelons in the world are grown.

Along the right bank the famous village of Añover climbs to the top of a low hill. Mounting the little rise one finds that the summit, or what appeared from below to be the summit, is rather a prairie, better described as a series of gentle undulations stained yellow here and there by clumps of broom among bare stretches of esparto grass and streaks of furze.

The plain is dominated by a tower which can be seen from many leagues away; it is the bell tower of Illescas, a miniature Giralda as graceful and elegant as the impudent one in Seville. But there is one absolute difference. The Giralda of Illescas does not laugh. It seems rather as if, amid the desolate sweep of the fields, it weeps for its missing palm trees and faraway orange groves. That tower is as miserable as a forcibly converted Moslem. Before Illescas we come upon a hillock crowned by a hermitage where the virgin Santa Bárbara is venerated, no one quite knows why. Skirting the slope are several large sprawling dwellings wrapped around and about in a multitude of petticoats of walls and under-petticoats of thatch, just as the peasant girls of those parts swathe their slender bodies in enveloping and billowing cloaks of colored baize. Almost every house has a large open gate under a tile-roofed penthouse as an entry for vehicles and a main portal with a more or less elaborate stone entablature and a coat of arms raised proudly between the arch of the doorway and the balcony corbel. On their first floors between the balconies are great spiked grilles, as on a monastery, which give rise to a malicious suspicion of possible scalings of walls.

In Esquivias there are many people of noble descent. The place is famous for its illustrious lineages and even more for its very illustrious wines.[1] In spring and summer the vineyards, abounding with foliage, tendrils and bunches of grapes, temper the aridity of the countryside and cover it with luxuriant verdure, even though the vine stocks are not lighthearted and unrestrained like those of Sicily, Naples and Greece, where the foliage wraps around the bodies of the grape-pickers and caresses their suntanned heads. The vine stocks of Esquivias are meager, stunted, barely reaching the ankles of the vintagers, and to pick the grape one has to lean over and bend the stalk as if about to cut it with a reaping hook.

The family of Doña Catalina de Salazar Palacios y Vozmediano was one of those whose serious and melancholy men would plant olive trees between the vines, not for any useful purpose but rather to frustrate the fresh young greenery of the vineyards. The Salazars were people of the old nobility who lived in Toledo. They may have come from Andalusian stock and they certainly had relatives in Andalusia. Both the Salazars of the older generation were dead: Hernando, the father of Doña Catalina, who died years ago, and Don Francisco, her uncle, who brought her up. He treated her very well and taught her to write and to read devout books, among which one on chivalry may have slipped in on the sly.

The Palacios were from Toledo but had been citizens of Esquivias for a very long time; they were serious people, orderly and devout, the men all priests and monks, the women very good housewives, silent, economical, early risers. None of them knew much of love. It is no country for love, much less for love affairs; no murmurings are apt to be heard at night save those of the partridge in rut billing his mate in the fields of vetch and carob beans. Catalina de Palacios, the widow of Hernando de Salazar, was one of those cold, stiff, intolerant, asexual women with straight and shining hair parted in the middle and pulled back, a jet pin in her knotted chignon, her sleeveless jacket fitting close. Her brother, the priest Juan de Palacios, was a pious man bent on making a profit in the exalted business of Heaven without neglecting that of earth. He was assistant priest of the Church of Santa María de la Asunción, parish of Esquivias, the patron saint of the village being Santa Bárbara in the hermitage.

Esquivias was a town belonging to the Chapter of Toledo, to which two irritating taxes had to be paid, that of the *onzavo*, or eleventh part of every bushel of wheat or other cereal, and the *alajor*, or ground rent of three and a half *mais* for every *aranzada* of vineyard.[2] However, it was possible for the clergy and people having influence with the Chapter to postpone their payments or even withhold them altogether without fear. The priest Juan de Palacios had a pretty way of arranging to avoid such charges, going frequently to Toledo and never forgetting to take with him a pot of grape preserve, an earthenware jar of pickled olives or a flask of old wine. The canons considered him a man of parts, and they also knew that he owned and collected rent from a house in Toledo next to Santa Ursula.

Juan brought up his nephew Francisco de Palacios, later to be Cervantes' brother-in-law, and imbued him with his own attitudes, turning him into another administrative clergyman like a hundred others in Toledo then and now. These good priests, faithful to their ecclesiastical duties, profess a devotion which fits in very well with arithmetic. God—they think—is the Creator of all the property on earth. We, Ministers of the Almighty, are here to administer that property circumspectly and conscientiously. And they do so most marvelously, nor do they lose anything by it themselves. One does not speak to these men of theology or of anything else purely speculative. Practical morality is their only science, the precepts of which appear to them as precise, indisputable, and invariable as the multiplication table, and thus do they live happily.

Who, then, is this Doña Catalina de Salazar Palacios y Vozmediano whom Cervantes aspires to take to wife? We can be sure that she is not a cold, calculating, worldly woman; neither is she devout in the fashion of those days. Doña Catalina de Palacios is a damsel of nineteen, buried in a dismal and joyless place. Then as now in all the villages of Castile there are thousands, millions of girls like her who conceal ardent hearts in breasts constrained by their tight-fitting sleeveless bodices, tormented by a hope for something which in most cases never does come. The power of women in Spain has not manifested itself other than in queens and nuns, and what queens and what nuns they were! But let us give a thought to the innumerable young and fertile feminine spirits that have withered away uselessly and lovelessly in those arid villages of Castile, of León and of Andalusia, and we must recognize a great error in our traditional upbringing that as yet shows no signs of being corrected. Doña Catalina was one of those poor girls who at nineteen looked ahead to the panorama of a dull and insipid life.

When Miguel went to Esquivias for the first time he was completely terrified. It was not enough to have been in the naval battle or to have looked so often on the face of death to prevent him from trembling before the forbidding aspect of one of those large Toledan houses where the ancient noble families reside, terrible in their arrogance. The large house in which Doña Catalina lived had a series of bedrooms and sitting rooms which were freezing in winter and intolerably hot in summer. There was a drawing room with some Russian leather chairs, a side table, and some very worn French tapestries on the walls, upon which also hung an image of Our Lady with a Child Jesus in alabaster, set in a carved walnut case, another image of Our Lady of Loreto in silver fastened on a board, and a picture of Saint Francis in oils, doubtless one of those gray and yellow Saint Francises which today are unhesitatingly attributed to El Greco and which his son Jorge Manuel, Luis Tristán, and other pupils painted by the hundreds.

The floors were covered with mats of plaited strands of bast woven during the rainy season by the day laborers and women servants of the house. In the drawing room and in all the rooms of the house coffers without number stood against the walls, nearly all filled with bits and pieces of old clothes, worm-eaten parchments and odds and ends of iron.

To comfort frozen bodies in those halls, cold as an Alpine plateau, a small brass brazier was lighted on days when visitors were expected or family ceremonies were observed. In the immense bleak bedrooms, each ventilated by a single window giving on the street or courtyard, one shivered mightily under blankets of Sonseca wool which had once seen service as cloaks or as blankets for the mules, but the bed was a lordly fourposter, a bed made to die in with dignity, as in historical pictures.

Beyond the living quarters were the spacious courtyards where the horse barns, sheds, granaries, and other buildings were situated. Among them forty-five hens were pecking away, and in the corner a splendid timekeeper of a rooster crowed. As in all decent houses there was an oven for baking bread, a storeroom for flour and bran, a board for kneading dough and a container of yeast; there was also a small winepress with its pressing-beam and its wine kegs and earthenware jars of all shapes and sizes. It was here that the famous wines of Esquivias were produced: wines serious, heavy, and treacherous, that deprive the brain of reason, or wines sweet and pleasant to the taste but which make stomachs burn—the wine of the imaginative gentleman and mystic who thinks to ascend to Heaven in a delirium of wind and heartburn with his stomach ablaze and his liver shriveled.

There is an unfounded tradition which holds that an uncle of Doña Catalina called Alonso Quijada de Salazar was opposed to her having any love affair with Miguel, who portrayed Don Quixote as a grotesque figure in order to make fun of him. Such an assertion is unbelievable. In the case of the Palacios their mean spirit was enough to put them into opposition, if opposition there was. But if Don Alonso Quijada, a member of the Salazar family, was given to reading books of chivalry and was therefore somewhat intrigued by them, it may have been he who served Miguel as the original model and possible basis for his creation. It is fatuous to suppose that Miguel did not love Don Quixote and it is not talking nonsense to imagine that he wanted to record a pleasant memory rather than make a malicious attempt at personal satire.

Miguel's triumph in Esquivias was not over Alonso Quijada but over the avaricious Palacios, narrow souls who would have preferred to marry Doña Catalina to another hidalgo from Esquivias itself. This Miguel who at thirty-seven years of age did not have a penny to his name or any way of earning a living save through the black profession of poetry, this Miguel who had not been able to gain anything from his success as a soldier or to emerge splendidly rich from the Court where he had friends, this loquacious poet who was in daily contact with actors and people who led wicked lives, and whose family, in addition, was always pawning possessions and living God knows how, was not a fit or appropriate suitor for such a ladylike and respectable young woman as Doña Catalina.

But in talking this way the Palacios did not take Doña Catalina herself into consideration. Perhaps they did not know that the quiet and discreet young lady had secretly read the *Amadís*; they certainly could not appreciate the irresistible attraction of Miguel's talk, the enchantment of his stories of prowess and misfortune, of the perils and hazards in which he had found himself; nor also the eloquence of those laughing eyes, the beauty of that dreaming white forehead and the proud martial mien of the blond-bearded soldier, the gallant and even honorable grace of his left hand, dead though it was. . . . As Desdemona loved Othello, as all women of such lineage love all men of such condition, Doña Catalina loved Miguel *because she saw him as unfortunate*, through the compassion the misfortunes he recounted inspired in her young breast and the warm emotion produced in her by the gallantry and valor of her suitor.

The hostility and reserve of the Palacios were in vain. On December 12 of 1584 Miguel and Doña Catalina were married in the Church of Santa María in Esquivias. The benediction was pronounced by the assistant priest Juan de Palacios, now an old man. The witnesses were Rodrigo Mejía, Francisco Marcos, and Diego Escribano. It would seem that no one from either of the two families was present. The Palacios had come to terms in order to avoid gossip, but it is almost certain that the Cervanteses could not or would not attend the wedding.

The notion that Cervantes married a rich woman has been greatly exaggerated. Doña Catalina's wealth, as her dowry reveals, was less than moderate and almost certainly of little use to a man who did not live in Esquivias itself, keeping a close eye on the vineyards and the farm work. Miguel, in view of his occupation, had to live in the capital, and he left his mother-in-law and brother-in-law, the administrative cleric, behind in Esquivias, where they were in a position to determine what money to send him. Miguel therefore could not rely on any yield from his wife's land, and upon arriving in Madrid he returned to his plays and his actors.

It is assumed that the couple lived with Miguel's family, since he was now the real head of the house. Old Rodrigo de Cervantes, never much of a man, was full of aches and pains. In the spring of 1585 he became very ill and on June 8 he drew up his will, "lying on his bed." In his testament Rodrigo named his wife Doña Leonor and his co-parent Doña Catalina de Palacios, widow of Hernando de Salazar, as executrixes, which shows that good relations existed between the two families at the time. He named as heirs his children Miguel and Rodrigo, Juan, Doña Andrea, and Doña Magdalena. Where and what had this Juan de Cervantes been, who appears only in his baptismal certificate and a couple of odd documents? Nothing more is known of him and it is thought that he died soon after.

The poor chirurgeon died five days later and was buried according to his wish in the Convent of the Fathers of Mercy. The sorrow felt by the family could not have been inconsolable. There was nothing handsome or noble about him, and in the whole of Miguel's works there is no evidence of filial love. Rodrigo de Cervantes was always a poor man whose lack of spirit was made all the worse by his deafness. Miguel learned nothing from him, and it is perhaps significant that whenever he mentions a chirurgeon he always calls him by the pejorative nickname "*sacapotras*" [boil-slitter], while on the other hand all of his respect and admiration was reserved for licensed doctors. It is easy to see that when speaking of chirurgeons he recalled his unfortunate father and when speaking of doctors he remembered the magistral figure of the wise Doctor Gregorio López who saved him from death in the hospital at Messina.

With the death of his father and his increased responsibilities as head of the family Miguel sought to establish closer relations with those who could help him in carrying out his enterprises. To this end he became intimate with the famous actor and playwright Jerónimo Velázquez, whose own talents and the favor of the Court had raised from being a bricklayer and floor-tiler to the position of leading actor and theater manager.

Jerónimo Velázquez and his wife Inés Osorio had a daugher named Elena who, when more or less a child, married Cristóbal Calderón, to whom thereafter she never paid the slightest attention. No sooner was she married than she established relations with a good-looking lad whose moustache had scarcely started to sprout, for he was only seventeen years old, but who already gave every indication that he would become one of the greatest geniuses of Spain.

The favors of Elena Osorio were so generous and the passions of the two lovers so inflamed that the fires of jealousy burned fiercely in the breast of the young lover. One day, around the year 1585, when Elena praised a *caballero* who jousted elegantly in the Plaza Mayor, the jealous lover in a fit of rage forgot he was a gentleman and slapped his lady-love furiously in the face. Elena was worthy of such a mad passion; she was lovely, a brunette with creamy white shoulders and breast, her hair chestnut with golden lights, her eyes bright and expressive. The entire Court knew the beauty of every part of her body through the infinite number of songs and ballads in which *Belardo* glorified the charms of *Filis.*

The Velázquez family lived on the ground floor in the Calle de Lavapiés, at the foot of the hill. One of the iron-grilled windows of the apartment gave on the street and it was so low that it was like a step up from the flags of the sidewalk; it was also deep in such a way that it formed a niche where a slender man could fit easily. One in particular used to hide there, partly screened from the gaze of the curious, and Miguel, who often visited the house of his friend Velázquez, had seen him there more than once.

The relations between Elena and her lover eventually became the gossip and scandal of the Court, reaching such a pitch that, although Jerónimo Velázquez was thick of skin, his wife Inés Osorio finally could stand it no longer. One day she lashed out at Elena, scratching her face, bruishing her flesh, and tearing cruelly at her hair.

A few days later when he came visiting Miguel saw Elena giving her lover through the bars of the window a braid fashioned from the hair her mother had torn out. As so many men hovered around Elena he looked closer to see if this was the one he had seen before. It was the same. Miguel saluted him with a friendly wave of the hand, but the other turned his face away like one who would not relish a jest or wish to be addressed in any way in such circumstances. Miguel said nothing and went on into the house.

Elena's lover was the secretary of the Marquis of Las Navas and *Belardo* (as the whole world now knows) was Lope Félix de Vega Carpio. Lope and Miguel looked at each other then and there was no meeting of minds . . . then or ever.

CHAPTER 29

The Farce of Moorish Ballads—Miguel Has Other Things to Do—Return to the Road

In Spanish poetry there are bloodlines that seem to be eternally fruitful, like some of the prolific old strains of sun-kissed peaches. That is what the illustrious offspring of the *Romancero* are—new ballads which for centuries have passed for popular works written for the people, while in fact they were composed in leisure hours for diversion and practice in writing, as well as to point up the amorous intrigues of friendly or mutually hostile poets who praised or reviled each other, traded gossip or related the shifts and accidents of their love affairs, assuming for the purpose Moorish or Arcadian names and at times even some taken from the ancient epic tradition.

Critics have not had to work hard to discover names by fitting them to events and thus discovering who were the counterfeit Moors and disguised shepherds. Among them were very well-known poets and dramatists such as Lope, Cervantes and Góngora, as well as others no less inspired though not so well known, such as Pedro de Padilla, Juan Bautista de Vivar and others.

It must be kept in mind that these ballads were born of any occasion whatever, on the most flimsy pretexts. They were the small change of talent, as today are the jokes or amusing turns of phrase of the Ateneo Club,[1] the social salon or the literary discussion group. But their use was such a current daily thing that, for example, when Lope had to leave the Court for a few days, before his departure he improvised, with his foot in the stirrup,[2] the ballad that says:

> The miserable Belardo,
> wracked by the jealousy of parting,
> humbly complains
> to the beautiful Filis. . . .

Between daydreams he recalled that his beloved Elena was the wife of Cristóbal Calderón, and he hastily composed that masterwork which in the *Romancero* has been called "Nest of the Turtle Doves" (*El Nido del Tórtolas*):

> The waters of the Tagus
> bathe the trunk of the green and white poplar
> dressed in seaweed
> amid reeds and rushes. . . .

The famous Felipe de Liaño painted Elena's portrait about the same time he was painting that of Don Álvaro de Bazán for the Emperor Rudolph II of Germany, and when Lope became the owner of the portrait he burst out in expressions of astonishment and delight with a number of ballads about

> The great Amoralife
> one of the strong men of Granada,
> he of the surest cutlass,
> he of the most feared lance. . . .

in which there is nothing Moorish save the names.

It was such common knowledge that Cervantes was one of the poets who were then turning out ballads on everything that happened that two years later, in a lawsuit against Lope de Vega, an unknown Amaro Benítez, who lived in the capital, declared that he heard Don Luis de Vargas in the courtyard of the Principe Theater use these curious words while commenting on Lope's satirical ballad about the Velázquez: "This ballad is in a style of which only four or five men are capable; it could be by Liñan but he isn't here, and *by Cervantes but he isn't here*, and since it is not mine it could be by Vivar or Lope de Vega." This is authentic testimony to the appreciation in which Miguel was held, and to the certainty that he was closely involved with the activities of the most highly regarded young poets of those days. A study of the ballads of that period might one day yield new works by Miguel, since he himself tells us that he composed a countless number of them of all kinds and on any subject. At present the only ones held to be certainly his are "Jealousy" (*Los celos*):

> Where the sun sets there lies
> between two sundered rocks
> an entrance to an abyss,
> I mean to say, to a cavern. . . .

and "Disdain" (*El desdén*):

> My heart is so accustomed
> to your ingrate disdain
> that now it feeds upon it
> as the asp on its venom. . . .

and the two well-known ones of *Elicio* and *Galatea*, in his pastoral novel.

In those days, however, despite the great surge forward that was already beginning to be felt in the theater, the writing of plays did not provide a livelihood for anyone. Plays and poetry were the fruit of idleness, and when a man had other things to do he cast aside the pen and got down to the serious and really important business of earning his living. When "twenty or thirty" of Miguel's plays were acted in the theaters of the capital in a brief period of two or three years one must be blind to say that he failed calamitously in the theater, and it is a monstrous injustice to tax his country as ungrateful and the public as ignorant when it had applauded his plays and bestowed the highest guerdon of popularity on the *Galatea* and his ballads.

Looking back without rancor late in life, he says it, as if it were natural and well known: "I had other things to do. I abandoned the pen and plays." And a few paragraphs later he adds, underlining the thought: "Some years ago I returned to my old idleness, and thinking that the time in which my praises were sung still lasted, I went back to writing some plays, but there were no birds in the nests of yesteryear. . . ."[3] There is undoubtedly some bitterness in this, but there is no sign that he seriously regretted having left the theater. It was the most natural thing in the world and a common way of thinking. The wishes of his wife Doña Catalina might have had some influence, also, for if she loved her husband she could not enjoy seeing him involved in the intrigues of wanton actresses and in the plots of crazy youngsters like Lope de Vega and his friends of the fencing school of Master Parades. Let us concede this, but recognize that it was at best a secondary motive for Cervantes' decision, since the new "things" separated rather than united him and his wife.

The man of action was also in rebellion. In his thirty-eighth year life attracted him, the air of the road tickled his cheek. A world of pleasing stimulation seemed to be opening up again before him. The eyes educated to the broad outlook of the soldier's life, the eyes which had seen so many actual tragedies and cherished so many real idylls in places that seemed to have been created for tragedy and idyll, now saw clearly the accoutrements, the incongruities of the fiction in which the poets of Spain were involved. For reality and robustness in Spanish literature that period of Moorish ballads and pastoral stylistics was a dangerous time. Fortunately Cervantes was able to avoid the danger when he returned to literature and on the basis of his accumulated experience raised the strongest and most daring towers of thought that existed in Spain: the long and pointed head of Don Quixote and Sancho's round pate.

The usual laments when reaching this point in Miguel's biography are therefore vain, and it would be stupid to condemn as sterile the years he spent in doing things that were not literary; it is a mark of innocence to think that without these things we would have had the *Quixote* to enjoy.

In 1584 the daughter of the love of Miguel and Ana Franca had been born and baptized Isabel. Either for this reason, whether she knew or presumed it, or perhaps because of the bad situation in which the family found itself, Doña Catalina returned to her home in Esquivias. But Miguel was not to spend a life of ease married to a landowner in the country. Soon he obtained a commission to make certain collections of money in Seville.

To see Seville once more is the dream of everyone who has ever been there. There is no need to say with what delight Miguel returned, eager to savor what as a child had barely touched his lips. It is also not possible to exaggerate the joy with which he sought again the rich flavor of life on the road, after having traveled over so many different ones, nor the good humor and gaiety with which he returned to the company of muleteers and the happy intimacy of inns and roadhouses.

Those plump and tranquil innkeepers whose daughters glanced half seriously, half jestingly, at the maimed hidalgo who flirted merrily with them, those incessant streams of prostitutes heading for Seville on their way to seek their fortunes in the Indies where there was a shortage of women, those lads who pounded along the road with their shoes hung across their shoulders, their short swords at their belts, singing the ancient couplet

> To the war am I led
> by my necessity. . . .

those thieves in gangs who wore on their breasts the S and H of the squads of the *Santa Hermandad*[4] and in their souls every petty vileness known to the world and many new ones, the country girls romping and skipping lightly in the dust, the Benedictine friars riding on mules as big as dromedaries, the squires from Biscay, the chattering Negroes, the vagabond students from the small universities, showing off and arguing like fencing masters, and all the immense and undisciplined popular masses of Spain were constantly on the move. That indeed was the true image of the world. Discerning eyes could find in every man and every woman a novel or drama considerably more interesting than any that had ever been written before. The world was the great and only theater, life the only great novel.

All this was far from the Court and its false, artificial, limited, and petty life. Upon crossing the great plain of La Mancha the windmills hailed him with their tattered wings, grinned at him with their gaping mouth-doors, winked sarcastically at him from their eye-windows. He heard the ancient song of *La Niña* sung by a muleteer or traveler, the words saltier and more amusing than ever:

> The girl
> when she sees me, winks;
> I call her
> she comes to my hand;
> I draw her
> under my cloak;
> I say to her
> face of sun and moon
> come with me. . . .

and the hoarse licentious voice, after a pause, adds the finale:

> for you are not the first
> who has come. . . .

He spent only a few days in Seville, busy with the collections entrusted to him, but in those few days he met and talked with one of his best friends, the best he had in that city. He was a poor actor, but a man of sweet disposition and generous soul named Tomás Gutiérrez. When he tired of the theatrical profession he became an innkeeper, and he served as a witness and gave bond for Miguel on several occasions. Tomás Gutiérrez and Pedro de Morales, two actors, were perhaps and without any perhaps the men who took the greatest interest in Miguel and to whom he was indebted for the most valuable favors.

CHAPTER 30

Conception of "The Invincible"—Miguel Makes New Friends

In the lucid intervals of its almost chronic delirium Spain has had a hundred opportunities to rehabilitate itself and emerge healthy and prosperous from the bad situations into which its excess of generosity and lack of self-control have led it. As Miguel approached his fortieth year there was daily evidence of this. At one moment a splendid flowering of good intentions emerged with great fanfare, only to dry up almost immediately; by evening the good intentions had fled with the sun after having lasted exactly as long as the lucid discourses of Don Quixote.

The Mediterranean was again abandoned to Turkish piracy and no one at all remembered the captives in Algiers or the endless evils that resulted from the insecurity of Our Sea. "What did I lose this hand for? For what did I suffer five years of captivity?" Cervantes often thought to himself. And again he thought of the anguished dread he had seen on the faces of mariners returning to Seville from the Indies, because the Atlantic was in like manner abandoned to English piracy. Miguel remembered Don Juan, now dead, and felt that he was better dead, since his heroism had borne no fruit; then there came to mind the image of the admired and feared Marquis of Santa Cruz and hope revived.

As he had already seen from his own experience that glory is of questionable value unless it serves to bring a measure of peace, he was not greatly impressed by the spectacular triumphs daily won in Flanders by Alexander Farnese, that brave captain from Parma he had encountered in the landing at Navarino. What was the most that could be gained in Flanders as compared with what the sea robbed us of daily? And Miguel, perhaps before any Spanish politician, saw Spain for what she was—a ship buffeted by waves from three directions in need of skilled navigators to keep her on a straight course.

It was so understood by Don Álvaro de Bazán, that great politician and great warrior, who was poorly rewarded in money and even less in gratitude, as were all the great men of his period. And if Miguel did not think as he did, the people had no doubt as to the need for a powerful navy to fight the Turks in the Mediterranean and the English in the Atlantic. If such a thing were possible the hatred for the heretical English was greater than that for the Mohammedan infidel. The old cry of "The Turk is on us! The Turk is on us!" no longer horrified the villagers, but rather that other more terrifying one, long preserved in some Spanish towns as a bogie to scare children: "The English are coming! Drake is coming!"

Hatred of the English therefore grew, unwittingly but fiercely, in the most remote villages of La Mancha and Estremadura, and in La Mancha the name of Anne Boleyn or *Nabolena* was a symbol for the most horrendous debaucheries, while in Toledo and in every cathedral or church where there was a *tarasca*[1] to be borne in the procession of Corpus Christi, this name was given to the allegorical figure of Lechery, shown mounted on a horrible scarecrow. The sermons of priests and friars further fanned the flames of hatred for the English among the ignorant, and the people unthinkingly loathed Elizabeth as much as Philip II himself did, and perhaps thought that the Virgin Queen was another monster of perversion, not like the familiar *Nabolena* but rather a horrendous *tarasca* which devoured men, ships, money, and all that inexhaustible Golden Fleece that the Spanish imagination envisaged as coming from the Indies as a reward for the achievement of discovering and Christianizing remote continents.

There came a moment when all these hatreds combined, and with the King and the people experiencing them in concert, all eyes turned to Don Álvaro de Bazán, who had not ceased making calculations and adding up numbers. When the King addressed himself to Don Álvaro the old man had already planned to assemble a fleet which the King and the people, filled with an Escorialesque faith, baptized with the name of the *Invincible*. The name was as quixotic as the purpose, and the new madness bore only an outward semblance to great wisdom, but Philip II was possessed by the conviction that often seizes upon the spirit when we are about to play a decisive card in life and that impels us to place in luck a confidence which might be put to better purpose.

Miguel, approaching his fortieth year, did not think for a moment of taking arms again, although he was to have a part in the victory, however humble, since he was already recommended for and almost certain to get a position as commissary for provisioning that part of the fleet which was to assemble in Andalusia. For him the heroic period was over. Writing, by which he had achieved as much fame as he could expect, had not satisfied all his desires. In his heart he still had too much energy to reconcile himself to living as a village hidalgo on the property of his wife, but at the same time one should not ignore the possibility that when he was in Esquivias the feel of land under his feet must have had a certain influence on him.

He who has never been a landowner and who suddenly becomes one acquires with the sense of proprietorship an endowment of portentous mental qualities of discretion and seriousness that the simple idlers, the mere poets who have only their lyre, or the common soldiers who possess naught but a sword at the belt can never acquire. This does not mean that Miguel's ideas were becoming conservative, as we would say today. Miguel always loved the road, travel, the variety of a peripatetic life. But now he was earning money with his plays, his name was respected and praised, and every once in a while he might take his siesta in Esquivias in the shade of the pear orchard. For a short time, therefore, he enjoyed the Horatian ideal of a peaceful, well-regulated life much like that of the Gentleman of the Green Coat whom Don Quixote visited.[2]

Miguel was thus enjoying the gentle Hesperidean tranquility of quiet fields and relative security for the morrow, a pleasure he had never tasted before, and during this interval of prudence and tranquility his mother-in-law and brother-in-law, who had never until then had much confidence in that soldier-poet whose speech they often could not understand, began to appreciate him as a sound and practical man. It was then that the promise of a dowry was made effective on the ninth of August of 1586, in Esquivias before Alonso de Aquilera. Such a document proves that confidence was being established between the stiff Palacios family and Cervantes, who was able to win them over by discourse as sensible and judicious as that of Don Quixote when it did not touch on the subject of knight-errantry.

It is almost certain that about this time Miguel had been somewhat disillusioned in his relations with the writers he had known but a short time before. Completely disgusted by the lad Lope, a trifle bored by the jests of the malicious Espinel, Miguel resorted to new friends of a more serious bent, not because they were older but because of their temperament and condition.

Among these there was a certain Lupercio Leonardo de Argensola,[3] an Aragonese nobleman who lived at the Court in a very aristocratic circle, falling in love but not madly, witty but not excessively so, elegant but unpretentious, a Latin poetizer and moralist like Horace, but like Horace one who fitted into the narrow grandeur and inhibiting spaciousness of the Escorial. Lupercio Leonardo was a friend of Cervantes from the moment they met, though at times he was not pleased by what he considered Miguel's excesses. All his life he was a man of good will, but it was obviously also a Horatian good will, involving no passion and no sacrifice.

Argensola was an academic rather than a memorable playwright, and Miguel's praise of the high-sounding and empty tragedies Lupercio wrote seems to have been dictated more by friendship than by liking them. Lupercio joined the *Academia Imitatoria*, established in Madrid in 1586 in imitation of those of Italy, and perhaps Miguel and his friend Juan Rufo attended some of its meetings. Epistles and satires in endecasyllabic tercets were read, sonnets and glosses were forged, and there were discreet criticisms that never offended anyone.

It is very likely that about that time Miguel also met Pedro de Isunza, who was later to become a great friend of his. Pedro's father, Juan Martínez de Isunza, had been a purveyor to the armies in Flanders, and in that predominantly industrial and trading land his spirit expanded, as did his pockets. He took his son Pedro with him so that he could learn to know world commerce, of which the docks at Antwerp were the emporium. The talents of Pedro de Isunza developed enormously, and around 1580 he established his commercial house in Madrid.

Before he left Antwerp, Isunza had met a hidalgo from Mondragón in Guipúzcoa named Don Esteban de Garibay,[4] who had gone there to have a very voluminous book of his, the *Comprehensive Chronicle of Spain*, printed in the establishment of the memorable and exquisitely scrupulous Plantin. The omniscient Benito Arias Montano[5] was also there, and with the help of Plantin he was working on that formidable monument, the *Polyglot Bible*, glory of Spain and Escorial of our erudition.

Garibay and Isunza soon became great friends, being fellow Basques and of similar condition. Garibay admired his friend Isunza as being "very sensible and without any vice or excess," and Isunza esteemed Garibay for those same qualities, so characteristic of the Basque race. Both of them were established in Madrid in 1585, and when Miguel met Isunza he also got to know his friend the chronicler. We can very well imagine how Miguel de Cervantes, having acquired a degree of seriousness and judgment that he perhaps never thought to attain for himself, should hold his two Basque friends in real esteem. It is possible and even probable that it was through a recommendation from one of them that he was nominated as a commissary under a commission approved by Don Antonio de Guevara, Purveyor General of the Fleet. Miguel was his representative in Seville until Don Diego Valdivia was transferred there from Segovia, where he had his home and properties.

The report which the Marquis of Santa Cruz presented to the King enumerating the supplies necessary to get the Invincible Armada ready for action insisted repeatedly and in great detail on the need to collect a great quantity of wheat with which to manufacture an enormous provision of ship-biscuit, since it could not be foreseen how long the fleet would have to be at sea. The matter was urgent, but Don Antonio de Guevara, old and sickly, accustomed to the quiet indolence of the Treasury Council, delayed his preparations for moving to the busy post of Purveyor General, and anyway he could not see how such great supplies could be obtained in such a short time, requiring as they did extraordinary purchases of wheat and other provisions. Licentiate Valdivia therefore had to start collections on his own responsibility and without money or any hope of getting it until Heaven knew when. Everyone realized that the provisions would be paid for late, badly and perhaps never, following the ancient habit of payments by the Spanish State. It was in these conditions that Miguel was named in 1587 to one of the most odious, difficult and ungrateful offices he had ever held in all his life.

CHAPTER 31

Cervantes the Commissary

THE silly, deaf, and blind people who speak of Cervantes without affection, only to show off and set themselves up as literary men, usually find fault with the very long period he spent requisitioning wheat and oil for the fleet and collecting arrears of excise taxes and tithes. Those who think thus do not understand that knowledge of life is taught by life itself and not by any other teacher, and that without those years of comings and goings, of calamities and hazards encountered by Miguel in towns, villages, farmhouses, inns, and along the roads and lanes of Andalusia we would never have had the *Quixote*, just as today we have no writers worthy of being considered sons of Cervantes save those who walked in their youth or walk today through lanes and roads, inns, farmhouses, villages, and towns. Life is a pilgrimage, and what can one who does not stir abroad know of it? And how can one who knows nothing of it, however talented he may be, have anything interesting to say?

Miguel had already known the heroic humanity of Lepanto, the lighthearted and free humanity of Italy, the savage and tragic humanity of Algiers, the courtly and cultured humanity of Lisbon and Madrid, but up to now he had no more than a glimpse of ordinary common humanity, the everyday one that formed and still forms the great source of energy in the nation, nor was he aware of that abject, retiring, and shriveled humanity that lives conventually in a corner of a village without ever leaving it, giving an impression of timidity, egoism, and parsimony.

The commissary for provisioning the Armada had to penetrate the very last corners of niggardliness, ferret out and turn up the smallest grain of wheat, suck up the last hidden drop of oil from the darkest cupboard or pantry. He was clearly and explicitly ordered to smell out everything by all possible means, to search, explore, and inspect the most private dwellings, to collect the last crumb from every private or public source, even to pry into the sacred property of the Church. He was instructed "to go with the tall staff of justice," visit the municipal government of each village, demand an assessment on all residents and if it had not been done already to do it himself, and to requisition, seize, and take away all the wheat, barley, and oil there was which might be useful in His Majesty's service.

"To go with the tall staff of justice" was to go on horseback into a hamlet with a staff of office like a constable who is investigating a crime or smelling out wrongdoers. It was taking along four or five or more arresting officers or catchpolls, who naturally would be the most abject and ragged specimens of the underworld, men used to the whip and the galley-oar, ex-assistants to the executioner, drunkards, ruffians and braggarts dismissed from any honest office for their light-fingered habits. It meant presenting oneself with this pacifying apparatus and sacred authority in a peaceful little village where men went to the fields to plough, singing their peasant songs while their animals ruminated placidly in the next field, the women spun, plaited bast, made clothes or sewed, or prayed for hours in the church or convent, and the monks and clergy strolled in the sun while the municipal authorities planned for the ploughing season and the harvest. It meant entering this peaceful village only to sow anxiety and unhappiness, breaking into the timeless monotony, requiring mayor and councillors to take actions that would harm their own interests and get them into trouble with their neighbors, friends and relatives, forcing them, by fair means if possible, by foul if they dared to resist, to go to the tithe barns or public granaries where grain was stored and to private granaries or storerooms, order the doors to be opened, and if this were not done willingly break them open, forcing locks or smashing planks, entering the granary or oil store and forcing the weighmasters of the village to cooperate.

It meant taking from trembling and weeping peasants those bits of their hearts, fruit of their loins and produce of their sweat that were called bushels of wheat or *arrobas*[1] of oil, leaving them as their only consolation a paper in which the commissary, in someone else's name, and that one in the name of the Purveyor, and he in the name of His Majesty, all of whom had a well-deserved reputation for bad pay, promised to pay for those fruits whenever it might be possible at a price they themselves had determined. After all this it meant looking around the neighborhood for muleteers and carts, if there were any, in which to load what had been collected and carry it to Seville. Behind the mule teams and the carts went the curses of an entire village despoiled of its wealth, the tears of the women, the excommunications of the clergy, and the target of all this wrath was the accursed commissary who had brought destruction and rapine to the village.

The small rural landowner is always and perforce has to be an apprehensive, mistrustful man, and even more so in those days when, besides being a landowner, he was a proud and pretentious hidalgo. He was also usually a man of scant culture, slow-witted, to whom it was talking nonsense if one spoke to him of the King, of military undertakings carried out for honor's sake, or of the Invincible Armada being assembled against the power and pride of the English.

What did he know of ships or care what England did? To get to that village in the sierras of Seville or Granada the Englishman would have a long walk. As for the King, the hidalgo owed him no favor, for he had taken his son to war, increased the sales tax, the tithes, the tax paid upon the marriage of the Queen and many other dues and contributions, and sent through the village a company of soldiers who, between their leather straps and plumes, carried off the best chickens of the barnyard and the honor of a virgin daughter. The unfortunate hidalgo foresaw a long series of days and months during which he would have to fast, and not out of saintliness, while his lean features became more wasted and ennobled from pure want.

In Ecija, where every summer the grain is parched by heat so excessive that the village is called "the frying-pan of Andalusia," the arrival of Cervantes put the inhabitants of that town in just such a predicament. Accustomed as they were to suffering spoliations and thefts, they had developed from ancient times a concept of property, noted by the most respectable authors, which won a reputation for the seven famous sons of Ecija.[2] In the present instance the inhabitants discussed with Ecijesque ingenuity ways in which they could protect themselves by hiding their goods from the scrutinizing eyes of the commissary and pretending, if he found them, that they had been stolen and did not belong to anyone.

In addition to the problems that such attitudes created for him Miguel inevitably got into a situation where for the first time he had to exclaim like Don Quixote: "We have come up against the Church." It was a matter of distraining a hundred and twenty bushels of wheat belonging to Don Francisco Enríquez de Rivera, a divinity-master in the Santa Iglesia Cathedral of Seville and a very close relative of the powerful dukes of Tarifa, great noblemen universally respected in the whole of Andalusia. The steward of that exalted ecclesiastic, a certain Damián Pérez, delivered the wheat to Cervantes against his requisition but not without warning him that some spiritual mischief might follow upon its seizure. At the same time he informed his master and Don Francisco called upon the Dean and Chapter of Seville, who claimed power over another kind of distrainment, to excommunicate Miguel de Cervantes for having seized this most holy wheat. What must have been the delight of the inhabitants of Ecija and its vicar when they saw at the door of the church the hated name of the tax collector on the list of excommunicates and heard it published from the pulpit by the sacristan with passion and scorn?

We must not exaggerate, however. Excommunications and interdictions were common in those days. Miguel must not have been too vexed by the decision of the Chapter of Seville, but he did not fail to ask his principal for protection. After a few months Don Antonio de Guevara wrote to the gentlemen of the Chapter to inform them that what was done could not be undone, since it was a matter of obtaining supplies for the service of His Majesty and to fight against the infidel. Not much attention seems to have been paid to Guevara's arguments, since Cervantes' excommunication had still not been lifted in February of 1588, but it must have been shortly thereafter, perhaps following receipt of moneys in the summer of 1588 with which to pay for the requisitioned wheat.

Miguel had flung himself into the adventure of Ecija with the same bold spirit with which he faced the savages of Lepanto and the Algerian pirates, but now he had to show tact and great ingenuity as well, and it is known for certain that he did just that, for not only did he carry out the commission entrusted to him very successfully, but he also achieved the miracle of making friends in Ecija who later were to pledge their credit and risk their possessions for Miguel's benefit. Such an almost incredible achievement calls to mind how the heroes of Spanish knight-errantry, while possessed of more than enough strength and valor in battle, combine it with cautious skill in negotiating. Thus the hero of Castilian independence, Fernán González, won kingdoms from the Moors, weapons in hand, and was able to achieve independence from León, thereby presenting his King with victory heaped on victory. Similarly El Cid Ruy Díaz, invincible in combat with the infidels, was a keen-witted weaver of pacts and raised money out of a coffer full of stones.[3]

Who has thought and said that the business of procuring wheat which Miguel carried out in 1587 in Ecija, Castro del Rio, Espejo, La Rambla and other villages was vulgar? Rather than vulgar, it was an occupation demanding great skill in dealing with men and making them serve one's purposes.

Miguel neatly solved the grave difficulty the excommunication would have created for a man with a propensity for humility, which must be all the more astonishing seeing that Ecija was a Levitical city where churches and religious houses darkened the streets, perennial prayers broke the silence of the siesta and the evening gatherings . . . and in this fanatical and ascetic community Cervantes retained his natural gaiety and managed to break through the shell, win friends, return frequently and find lodgings and smiling faces, and even to learn of the ardent love stories that circulated in the enfevered town and its surroundings.

His services were held in such esteem that no sooner had Miguel finished one commission than he was charged with another, and in this way he travelled all the highways and byways of the kingdoms of Cordova, Seville, Jaén and Granada. On the twenty-second of January of 1588, upon giving him another mission, one of procuring four thousand *arrobas* of oil from Ecija, Don Antonio de Guevara says that "it is advisable that the person to be appointed should be careful and diligent . . . and that Miguel de Cervantes, a resident of this city [Seville] is the kind of man needed for it because of his achievements and experience in similar things and because of my satisfaction with him as a person."

On June 15 Don Antonio ordered Miguel to go to Ecija again as quickly as possible to collect the wheat requisitioned the year before and to mill it in all haste. Some pious soul had told the Purveyor that the requisitioned wheat, which had not been shifted for a long time, had been invaded by moths, as was natural with the arrival of the summer heat. And since there were no funds with which to pay for it, nor was it right that it should all be eaten by moths. Miguel was to get hold of it without paying a maravedi, carry it to be milled and compel the millers to turn it into flour, even against their will, and finally to look for someone who would cart it to Seville, all of which was to be done in the presence and with the knowledge and consent of the mayor and the authorities of Ecija, whose feelings at such a cruel and arbitrary levy can well be imagined.

Miguel arrived in Ecija to carry out this most difficult mission on the eighteenth or nineteenth of June and met with the authorities, who demanded that he name sureties to guarantee his signature and go bond for his promise to pay. History has preserved the names of these unknowns who demonstrated their confidence in Miguel in such critical circumstances. They were Fernán López de Torres, Francisco de Orduña, Juan Bocache, and Gonzalo de Agular Quijada.

When the granaries and tithe barns were opened there were more problems. The wheat had to be examined and reweighed to determine the amount of wastage and it had to be winnowed, freed of dust, turned over and sieved. It then had to be taken to the mill and arrangements made to ensure that the flour would be of good quality with the refuse and siftings separated out. To do this the mills were requisitioned and private people not allowed to carry out their urgent millings; to sum up, it bothered and prejudiced everybody. Finally the carts had to be lined up before the magistrates and scriveners and an accounting and justification for all this entered in detail in the appropriate registers, which showed the totals and the supporting data.

Miguel spent all the rest of the year 1588 in Ecija, winding up the complicated and tiresome operations implicit in his mission. Fortunately by June 28 the paymaster, Agustín de Cetina, began to send his payment orders so that compensation could be provided for the wheat and the expenses of milling and cartage. Cervantes made payment and this calmed everyone down to such a degree that in October the city of Ecija offered to make a voluntary contribution to His Majesty of twenty-five hundred more bushels of wheat.

Miguel had carried out his missions in excellent style, and each of the operations that the sale, milling and carting of the wheat required was for him an opportunity to make new conquests in understanding humanity. The workman is judged by his work. Miguel received his due and noted down what he received. He paid out and noted down what he paid. He had to eat and live on it, for his daily pay of twelve reals was the last entry to figure on the general account.

During this period he went to Seville from time to time and he may have been there on the twenty-fourth of October, a day when the city celebrated with great clamor and rejoicing the installation of the great bell in the Giralda. Perhaps it was then that he met a wise and clever clergyman who became a great friend of his, Licentiate Francisco Porras de la Cámara.

Miguel was not dissatisfied with his career. He already enjoyed an excellent reputation as a public functionary. At times he thought he had found his true vocation.

CHAPTER 32

The Invincible Armada

THE great question of the projected war against Great Britain was now constantly to the fore. Pope Sixtus V, remembering that happy time when the grunting herds of swine would answer to the sound of his horn from the oak forests of Montalto, wanted to lure back to the pale of his church the many beings who had wandered from the right path. Philip II for his part could not forget his ancient hatred of the English and was ever conscious of the insults that the pirate Sir Francis Drake heaped on the ships and ports of Spain.

As secretly as possible naval preparations had been started long before in the dockyards and arsenals of Antwerp, Dunkirk, and Nieuport; much naval artillery was collected from Italy; great numbers of troops were levied in Spain, Germany, Lombardy, Naples, Corsica and Burgundy; the *tercios* of Flanders were reinforced. Alexander Farnese took care of the land forces, those of the sea fell to the Marquis of Santa Cruz, Don Álvaro de Bazán, now old but still spirited and vigorous.

As always these two experienced leaders carried out their duties, but without letting enthusiasm run away with them. To fight England at sea did not appear to them a trifle. To confront the terrible Drake, Frobisher, and Hawkins, corsairs of the high seas, was a very different thing from attacking Mediterranean pirates.

They did not see clearly, as we do now, but those illustrious generals probably had a presentiment that what had been achieved by Drake and his English pirates was a very great and radical transformation in the art of naval warfare. To privateer in the Mediterranean required only boldness and a knowledge of the gulfs and ports; to practice piracy on the Atlantic required in addition great tenacity, incredible endurance, and above all iron discipline on board ship. The picturesque Greek, Italian and Illyrian renegades were of no use for this, nor were the cruel and avaricious captains of the Turkish galliots, whose crews were the lowest of the low. Drake organized, disciplined, and had at his disposal extremely patient people, blindly obedient, and it was thus that he succeeded in establishing mastery of the ocean.

Nevertheless the besotted King was convinced that the fleet being prepared would be the *Invincible* Armada. That insolent, boastful adjective ruined Spain. The Castilian valor of old was being transmuted into the empty arrogance of the bully who threatens death and proclaims victory before doing anything at all. It had occurred to no one to qualify the navy of Lepanto or the fleet of the Azores as *Invincible*.

When the Marquis of Santa Cruz heard of this dictum he shook his head uneasily. As great in preparing for action as in action itself the immortal Don Álvaro had been laboring to have everything ready, from the armaments most needed for naval artillery to the minute details of provisions and harness. As was his habit, as was the habit of all illustrious captains of history, he went about this carefully and deliberately. His composure irritated Philip II and inspired him to launch this icy arrow from among the frigidities of the Escorial: "In truth you respond badly to the good will I have always borne you." Such cruel words, levelled at an old man who had placed the service of the King above everything else and was working himself to death in that service, were enough to make an end to the greatest living glory of the nation. An official communication from Lisbon dated February 15, 1588 reported that the Marquis of Santa Cruz had died "overwhelmed by heavy labor and accusations against him regarding the failure of the enterprise."

After this the unexpected, the absurd, the incredible happened. It was necessary to name an admiral for the Invincible Armada, already mustering in the port of Lisbon. Philip II looked about and his eyes fell on the undersized and rickety figure, the bandy legs and curly locks of Señor Don Alonso Pérez de Guzmán el Bueno Manrique de Zuñiga, etc. He was the seventh Duke of Medina-Sidonia, a great horseman and famous for his skill in spearing wild bulls, as also for his avarice and his incapacity in anything that did not concern money or the running of bulls.

The Duke, whose ineptitude and cowardice were proclaimed in the Court by his own wife, was thirty-seven or thirty-eight years old. His wife, ten years younger, was the beautiful Doña Ana de Silva y de Mendoza, daughter of the Princess of Eboli. Philip felt a great, almost paternal love for Doña Ana, who was as lovely as she was clever. He did not hesitate, therefore, to give the command of the Invincible Armada to her husband, and even before Don Álvaro de Bazán died the King's secretary had already written to the Duke, who replied with the following letter, the importance of which justifies quoting parts of it:

I am replying to the letters of Your Honor which I have, all dated the eleventh, in the first of which Your Honor wrote me by order of His

> Majesty regarding the news that had been received there of the difficulty created by the illness of the Marquis of Santa Cruz and the small hope there is of his life and the need for his presence at this moment, the Armada being so far advanced, in order for it to leave in the middle of this month, with its departure impossible to postpone for a thousand reasons, His Majesty has turned his eyes on me to take charge and direct this expedition. . . .
>
> In connection with this matter I will respond first by kissing His Majesty's royal hands and feet for having thought to make use of me again for such a great undertaking, for the accomplishment of which I would like to have the strength and talent that are essential for such service. These, Sir, I do not have. I am not well enough to sail aboard ship, for I know by the little experience I have had at sea that I get seasick, because I have much rheumatism.
>
> Besides this Your Honor knows, for I have said and written it many times, that I am hard pressed financially, so much so that to go to Madrid, the few times I have done so, it has been necessary to try to borrow money and part of the outfit. My family owes nine hundred thousand ducats, and it is therefore not financially possible for me, nor do I have a real to spend on the expedition.[1]
>
> Together with this, neither in conscience nor as a duty can I take on this service, because it is such a great project and such an important undertaking that it is not right for it to be accepted by someone who has no experience of the sea or of war, because I have neither seen or experienced it. . . .
>
> Besides this, for me, inexperienced as I am, to join the Armada without knowing anything about it or the people who are in it and the service that is required, nor of the intelligence that is had from England, nor of its forces, nor of the correspondence on this matter which the Marquis had through the years in which he handled this, would be to do so altogether blindly, even if I had much experience, entering me in the race so unexpectedly, and hence, Sir, all my reasons are so strong and expedient to the service of His Majesty that for the same reason I shall not attempt to embark upon something that without any doubt I would carry out badly. . . .

Cowardly, stupid, and miserly, the Duke drew a true picture of himself, and responsibility for the disaster must be imputed above all to the obstinacy of Philip II, who had already reached that state of mind in which the willful and capricious great man tries to challenge reality and make his own wishful thinking triumph over every issue. On April 25 the royal standard was entrusted to the Duke and on May 14 he gave notice that the fleet was ready but the weather bad. He added that

> in the Benedictine Convent which is in Loyos, past Xobregar, there is a saintly monk called Antonio de la Concepción. I have, these past

> days, been in touch with him as often as I could and he is certain that Our Lord will grant Your Majesty a great victory. He told me to write this to Your Majesty and he begged Your Majesty not to carry out the undertaking as revenge against the offenses which the infidels have inflicted on Your Majesty nor in order to extend Your Majesty's realm, but only for the glory and honor of Our Lord to bring back to the Church those heretics who have left its pale.

For the honor and glory of Our Lord there sailed from Lisbon 130 ships of 57,868 tons burden with 2,431 artillery pieces. Aboard them were 19,259 soldiers, 8,050 seamen and 2,088 rowers. Accompanying the Duke of Medina-Sidonia and keeping close to him were the Prince of Asculi, the Count of Gelves, the brother of the Lord High Constable of Castile, the sons of Aguilafuente, Noves, Medellín, Orgaz, Lemos; Don Pedro Portocarrero, who had had some connection with the Cervantes women; and Don Tomás Perrenot de Granvela, who took from Lope de Vega what he held most precious, the love of Elena Osorio, better known as *Filis*. There were 228 cadets, not as noble as the above, with 163 servants. Finally, to care for the souls of those who might perish the Duke of Medina took 180 monks of different colors, and to cure their bodies five doctors and five surgeons.

The King sought to anticipate everything, and he even gave Medina-Sidonia secret instructions regarding peace conditions. "That the free enjoyment and practice of our Catholic faith be permitted in England" was the main demand . . . "the greatest effort must be made to get it."

This fleet made up of extremely heavy vessels, manned by noble and devout gentlemen, set forth to serve an ideal, led by a lancer of bulls assisted by a bevy of monks whose first and only aim was a purely religious and spiritual triumph. . . . Was there any other nation save Spain that in modern times armed ships and provoked a war for such purposes and in such absurd conditions? The hidalgo from La Mancha with his battered helmet and his flimsy lance dared to combat windmills, to tease lions.

Upon receiving the first news, which arrived around the end of July or early August and told how the Armada met the English ships near Plymouth and how the Duke did not dare to attack them and had to retreat, finally taking refuge in Calais, Miguel composed the first of his two extremely interesting *Songs to the Invincible Armada*. He entitled this one "Song inspired by the various accounts which have arrived of the Catholic Armada which went forth against England," and in it he portrays his state of mind, which was that of the whole nation. It is not so well known that its principal strophes do not merit reproduction.

Bard, swift report, on speedy wings;
break through the thick mists of the North;
on winged feet, come and counteract
the confused rumor of evil news,
and with thy light disperse the shadows
of Spanish faith which flees before thee,
put an end to this uncertainty
by bringing forth something apt to show
a happy ending for the glorious plan
whose outcome suspends us 'twixt relief and pain,
whether in the naval fight or that on land,
until with your eyes and tongues
telling us of the other's ignominy
you sing the valor of the sons of Spain
with which you glorify Heaven and terrify the earth . . .

Tell, as in the end you will, how
bodies flew through the air
propelled by the fiery engines of war;
how the waters changed their color
and the blood of fearless hearts
soaked the enemy soil;
how this ship or another fled
or fought fiercely; in how many forms
the shadows of death appear;
how fortune intervenes with fate
not showing itself even-handed or consistent
until through a thousand different obstacles
the Spanish power,
bursting through air, land and fire
declares the deadly game as won. . . .

After this you will tell: how in deep
serried ranks our invincible Christian army
goes marching with victorious banners,
adorned with the Cross, fluttering in the breeze,
a proud and pleasant sight to see;
making that fearsome sound
which hollow metal gives forth,
as does that of the drum which begets and nurtures
valor in fearful breasts
transforming and reducing natural fears;
reflecting the gleaming lights,
fair and bright as stars,
the sun makes on polished arms
when it is pleased to look down on this squadron.

Having said this, return in haste,
and in the ears of the two wise,
famous Generals quickly give the message
which will tell them of the glorious
race of their illustrious forbears,
symbol of more than human valor;
to him who leads the ships
show him a knight upon a wall[2]
armed with courage rather than with steel,
and mid the Moorish mob a child, bound
like a lamb among ravening wolves,
and show the second Abraham who cast the dagger down
with which the barbarian makes
the horrendous sacrifice, winning thus
immortal fame on earth, glory in Heaven.

To the other you will say he has the blood[3]
of Austria in his veins, that with this alone,
you will tell him of a thousand famous deeds,
which in all that the broad seas encompass
and the two poles look upon
were by his ancestors achieved;
these having thus been informed
go among the army of our people
and looking everywhere you will find
a thousand Cids, a thousand Rolands and a thousand Mars,
that one brave, this one braver still,
you will tell them only to look ahead
so that later they may aspire
to complete this most hazardous feat:
sons, behold your mother Spain. . . .

Neither Miguel nor anyone else could specify any merits of the Duke of Medina-Sidonia save those he might have inherited from his noble ancestor Guzmán el Bueno, but in any case in this song, where there already is a bit of fanfaronade and quixotic *Spanishness*, the first step toward total degradation can be seen. The bad news is doubted, but in case it should turn out to be confirmed this is anticipated with a touch of resignation. Before this when were resignation and acceptance ever found in Spanish souls?

The second "Song of the loss of the Armada which went to England" is the reflection of what we now call a "state of opinion," repeated a hundred times in other disasters. All kinds of reasons, shadows of reasons, pretexts and palliatives are dragged in to justify the defeats. The fanfaronades and theological invocations swell and burgeon more and more.

Mother of the heroes of the war,
confidant of Catholic soldiers,
crucible in which the love of God is purified,
land where it is seen that Heaven buries
those who to Heaven will be borne
as defenders of the purest faith,
let it not seem to you only mischance
Oh, Spain, our mother!
to see your sons returning to your breast
leaving the sea full of their misfortunes,
adverse favor was not cause of their return,
but by the force of an irresistible storm
of sea, wind and a Heaven which permits
the enemy head to be slightly raised,
odious to Heaven and hateful to earth,
for then the fall is certain
when the rise is presumptuous and vain.

Open your arms and gather in them
those who return, perplexed, not conquered,
there is no apology for what Heaven ordains
nor can the hand at any time
seize by the forelock the bare
pate of danger for good luck,
nor is the chain that binds and knits
the good issue in martial matters
made of steel or diamonds
and the strongest spirits are beaten down
by what the wind does to their arms;
and this disorderly retreat you see
I understand is undoubtedly that twist
of the bull to launch its deadly swerve
upon the people with impious bodies,
since Heaven is not inclined, though it may tarry,
to leave such abominations unpunished.

They have trodden on the tail of your lion;
shaking its matted mane it returns already
to a just vengeance for the offense,
not only to itself, for if it were only so
it might perhaps be forgiven; the return
is for that to God, and in restoring it thinks,
unique in valor, in strength immense,
clear its understanding,
indignant with reason, and such as
any Christian breast, though it were marble
would be moved to just and vengeful purpose,

and more even than the Gaul, the Turk, the Moor,
look sharply and with mind perplexed
as to what the beginnings, what the ends
and on what this lion has set his sights,
for it knows that its fate is happy
when with ague the lion is possessed.

Well then (Oh Philip) our lord,
second in name, and second to none,
pillar of strong and sure faith,
turn into happy and more propitious result
this design which the world contrives
which thinks to see you meek and without courage
as if it were not enough to move you
your ports assaulted
in the distant Indies
and at home your ships on fire,
in foreign lands your temples profaned;
your seas filled with cruel pirates,
your fleets reduced by them
and in them a thousand lives and fortunes
subject to a thousand barbarous steels,
things that each does what is possible for him
and seeks to achieve the impossible.

Ask for, take, Sire, everything
that your vassals have to offer you
with generous and valiant hand
in exchange for your putting on the neck
of the perfidious English the yoke that
their faithless hearts and insane acts deserve;
not only gold, which is vain to love,
but their dear sons will they give to you,
as did Don Diego with his
who in his own blood and alien fire
purified the deeds ever famed
of the House of Cordova, which has given
fourteen first-born sons to the lances
of the Moors, and with firm confidence
their works and their names have spread
over the spacious roundness of the earth
for he who dies thus lives to gain Heaven. . . .

In spite of this, saddened, deeply saddened was Miguel when he learned the whole enormous extent of the catastrophe. Thousands and thousands of soldiers had perished, some in combat, others of shame and sorrow, as did the brave Captain-General of the Biscayan fleet

Juan Martínez de Recalde, as did the valiant General of the Ships of Guipúzcoa, Miguel de Oquendo, as did the doughty Alonso de Leiva. The Duke of Medina arrived at Santander with his ships destroyed, himself destroyed, stupefied and out of his mind, his hair blanched. As he passed through Valladolid and Medina del Campo indignant crowds pursued him with whistlings and insults; the boys threw stones and balls of mud. Only the King had for the vanquished imbecile and for the defeat a phrase appropriate to a comic opera that historians obstinately insist on presenting as a poetic flight of the imagination.

Philip instructed all the churches and monasteries of the realm to offer thanks to God for the defeat of the Armada. Since God had ordained what had happened, for ends inscrutible to men but necessarily good since they were His, it must be for the best, for the glory of God and the good of souls. Hence the disaster was not a matter for lamentation but for rejoicing.

At times Miguel wept, at times he laughed, and when he laughed he thought to weep and when he wept he thought he was laughing. The Iliad of the dream had been changed into a *Batrachomyomachy*,[4] the ever-victorious Amadís into the always beaten Don Quixote.

CHAPTER 33

The Poets of Seville—The Sevillian Underworld

CERVANTES' business affairs kept him so occupied from 1588 to 1590 that he scarcely had time to remember that a few years back he had been a literary man and a poet. When he was staying in Seville he had to pay more attention to getting his wages paid than anything else, something which, as always happens in Spain, was much more difficult than earning them. With painful delays, in dribs and drabs despite his friendship with the accountant Cetina, the diligent commissary collected part of what he had spent and continued to spend on his trips and his sojourns in Ecija, Carmona and other places. However, poets and poetasters were in ample supply in Seville and in the whole of Andalusia, more than enough so that Miguel, busy with collecting and milling wheat, did not miss the company of the poets of the Court.

In this land of Spain poetry can sprout from the most humble incidents of life and there is no impediment to a poet dedicating himself to that craft regardless of his condition. In Seville, according to witnesses of the period, there were poets in that beautiful city ranging from the chief magistrate, the Count of Manteagudo, who wielded the supreme local authority, down to the executioner, and moreover two town criers, five scriveners, three judges, two from the Steps and one from the Contract House, two practising advocates, six doctors, four silversmiths, two foundrymen, one weaver, three woolcombers, and a goodly number of persons with unmentionable and unadmitted trades and occupations.

The banks of the Guadalquivir and its crowded inns and taverns offered pleasant asylum to the castanet-playing Muse of the *seguidillas*,[1] and the Steps of the Cathedral welcomed the semireligious, semibuffoon inspiration of the petty poets who composed verses and lauds to the Virgin and to Saints Justa and Rufina, less inspired but similar in that respect to the great Castilian poet, father of the poetry of saints,[2] that blessed cheerful clergyman from Rioja who, on beginning the devout life of the most esteemed saint of his land, exclaimed, licking his lips with pleasure in anticipation: "It will, I believe, be like a glass of good wine. . . ."

The great preaching saints were devoted to poetry of the most deeply Castilian quality, as also were their priestly pupils who, in Ecija, in Cordova, in Montilla and other places, found themselves succumbing to divine love, consumed in the purest ascetic flames under the magic of the burning words of the Master of Avila,[3] who went everywhere lighting fires in the tinder of souls. The mystical blaze of Saint John of the Cross who, to feed them, cast bits of his heart into the flames, burned with an otherworldly splendor, and his verses were on everyone's lips, especially on feminine lips, poems that could be recited with equal fervor by a seeker of better worlds or by a lover mad with passion in the hot silence of the bedroom.

There were also many great poets in Seville whom Cervantes had known by reputation when he was young and whom he praised with some exaggeration in the *Song of Calliope* which he inserted in the *Galatea* in order to earn goodwill. But if he tried to get near the divine Fernando de Herrera, whom everyone regarded as lord and master, his disappointment must have been very great. "He who rose by never trodden paths," the faithful Platonic lover of Doña Leonor de Milán, was poor, aging, retiring, and what today is described by that untranslatable word *raté*, a soured man, unable to temper the bitterness of his heart with the sweetness necessary to make disappointment in love pass as poetic. Nothing brought him out of his cloying melancholy but the trumpet calls of the victories in the Alpujarras and at Lepanto, or the defeat and destruction of King Sebastián. He also sought to distract himself by preparing the publication of an out-sized book, the very title of which is alarming: *History of the Most Notable Things That Have Happened in the World.* This book has not survived, and there is no reason to regret it, since for Herrera the most notable thing that had happened in the world was that he had been loved a little by Doña Leonor de Milán and that she had left him to marry the Count of Gelves, who was probably better-looking than Herrera, most certainly richer, and able to compose verselets as well as any other man. At any rate Miguel could observe that the divine Herrera also took up prose, as did other Sevillian poets who grew up in the house of Master Mal Lara,[5] as much or more than he.

Miguel must have admired the gay Baltasar del Alcázar, that fine poet with the ruddy face of an epicure, white beard and laughing eyes, but he can have had little or no contact with him since Baltasar del Alcázar held high position and was a man disinclined to inconvenience himself for anyone and least of all for needy poets. On the other hand Miguel himself says that he knew Don Juan de Jáuregui, that noted painter and poet who had shown by his translation of Tasso's *Aminta*, now so famous, and his magnificent version of Lucan's *Pharsalia* how it was not true that translations were always the wrong side of a tapestry.

It is logical to believe that if Miguel was acquainted with any writer during those years it was by chance, but for all great and even for all minor poets it is advisable to take a healthy dip into prose from time to time, all the more so when the poet is so vigorous that he can get artistic substance out of what is most vulgar and coarse, as was the case with Cervantes. His friends and associates were now his assistant and colleague in collecting and requisitioning, Miguel de Santa María, the paymaster Agustín de Cetina and his clerk Juan de Tomayo, and other men of like manner, without forgetting the actor Tomás Gutiérrez, to whom Miguel owed much.

As always, he was more interested in the enormous variety of the life of the people of the city than in the wealth and ostentation that dazzled newcomers. Seville was then on the way to the Indies[6] and all the idle folk of Spain and other parts of Europe gathered there. Every known language and others just beginning to be known were spoken on its docks and streets. Mingling on them were the hapless folk among whom the legend of the Indies induced hopes of a new Golden Fleece, as well as the rogues and knaves of all Spain who came to practise their skills in thievery, together with the hangers-on who followed them to pick up anything left over and sell it in the dens of the *peristas* or receivers of stolen goods.

Clever and diligent pickpockets began by working individually on their own account, but such irregularities were quickly put an end to, for no sooner did they become known to the chiefs and overseers of the gang that spread its net over all of Seville than the men guilty of them were promptly picked up and taken to the patio of Monipodio to be made subject to his orders and regulations.[7] Close to the port of Camaroneros where the fishing boats tied up was the Fortaleza; passing under the arch one entered a lane of small low houses. The penetrating smell of a common sewer which emptied into the river just there was only too perceptible. A small whitewashed house with a narrow grilled door on the ground floor and a balcony with another grille on the first floor seemed to hide itself timidly among the other houses. A little porch, a tiny brick-paved courtyard, a low hall, a gallery with balconies—this was the patio of Monipodio.

The Arenal, so often visited and long remembered by Cervantes as well as by Lope de Vega, was a school for vagrants and an academy of ruffians. In the evening it was an ant heap or rather a worm hole peopled by folk of dubious ways of life in which every kind of purely Spanish amusement could be tasted and experienced, in which there is no fulfillment or complete satisfaction if there is not mixed with it a little cruelty and a great deal of mocking at misery, pain and death.

A bridge of planks connected the Arenal with the Triana across from the port of the Camaroneros, supported by boats which served as a refuge and dormitory for the scum of all that was evil, that lawless rabble which at the same time was lurking under the bridges of Paris and pillaging around those of Constantinople. The mischievous smile that the houses of the Triana, bathed in sunlight and looking like a row of young teeth, directed at the Arenal each morning, the Arenal would return in the afternoon, embellished and augmented with grimaces from the fat face of the Torre del Oro and with enticing reflections from the Giralda. Between the two smiles a whole world circulated morning and evening, tarrying in the Resolana where as evening fell the quarrelsome nymphs of charcoal held out wretched and ill-packed bundles as they scratched at the itch and the lice when not at more terrible wounds and more biting parasites. At other times they went from the Resolana, passed the wall, entered the famous Compás, and sank into the slough of the Laguna where all the obscene waters and all the fetid passions of the great cosmopolitan city ended up. There, to seek out and exploit the poor women prostitutes, came the gallants of Seville, lusty fellows, marked by the slash of a knife or by the hand of the executioner, sporting long drooping mustachios, watchful of eye, insultingly supercilious. Among themselves they discussed tidings of robberies and fights along with their amorous adventures. The arrival of other famous valiants from Castile was awaited eagerly, one such being the memorable Campuzano, who

> marvelously skilled with sword and dagger,
> sliced noses in Castile
> and always remained whole.
> One summer he decided to go to the Indies
> and quarrelled with Montalvo from Seville;
> from the argument he came out lame in one foot
> blind in one eye and lacking one hand. . . .[8]

Today we can hardly imagine how people lived in that sink of pestilence which was called the Compás. One house remains, however, from which we can infer what the others were like. Around the Lake of tainted waters there were thirteen houses belonging to the Municipality, thirteen to the Chapter of the Cathedral, and four or six privately owned, all used as brothels. They were low buildings with hardly any facade. A narrow door with a grating opened into a long covered passage. Copying the cell system of the ancient Greek and Roman brothels, there was a long narrow yard paved with *chinos* or pebbles, on both sides of which were miserable rooms, each with a door and window. In each of them lived a woman, or rather a hot-bed of corruption, since infection was universal and inevitable, as demonstrated in 1593 when a tour of inspection gave the doctors so much work that the Municipality agreed to pay fifty thousand maravedis as a gratuity to each of them to compensate for the horrendous sights they had looked upon.

All those luckless creatures were subject to the authority of the "mother," mistress in charge of the brothel, and it would be well to note, as an indication of the spiritual condition of that society we think of as so Christian and devout, the infamous and appalling use of what is the most sacred word in all languages. "Mother Celestina"[9] were two words which together were considered synonymous, and in Seville to mention "mother" was considered the greatest insult of all.

This, then was a different world from that which Miguel had seen, although he had seen so much, but do not think that this loathsome social ferment was something apart from the circulation of other classes; very much to the contrary. The women of the brothels wandered about freely at all hours in the city and its surroundings. To prevent them from mingling with virtuous folk they were ordered to wear saffron-colored hoods held by a brooch of gilded brass . . . and very soon many women of good repute and regarded as very respectable took to wearing the saffron-colored hood and the brass brooch, as the most illustrious ladies in Paris wait until the kept women show them what is the fashion at the races of Longchamps.

The wicked lives they led did not keep these women from being true believers and very devout. When Lent arrived the "father" and the "mothers" of the brothel would take the women, dressed in dark colors and with veiled heads, in a group like a school, to confess and communicate, to take part in spiritual exercises and listen to sermons and pious discourses. Some of them repented, spent a lazy period in the convent of the Sisters of Repentance, and then returned to the company of their comrades, the prostitutes, and their friends, the pimps and panders.

Among them and in his dealings with them Miguel met Chiquiznaque and Maniferro[10] and learned of the marvelous achievements of the famous Cristóbal de Lugo, out of which he built his finest play, *The Fortunate Procurer*, one of the first if not the oldest of a long series of theatrical works whose protagonists are great criminals or libertines and hotheads who repent and retire to lead a saintly life. Even more than in *Rinconete and Cortadillo*,[12] wherein these matters are touched upon incidentally, we find in *The Fortunate Procurer* abundant traces of sciences and disciplines which Miguel, now in his forties, learned in the academy of the Lake District.

This insufficiently studied and even less appreciated play by Cervantes is the mother of all the popular poetry of Quevedo and of those who imitated him. In it we encounter the original source of the most licentious ballads in Quevedo's manner and the most successful effort to introduce in the theater the picaresque types and scenes already found in novels.

Read the first act of *The Fortunate Procurer*, an even more lively, sanguinary and vivid picture than *Rinconete and Cortadillo*, and you will find no logical explanation for the way in which Cervantes could tread in so much slime and such varied filth without being soiled. How and by what miracle Spanish genius has reached such low depths without exceeding the bounds of art can only be explained if you have seen how Nature teaches white doves to dabble in slime and dung without staining the polished rose of their beaks or their snow-white feather pantaloons. For this they were given wings.

CHAPTER 34

Miguel Applies for the Indies—Pedro de Isunza

By now Miguel was much more Andalusian than Castilian. His mind was dominated by the infinite variety of experiences he was encountering day after day and they were molding him as the wheel of the potter molds the lump of clay. This discipline was an excellent thing, so much so that it put Miguel above all the other talents of those times. The Spanish genius is very apt to coagulate into tight lumps and sticky poultices of thought, as we find in Quevedo, in Gracián, even in the gay Espinel and in Mateo Alemán, the uninhibited author of *Guzmán de Alfarache*. Meditation and thought form a crust over events and hide them from sight; rationalization absorbs and obliterates all the substance of reality, and when one seeks the real meaning of what has been written it is not to be found. But Miguel was a man of action and of the kind of swift and decisive action which stimulates and inspires. Every happening may have suggested hundreds of thoughts in him but they were overwhelmed by the necessity of making a living and the pressure of urgent commissions, so that the thoughts themselves had to be concise, fleeting and adjusted to the pace and pattern of events.

From time to time, however, Miguel remembered his wife, who remained in Esquivias in the shade of the pear trees of the orchard, taking care of the forty-five hens and the cock and the newly planted vines which her brother Francisco watched over faithfully, doing for himself like a good Christian who knows where well-regulated charity should begin.

It is a curious thing, this, which the historians have not noticed, how Cervantes spent the best part of his life separated from his wife without that excellent lady seeming to be at all perturbed. What did Doña Catalina expect of Miguel? Did she still consider him a reckless fellow accustomed to living among actors and dancers, and was it because of this that she let him wander at will in Andalusia on dubious missions? Did she think that Miguel stayed there to build a profitable career with a future? And whether she believed the one or the other is there any indication that she loved her husband?

It is true that the men of those days and of Cervantes' temperament were much stronger and tougher than we are, but did the most human of all Spanish writers escape the law of humanity which makes us at the age of forty seek a familiar shelter and warm intimacy to soothe our pains and heal the wounds in our hearts? We know very well (we follow him almost step by step, thanks to the patience and shrewdness of scholars) the places where Miguel stayed during all the years he spent in the office of commissary; we can say with complete certainty that on such and such days he got from such and such places a certain number of bushels of wheat and barley or skins of oil. We also know that the spectacle of life was always for him an inspiration, a diversion in the midst of his labors, but we must not think that with knowing all this we have found out all there is to know about Miguel's life during those years.

He was neither a simple collector of provisions and requisitioner of grain like his good friend and comrade Diego de Ruy Sáenz or his assistants Miguel de Santa María and Nicolás Benito, nor is man only a literary machine for transforming the things he sees into material for novels. What the very numerous documents we have of this period of his life do not say anything about are the anxieties and griefs that afflicted his spirit and how they were transformed by the passage of time into gentle witticisms and a broad and benign outlook on life.

The constant movement of riffraff from the Arenal to Triana and from Triana to the Arenal which might have interested our commissary as a curious fact of life soon became tiresome and offensive to his native fastidiousness. The atmosphere in the lower quarters of Seville and in the villages where he went to requisition finally became insufferable. He saw only people of low quality around him, such as his coworkers Tamayo, Santa María, and Benito, good-hearted fellows but of scanty refinement, or the rustic rabble, malicious and mistrustful, which he encountered in the villages.

The odious function of commissary weighed upon him and in the spring of 1590, on returning from Carmona where he had been turning up and distraining oil, he found out from someone in the Contract House[1] that there were three or four vacant positions in the Indies, one that of auditor in the new Kingdom of Granada, another with the galleys of Cartegena de Indias, another the governorship of the Province of Soconusco in Guatemala, and finally the office of magistrate in the city of La Paz.

Miguel wrote a brief memorial recalling his services and those of his brother Rodrigo, who at the time was an Ensign in Flanders; without exaggerating he recounted his misfortunes and humbly prayed that one of the positions mentioned be granted him. We do not believe that at such a time Miguel thought, as did Don Quixote, that he was going to conquer the Kingdom of Candaya nor become the lord of the island of Malindrania, nor yet gather the riches of Cathay; we do think though that having experienced the present and the past he regarded the Indies as "something else," for better or for worse but different from what he had already seen and tasted. The memorial was accompanied by the famous certificate of the Duke of Sessa and that of the captivity.

As Miguel had no recommendations or did not know how to use them he did not have to wait for long to see his claim turned down. His memorial addressed to the President of the Council of the Indies is dated May 21 of 1590. On June 6 of the same year the chairman, Doctor Nuñez Morquecho, wrote his short, steely, cutting phrase, which left no room for any hope: "Look for something here in which we can be of service to you."

One can see clearly how the petition was dealt with. Doctor Nuñez Morquecho quickly scanned the qualifications and services of Cervantes. In the Council of the Indies many similar memorials were received daily. Doubtless this Cervantes had been a good soldier in the naval battle, as many others had been; like many others he had been a captive in Algiers. He was backed by the defunct Don Juan, whom no one had any good reason to remember, and by the Duke of Sessa, who was always regarded as a poet, which in the parlance of the Court, in politics and in the administration was equivalent to being touched in the head. Certainly none of the fat sinecures in the Indies could be given to a man of such small importance.

In this terrible year of 1590 Miguel faced an extremely bad situation. He would not be named to undertake any new commissions until he had settled the accounts of the last one, and as everything in them had to be justified with the scrupulousness and detail as traditional in the Treasury as its own carelessness and slackness in paying its debts, Miguel had to get together all his facts and figures, add and re-add them, prove the smallest item, and provide receipts and discharges for every expense incurred. These settlements referred to the collection and bagging of wheat during the years 1587, 1588, and 1589, in Ecija and other places. The sworn deposition regarding the wheat of Ecija that Cervantes signed on August 27 of 1590 contains a charge of 43 *arrobas*[2] and 5 pounds of flour and 14,594 maravedis that Miguel could not justify. The outstanding balance and charge against him are clear and it would be childish to deny them, but by the same token it would be punitive malice to blame Miguel, who acknowledged the balance and showed himself willing to pay it but declared at the same time that 112,608 maravedis of salary were due him for 276 days at the rate of 12 reals per day.

The extraordinary and surprising thing is that the balance was not much higher. Do the account over and it will be seen that Cervantes lived on those maravedis and that flour for nine months in a hostile city where he had gone to extract the last ounce of fat from the poor peasant. What did he eat during this period? Where did he find shelter? How did he clothe himself? It seems logical that he owed his very existence to the kindness of those four quixotic friends of his in Ecija who went bond for him.

The summer and autumn of 1590 went by without Cervantes doing anything to more purpose than presenting the auditor's office of the Exchequer from time to time with the receipts and justifications for his accounts. On November 8 unusually cold weather descended on Seville and Miguel found himself so ill-clothed that he was obliged to have recourse to his friend Tomás Gutiérrez, the former actor turned innkeeper, to stand surety for him with the merchants Miguel de Caviedes & Co., who had sold him five and a half yards of coarse mixed cloth at twenty reals the yard.

This might mean many things, but among them the principal ones were that Miguel had no credit in Seville unless a man like Tomás Gutiérrez vouched for him, that he did not have ten ducats nor was there any hope of his having them for some time, and that he dressed in a very humble kind of cloth, something on the order of what today we call serge, cheviot or any other nickname by which clothiers misrepresent coarse material.

It is probable that at the same time Miguel lived with Tomás Gutiérrez, since both called themselves residents of the parish of Santa María. Sevillian hospitality was so generous that the wine merchant or innkeeper did not usually refuse lodging in his house to some unfortunate writer or artist, and even today this happens. One can live on little and the favor is not great, but it should at any rate be acknowledged. Perhaps Miguel took advantage of the good Tomás Gutiérrez' hospitality during the whole of 1590 and the first few months of 1591, since during that period he was not entrusted with further commissions; he may have been somewhat discredited by the outstanding balance from Ecija.

The spring of 1591 brought him hope. In April of that year Pedro de Isunza, the shrewd merchant whom Miguel had met before in Madrid, was named Purveyor General to the Spanish galleys. As a man who had been taught in the school of the greatest merchants of Antwerp, Isunza was not one to quibble over minor matters and he paid no heed whatever to that outstanding balance. From the start he named four commissaries, "honest men and entirely trustworthy," as he wrote to the King on January 7 of 1592; they were Gaspar de Salamanca Maldonado, Bartolomé de Arredondo, Diego de Ruy Sáenz and Miguel de Cervantes.

Pedro de Isunza, a man of the world and an administrator, was a very different person from the elderly Don Antonio de Guevara. He paid his commissaries punctually and defended them from the ill will they encountered in the villages in the exercise of their unpopular mission, which at times reached the Court in the form of protests and complaints. Miguel felt that his lot was greatly improved when he began to work under Pedro de Isunza.

He now returned to the days of wearisome forays in the course of which he scoured all the most notable Andalusian towns and cities. It was then that the body of his speech acquired the infinite number of idioms from Andalusia and not just from Seville which can be observed in the *Exemplary Novels*, in the *Quixote* and in the *Persiles*, although they are fewer in the last of these. It was then, also, that he heard and came to know the Andalusian love stories that he interpolates in all his works.

As he moved about by roads, paths and narrow lanes Miguel arrived at the devout town of Úbeda, famous for the hills where the imagination of all Spaniards takes refuge,[3] and the whole village recounted in consternation how on the fourteenth day of December of 1591 the "flame of living love" had been extinguished there and the soul of the Carmelite seraph John of the Cross had plunged forever into the "dark night."[4]

It was said that the holy dead body of the divine poet gave out a most sweet fragrance which had penetrated all Úbeda, and Cervantes saw the exalted imaginations of these good people expanding and losing themselves in the legendary hills in pursuit of the Knight of the Cross bent on the conquest of the spiritual and occult Kingdom of God.

Such adventures were not so very different from those of knights-errant that they failed to impress themselves forcibly on Miguel's imagination. The not-yet-created Sancho told how the blessed John of the Cross had died of pestilential fevers and how his body emitted a fetid odor like that of all victims of typhus, but Don Quixote took flight and declared loudly that it was not the stench of a corpse but a most sweet aroma and Arabian perfume, a fresh and delicious exhalation of roses and apples.

Farther along the road Miguel passed by Montilla, and since his conversation inspired that of others they spoke to him of the craft of the two famous witches called La Camacha and La Cañizares. They told of La Camacha how she had changed Don Alonso de Aguilar, son of the Marquis of Priego, into a horse, and how the Inquisition of Cordova held the lad prisoner for having allowed himself to be subjected to such an incredible metamorphosis.

La Camacha may have been dead by then but Miguel did not fail to see La Cañizares, to talk to her and to witness her sorcery and her incantations, in which at that time all Spain believed, even the most intelligent and cultured people, with the complete approval of the Inquisition, which could not have survived without similar raree-shows.

In the low, narrow and dark room of the witch, lit only by the feeble light of a clay lamp, Miguel saw that figure, "just a bony skeleton covered by dark, hairy and weatherbeaten skin. Her parchment-like belly covered her lewd parts and hung down to the middle of her thighs. Her drooping breasts were like two cow bladders, dry and wrinkled, her lips were blackened, her teeth few, her nose hooked and bony, her eyes bulging, her hair dishevelled, her cheeks sunken, her throat shrivelled. . . ." Next to this disagreeable vision Cervantes saw a black dog jumping and twisting in devilish contortions, posessed of human speech and spirit, or perhaps the Devil's. This fantastic dog, which appears with the witch in the *Dialogue of Scipio and Berganza,* we will not encounter again until we climb to another summit of art, the laboratory of Doctor Faust.

CHAPTER 35

Opposition to Purveyors—Miguel in Prison—Isunza Dies

PEDRO ISUNZA, as has already been said, was a man of clear mind and extraordinary common sense, just the opposite of what the men were like to whom the affairs of the Treasury and Public Administration were usually entrusted in those days. He was the first Spanish free trader and was very much in favor of coordinating the principal aspects of commercial activity, which were then disorganized, dispersed and full of uncertainties, and he proposed that three fairs, each of a month's duration, be held in Valladolid or Medina del Campo. He also advocated creating banks in Seville, Lisbon, Zaragoza, Valencia and Barcelona, strengthening and diversifying their operations and fixing a legal discount or interest rate for bank drafts and money orders to be approved morally by His Holiness.

It is easy to understand the difference between this shrewd and able man, indoctrinated in the methods of a great mercantile metropolis, and the preposterous little people appointed by the King to posts in the Treasury on the basis of recommendations or family influence. Pedro de Isunza presented his accounts on time and obtained that they be properly approved, and since punctuality was the rule in his official dealings he was not greatly loved by the tale-bearing officials of the Accountant's Office and the Treasury Council, so given to procrastination and fault-finding, and fearing complaints and disputes more than anything.

These differences became even greater when Pedro de Isunza, discharging his function as Purveyor and very zealous in carrying out his duties, attempted to carry things off rather high-handedly, as he had been accustomed to do in Barcelona. And since he was making payments promptly and meeting his responsibilities fully his commissaries also became exigent, confident that such a strong man would protect them in case of difficulty. Inevitably the diligence of Isunza and his commissaries earned them nothing but hatred and recriminations from the villages. These were supported by the royal officials and accountants, among whom Isunza must in any case have enemies for the very reason that he was not, like them, a man with pen in ear and hatchet tongue, and they were subscribed to by ecclesiastical folk and members of religious chapters with interests damaged by the requisitionings of wheat. The cassock-wearers no doubt intrigued busily in the Court, whereupon the King ordered the Corregidor[1] of Ecija to visit the villages and hear all complaints against the royal commissaries that the people wished to lodge, also ordering that no wheat be taken without payment for it.

With this order the authority of the commissaries and the respect in which they were held were practically nullified. Miguel de Cervantes and Diego de Ruy Sáenz, whose duty it was to collect and ship wheat from the bishoprics of Jaén and Guadix to provision the Navy in the Straits of Gibraltar, wrote to Pedro de Isunza declaring that it was useless for them to present themselves in the villages with the tall staff of justice and the authority it represented if the villagers knew that as soon as they left, or even before, they would be followed by an inspector of commissaries who cast a protective shadow over the granaries and tithe barns, and with all the prerogatives and solemnities of ordinary justice undid everything the commissaries had done, halting the requisitions and embargos, grindings and shipments. If Don Francisco Moscoso, the Corregidor, was a native of Ecija it is not surprising that he understood the dispensing of justice in the same light as did the Tempranillo José María,[2]

> he who robbed the rich
> and gave succor to the poor

and achieved an easy popularity among the people of the villages for having righted wrongs and satisfied grievances.

As a frank and sincere Basque who scorned subtleties and complexities, Pedro de Isunza complained to the King on February 22 of 1592 without appreciating the kind of temporizing and blowing hot and cold with which Philip II inaugurated the politics of connivance and petty compromise and the system of deceitful procrastination still with us. The clerks of government offices, the business agents, the office worms and shufflers of paper that the villages and chapters maintained in Madrid constantly exerted their influence to harass the Purveyor and his commissaries, threatening them, demanding accounts and settlements, accumulating charges, overwhelming them with questions. In particular there were two accountants called Pedro Ruiz de Otálora and Francisco Vázquez de Obregón who would have been capable of asking the All Highest for a detailed justification of the expenses incurred in organizing Paradise. Thus Miguel, like the other commissaries, persecuted by the hatred of the villages, tormented by continual demands that accounts be submitted, constantly threatened by the black shadow of the inspector of commissaries, who would call him to account for every step he took in each village, dragged out a most harassed existence through the districts of Jaén, Granada, and Málaga, the disagreeable character of which no one can form an exact idea who has not had to appear before present-day representatives of the Treasury, the employees of which with very rare exceptions are legitimate descendents of those government clerks.

In August of 1592 Miguel was in Seville to answer the charges which had been filed. The famous actor from Toledo, Rodrigo de Osorio, was there with his company; they may have stayed at the inn of Tomás Gutiérrez, the retired actor. When Miguel found himself in the company of actors all his past glories returned to the mind of the bored and weary commissary of provisions as he chatted with Rodrigo Osorio about the progress the theater was making in all parts of the Realm and about how from one day to the next new playhouses were being opened and the love of them was increasing, even in the villages where there had never been anything more than a morality play for the Feast of the Corpus put on impromptu or by strolling players.

Osorio recalled, or Tomás Gutiérrez may have told him, that Cervantes in the not too distant past had been one of the famous authors whose works had been staged in Madrid and other theaters and that they had run their course without whistles, yells and tumult and without receiving the accolade of cucumbers or other throwable objects. Mentioning plays to Cervantes was like encouraging Don Quixote to become absorbed in the subject of his knight-errantries.

This was a moment of doubt and wavering for him. He wondered once more whether he had been mistaken and whether perchance he could not find his salvation in playwriting as a relief from the wretched trials in which he was involved. Rodrigo Osorio offered to stage half a dozen plays if Miguel would write them and on September 5 Miguel and Osorio signed a contract before the notary public Luis de Porras by which Cervantes obligated himself to write six plays with plots and titles of his own choosing, as soon as possible beginning on that day, and to deliver them to Osorio one by one, written in a clear hand. For his part Osorio undertook to stage each of these twenty days after receiving it and to pay 50 ducats "which are" 550 reals for each. There was only one restriction on Miguel, namely that he would receive nothing if the play did not seem to be one of the best that had ever been performed in Spain.

We do not know that Miguel wrote the plays he promised Osorio, but it does not seem probable, for he had no time for it. Financially attractive as the agreement was, Cervantes did not have the prodigious facility of Lope for producing a play "in twenty-four hours from the Muses to the theater," and it is almost certain that he could not write six dramatic works in forty days or so, even if they qualified for the fifty ducats each, without making too great demands on his imagination and compromising his reputation as a commissary still in the service of Pedro de Isunza. Plays, even if their success had been assured, were chancy things and short-lived; not even Lope himself could live by writing them. If Miguel could have achieved a secretaryship or entry into the service of some grandee, like those who protected Lope, he would not have been one of Isunza's commissaries, but he was now too experienced to abandon a certainty for something dubious. Thus the problem presented itself to him in those dismally prosaic terms.

Having reached this conclusion he returned forthwith to his commissions after a brief interval when he may have thought of writing plays one day. No sooner was he back a few days after signing the contract with Osorio when the black shadow of the Corregidor of Ecija, Don Francisco Moscoso, caught up with him in Castro del Rio and slapped a prison sentence on him. In those days it cost very little trouble to have a man put in prison and even less to see to it that he did not get out for a very long time. With Miguel in prison Moscoso charged him with having seized illegally three hundred bushels of wheat held by the custodian of the public granary of Ecija and with having sold them without permission. He was told that he must return the wheat and deposit it again in the public granary of Ecija or pay its value at the rate of fourteen reals per bushel, and a fine of six thousand maravedis was imposed on him as war tax and to cover the costs of the lawsuit.

Miguel's prison term must have been very short, however, and not too rigorous. In that village where the current popular saying was "Where there are no oranges what is there to eat?" nothing too extreme can happen and even less so in the month of September. At the same time Miguel could count on the protection of Isunza and on his own charm and ingenuity. He soon found sureties, came out of the prison and continued his travels. It does not seem reasonable to think that Cervantes could be greatly alarmed or aggrieved over his imprisonment in such a pleasant city as Castro del Rio, although it is true that to find himself persecuted by the law and thrown into jail was the only thing lacking for one who had known the galley and the barracks, the hospital and captivity.

A much worse affair than this was the Teba case. A certain citizen of Teba named Salvador de Toto Guzmán, chief collector of the royal tithes, brought to justice Nicolás Benito, assistant to Miguel de Cervantes, because he had appeared in Teba and the authorities having opposed him he went to the tithe barn, forced the doors and removed 1137½ bushels of wheat and 58½ of barley which, according to Salvador de Toto, belonged to the tithes. On these grounds a lawsuit was filed in Madrid with charges directed, not against Cervantes nor against Nicolás Benito, who was simply a servant, but against Pedro Isunza in an attempt to entangle him in a discreditable affair and deprive him of his Purveyorship. The plot against Isunza had prospered thanks to the intrigues of the Court, and His Majesty's Attorney General was now asking the Purveyor to pay out of his own pocket the value of the wheat taken illegally in Teba. There were so many documents with which the Treasury tribunal overwhelmed Isunza and Cervantes that, finally exasperated, the good man from Vitoria decided to go to Madrid to untangle the wicked plot contrived by his enemies, and to do so better he took Cervantes with him.

Isunza and Miguel were at the capital around the middle of November, and on December 1 Miguel requested His Majesty to surrogate to himself all the charges brought against Isunza for the business in Teba. This quixotic document proves that the flame of generosity continued to burn in Cervantes' heart when he was forty-five years old, just as it had when in Algiers he faced up to Hassan Pasha and risked his life to save the other captives.

Those who admire a noble gesture can learn much from this humble legal petition in which Cervantes, as great and resolute as Don Quixote himself, writes in superb language, addressing Philip II and his haughty magistrates:

> I have taken on myself the responsibility of accounting for everything in addition to what is charged to me and it is not just that such charges be laid against the said Purveyor or against me nor that the said Purveyor be unjustly molested. And that this truth be understood I offer to come and render an accounting at this Court or wherever it would please Your Majesty and to give adequate legal sureties besides those I have given to the said Purveyor. . . . and may it please Your Majesty that upon my giving the said sureties and the accounting which I offer neither the said Purveyor nor his goods be molested, for he owes nothing, and I beg that justice be done.

And judging that even this was not enough, after his signature he adds:

> Moreover, I implore Your Majesty to order the judge to discontinue the action until the truth of this business is known for it is not just that the simple unsupported petition of an informer be believed, espe-

cially when it is against such a faithful servant of His Majesty as the said Purveyor Pedro de Isunza.

Let us note this well as assurance that Cervantes' spirit showed no sign of being crushed by the daily frustrations of his position. Like Don Quixote, he was convinced that justice will triumph in the end and because of this he can speak in such a serene and confident tone. He stands far above the petty intrigues and trickeries of ink-stained clerks; it is not for nothing that he has reached forty-five years of age, during which he has risked his skin and been ready to pay with his life. The state of mind of Miguel on this visit to Madrid is not that of a beaten and disillusioned man, as some people claim who would like to present him as a precocious romantic. No. Miguel is a civil servant who defends his rights and who risks himself and his goods for Isunza, his friend.

There is no sign whatever that in this brief period Miguel did any literary work or renewed his former friendships with the poets of the Court. The moment of indecision he had experienced in Seville which made him engage himself in the matter of plays for Rodrigo Osorio has passed. On the other hand Pedro de Isunza is grateful and is not going to change helpers suddenly when he has such a good and reliable one. Nor is Miguel's own character changeable like that of Lope, in whom we can recognize a bit of the lad of many masters that existed then in every clever Spaniard.

The prudent and honest Pedro de Isunza had seen at Court how his enemies had worked and would continue to work against him, and upon coming up against so much injustice and paltriness his bodily humors rose in revolt and he fell into a profound melancholy followed by fever. He became seriously ill in Madrid and his friend Don Esteban de Garibay says at the beginning of the year 1593 that "they thought he would die." In May he was a little better and moved to Puerto de Santa María hoping to recuperate in the good climate, the sea air and the care and comfort of his home and family. Unfortunately it was not to be. On June 24, after a very short illness, Pedro de Isunza died in the arms of his wife.

Once more Cervantes found himself in the street like a dog without a master. Now he could hope to depend only on his own ingenuity.

CHAPTER 36

The Three Courtyards of Seville—Celebration of the Corpus—Death of Miguel's Mother

THE courtyard of Los Olmos [The Elms] near the Cathedral was one of those convivial places where all kinds of people gather and where gentlemen mingle with thieves and solid citizens with inveterate gamblers. It was a closed precinct, but with a wide entrance and a gate open at all hours of the day and left ajar at night. It had always been a meeting place for the famous winetasters of Andalusia, who, with their eyes closed, could tell by its aroma the difference between the must from Alanía and that from Guadalcanal. It was also the haunt of gamblers with cards or dice, grave robbers and looters, as well as of the swaggering brawlers who killed for hire and sliced noses without any special skills other than those of the common and ordinary art of sword fighting, as it was called contemptuously by writers who were beginning to theorize on the use of the foil. And finally it was a place for rogues, pimps, homosexuals, and a rabble described by such names and many others, familiar and unfamiliar, by Juan Hidalgo, the lexicographer of thieves' jargon.

In those days there were three courtyards where the best and the worst of Seville could meet. One was the courtyard of Los Olmos. Another was the courtyard of Los Naranjos [The Oranges], the only one which still exists and is nothing more than a patio of the Cathedral, entered by the Arabic doorway of El Perdón in which the pulpit can still be seen which many preachers and teachers mounted to lecture a society even more corrupt than it is now. Another was the courtyard of Don Juan, where plays were staged, which had recently become fashionable.

No one could be a true Sevillian if he did not frequently visit the three courtyards: that of Don Juan to predispose him toward sin by the example of plays with seductive ladies and insinuating gallants, that of Los Olmos where he could sin in every way without let or hindrance, and that of Los Naranjos in which to repent of his sins and prepare for absolution. In a hand's breadth of ground, as the saying goes, the Sevillians had the solution to all of life's principal problems, for undertaking to lose one's soul and for rehabilitating and cleansing it afterward.

Miguel wandered idly from one to another of these courtyards while he waited for the new Purveyor to the Galleys, Miguel de Oviedo, to give him some commissions. Since 1592, when the benches of the Steps had been demolished, many of the peddlers, singers, chess players and card players who formerly clotted around the Cathedral had taken refuge in the courtyard of Los Olmos or against its walls. In his periods of idleness Miguel to a certain extent lived the life of these people, for whom there were no fixed hours, no sure food, no untroubled sleep.

Seated on a bench or leaning against a wall, he let his mind wander in the warm and scented atmosphere of spring in Seville. Examining his life in those relaxed moments, the most fertile for the artist who catches in them a glimpse of the vague outlines of his creations, there started to take form in Miguel's mind, in a mysterious and arcane way, at times in grave and deliberate progression, at others in wild flights of the imagination, the visionary fantastic figures that were to acquire immortal life under his pen. Bloody and dissolute reality confronted him in the courtyard of Los Olmos, roaring out oaths by all the saints and mouthing vainglorious boasts, whereas he was penetrating the deep human truth that belongs to all times in contemplating his agitated life and recalling his dead illusions and fading delusions.

As a matter of fact the courtyards of Los Naranjos and Don Juan competed with falsehoods and lies against that of Los Olmos with its sword thrusts of cut-throats, flourishes of gamblers, drunkenness of wine-bibbers, and caresses of the whores of the Compás. Truth resided within man, according to Holy Writ, and must be sought there, and on thinking thus Miguel remembered the miraculous fragrance that the villagers of Úbeda had scented in the putrefied corpse of St. John of the Cross. The outward semblance was illusion, and many people had no other. The inner life began by working on souls, not to produce tangible results but to put an end to action, to annihilate "the other," the material, the "little ass" of the Saint. What, then, was life?

The reflections accumulated by Miguel in his interminable and hateful days in Ecija, while the powder of the sifter flew like golden dust sifted in turn by the sun, were followed by his thoughts as an idler in the courtyard of Los Olmos amid the noise and turbulence of the Sevillian rabble. At times in the limpid sky, at times in a dark corner of the tavern under the shade of the top-heavy elm trees with their foliage fouled by the dust of the dance floor and with nails artfully driven into their trunks to hang cloaks and caps upon, as miserable as hat-trees in a restaurant, Miguel saw delineated, as yet no more than a diaphanous shadow emerging from his own life, the figure of the vagabond knight who thought to reconquer the dead Golden Age, to revive the happy centuries when illusions could be realized, like the canon who boasted of the facade of a cathedral which had been over-ornamented in stone and appeared to uphold the vault of Heaven: "Let us build a church such that future centuries will believe we were mad."[1]

In Ecija, in Úbeda, and in Montilla, Miguel had learned that the former lunacies of the age of chivalry were already being replaced by the knight-errantries of mysticism and asceticism. Here and there in the villages of his miserable commissions he had learned, like the miraculous spider feeding itself on the blood of ardent hearts, to spin his web of tenuous threads throughout all Spain. In the same way the emaciated Knights of the Cross and the mortified Ladies of Divine Love wandered through inner castles and in ineffable ecstasies scoured the seven heavens of their mansions, burying themselves in them and losing sight of the world. In those convents of monks and friars pulses fluttered and hearts pounded upon recounting the latest deeds of the Knight of Loyola and his swift squadrons, or the merciless triumphs of the Man of Almodóvar del Campo and his battles against the giant Caraculiambro, which before was called human love, and finally the wanderings of the heroic Woman of Avila.[2]

Cervantes also knew very well what could be done simply by observing closely all that he saw around him in the three courtyards: Cristóbal de Lugo and Pedro de Urdemalas, Monipodio and his confraternity had nothing new to tell him. They were brothers of Lazarillo and Guzmán de Alfarache, and they behaved and talked like them. But that was not much; it was only the outer skin of life, and one had to dig below the surface and squeeze hard to get its bittersweet juice.

One day he was awakened from these imaginings by the appearance in the courtyard of Los Olmos of two friendly figures who stretched their arms out eagerly toward him. They were the ex-bricklayer and famed actor Jerónimo Velázquez and his comrade and crony Rodrigo de Saavedra, who had come to Seville for the celebration of Corpus Christi. In the coolness of Los Olmos, tankard at the ready, the three old friends communed together sitting around a table. Miguel's heart was refreshed by talking with these wanderers who had crossed all Spain dispensing gaiety.

They had great news to tell and great insults to hurl, especially against Lope de Vega. The scandals of Lope and Elena Osorio, the lampoons he composed against Elena and Ana Velázquez and against their neighbor Juana de Ribera and the macaronic satire he wrote against Doctor Velázquez de Contreras had forced Jerónimo to complain about Lope, who was condemned to banishment, at first from the Kingdom of Castile and later from the Court. Cervantes knew all this, having heard of it on his last trip to Madrid, but perhaps he had not heard until then the many malignant things to say about Lope that occurred to these bitter enemies of his.

Certainly—Miguel thought—it was not worthwhile to be called a great poet and to be applauded and praised in all Spain if the word of an actor, a onetime conniver at lechery, could condemn a man to exile. In this respect the commissions were not so bad, for one was at least in the service of the King and could hope for some advancement.

Cervantes compared his own situation and even that of Lope, at that time a servant in the house of Alba, with the position of Jerónimo Velázquez, a wealthy property owner with influence at Court when he needed it, even to the point of indicting Lope and having him exiled, and of obtaining rich appointments in the Indies for his son, Doctor Velázquez, of whom it was not known that he had ever rendered any service, and he saw falseness grow and spread, taking possession of all Spain with the huge farce of a hypocritical and corrupt way of life in which everything was governed by intrigues and recommendations, wiles and deceit, favors achieved by petticoat influence and advantages gained with wigs and paint.

In order to develop the business of the triumphant histrionic art even further the companies of actors, in which women had not figured in the past and up to 1587, female roles being taken by beardless lads, now carried with them their henhouses of actresses, the wives or semiwives of the actors, as Quevedo said, there generally being two for each man.

With the added attraction of petticoats, love of the theater grew enormously in the villages. In many places, then as now, it was the vehicle for *autos*[3] or comedies which brought "fleeting happiness," a moment that never returns, or returns too late when the flowers it made to bloom in the hearts where it had been born have already wilted.

Let us try to imagine what it must have been out there, say in the hills of Úbeda in the days when men and women were bathed in a mystic perfume, guarding the secret of their great pious fiction, to see the wagon of the actors appear, to witness the shameless clowning of the members of the company, the impudence, the picaresque dances, the inciting movements and licentious songs of the comic actress who always had to be a dancer. What must it not have meant to hear the silence broken and made pregnant with tempting suggestions, the clicking of the castanets and dances on which to feast the eye, the clothes of shining materials, the dazzling finery of jet and spangles, and then to see that unholy crew recite with most reverent intonation the metaphysical arguments already heard from the pulpit or read in spiritual epistles and devout books, but which from the lips of the actors tended to have a deeply disturbing, amorous and worldly tone. Mari Flores or Ana Ruiz, playing the parts of Guilt or Lust in the most devout *autos* of the Corpus and managing to appear gallantly decked out, as Guilt and Lust usually do present themselves—what ravages would they not make in young hearts and what a trail of disappointed passions would they not leave behind on departing from each village? Thus the hypocrisy emanating from the highest sources soon penetrated the whole social fabric and was beginning to dominate religious life.

Jerónimo Velázquez had already been in Seville to present the *autos* of the Corpus in 1582, but at that time he did not have women with him. When he came in 1593 the Sevillians of the three courtyards licked their lips with pleasure at the thought of how delightfully they were going to be entertained and how they could celebrate equally their devotion and the marvelous efficacy of the Most Holy Sacrament, a beautiful metaphysical belief upon which Spanish talents have based the greatest displays of their religious processions. Velázquez presented himself before the Chapter and after some discussion he offered four *autos* he had already tried out. They rehearsed some of the scenes before the canons and aldermen and Miguel saw how the profession of actor had risen from its former low estate and how machinery and stagecraft had reached a level of unanticipated perfection.

The Corpus of 1593 was long remembered in Seville. Besides the floats which carried the *autos* and religious images, with an award for the best-liked work, prizes were given for the most splendidly dressed confraternity and for the arches raised where the procession was to pass, whose merit consisted less in their artistic or architectural aspect than in the ingenuity and complication of their allegorical figures and in the couplets and verses on posters and placards written in Latin and Castilian.

There were also prizes for the dances which followed the Most Holy Sacrament in an extremely long procession of puppets, acrobats, Negroes, Moors and every kind of wild and noisy folk, the top prize going to the *Triumph of Seville*, a dance in which Moors and Christians necessarily figured and the saintly King Fernando III appeared. There was a dance to accompany the *tarasca* with the *Anabolena* mounted on the float, and on another float a tumbler did death leaps celebrating the triumph of the Sacrament, like the juggler before the Virgin (for there is nothing new in this world).

The crowning height of frenetic shouts and unbridled demonstration of joy was the scandalous, insolent, vibrant, lubricious, and cynical *saraband*, that dance which, from the moment when it first appeared until the days when it was danced in the salons of the Sun King of France, sent a spasm of incandescent voluptuousness, first through the whole of Spain and later through all France. When the moralists and lawgivers rushed to provide a remedy it was already too late.

Whoever did not believe in the existence of the Devil or had not heard of him would have been forced to invent Satan and to recognize him as the author of that arch-lecherous *saraband* presented in the Corpus of 1593 in Seville. What the gentlemen of the Chapter did not see during the rehearsals—or if they did, said nothing—could not fail to be noticed by anyone as discerning as Cervantes. The appearance of the *saraband* with its whirls, leaps and clapping hands was a sign of decadence. The heroic Don Juan and the wise Don Álvaro, stereotypes of Achilles and Ulysses, had already died, and well dead and buried were they. Spanish courage at sea had been sunk with the Invincible Armada and what was left of it on land was being worn down in Flanders. In the heart of the country the response to these disasters had been mystical ecstasies, ascetic extravagances and theatrical fictions. In the Escorial the hard gray monarch, grayer and harder than the stone itself, rotted under the shadow of its square blocks, condemned to a life of pain.

Miguel knew then that a conquered people had finally tasted the fruit of despair and the visions flitting through his mind began to take the form of beaten hidalgos with shattered ideals, of enchanted princesses changed into coarse peasant women. The first appearance of the *saraband* had routed the knights of the ideal.

When the *fiestas* of the Corpus were over and the temporary gaiety dissipated, Miguel returned to following the road, which by now had little or almost nothing to teach him, commissioned by Miguel de Oviedo as he had been in the past by Guevara and Isunza. During the last months of 1593 and the first of 1594 he covered the country for twelve leagues around Seville, collecting supplies of oil and wheat for a Navy in the existence and usefulness of which no one now believed. And around this time he may have known and frequented the ultimate of roguery, the tuna fisheries of Zahara.[4] It is certain that in all the villages he heard the Duke of Medina badly spoken of, and he may have made a note in his memory or among his papers of the facetious scoffing nicknames that the knavery of Medina-Sidonia, Zahara, Los Puertos, and Cádiz gave to the most important people of the country. Genuinely gypsy are the names of Don Timonel of Carcajona, of Pentapolin, he of the bare right arm, of the powerful Duke of Nervia, of Alifanfarón from Trapobarna and the baronies of Utrique.[5]

While Miguel was pursuing his roving life as a commissary in the first days of November of 1593, Doña Leonor de Cortinas died in Madrid, where she lived in the Calle de Leganitos with her daughter Doña Magdalena in the house of Pedro de Medina, a leather-dresser.

We know nothing of the pain which the sad news must have caused Miguel. We do know of the tender solicitude, the industrious constancy with which Doña Leonor achieved the ransoming of her captive sons; we can infer the gentleness and benevolence of her loving spirit and the tenderness she always bore her children. In her we can also distinguish the great qualities of the determined and vigorous women who were then more numerous than they are today, those Spanish mothers who never break out into the kind of shrieks which this or that actress might translate into theatrical language, those mothers who gallantly follow with dry eyes the son who departs to a cruel war or an uncertain future and who do not permit the tears to flow until they are alone where their sorrow will not distress others.

Nevertheless it is difficult to project an image of her. In Miguel's works this holy image of the mother does not appear and it must be so and must be expected from a writer who is sensitive enough to understand how the great, the superlative test of our best writers and poets is exactly what they are reproached with and censured for by some who regard it as a demerit. It is commonly said that in Spanish literature "there are few mothers." Let us be proud of it because our great poets have been, at the proper time, men of such refinement that all had tacitly understood that mothers have nothing to do with literature, which, however noble and lofty it may be, cannot but profane the deepest and purest of human sentiments. The silence of Miguel, like the silence of Lope in similar circumstances, is not only a sign of delicacy but also of strength, and what delicacy is worth anything without strength?

When Lope's father dies he writes one of his best sonnets. His mother dies and he is silent, he who could never be silent about even the smallest afflictions. In Lope's theater we find some fathers and magnificent, venerable and stately grandfathers, like Tello de Meneses; there are few mothers and they do not fit into the spirit of the author or the quality of his other characters. The mother of Miguel died. Miguel was silent. His silence on such an occasion is one of his best works and the most Spanish in style.

CHAPTER 37

St. Martin's Summer for Miguel—Anxious Times—Granada

WE cannot assume that Cervantes now felt himself completely cut off from his home and family ties like so many men of the highways and byways who were criss-crossing the nation in those days. Outwardly toughened and hardened by his forty-seven years of ceaseless travel, his heart was certainly still tender and sensitive despite the blows it had suffered. He did not have a stone upon which to lay his head, but it was difficult for him to believe that as an individual he was no longer of interest to anyone.

Let us not deceive ourselves into thinking romantically that Miguel's cheerfulness saved him from such apprehensions. A soul like his cannot live in a state of perpetual conviviality; a spirit like his cannot be satisfied forever with the attractions of the picturesque as perceived in vagabondage by those who have never been vagabonds or have been so for only a few days, just for fun and not out of necessity.

One is forced to conclude that for this man the restlessness of the life he led finally tired him out. While he went from village to village and from inn to inn, harassed and pushed around, on assignments and commissions which he disliked, as anyone would, his faithful Doña Catalina de Salazar led a soft life in the big house in Esquivias, communing with her brother the administrative clergyman about the looks of the fallow or the sample of olives, dropping off to sleep in her chair, losing some stitches of the stocking she had started or abandoning her sewing basket for the cat to play with.

The problem of earning a living still presented itself before Miguel's weary eyes and there were no suitable new ways of solving it. He must continue without any hope of relief the wanderings in which he already knew or could imagine everything that might happen, or bury himself in Esquivias and vegetate, if his wife and brother-in-law permitted.

Saddened and downcast, Miguel once more traversed the beaten track from Seville to Madrid and stopped off at Esquivias in the spring of 1594. Do you think that his wife received him with open arms? On the contrary. These gentlewomen of small villages are what the priest orders them to be when he reads the Mass to them: sealed coffers. There are some who accept the idea that there is nothing inside, along with those who are not accustomed to opening many coffers and to appraising the tarnished remnants, the worn ribbons, the yellowing papers that are usually kept in them.

While Miguel has acquired the virile beauty of a mature man, Doña Catalina had preserved the beauty which is guarded and stored up, that rare and wonderful delicacy of the small pictures painted on wood kept in the chapels and sacristies of cathedrals covered with a little curtain once purple and now violet fading to gray. The features have dried up a little, possibly the bony structure begins to draw slightly angular lines on the jaw, the chin, the bridge of the nose. The cheeks are a shade thinner, the hair a bit faded, but in compensation, amid all this which spiritualizes and sanctifies the face, the eyes are still young. In them is life, stored-up love, and anyone who knows how to awaken it will find out whether the sealed coffer is empty and will discover the hidden perfumes, which are the most delicate, and will finger the withered silks, which are the most alluring to the touch.

It was a pleasure like this for Cervantes to enjoy interrupted love, stir the deep waters, taste the first dryness of his Doña Catalina, the handsome childless lady who by now had become accustomed to the idea and the fact of a premature widowhood, and who may have spent long hours, days and months free of any obsession with love or with the memory of her husband. Doña Catalina was then twenty-nine years old, and you who are expert in such matters consider what twenty-nine years old means in enjoyment for a robust and healthy man of forty-seven. It is possible that at this time Miguel had the most deeply happy moments of his life.

They did not last long. The Ingenious Hidalgo knew all too well that the sweet pleasures of repose were not for him. He understood perfectly that even though the gold of his hair and beard were untouched, youth was leaving him from one moment to the next. He was beginning to experience the shiver produced by a young soul within a body that is beginning to age. A wise man, he savored the pungent scent of the quince locked away in the coffer; a prudent man, he got ready to confront the approaching autumn. But the hour of rest had not yet been sounded. It was still necessary to earn it, and consequently Miguel moved to the capital.

He found his sister Magdalena there, her former beauty faded and dulled, her aquiline visage concealed by the black veil which was to frame it from then on. Her tender heart was now very inclined to melt and stream from her eyes in a rain of tears. As always he found his sister Andrea determined and spirited, and again as always ready to start a lawsuit with the morning star if it approached herself or her daughter to seek their favors.

By then Doña Andrea was widowed for the second time and in her we can see a glorious forerunner of the illustrious and memorable generation of attractive and clever widows who have spun the greater part of our social history and woven their threads into the woof of political life. Doña Andrea was doubtless a lady who was good to look at, fresh and seductive. The proof of this is that later, as the widow of her second husband, the Florentine Santes Ambrosi, she was married to General Alvaro Mendaño, of whom we know nothing. She was one of those women who in their fifties look like the sisters of their daughters and are loved by generals with white goatees whose spirits are still a bit like that of Don Juan. Doña Andrea and her daughter must have circulated rather freely in Madrid with gracious assurance. They were both free to marry and had no need to fend off the suitors who appeared.

One of these was the noble Aragonese gentleman Don Pedro de Lanuza y de Perellós, a Knight of Santiago who had come to Madrid to lift the confiscation of his family properties three years before through the cruelty and ill-considered behavior of Philip II. Walking the streets or visiting the steps and porches of churches he had come upon the Cervantes women and made love to Doña Constanza. He had thought this an amusing game when he was penniless and with his possessions in pawn, but when he saw that the King was in a mood to make up for past injuries and grant him a commandery in his Order he thought it prudent to disengage himself. When Miguel arrived in Madrid things were going very badly between the lovers and the Cervantes women did not hesitate to demand from Don Pedro the usual indemnification in such cases, at first in an amiable and friendly way and later through a lawsuit.

It must have weighed heavily on Miguel to see his clever sister once more mixed up in a lawsuit of the same nature as in the past. He and the members of his family were developing the painful tenseness that papers bearing official stamps leave in all houses which they visit frequently. It is an unhappy state of affairs to be condemned to living always in the company of legal papers; even more unhappy was the sight of how almost every house in the capital was entangled in intrigues similar to those of Doña Constanza and Don Pedro de Lanuza, promises of marriage, commitments and lawsuits, secret and hidden frauds and plots, all boiling in the pot of Madrid. Miguel could sniff what was approaching at top speed, and now he knew that the times were no longer for him nor the season proper to his genius, but rather the beginning of decadence; but if he could sniff it, it is obvious that not everyone noticed it, and more than half a century had to go by before anyone did.

In the royal halls hardly a trace remained of that military Court which surrounded Philip II in the first years of his reign, inherited from his father and upheld by the example of Don Juan de Austria. The warrior had disappeared completely from the Court and was kept at a distance from the Escorial, the last stone of which was then about to be put in place, but he was ordered to take some outstanding action that could then be painted in the Hall of Battles.

Widowed for the fourth time and now very poor in health, the King was preparing to swear in his son Prince Philip as heir to the Crown. This future king was an enigma; all that was known was that he was an affable and discreet courtier. There was talk of his having had some early love affairs with certain Andalusian great ladies, although his exemplary piety was spoken of endlessly. Miguel heard all these things about the Court and was sadly convinced that the heroic race of Don Juan had been extinguished.

His old friend Agustín de Cetina, possibly through the recommendation of his clerk Juan de Tamayo, who also knew Miguel, lost no time in obtaining a new way for him to make a living, if a new way can be described as the position of executive agent, commissioned by the King or rather the Treasury Council to collect 2,459,981 maravedis owing to the Treasury from the Kingdom of Granada for royal tithes and sales taxes.[1] On the face of it this task was no less difficult than that of commissary of supplies for the Armada; actually the obstacles were even greater, since it was not a case of collecting wheat and oil, commodities usually to be found in the villages, but rather of collecting money, of which there never was any abundance, and obtaining it as arrears of taxes. To do this Miguel had judicial and executive powers and he could sue and imprison people, attach their possessions and if necessary auction off the very guts of poor debtors.

Obviously the bone thrown to Cervantes by his old friend Agustín de Cetina or those to whom he spoke in order to obtain this commission was not an easy one to gnaw. In addition it was necessary for Miguel to present a surety bond, since it was clear that his own personal credit was not enough for granting him so much authority and putting at his disposal a sum of money he was to collect himself and deliver to the Treasury. There had to be ample security, and the few friends Miguel had in the capital were not rich. It is not known how he got in touch with a certain Don Francisco Suárez Gasco, a rich man but contentious and with a bad reputation, who offered to go bond for four thousand ducats to get Cervantes out of the difficulty.

Cetina backed Cervantes, but he could not get an agreement that Suárez Gasco's bond be considered sufficient. Nevertheless on August 13 Miguel was given a royal commission to recover the indicated sum from the reserves of the mint of Granada and its revenues, from the tithes of Ronda, from the sales taxes and tithes of Loja, Alhama, Guadix and its district, Baza, Almuñécar, Motril, and Salobreña. All of this was to be collected in a period of sixty days at the outside and delivered in coffers with three locks to Don Pedro Mesía de Tovar, who was then the Treasurer General, and he must do this in person, delegating it to no one, and receiving 550 maravedis daily in wages for himself and his assistants.

Perusal of the letter of commission must have given Miguel pause. It is drafted in such a way that had it not become history because of its reference to Cervantes it would deserve to be preserved as a model of administrative literature and example of bureaucratic habits. In it the duties of the commissioned officer are specified with inquisitorial rigidity, but when telling him what he has to collect it falls into gross inaccuracies. Those who ordered the collection of some of the taxes did not even know their amount or whether in fact they had or had not been paid.

Nevertheless Cervantes undertook this commission and on August 20 he again pleaded before the King for Suárez Gasco's bond to be regarded as sufficient, "in consideration of my having no other sureties and that I am a well-known man of good repute married in this place." By this last hook he caught the scrupulous and excessively cautious accountant Araiz, who said that if his wife had possessions they would be acceptable as surety for Miguel. It was then necessary for Doña Catalina to obligate her possessions on her signature individually and jointly with her husband, which was done on the twenty-first of August, the day after the petition, both of them being in Madrid and Doña Catalina therefore well away from the influence of her brother, but convinced by the eloquence with which Miguel painted the absolute need for such a commitment.

Miguel then left for Granada, and it is obvious that if the other great cities he had visited made a strong impression on him, all the more was this bound to occur in that most perturbing city, which has given birth to the Andalusian talents most similar to those of Castile and most classically Castilian.

If Cordova is the city for the dogmatic and contemplative man, Granada is the city of the revolutionary thinker, of the forger of fruitful contrasts and fertile contradictions. This is due to the constant presence of snow-capped heights and of African vegetation in the lowlands. Though busy and overworked by the pressures of his commission, Cervantes had time to observe on one side the peaks of the Veleta and of Mulhacén, eternally white and impassable, and at their feet the fruitful and flourishing plain of Granada upon whose green foliage nostalgic captives and poet kings made restless by their memories had refreshed their eyes. The snow of the peaks at each break of day seemed a little closer to the sky and the splendid greenery of the earth appeared to spread and multiply from day to day, threatening to cover all the surrounding earth where the prickly pears dragged on the ground, the agaves stood erect and the untamed canes burst like hundred-branched candelabras over the walls of the orchards. In the patios and gardens of the houses the acrid odor of myrtles rose to the nostrils and upon raising one's head the eyes lighted on the kindly shade of pomegranates, the fruits of which were starting to redden, painted in gold and blood by the vermilion sun which sailed through the cobalt sky. There men paced gravely, as hidalgos should, without the noisy gaiety of Seville; there the women, locked and double-locked behind bars and blinds, courted and allowed themselves to be courted without showing more than a hand or an arm to the street. The splendid calm of the rich Moors and the intolerant and suicidal fierceness of the fighting Moors had left here and there deep traces in character and in speech from the last days of the Nasrids.[2] The contrasts in the landscape were also found in the spirit. The Christians of Granada seemed yesterday's Moors, and the Moriscos, of whom a great number still lived in the city, were most restrained and smooth, as if they had been converted by the Evangelist.

Granada was the appropriate city for the Ingenious Hidalgo to examine when a mature man. She it was that made Miguel go deeper and deeper into the ideas he had already conceived, or at least sketched, of the great and fundamental contrast in which the whole of life might be viewed. To the snowy heights of the Veleta and the Mulhacén seen face to face with the green pomegranates, the fleshy prickly pears and the untidy sharp agaves of the Granada plains we owe in large part the ideal antithesis and the masterly synthesis of Don Quixote and Sancho.

CHAPTER 38

A Difficult Commission—A Banker Absconds—Return to Poetry

From Granada to Baza, passing through Guadix, Cervantes always had on his right the majestic Alpujarras, their summits gilded by the setting sun. On the left the fertile plains of the district of Guadix and the Hoya de Baza again present the same contrast as in Granada, where the prairie humanizes the spirit, the mountains elevate it. In his youth Miguel had tasted one of the greatest delights given us to enjoy in the limited sphere in which we move: that of looking down on Italy from the Alps. He now walked the slopes of the Alpujarras and contemplated those places where untouched Nature offered the ancient peace of its centuries-old pines and its everlasting live oaks, the ground covered with a thick carpet of the thorns, furze, heather and hips which begin where the perfumed broom and the rugged hawthorn end.

The very name of Baza, in past centuries known as Basti or Batis, was the baptismal name of the father of Andalusia or *Bética* and its patriarchal river Betis nourished by the snows of the Alpujarras. Granada is good for renewing a forty-year-old spirit; the sierras are best for making it more serious. The clear air of the mountain ridge, the September breeze that rose from it, the chill that came from the lightly singing threads of crystal clear water, caressed and refreshed the cheeks of the traveller.

On September 9 Miguel arrived in Baza and presented his credentials to Licentiate Antonio de Rueda, Mayor and Acting Corregidor of the city and its territory. Together they summoned a certain Alonso de España who was the successful bidder for the collection of royal taxes in Baza and its district, and Miguel immediately discovered the first of the infinite number of common frauds he encountered daily. Alonso de España, upon receiving the tax concession, had provided no guarantees of performance, and those Treasury functionaries who were so very scrupulous in demanding guarantees from Miguel had been satisfied in Baza with Alonso de España's naming as Treasurer one Gaspar de

Tejeda, who probably had no one to answer for him either. Thus, then as now and long before, ancient and knotty as the evergreen oaks of the sierra, *caciquismo*[1] entangled all the villages of the nation in its ramifications.

Miguel tried to formalize the account, to establish exact figures, and everywhere he was confronted by exemptions, privileges and formulas for postponing payment. Four villages, Cúllar, Zúgar, Caniles, and Benamaurel, had compounded[2] and paid sales taxes and tithes. Three villages, Roya, Freila, and Macael, famous for its marbles, jaspers and serpentines, had not compounded but they also had paid. Another two or three managed to escape taxation because they were assessed as between land and sea, which gave them a possible pretext for not paying sales taxes, and in fact they did not.

Furthermore, the people who had influence at the capital, in short the *caciques*, had induced the King to respond favorably to the petitions of gentlemen and ladies whom it was thought desirable to keep well disposed. Carelessly and without knowing what he was doing, the King granted so many annuities chargeable to so many revenues that when all of these capricious and more or less legitimate abatements were deducted the paper figure of 3,342,320 maravedis Miguel was to collect was reduced to 83,713 maravedis—that is to say, to one-fortieth of what the gentlemen of the Treasury in Madrid had calculated. The Court with its frauds and pretenses had barely been born and begun to centralize its services in the capital and already Madrid and the villages began to cozen and distrust each other, and there was no sure way of knowing what was the actual wealth, the real resources on which the country could count. When he closed out and signed for this account stripped of the farthingale figures that the accountants of Madrid had dressed it in, Miguel must have given a great shout of laughter.

But it was not only that the shortages in the account amounted to forty times more than estimated but even that amount had to be divided into three parts,[3] thus reducing it to 27,940 maravedis or 820 reals . . . and worst of all there was no one who would pay this sum because from what he could gather Cervantes finally realized that Treasurer Gaspar Osorio de Tejeda also had neither provided a guarantee nor collected any of the amounts promised. All those millions of maravedis had thus evaporated into thin air, like sums dreamed up by Portuguese financiers and managements and realized by Spanish investors.

In truth it was a most incredible and tiresome practical joke, by reason of which Cervantes, after he stopped laughing, pulled himself together and, provided with the powers that his commission gave him, told Mayor Rueda to point out a solvent person who would pay him at least eight hundred reals. The mayor, under pressure of the credentials which Cervantes brought, said that those who could pay some or all were a certain Simón Sánchez, a city steward who should have the revenues from the tax roll in his possession, and a certain Juan de Cuenca, tax contractor of Zujar. They went to their houses in search of them but they did not appear until the following day. They finally paid unwillingly, and Miguel charged them a day's salary for having had to wait for them. But this chapter out of a picaresque novel had still to end with another example of close-fisted behavior.

Although he had paid nothing, in the final analysis Alonso de España held the position of Treasurer and Cervantes required him to pay his salary for five days, two of which corresponded to the part of the road between Madrid and Baza, two others to the journey to and from Guadix, and one for staying in Baza going over the accounts, and he even collected for the cost of transferring the money to its destination; and recognizing his type as soon as he saw him, Miguel added that if he did not pay this sum, the total amount being a scant eighty-six reals, he would pay himself from the Treasurer's salary, for the worthy Alonso de España had a salary entailing neither responsibilities nor obligations, this being the true and only ideal of the sons of *caciquismo*. The man defended himself desperately, but faced with the judicial powers of Cervantes he ended by giving way and paying up, declaring that he did so "under compulsion and threatened by legal process, and to relieve his vexation and the loss of his money he would recover it by collecting from anyone who might have any."

Is there not something symbolical in the name of this Alonso de España who is being paid to exercise an imaginary function and of whom the only characteristic one can see clearly is his tenacious refusal to pay anything, adopted as a system with complaints and protests and the obvious intention of extracting those eight hundred reals from the bowels of the first available unfortunate?

As Cervantes returned to Granada and went from there to other towns, transacting business with their treasurers, accountants and tax contractors, more disappointing items came up and more muddles and carelessness in the books of the Treasury Auditor's office became obvious. Thus he had to write to the King from Granada on October 8, asking for an extension of time in which to complete the commission.

Toward the end of November Miguel received a reply to his letter, a royal writ extending the commission for twenty days or for as many more as necessary. Miguel thought to go to Seville with what he had already collected and to remit it to Madrid from there, for which purpose he bought bills of exchange from Pérez de Vitoria in Málaga drawn on Juan Leclerc, a Flemish merchant established in Seville.

On December 9 he was in Ronda collecting certain sums due him. He crossed the Alpujarras during the season of most extreme cold, and in four or five days he appeared in Seville where he cashed the bills of exchange at Leclerc's bank. But he was not a man to feel safe with money in his possession, and he went immediately to deposit it at the office of a Portuguese banker and merchant named Simón Freire de Lima, who gave Miguel a bill of exchange on himself payable in Madrid. After spending some time in Seville Cervantes returned to the capital, where he expected to cash the sum he had entrusted to Freire and close out the accounts of his mission; but a few days later Simón Freire declared himself bankrupt, or as was then said he absconded with 60,000 ducats. It was not difficult to arrange a passage in one of the galleys leaving for the Indies, a common refuge then and since those days for all the spendthrifts, embezzlers, bankrupts, and insolvent debtors of Spain. Overwhelmed by such an unforeseen calamity Miguel returned to Seville in order to arrange quickly for the 7,400 reals which he had entrusted to the fugitive to be excluded from the lien on Freire's property placed by the other creditors, since those maravedis were sacred as belonging to the Royal Exchequer.

Miguel once more found himself alone in Seville without influence, without money, trying to collect an almost impossible debt and without any possibility of returning to Madrid or of obtaining new commissions on which to make a living. The truth of the matter is that this misfortune put an end to his life as a civil servant. His supporters, if he had any other than Agustín de Cetina, did not bother to investigate or establish whether what had happened could be ascribed to negligence on Miguel's part or to some other cause. It was indubitable that in the sales tax commission he had collected very much less than the imaginary amount assumed by the Treasury Council and to top it off there was the loss of what he, ill-informed on how the affairs of the bankers and moneyed people of Seville were handled, had imprudently entrusted to the Portuguese. It would therefore be out of the question to give new commissions to an official who had carried out the last one so badly, and who besides had no one to speak for him.

How he lived in Seville during the next few years we can imagine; of what he lived on we know absolutely nothing. After the end of his heroic period the life of Cervantes is monotonous, like that of every poor man who struggles for a livelihood. With the passing of his epic days he did not have a brilliant and exciting period as did Lope and Quevedo.

Walking the pavements of Seville in 1595 Cervantes again felt himself bogged down and unable to see a way out. He then remembered, as he always did during one of these interludes, that he was a poet. Poetic tournaments in honor of Saint Hyacinth had been convoked in Zaragoza, and a prize was offered for variations on this extraordinary roundelay:

> Today Heaven offers the Church
> a stone so perfect
> that it shines resplendent
> in the crown of God Himself.

Four stanzas of double *quintillas*, written without enthusiasm and with many stumblings, were enough for Cervantes to be given the prize by the judges in Zaragoza, and his poem was read and greatly praised by the jury in a decision written in two appalling *quintillas* in which Cervantes is called the genius from Seville. He must have laughed immoderately over this judgment and the nonsense contained in his own ten verses.

All of the year 1595 went by in quibbling with the Treasury over the recovery of the money collected by Miguel during his commission. The matter caused him so many headaches, so much grief and disgust, that it was probably then that he definitely hung up his habit as a public functionary and once more flung himself into poetry and prose, much as he might have flung himself into the Guadalquivir.

CHAPTER 39

Assault on Cádiz—Cervantes, Voice of the People

THE tenth Count of Niebla and seventh Duke of Medina-Sidonia was, as we have seen in an earlier chapter, one of those gentlemen typical of the period in which lances were turned into reeds. He was the prototype of disastrously feckless courtiers because of his cupidity and his worthlessness, the like of which had not been known in the Spanish Court for many years. He made up for these defects by the elegance of his person, the fruit of his rich inherited blood. Most appropriate to him are those artificial verses in which Don Luis Góngora[1] depicts the Count of Niebla withdrawing for a moment from the chase and taking refuge in pastoral peace, solacing himself with bucolic poetry:

The hand of the master idly strokes
the plumage of the noble bird,
mute and idle on the falcon's perch,
even daring to ignore the bell.
The Andalusian horse, champing
the golden bit, makes lazy foam,
the greyhound whimpers on his silken cord
and the zither finally supplants the horn . . .

The affectation and far-fetched style of these verses is compensated by their elegance and they include unsurpassable polished phrases which convey feeling:

The Andalusian horse, champing
the golden bit, makes lazy foam,
the greyhound whimpers on his silken cord . . .

together with other prosaically twisted ones: "even daring to ignore the bell. . . ." This was what was taking place in Spanish society during the last years of Philip II. We have already noted that fighting men had disappeared from the Court without being replaced by men of ideas. Instead it was intriguing and scheming men like Cristóbal de Moura and Mateo Vázquez who ruled it.

The despotism of Philip II was the first sign of what was to follow among the great Spanish politicians and leaders, men so egotistical and self-opinionated that they could not tolerate the collaboration of any other intelligences. Philip II always loved obscure and mediocre men; he believed that the greatness of his thought carried with it effectiveness in carrying it out, even when he entrusted this to weak or clumsy hands.

By reason of this, and perhaps for other sentimental reasons that should not be rejected by careful historians even though conveyed in only the slightest of whispers, Don Alonso Pérez de Guzmán had been entrusted with the position of Captain-General of the Ocean and of the Coast of Andalusia, having been kept on even after the disaster of the *Invincible*, for which he was not wholly responsible even if he was blamed for it. To protect and make much of unpopular people is another failing of Spanish absolutism. The man who reaches the top not only wants to impress his personality on all around him, but he delights in opposing the general opinion in a show of what he regards as magnanimity.

As usual England knew perfectly and in detail everything that happened in Spain and more especially on the Andalusian coast, which has always had an extraordinary interest for the English. They had had experience of the incapacity of the Captain-General of the Coast and knew all about the limited number and negligible strength of the ships which Spain had dispersed between Cádiz, Málaga and Algeciras. It was a unique opportunity for a daring blow and the English undertook to deliver it promptly and forcefully.

A fleet under the command of the favorite of Queen Elizabeth, the luckless Earl of Essex, entered the bay of Cádiz as if attending a theater or a social function, attacking and sinking the four obsolete warships stationed there. The people of Cádiz did what they could to resist, hastily organizing guilds and other groups into military companies, among which was one of Franciscan and another of Augustinian friars, but the English captured the city, looted its riches, took prisoners, and behaved like a gang of bandits in an unguarded camp. This went on from June 29 to July 16 of 1596 and was a repetition in miniature of the sack of Rome by the troops of the Spanish Caesar.[2]

The news of the sack of Cádiz spread all over the whole of Andalusia and in the first half of July groups of terrified inhabitants of Cádiz, fugitives from the sack, arrived every day in Seville. All of them asked, with the urgency of those who had been despoiled, what the Captain-General had done and what he was going to do. They all received the same answer: the Duke of Medina-Sidonia was at the tuna fisheries of Zahara, one of the healthiest and richest sources of income for his house, preparing either to catch more fish or to organize their protection. Little he cared whether Cádiz was lost or won as long as the fisheries were abundant and profitable.

Miguel, who was present at these events, being unemployed and aware of all the rumors in the city, then felt the greatest desire to burst out in Homeric laughter that he had ever had in his life. What else could a former hero do when he saw tumbling down in a few years not only the naval power of Spain, always a trifle fortuitous and unsound, but even the legend of the past, which in truth for him was the history he had seen with his own eyes, touched with his own hands and sealed with his own blood, as well as the skill, sagacity, alertness and resolution of the Spanish captains he had known at Lepanto, at La Goleta, at Terceira? It seems that when he died, Don Álvaro de Bazán had taken with him not only the skill in command but also the calm, the serenity, the composure in awaiting events and dealing with them that a strong man can impose even if it be not dictated by intelligence, dignity and proper pride.

A wave of picaresque humor welled up from the Guadalquivir where the satires and jeers of both poets and people were directed against the Duke of Medina-Sidonia, but perhaps Cervantes thought, and with reason, and we think it today, that in that critical tragicomic moment it was not the Duke alone who failed, they all failed; there was not a single man who knew how to face the situation, put himself at the head of the forces, and attempt a serious and orderly defense. It is true that there was patriotism and unselfishness, but it was disorganized, crack-brained, uncertain and ill-advised.

Of what use could a company of Franciscan friars be in the event of war and a need for quick action? Those two platoons, one of Franciscans, the other of Augustinians, shouldering their pikes and muskets, were something appropriate to musical comedy, something that deserved only laughter. A people who could provide only a few men dedicated to the service of God in defense of its most important maritime stronghold deserved the *Quixote*. The personal politics born under the cupolas of the Escorial were already beginning to bear fruit.

To provide what seemed a comic theme there came to Seville an outrageous captain who answered to the high-sounding name of Marco Antonio Becerra. Somebody had told the Duke that the city should prepare to defend itself as Cádiz had done, and without moving from his tuna fisheries he ordered the organization and training of a militia.

The people who turned out to join the companies of Becerra were not ragged and venal folk but rather those demi-bourgeois, demi-artisans who just then were defending the forts in Flanders successfully: people in whom the martial spirit surges in time of danger when they think they are going to fight to defend the home or the business, the fat wife and the soft armchair, without prejudice to that vanity and preoccupation with uniforms and with deeds real or imagined which remains after the first ardors have cooled. What is certain is that the militiamen of Captain Becerra must have organized themselves more or less like the confraternities of the Holy Week and bedecked themselves with the showy extravagance proper to such corporations.

Never had such a theatrical display been seen in Seville; neither the processions of the Corpus nor the *autos-de-fe* of the Tablada nor the hangings and whippings in the Plaza de San Francisco had ever attracted such a crowd of idle folk and shrieking children as did the resplendent soldiers of Becerra drilling in the fields of San Sebastián. The multitude from the Meat Quarter of slaughterers, butchers, flayers, and assistants and the whole rabble from the Slaughter-house, as also the fops and pimps with their servants and their mistresses from the precinct of San Bernardo, had never had such a pleasant diversion as that of hearing the stentorian bellowing of Captain Becerra and watching the clumsy movements of his raw troops.

They went down there for the fun of choosing nicknames for their many friends who were organized in companies, the Marketeers of El Salvador, the Mulattos of the Fish Market, the Hucksters of the Costanilla and the Caza; it was the diversion of a whole people who felt that the time had come to make a jest of everything. The satiric good humor of Seville, the mockery, witty and at times pitiless, though devoid of rancorous bitterness, had begun to penetrate the consciousness of a people saddened by disasters and the preachings of the black-clad men who were spreading their net of asceticism and melancholy over the whole nation.

In those fifteen ridiculous days Becerra and other captains and old soldiers who came to Seville to strut like military men in all their glory were the targets of amusing jokes for the Sevillian poets, but in this none of them could touch the famous sonnet of Cervantes, the first one in which a clear perception of the absurdity of what was going on begins to appear. It goes like this:

> In July we witnessed another Holy Week
> replete with certain confraternities
> which soldiers call companies
> who terrified the mob and not the English.
> The multitude of plumes was such
> that in less than fourteen or fifteen days
> their pygmies and Goliaths flew away
> and their edifice collapsed on its site.
> The Becerra bellowed and set them in rows,
> the earth thundered and the sky darkened
> threatening complete destruction. . . .
> and finally into Cádiz with extreme caution,
> the Earl having left without the least misgiving,
> the great Duke of Medina entered triumphantly.

For in fact that is the way it happened. The English left Cádiz on July 16 and very shortly after came the "god of the tuna fish," as the Sevillian bard Juan Sáez de Zumeta called him in another sonnet, more sour than amusing. But neither he nor Juan de la Cueva nor Alvarez de Soria could laugh at those improvised soldiers with their fanfaronade of plumes as could Miguel, who had known the bravest and truest soldiers of his century. None of those poets possessed the art which transforms indignation into laughter without any apparent malice.

At the same time the sonnet reproduced above, the other which says that "a master of fence was Campuzano. . . ." and another two or three similar backstairs subjects which unfortunately have not been preserved, were sufficient to win popularity for a poet. Rather than the diffuse poems which were printed and no one read, those clever and timely little pieces that circulated by word of mouth were appreciated, learned, and remembered by the whole world.

The public always demands to be made to laugh with a few words or brief phrases, categorical, precise and easy to remember. They like a voice they understand to tell of events witnessed or surmised and the feelings they aroused. For the first time, then, motivated by what happened in Cádiz, Cervantes became the interpreter of what everyone thought and felt. His voice was the voice of the people and perhaps because of this he was not appreciated nor was his genius sensed by the lordly poets. For them the public did not exist, for what had the masses to do with, what did the crowd care about, the "clear eyes, serene" of the lady loved by one of them, or the charming pranks with which the other, consummate artist of erotic tricks, diverted and excited his Inés to jealousy?

It is important to determine what concept of literature was then forming in order to appreciate the perspicacity of Miguel, who, abandoning his previous false concepts and prescinding the style and practices of all the writers and poets, was later to understand that he must write for a universal public without letting the pettiness and political intrigues of militant literature disturb him.

From the time in 1596 when he composed the sonnet mentioned above one glimpses how a way was being opened in his mind for the opinion later revealed in a hundred passages of the *Quixote* that literature was no longer an amusement for idle gentlemen, but that the writer was discharging a social function and must satisfy the desires of the public, cater to it and stir it up for present advantage and future fame. In the mind of Cervantes that concept expressed not so long ago: "I had other things with which to occupy myself," had already changed, or at least was beginning to change from then on. It seems certain, although there are no authentic documents to prove this, that the conviction was taking hold of him that writing was also "a thing with which to occupy oneself" and not just a pastime. It was still that for many other writers and may be so always for those who are merely lyricists whose inner feelings, if they are truly such, will never manage to move a great number of people.

How can we not think that it was in those years that Cervantes conceived ideas, planned, sketched out and composed plays, interludes, exemplary novels, the second part of *Galatea* and was on the threshold of the *Quixote*? His worries in those days were so great and his resources so few that he was unable to go to the capital, whither he was summoned by the importunate gentlemen of the Treasury Council to settle the account pending from his former commissions. Such were the harassments he suffered in this most critical moment of his life that he must have been incommunicado and barely in touch with his family.

Meanwhile the worms of legal procedure continued gnawing away at the papers of the commissary, implacably fixing responsibilities and demanding settlements. The addle-pated Suárez Gasco, his guarantee threatened in the business of the tithes, demanded before a judge that Cervantes present himself in Madrid to produce documents and settle accounts. On September 6 of 1597 the President and Accountants of the Auditor's Office of the Treasury, on petition of Suárez Gasco, ordered Licentiate Gaspar de Vallejo, judge of the Royal Court of Appeals of Seville, to require Cervantes to present himself before the court and account for the maravedis in the balance of his account or provide bail for his appearance, and that, should he not do this, he be seized and conducted to the Royal Prison until such time as the President and Accountants should decree otherwise.

Licentiate Gaspar de Vallejo carried out the orders given, and being unable to collect the said bail he put Miguel de Cervantes Saavedra in the prison of Seville.

CHAPTER 40

The Prison of Seville—Genesis of the Quixote

THE narrow lane of Entrecárceles, formed by the back of the Audience Chamber and the front of the Royal Prison, was not a place for people to pass through but rather a swamp of misery, a sink of iniquity and corruption, where all the worst of Seville and its environs collected. Four paces apart, eyeing each other and breathing on each other like two brawlers ready to fight, the Royal Prison and the Prison of the Audience Chamber challenge each other constantly; from time to time the Royal tossed at the Audience some human debris of no use for either the galleys or the gallows, although the gallows were readily available. All kinds of filth spilled from the jail into the lane, and since it was always full of a fetid and stinking mob fed by the comings and goings of the prisoners, just a peep into it dealt one a slap in the face from all the putrefactions of the world.

Followed by bumbailiffs, Miguel crossed that human dung heap to the threshold of the Royal Prison. There first of all he encountered the porter of the "golden gate," who took his name and asked what his crime was. A scrivener noted both facts in a grimy book and the guardian of the golden gate inquired no farther, since there was no chance of extracting any Mexican salve [bribes] from a man imprisoned for debts to the Treasury, just as there would be none from those who entered there as bullies or *hombres*, or their exact opposites, so to speak, as sodomites guilty of the abominable crime, or as thieves, prostitutes and pimps.

The porter of the golden gate approached a staircase, and telling Miguel to go up it he murmured in a thin, flute-like voice "Ho-lá!," making a whistling sound which went gliding up the walls and was answered by another which said "Ai-lá." This meant: "Prisoner coming" and "Let him come." After this he of the golden gate informed him of the silver what the crime was: "There goes Señor Hundred-ducats!," since Miguel was there for debt, and when he reached the top of the staircase the man of the silver gate said: "He is here!" This established that Miguel was destined, not to be put in irons or assigned to the galleries, prison areas where dangerous prisoners were confined —highwaymen, murderers and sodomites—but to the upper halls next to the infirmary and near the warden's quarters. Miguel's crime was considered a misfortune or misadventure rather than a crime as such, and it would not be fit for a prisoner of such minor importance to be confused with the mass of killers, ruffians, swindlers and gypsies.

On the way to the upper halls Miguel was to see the only aspects of life he had not yet experienced. Thanks to the famous *Account of the Jail of Seville* (*Relación de la cárcel de Sevilla*) and the similarly entitled farce composed by the clever and amusing Sevillian lawyer Licentiate Cristóbal de Chavez, which Gallardo attributed to Cervantes in obvious error, we know in detail all about that incredible corner of Spanish life in the last years of the sixteenth century.[1] From such works we learn how the eighteen hundred prisoners immured in that huge building lived, ate and enjoyed the hundred and fifty or more women who slipped in daily, and how they fought each other, killed each other, gambled away everything down to the skin, got drunk or wallowed in other worse vices, and how they emerged so bravely for "*His Majesty's service*" or for the gallows. We get to know their evil habits, tricks, wiles, extortions, frauds, their life or death devices to win their daily bread, their incurable bragging, their incredible courage under torture and sentence of death, their extraordinary devoutness, their lunacies, simplicities, and childishness. The man who had ten or twelve killings to his account and who had had his belly sewn up and his entrails patched without batting an eye would give the greater part of all he possessed to another prisoner with a clever pen who could write him a love letter to his mistress in the Compás or in San Bernardo where she was staying with a well-known father and mother (those of the brothel). The message would drip with the most elaborate conceits of love and tenderness, and at the end a heart would appear, pierced by many arrows and colored in saffron or ochre, or a man in fetters and shackled by a chain to the lips of his loved one whence erotic declarations came tumbling out.

Battening on the prisoners and on their needs, vices and whims were some hundreds of individuals worse than their wards since they served them voluntarily. Some would tattoo horseshoes, serpents or "esses with nails" [*ess* + *clavos* = *esclavos*, i.e., slaves] on the legs, arms and chests of future galley slaves; some shaved their heads and tended their moustaches; some ran busily about stealing from this one to sell to that one crooked daggers or yellow-handled knives, to say nothing of the "little shepherds," which were sharpened sticks with fire-hardened points that went through a man like a barber's razor. Some were clever at "flowers" [card tricks] and had a talent for "branding oxen," which meant marking packs of cards for the benefit of gamblers, at times for cheating, at others out of pride in playing to win. Others were eagles at using the cold chisel and saw to break through iron gratings, walls and roofs; others at hiding women under beds, stacking them up, in their shifts or naked, as if they were blocks of wood.

During the day and up to ten o'clock at night there was an incessant movement of people in and out of the prison; no one was asked the reason for his coming or going unless he were a prisoner, and even they, if not among the dangerous ones, also went out by paying money to the warden, the underwarden and the assistant jailkeepers or guards, who were themselves prisoners, for there was no one in the whole building who was not a criminal or accomplice, friend or servant of criminals. That entire rabble was fed by four taverns which flourished in the prison and by what each man could get for himself, for it must be understood that no one there could claim rations or obtain food except through charity and the collective generosity of the inmates. Posts in the prison, such as those of warden, assistant warden, shopkeepers, porters and others were considered enviable because of their profitability; that of the executioner was as lucrative as that of the warden, since he never tortured anyone without first collecting for tightening the cords less severely, and the unfortunate man who had to undergo torture would get escudos from the very bowels of the earth lest he come out crippled, maimed, or ruptured.

Cervantes makes it plain that the noise and discomfort of the prison were insufferable. During the day the bustle and confusion of so many people coming and going was supplemented by the clamor of the many quarrels and scuffles, yells, songs, gypsy dance music and the disputes and grumbles of losing gamblers. Separated from the male prisoners but in the same building the women prisoners spent the whole blessed day singing the latest *seguidillas* in chorus, accompanying themselves on the guitar and the harp or lute:

> For a Sevillano
> curled in Walloon style
> my whole heart
> is on fire. . . .

At other times their guitars and stringed instruments were taken from them and that was worse, because then they would keep time by rattling the shackles which they bore on their hands and legs. At the top of their voices they communicated with their men through the walls and made declarations of love such as were never heard in the hell of lovers. "Ah, my soul, come to the window for I am getting out tomorrow! Send me a release, my life! Darling, the present is for the whole of my life! Safe and sound may I see you, my hero! . . . " The gaieties were noisy, the quarrels silent. The *hombre* with his guts gaping kept as quiet as if nothing had happened. It thus came to pass that the least guilty were usually the ones who were netted to be whipped or sent to the galleys.

The clamor and the raillery were greater when there was a death sentence. Then the whole prison hummed with excitement. Men and women made much of the condemned man, all the more the greater the serenity of his face and the calmness of his speech. In that place men diced with death and lost everything except the body to pain or to the gallows. The condemned man imperturbably continued his game of cards and if he could, at two steps from the rope, he would pull off four or five fancy tricks to win some cuartos from his cronies.

There was no joking about religion either. In each hall and in the rooms or cells of those who were kept separate there were one, two or more images before which little wax or oil lights were constantly renewed. Horrific Christs were painted in saffron on the wall or prints of the Virgin and miracle-mongering saints were illuminated in the most fantastic colors. When the doors of the prison were closed all the little altars and images had their lights lit. Those of the altar at the back of the big patio were also lit and the sacristan, flogging rope in hand, went around forcing the prisoners to kneel. They let go the pack of cards or the woman with whom they were toying and eighteen hundred voices, some rough and brandy-soaked, others high-pitched and feminine, intoned the *Salve* with the ancient tragic singsong of prison *Salves* which chills the bones of anyone who hears it for the first time. Important and minor prisoners alike, short-termers and those sentenced to death, sang with the same devotion, either gnawed by fear of the other life or believing in miracles which might save them to return to their predatory banditry.

While he prayed with them, following the terrifying chorus of those voices, Miguel felt how an ideal hovers above all human miseries, an ideal which is different for each individual but which unites them all as male and female voices joined in that unexpected concertedness of the *Salve*, and what for him had always been a presentiment was now transformed into a profound realization of how interesting humanity, both high and low, is and can become if it is conceived and represented as in search of something, going on a pilgrimage with noble intent and fighting for an unrealizable and extravagant end. In the fetid darkness of the patio and of the corridors and rooms that gave onto it the lights of the little candles and wax tapers flickered, blinking on the doors and windows. Some voices lisped menaces, others voiced sly threats, and above them all there was likely to sound a clear feminine note that intoned the religious chant with angelical sweetness. Miguel recognized that voice as the same one that had sung to the sound of fetters the ardent *seguidilla*:

> For a Sevillano
> curled in Walloon style. . . .

That squalid little world of the jail of Seville thus epitomized the ardent desires, loftiness and pettiness of the great world, and all were important, exciting, moving, making one laugh, bleed, shudder; all were just as interesting as the heroic events that the historian and epic poet extolled.

That suggestive contrast between the snows of the Valetta and the luxuriant open plain of Granada which Miguel had observed held the secret of life and art. And it was then, sunk in all the horrors of prison, feeling misery course through his body, seeing the lice, fleas, bedbugs, crab-lice and ticks on that same body, that Miguel remembered his past days of glory, recalled the golden sun which lighted him at Lepanto and caressed him in Naples and in Lisbon, and he reflected that the sun was not another one, nor had he changed, but that in life we innocently delude ourselves into thinking that what is big is great and what is small is negligible.

Miguel did not arrive at these reflections alone and he might not have done so at all if there had not also been there in the jail a prisoner like himself, a Treasury employee who was there for similar reasons in connection with the settlement of accounts. In former days he had been one of the high officials of the Auditor's Office of the Treasury, and even better than Miguel he understood the intrigues of the Spanish Court, the exuberance of Italy and its free life. He was at least fifty, a calm and most sagacious man, a master of life with a gift for reminiscence and a skill in recounting events of major or minor import greater than that of anyone else. Besides this he was a man so buffeted and toughened by life that he could give the god Saturn lessons in experience, and so much the philosopher that perhaps Spain has had no one to equal him. He and Miguel soon became friends as intimate as two unfortunates can be when they meet each other upon reaching their fiftieth year. Very soon he told Miguel of a book he had written which, unless he was mistaken, was to be one of the most entertaining ones that had ever been composed in Spain.

This friend was called Mateo Alemán[2] and the book which Mateo read to Miguel in the jail of Seville was entitled *The Panorama of Human Life, Adventures and Life of the Rogue Guzmán de Alfarache* (*La atalaya de la vida humana, aventuras y vida del pícaro Guzmán de Alfarache*). So we see where and how the same quill pen which had written the last chapters of *Guzmán de Alfarache* was perhaps used to write the first pages of the *Quixote*, begotten in a jail. It could have happened nowhere else but in the prison of Seville, where Miguel spent the whole of that autumn, quitting it in the first days of December.

Miguel had had many fruitful autumns, but none more than the one he spent in the prison where the unique book was born. Who can depict his joy when he came out of there and found himself again in the broad Plaza de San Francisco, walking under the porticos with some manuscript sheets under his arm? What he had got out of those months in jail, aside from the gray hairs in the gold of his beard, was the greatest gain and richest reward of his life. And having made a beginning, happy and confident that he had entered with a firm step on the road to immortality, Miguel laughed, and he laughed thinking that this was not brought about by consorting with the greatest heroes of his day. What he did not acquire under the orders of Don Juan de Austria and Don Álvaro de Bazán he attained in those days of lice and bedbugs, wounds and stripes, in the prison of Seville.

Like many others Miguel lived somewhat at the mercy of circumstances and just kept afloat in Seville while he put together, drafted and gave form to his book. There is no doubt that while he was composing it his temperament would not permit him to keep such a treasure hidden, and thinking only of satisfying the joy and gratification with which the work was conceived and written he would read it aloud to other writers. In this way, long before the work was printed and even before the first part was finished, its natural excellences began to be published by word of mouth throughout Seville, and thus the fame of Cervantes as a man of extraordinary talent and of unparalleled inventiveness was spread abroad.

As few other books, perhaps as no other book, the *Quixote* has the exceptional merit that its subject can be presented and summarized in a few words, and it therefore can come within reach of all intelligences and suit all tastes. The striking antithesis glimpsed by Miguel in Granada, or perhaps even before, and recalled and thought out again in the jail of Seville, captured minds immediately, interested them, persuaded them. Not that the Sevillians pointed Cervantes out, as the Florentines did Dante when they learned he was going to publish the *Inferno* and declared that he had been there, but in Seville there were many people who knew Don Quixote and Sancho and who talked about them five or six years before their adventures were published. Only a man as vulgar as the chronicler Ariño did not know the name of Cervantes. On the other hand Licentiate Collado, when copying Miguel's verses for the funeral monument of Philip II says very clearly: "Some other miscellaneous verses were put in and some *décimas* composed by Miguel de Cervantes *which, because they were his, it was agreed be put here*."

This means that Miguel was not only well known but was reputed to be one of the most gifted writers of Seville, not so much for his poems as for the news about the *Quixote,* of which some knew more, others less. Nevertheless, as had always happened to him, when the autumn of 1598 arrived he found himself very short of clothes and even shorter of money. On September 15 of the said year he had to ask for eleven yards of coarse cloth on credit with which to make two suits or a suit and a cloak, perhaps a short one without a hood. A month and a half later he was busy selling provisions at retail to the biscuit-makers of Triana and to the masters of the tenders and schooners which tied up to the dock.

Meanwhile one of the most important events in history had taken place in Spain. Gouty, covered with sores, worm-eaten and putrid, King Don Philip II died on the thirteenth of September at the Escorial. With him the glory of the Austrias was extinguished.

Great Seville, "Rome triumphant in spirit and nobility," resolved to celebrate the funeral of the King by raising such a monument that it would be talked of in the whole world. Its planning and execution, after a fiercely contested competition, became the responsibility of the leading master builder of the city, Magistrate Juan de Oviedo, that famous architect and military engineer to whom Seville owed the most important works of the period. The statues for the funeral monument were made by the sculptor of grief Juan Martínez Montañés and his colleague Gaspar Núñez Delgado, the paintings by Francisco Pacheco, Juan de Salcedo and Alonso Vázquez Perea. On November 24 the funeral ceremonies began. On the following day, at the Mass, the members of the Audience Chamber and those of the Inquisition quarreled over a question of protocol, the Mass was held up halfway through and its celebration had to be concluded in the sacristy. Amid the shouts and cat-calls of the Sevillian people the clergy retreated under the pulpit of the preacher, the gentlemen of the Inquisition left infuriated, sweeping their long black gowns around them, and those of the Audience departed muttering between their white laces and black Councillor's robes.

For some time the incident provided matter for gossip and the titillation of the Sevillians. The funeral monument was raised, but the funeral itself was not celebrated until the end of the year. Every day people would go to see if the rites were going to be performed or not.

On December 29 Cervantes entered the church by chance and upon seeing so many Sevillians gaping at the preparations which were finally being made to celebrate the funeral honors the following day, he looked upon the monument for the hundredth time and, unable to contain himself amid the general derision, he intoned that sonnet which was always to have first place in his writings:

I swear to God this grandeur doth astound me
and a doubloon would I give to describe it;
who will not be amazed and marvel
at this famous structure, this richness?

By the living Christ, each part of it
is worth more than a million, and what a sin
were it not to last a century, oh great Seville!,
Rome triumphant in spirit and nobility.

I'll lay a bet that the spirit of the dead,
but to enjoy this place, today has left
the glory in which it lives eternally.

A bully-boy heard this and said: "For sure
what you say is truth, Sir Soldier,
and he who says the contrary lies."

And then, incontinent,
clapped on his hat, hitched up his sword,
looked askance, departed, and nothing happened.

CHAPTER 41

The Academy of Pacheco—Books of Knight-Errantry— Don Quixote *Grows—Ana Franca Dies*

THE painter and poet Francisco Pacheco, actually a mediocre painter and unattractive poet, left us a real treasure in his *Descriptive Book of True Portraits of Illustrious and Memorable Men.*[1] Thanks to that amazing book we know better than by any written description what the artistic and literary society of Seville was like in the last years of Philip II and the first of his son. Without its author intending to do so this book shows us how in the reign of Philip II the various arts and sciences began to coalesce and form a solid and compact body of knowledge. The illustrious and memorable men portrayed in it, although neither they nor their portrait-painter harbored any such intention, constituted an Academy with all the merits and all the evils inherent in that name.

In it there are people of marked academic temperament, one such being Doctor Luciano de Negrón, flabby, mild, soft-eyed, his face timid, full of false modesty and sham goodwill, who would soon slip quietly into the seat of Vicar-General vacated by the death of Cardinal Don Rodrigo de Castro. In due course he would assist with the greatest evangelical docility in the degradation and execution on the gallows of two Portuguese monks, a Dominican and a Franciscan, whom he himself had condemned for complicity in the imposture of Marco Tullio Carsón when he claimed to be King Sebastián, lost at Alcázarquivir.

There are also medical men like Doctor Bartolomé Hidalgo de Agüero, a disciple of the famous Doctor Cuadra. After twenty years of trepanning and perforating the skull with the usual iron tools, he saw that no great results were obtained by such inhuman methods and he invented a gentler kind of treatment, "he cast aside the instruments and strong medicines, the digestive ointments and wet packs and in their place used drying and preservative materials which are called cephalic, such as his '*magistral powders*,' the blessed oil which they call Aparicio, and other things proper to setting bones and drawing out pus and humors with the greatest lenity." As a result he effected so many cures that a wounded bravo in Seville, though he might have had all his bones broken, would say full of faith, "Commend me to God and Doctor Hidalgo," because he cured everything with gentleness and skill. In it there are friars with lowered eyes and jutting jaws like Master Juan Farfán, who preached to corrupt and depraved Seville from the pulpit and in his moments of leisure knew how to wield a satirical pen briskly and fearlessly, as is shown in that almost unknown sonnet of his, *To a Cuckold* (*A un Cornudo*), which begins

> Oh, tame sheep, oh, handsome ox,
> working ass always content,
> blanket and cover for your wife,
> docile mastiff to him who comes seeking . . .

In it are correct mannered painters, for whom the art of composition was a part of dogmatic theology and the use of color a study derived from the liturgy, like the rationalist Pablo de Céspedes, whose insufferable pictures still to be found in Seville are the prelude to all the coldly academic painting of the eighteenth century and the beginning of the nineteenth (if during this period one can call painting anything not done by Goya), which is to say that in a marvelous way they exemplify decadence prior to a later flowering. There are dried-up Jesuits, emaciated, care-worn and pale, keen-witted, with circles under cold blue rheumy eyes, one such being Padre Luis del Alcázar, a cunning and prescient person who appears in this work, souring and embittering the happiness of others. There are learned archaeologists and lovers of antiques, such as Master Francisco de Medina, a professor from Osuna and secretary of Cardinal Castro, and other collectors and owners of museums and libraries like Gonzalo Argote de Molina, the Lieutenant General of Andalusia, talented chronicler, historian, bibliophile, and man of the world. There are prodigies of learning like the great Benito Arias Montano and of eloquence like Fray Luis de Granada. There is no lack of wealthy burgesses who know how to combine the art of administration with that of the festive muses, like the great Baltasar del Alcázar, majordomo of the Duke of Alcalá in Los Molares, a connoisseur of the properties of stones, herbs and metal. His brother Melchor del Alcázar, Governor of the Royal Castles of Seville, is also there.

This mixture of burgesses and aristocrats, friars and clergymen, who believed in hanging those who should be hanged and in preserving the treasures of antiquity and the good posts and benefices of the current era, was doubtless an academy of brains, settled, conservative, full of that peaceable and pleasant serenity which beautifies and ennobles fertile old age and justifies sterility.

All these people are affable, calm, and if any prank ever occurs to them they communicate it secretly, mouth to ear, laughing briefly and measuredly and then resuming their gravity. Apologetically, without any biography underneath, without even a name, a Knight of Santiago with sweeping moustaches, expressive eyes and enormous round spectacles has slipped into the book. You recognize him immediately but the author, the prudent and cautious Pacheco, has not wanted to give his name; he is Don Francisco Gómez de Quevedo.[2] Missing from the "true portraits" is that of the Equerry to the Queen, Don Juan de Jáuregui, whom Pacheco doubtless did not paint since he was a fellow artist, and there is no portrait of the great Sevillian poet Juan de la Cueva de Garoza.[3] Finally, the portrait of Vicente Espinel and the image of Miguel de Cervantes are absent.

What does this signify? To me it means that Cervantes from the first belonged to the caste of the satirists, the independents, the poverty-stricken, the antiburgesses, the antiacademics. He may have known and dealt with some or perhaps with many of the calm and sensible men whose portraits Pacheco painted, but surely they neither understood him well (aside from the fact that many were old by then) nor did he appreciate them, perhaps because they did not deserve appreciation.

During those years when he had no regular occupation nor a post like the one he had before, Miguel was little more than a vagabond, always on short commons. So he walked through the streets, through the Arenal of Seville, with idle hands, an empty stomach and the awe-inspiring project of the *Quixote* in his head. And he did not think only about the *Quixote*, for surely some of the *Exemplary Novels* were composed at this time, certainly *Rinconete and Cortadillo, The Anglo-Spanish Lady* and *The Jealous Estremaduràn*, possibly *The Two Maidens*. From them and from the part of *Don Quixote* that he was writing he would read bits to his friends, both writers and others. It was then that Cervantes took the fancy of a gentleman from Toledo who most certainly helped him. Don Fernando Alvarez de Toledo, Seigneur of Higares, related in some way to the House of Alba, was a near relative of the Duke of Lerma, with whom he was not on a very friendly footing. About this time Cervantes also cultivated his old acquaintance Licentiate Porras de la Cámara, to whom he read his works to their mutual satisfaction. With these friendships, which he knew were useful to him, the future was opening up a bit. He had little news of his wife or sisters, nor can they have worried much about what might be happening to him.

Miguel now felt himself alone in the world, and for this reason he seems to have been searching for a way to get ahead, trying to please noble gentlemen like the Seigneur of Higares and the young Duke of

Béjar, attempting through Porras de la Cámara to get support from the Church. It was becoming ever more powerful, in particular since (whatever myopic historians may think to the contrary) with Philip II dead the civil power lacked a strong hand determined to check an excessive growth of ecclesiastical influence. Miguel, then, while he pounded the pavements of Seville in search of some connection in order to earn his bread, such as a deal with the biscuit-maker Pedro de Rivas or others like him, recalled with nostalgic gloom the abundance of the Vatican in which he had lived for a few months, the splendors and pomp of those Aquavivas and Colonnas whom he had rejected when he was young. On the other hand he saw all the great gentlemen whom we know through the *Book of Portraits*, so sleek, well-fed and happy through having taken refuge in the bosom of the Church or through establishing a close relationship with it.

Times were changing. Philip II had been a man capable of confronting the wrath of Popes and of other Catholic nations. A great sinner, the manly fortitude he had inherited from his father was mingled in him with some meanness of spirit and lack of confidence, offspring of the feeble and easygoing character of his mother. This he managed to overcome in time of danger, however. Then, by taking command of himself, he was able to take command of others.

His son Philip III, on the contrary, was all lymphatic softness. He was a small sinner, and his backslidings, which at that time were minimal, so weighed upon his uneasy conscience that he needed to relieve the burdens oppressing his weak soul by entrusting them to whatever saintly man would absolve and pardon them. It was then that consciences started to be troubled and the Church, and more particularly the friars, began to move in, conquering all the inner castles, subduing an impoverished and unstable society that had lost its gaiety, banished from Spain by the malignant voices of bilious preachers. It lost confidence in itself and in the help that God always lends to the individual who has faith in himself without benefit of intermediaries or talebearers. The people lost the power to solve their inner conflicts and cure their spiritual troubles. The growth of the Court and changes in courtly customs also contributed a great deal to this situation, uprooting the provincial nobility from its rude solitude and plunging it into demoralizing promiscuities.

Miguel, spiritually exhausted and increasingly battered by the blows of adversity, was beginning to realize how greatly needed were superior people, powerful individuals, charismatic, capable of leading men, controlling events, inspiring emotion and guiding ideas. Miguel saw the heroes of reality disappearing from the scene in Spain, replaced by the heroes of extravagant fiction.

Neither the petitions of the courts of Valladolid in 1555, followed by numerous protests from such wise and eminent men as Masters Luis Vives and Alejo de Venegas, Melchor Cano and Fray Luis de Granada, nor the arguments formulated by the venerable Arias Montano, the man whose sagacious eyes were always wide open, were able to banish the plague of books on knight-errantry, the reading of which destroyed minds longing to see past adventures on land and sea repeated and amplified until they reached the impossible and crossed the borders of honest fiction to enter those of delirium. Were not books of knight-errantry perhaps in a certain way accounts of spiritual conquests, secret kingdoms, invisible mansions and inner castles? Were they not also the spoken or written narratives which in passionate and imaginative Seville or fantasy-loving Cádiz told of the prowess of the conquerors and discoverers of the New World?

There was nothing to oppose the appeal to the imagination, the insatiable avidity for the kind of reading matter in which the epic became a lunacy. The pastoral novels were a weak defense against such an invasion, and Cervantes knew this well, having been one of the first to oppose Arcadian sweetness and softness to the noisy bustle of the knights-errant. He was becoming persuaded that neither his efforts to follow the path of Montemayor and Gil Polo, nor those of Suárez de Figueroa, Gálvez de Montalvo, Lope de Vega, Valbuena, and the rest of the bucolic crowd would do more than cloy the public taste.

To give pastoral poetry and bucolic novels to one who asked for knights-errant was like trying to satisfy with honey and puff-pastry a hungry stomach which craved raw meat and three-pound loaves of bread. To call people's attention to what is base and prosaic in humanity, as the author of the *Lazarillo*[4] had done and as Miguel himself and his friend Mateo Alemán were now trying to do, could be a means of bringing the accumulated nonsense of knight-errantries to an end if the picaresque novel could manage to move in and reach all social circles, but its very character prevented it from doing this. The novelistic novels, as they are called today, had not yet occurred to Cervantes as an eclectic remedy for mitigating the evil, while imitations of the Italian *novellas* in the form of "exemplary novels" were inadequate. The "world" and the "mob," as he said, echoing his friend Alemán, should be treated as an ill-bred child, not frustrating him but playing on him cleverly by giving way and cajoling him.

As the matter stood, the books on knight-errantry were lively and rewarding, in the opinion of the populace. They had deep roots related to the *Romancero*, to the ancient *Gestes* and to the very origins of the nation, continuing through the Middle Ages with true histories of real soldiers of fortune. There was no way to cope with them other than to write still another book on knight-errantry greater than all the previous ones and to bring on the scene a flesh and blood knight and then make him fight, now with imaginary giants, now with real thick-headed rustics, merchants and traders, now with imaginary troops of Alifanfarones and Pentapolines. For the intelligent reader these would personify all the characters begotten of Andalusian and Portuguese *rodomontade* and figments of the imagination.

Pleased with this conclusion, Cervantes plunged into all that incredible cosmos of vacuous absurdity, sprung from God knows where. He caught echoes of ancient tales of the magic horse from India, perhaps coming to rest in the Homeric poem, after which came the very old legends of Clamades and Clarimunda converted into Pierres and Magalona. The primitive heroes of knight-errantry—Fierabrás, Partinuplés, Oliveros de Castilla—ran wild, mounted on magic chargers, on hippogryphs, on zebras, on dragons, the tales of marvels all mixed up with demoniacal and pious legends such as that of Robert the Devil from Brittany and with true tales of the travels of Dom Pedro de Portugal.

Behind this first squadron followed an infinity of knights conceived by people who had not the slightest notion of knight-errantry, such as the absurd Feliciano de Silva, father of *Florisel de Niquea, Don Rugel de Grecia*, and so much other nonsense. Bernardo de Vargas, a Sevillian, was author of *Don Cirongilio de Tracia*, offspring of the noble *Elesfrón de Macedonia*, while we owe to Pedro de Luján the invincible *Lepolemo*, also called the Knight of the Cross. Jerónimo Fernández from Burgos gave *Don Belianis de Grecia* to the world from his law office in Madrid; a Portuguese lady carried on the story of *Primaleón and Polendos*; the noble Don Melchor Ortega brought *Prince Felixmarte de Hircania* out from the hills of Úbeda, his home country. At the very time when Cervantes was thinking of the *Quixote*, Don Juan de Silva y Toledo introduced the outrageous *Don Policisne de Beocia*, and in 1589 the Franciscan friar Fray Gabriel de Mata turned none other than the seraphic father Saint Francis of Assisi into a knight-errant, entitling him *El caballero Asisio*. Friars, ladies, gentlemen, poets, naturalists, secretaries, accountants, and people of every kind were dedicating themselves to composing and reading the iniquitous books of knight-errantry.

To attack and demolish them was an undertaking requiring the greatest creative ability, but it was clear to Miguel that he should make the attempt, a resolve which did not precede but rather came after the great conception of human contrasts as the basis for a grandiose and definitive composition. He was convinced of the enormous moral and literary consequences of overthrowing the knight-errantry fiction which incorporated the eternal illness of Spain, in recent times called the golden legend, that delusion and exaltation which seizes upon Spanish spirits when, exhausted by excesses of heroism and energy, they fling themselves down to dream of unknown worlds and fantastic conquests.

This lack of balance between thought and action, this impracticality and consequent absence of mental capacity to see things clearly, this complete and purely Spanish divorce between theory and practice, leads either to the Utopia of the knight-errant or to the routine of the paunchy squire and his cronies. . . . I will not say that Cervantes reflected on all this, but I will maintain that misgivings about all these things and many more were taking hold of his spirit and adding new substance of reality to what he had already thought about his work.

Before any politician had smelled it out, with the exception of those prescient Italian ambassadors who went all over Europe from the very first days of Philip II attempting to discredit Spain, Miguel knew that his country was beginning to follow the downward path. He also was losing ground, but without anxiety or misgivings he found himself in the bright autumn of life, full of visions of glory and immortality, as in so many other autumns of his ill-spent youth.

About that time a great sorrow befell him with the death of Ana Franca, which he could not mourn publicly but which affected him spiritually and gave his life a new direction. She was the woman Cervantes had loved and who was fertile for him, although they both married elsewhere, he with Doña Catalina and she with Alonso Rodriguez. Now Ana Franca was dead, a widow with two children, so that Cervantes' daughter Isabel and her older sister Ana Franca were left orphans.

Miguel received the news through his sister Magdalena, and he thought of his approaching old age, he remembered his daughter whom he scarcely knew, and from Seville he arranged a way to provide for her, counting on the good feeling of the generous and kindly Doña Magdelena. He sought out a pseudoguardian for the two orphans, a certain Bartolomé de Torres who hired himself out for such purposes, and three days after he had been named guardian he contracted to place Isabel in service with Doña Magdalena, who was to teach her needlework and embroidery, give her food and drink, bed and a clean chemise, and treat her well.[5] Doña Catalina de Salazar must have been informed of all this, and Miguel intended in this way to prepare gradually for introducing his natural daughter into the legitimate family and providing for her there. He discerned that the days of his old age were near and every day he felt more urgently the need for a measure of tranquility in order to complete the work which burgeoned from the tip of his pen. He did not yet see that Don Quixote must die in his own bed and in possession of his senses, but he did see that he must return home either by force or of his own free will after having been well beaten up.

An event much talked of in Seville reinforced his conviction that Spain was going down hill fast. In the days following September of 1599 the *Asistente*[6] of Seville, Don Diego Pimentel, received a letter signed by King Philip III ordering him to provide a very good reception for the Marquesa de Denia, who had gone to Sanlúcar to be present at the lying-in of her daughter, the Countess of Niebla. The Marquesa de Denia was the wife of the favorite of Philip III, the overbearing Lerma, progenitor of all Spanish *polaquería.*[7] It was said that Philip III, when barely a child, had enjoyed a very good time with the Marquesa, and it was this amiable lady who initiated the devout monarch into the sweet mysteries which the cunning Lyceus taught the innocent Daphnis.[8] What is certain is that what today is usually called the "official element" of Seville got ready to entertain the good lady. The famous alderman and most elegant poet Don Juan de Arguijo received the illustrious visitor in his country house of Tablantes, and in doing so he made so many luxurious preparations that he cast his fortune to the winds.

The city, devastated by an epidemic of carbuncles and boils and by the consequent misery, saw its money being thrown away on masquerades, plays, simulated naval battles on the Guadalquivir, jousts with reeds and bulls that turned out to be tame in the Plaza de San Francisco. As if this were not enough, the town corporation agreed to make a present of ten thousand escudos in gold to the roving lady, in whose hands, it could be said, the entire fortune of Spain then rested. The municipal government of Seville acted in this matter like the most servile courtier, and there were only two independent and worthy men in it, Diego Ferrer and Juan Farfán, who opposed such mad and unwarranted prodigality.

That disgusting permissiveness of all the representatives of the people toward the monarch's weaknesses was a sign of the times. All the satirical poets of Seville, those whose portraits were not included in the academy book of Francisco Pacheco, let loose rivers of jeering verse on the subject. It is just possible that the pen which was busy with the *Quixote* drafted this sonnet in a moment of leisure:

> *Quae es ista quae ascendit de deserto?*
> a sly fellow asked a Licentiate,
> a graduate *in lege bellacorum*,
> with waxed moustache and open collar.
> Dying with laughter, he replied:
> This performance, Señor soldier, keeps me

so amazed and engrossed, so stupefied,
that I still cannot find out what it is.
They say this tumult and feasting comes
from Seville having received a woman
who will repay with a *pax vobis.*
Then she climbed calmly into her litter
and he, striking his breast, cries: Long life,
great Marquesa, now the King *ora pro nobis.*[9]

CHAPTER 42

Miguel Seeks Asylum—The Anglo-Spanish Lady—*Lope Attacks*

CARDINAL Don Fernando Niño de Guevara,[1] whom we know personally from the full-length life-sized portrait painted by El Greco, was a polished man, elegant, with long generous hands on which four rings gleamed, splendidly vested in ample bishop's robe of heavy watered silk and impeccable alb lavishly adorned with Venetian laces. Everything about him indicated great perspicacity and aristocratic refinement. He was a Spanish Cardinal who resembled an Italian, and what was Sevillian artfulness in his predecessor, Don Rodrigo de Castro, painted by Pacheco, in Niño de Guevara might be taken rather as a subtle kind of dissembling wholly consonant with his facial expression and his worldly tastes. In short, it can be said that Don Rodrigo de Castro, who died on September 20 of 1600, was a man of the sixteenth century and that Don Fernando Niño de Guevara was a man of the seventeenth century, and even though this comparison by centuries may seem arbitrary, in the present case it is not.

Philip II, with all his greatness and all his failings, belongs to the sixteenth century, as do the heroic part of Cervantes' life, the *Galatea,* his plays, and the novels that reflect what he saw and learned in Italy. Philip III and Philip IV belong to the seventeenth century, as do the novels on picaresque subjects, the *Persiles,* the later plays, and the *Parnassus.* Only the *Quixote* rises above those two centuries and all others, without losing sight of the sixteenth and seventeenth which it bestrides, since in it is comprised the great Spanish crisis that is essentially the crisis of all humanity in modern times.

When Niño de Guevara was named Archbishop of Seville he determined before anything else to get a clear idea of the conditions to be found in his diocese. He knew that the epidemic continued, or rather the various epidemics caused by wretched conditions, and he donated many thousands of ducats to remedy whatever could be remedied. He also knew that the sores, carbuncles, and manges of the body were as nothing compared to the moral and social rot which invaded the city and the diocese, and in order to be better informed he ordered a report to be made by the prebend Francisco Porras de la Cámara, a friend of Cervantes and a man with the kind of clear mind needed to carry out such a mission successfully.

Porras de la Cámara had assembled for his private amusement an archive of papers and writings in prose and verse divided into three parts, one of profane poems which has disappeared, one of religious verse which has ended up in the possession of the distinguished North American Hispanophile Mr. Huntington,[2] and another which is the much consulted codex entitled *Collection of Cervantine Curiosities.*

These curiosities collected by Porras de la Cámara were "fabulous events" or those the good prebend wished to be taken as such: jokes and bright ideas of the already mentioned Master Juan Farfán, gossipy stories and anecdotes of other talented Sevillians, an account in prose and verse of a trip to Portugal in 1592, a sketch of the state of Sevillian poetry in the middle of the sixteenth century, a laudatory biography of Licentiate Francisco Pacheco, the Canon, an uncle of the painter of the *Book of Portraits,* and finally the manuscripts, with considerable variations and omitting the author's name, of *The Pretended Aunt, Rinconete and Cortadillo* and *The Jealous Estremaduran.*[3] With these and other materials Porras de la Cámara was able to fashion a composite as pithy as the confidential letter in which he informed Cardinal Niño of what was to be found in his diocese. Modern studies of actual conditions tell us that Porras de la Cámara fell somewhat short of the reality in his portrayal, but the notable fact which emerges from this report is that in order to show the state of society in his time he found nothing better than to copy these works of Cervantes, whose pen told the unvarnished truth.

It can also be inferred from this how close was the friendship of Miguel and Porras de la Cámara, who must have recompensed him in some way for the generosity with which he lent him his manuscripts although they had not yet been published. Perhaps from the moment when Porras de la Cámara was interrogated by Don Fernando Niño, Miguel glimpsed hope of seeking the protection of the Church as a final resort in view of his penury, and he may have envisioned future support from a rich and generous Maecenas, splendid and Italianate, like the

Archbishop of Seville. It is accepted as a certainty among Cervantes specialists that Porras de la Cámara read Cervantes' manuscripts to Cardinal Niño during the long summer siestas when the two of them sought relief from the heat of Seville in the Archbishop's property of Umbrete. Doubtless Porras de la Cámara spoke to the Archbishop of the abject poverty in which a man of such wonderful talents was living. Then, as on so many other occasions, Miguel was knocking at the portals of the peace he longed for but was unable to cross the threshold.

One day he was walking deep in thought in the lanes which wind around the parochial church of San Marcos in charming complexity. A great crowd of well-dressed people was approaching the small square before the Convent of Santa Paula, and the patio in front of the convent was also full of people. The sun caressed the magnolias, laurels, and balm-gentles which adorned the patio and left in the shade the noble ogive of terra-cotta with broad yellow and red moldings on which a pediment displays the arms of the Catholic Kings in varied hues of majolica and medallions of glazed tiles in relief show episodes in the holy life of the saint to the small birds and pigeons.

Moved by curiosity Miguel entered the church, which sparkled in holiday dress, from the Mudejar trelliswork of flying beams down to the floor of glazed tiles fashioned in a wavy pattern like those in some of the rooms in the Castle of Don Pedro el Cruel. In the two little side altars a St. John the Baptist and a St. John the Evangelist, recent works by the already famous Martínez Montañés, seemed to be telling each other their sorrows, singing of them in low tones to the sound of an angelic guitar. On the twin pilasters of the main arch two little angels flew with joyful abandon, dancing *seguidillas* with the candelabra hanging from their right hands. In the back of the choir through the curtains was heard the hum of the community, the lisping voices of the Sevillian nuns, who are the most gentle and lovely nuns in all the world and who speak of God as of a sweetness infinitely superior to that of the rich egg candies made by their white hands.

Miguel learned that a novice was to take the veil and he saw the approach of the procession which followed the new religious, "one of the most distinguished retinues that had ever been seen on such an occasion in Seville." Miguel saw the bride of Christ, so graceful, lovely and well accoutered that seeing her was a blessing from God, and all those present pressed forward to gaze more closely on such peerless beauty. Miguel was the first to catch sight of a man pushing through the crowd, dressed as he himself had been when he arrived in the ship of Master Antón Francés after being ransomed by the Trinitarians, with his cross hanging on his breast, one arm red, the other blue, and a round blue bonnet on his head. He recognized in the frantic eyes of that man not only the anxious spirit of a captive, as he had been himself, but the appalling situation in which he had found himself so often, thinking to grasp happiness by the hem of its tunic and losing his hold only to fall once more into black despair. Miguel then heard the voice of that liberated captive cry out in urgent tones: "Stop, stop, for while I live you cannot be a religious. . . ." Thus he was present at the climax of that dramatic scene and he returned home with his mind seething.

The event was much talked of in Seville. Miguel, his spirit still moved, told his friend Porras de la Cámara about it and the latter begged him to "put all that story down in writing so that the Archbishop can read it." That is the story of *The Anglo-Spanish Lady*, modified and dressed up by Cervantes to give greater pleasure to the Archbishop; it was written after *Rinconete and Cortadillo* and *The Jealous Estremaduran*, and like them was based on things he had witnessed in Seville.

Miguel felt that he was making an auspicious beginning for a career as a writer in favor with men in power. If the sonnet against the Marquesa de Denia were his perhaps Señor de Higares, with whom his relative the Marquesa had quarreled, was aware of its authorship. It is certain that Miguel wrote *The Anglo-Spanish Lady* to order, as Lope and many other talented men did, but we do not know whether it was rewarded or in what manner.

At the end of the year 1600 Lope de Vega, having quit the service of the Marquis of Sarriá, arrived in Seville where he lived in Triana, perhaps in the house of his uncle the Inquisitor.

For a man without a patron the craft of writing was only a way of living from hand to mouth, but for Lope it was a glorious, felicitous, and gracious way of leading an entertaining and carefree life. His plays and poems were for him the bed on which he rested, the coffer from which he drew whatever he needed for his daily wants, the spies and go-betweens for his loves and flirtations, forgiveness for his frailties and blunders, and the means of acquiring rich and generous protectors. Over and above all this was something else which up to then had never been achieved by any writer, something that Lope was the first to enjoy in Spain, and that was popularity, universal appreciation, being known and admired for his achievements and not just within the circle of other writers. It penetrated the secluded boudoirs of ladies and found its way among the multitudes who were beginning to turn their heads when someone would say, "There goes Lope." This sun of popularity which perhaps had never had a name given it up to then, emerged for the first time in Spain to shine on Lope de Vega.

It was therefore only natural for the satirical Sevillian genius, that wild and dishevelled Muse of the streets that Pacheco had been so careful not to include in his book, to direct a salvo at him. One of the first bows in his direction was a sonnet by a certain uninhibited Sevillian, half ruffian, half poet, called Alonso Alvarez de Soria. This is the famous invective which begins:

They say Lope has arrived. It is not possible.

and ends with these not too proper phrases:

Should he not be as great, then, as his renown
I sh.. on you, on him, and on his poems. . . .

Lope got wind of the sonnet, although at that time he had nothing to do with cheap poets and associated only with his uncle, with the elegant gentleman Don Juan de Arguijo,[4] and with some of the complaisant academicians of the *Book of Portraits*. For the moment he paid no attention to it nor to the other satires, popular songs and ditties with which he was greeted as a new arrival; but what always happens in such cases came to pass. Lope maintained his silence and when he had finished his famous work *The Wanderer in his Homeland* (*El peregrino en su patria*) and sent it to his friend Arguijo so that he might honor him with one of his amber-gloved and frilly-ruffed sonnets, the malevolent Alvarez de Soria assailed him more furiously and returned to the attack with a *décima*[5] of broken endings, one of the first to be composed in such a form:

Sent by Lope de V-
to Señor Don Juan de Argui-
the book of *Peregrí-*
for him to say if it is goo-
and he is so noble and discre-
that being as it is ba-
he says it's another Garcilá-
in its outline and composi-
but later, to himself, who dou-
that he must say it is a swind-?

The aggressive tone of the *décima*, the effrontery of breaking off the ends of the lines to make it into impertinent babbling, making faces and playing games, and the fact of attributing to his friend the noble Arguijo a pious fraud regarding the value of his work, must have roused Lope, whose fathers had not made him one to suffer jokes at his own expense. He made inquiries and searched around for the author of such verses, and since Alvarez de Soria was unknown and the other satirical writers were probably friends of his, it did not occur to Lope to think of any other person than Cervantes, with whom he still felt at odds because of the old incident of Elena Osorio, and perhaps he also bore a grudge against the actor Morales, a great friend of Miguel. What is certain is that Lope replied to the attacks against him with this venomous and ferocious sonnet:

> I know nothing of la-, of lí-, nor le-,
> nor do I know if you, Cervantes, are ba- or bu-
> I only say that Lope is Apollo and you
> are the cart horse of his coach and ever a pig.
> So that you would not write it was ordained
> by Heaven that you be maimed at Corfu:
> you talk like an ox, but you did say *mú.*
> Oh, may it bring you bad, quixotic luck!
> Honor Lope, old ass, or look to yourself!
> For he is the sun and if he angers it will rain
> and that despicable *Don Quixote* of yours,
> from bu- to ba- goes round the world
> peddling samples and bastard saffron
> and finally ends up on a dung-heap.

Lope had certainly not forgotten Miguel, as an inopportune witness of youthful adventures is not apt to be forgotten, and having reached the peak of his glory he took a savage revenge on that unfortunate poet whom he knew only from his *Galatea* and a few theatrical works which perforce must have seemed poor to him, being as they were in a field in which he had been so remarkably successful.

Lope thought that with that sonnet he had buried Cervantes forever and he still did not realize that this was the only person who might one day outshine him. He did not know Cervantes well and he knew the *Quixote* only by hearsay, from inadequate descriptions or references provided by people to whom Miguel may have read only a few chapters. Nevertheless it is obvious that from then on Lope scorned Cervantes as one of the vulgarly envious, of whom there were many, and he lived in this error for some time.

On the other hand, it would not have been unnatural for Cervantes to feel jealous of Lope, to whom had fallen, thanks to life's injustices, nothing but satisfactions and the coddlings of fortune. Lope, constantly sought after, rejected protectors, discarded mistresses, and lived in a perpetual war with himself because he had no need to struggle for a living. Lope triumphed, Lope was famous, the elegant ladies and gentlemen from the highest social circles contended for him, he rose with the rise of the theater, he had reached the summit in two strides, he was Nature's prodigy. Meanwhile Miguel lived beaten down and almost obscure, at his age still circulating from the courtyard of Los Olmos, where at that time the offensive Alvarez de Soria was reigning, to the courtyard of Don Juan or the orchard of Doña Elvira, playhouses where he was sure to encounter the works of Lope being played, with the actors who were the friends or servants of Lope on the stage. And to show how great was Lope's error in attributing the *décima* to Cervantes one has only to think how any attack by Miguel was limited to the prudent, measured and purely literary criticism of Lope's playwriting included in the dialogue between the canon and the priest in the *Quixote*, which he must have added at the time to what he had already written in Chapter 48.

Cervantes was in no mood for violence; his autumnal spirit was becoming subdued. The immortal work on which he was engaged had broadened his talent and made it more sure, as must always happen when the writer is humble and thinks only of pouring out his soul on paper whatever others may say or think. Miguel always knew the value of his work, but as it progressed he understood it more clearly and the friends to whom he read bits of the *Quixote* helped in this.

Don Quixote became popular in Seville long before he saw himself in print, and the names of Sancho Panza and Don Quixote were used as nicknames, as they are today, to specify one known individual or another. It is possible that Lope, stirred by curiosity on finding the name of Cervantes' work frequently mentioned, may have wanted to get to know it and that he then tried to approach Miguel. It is not reasonable to suppose that the enmity between them lasted, since in 1602 a third edition of *La Dragontea*[6] was published and it included an extremely laudatory sonnet by Cervantes.

It is almost certain that Cervantes had softened many of the more critical conceits in the conversation between the canon and the priest and that Lope, although he did not know Miguel's work well, now modified his judgment as much as it was possible for a man so full of himself to do. There is evidence, however, that there was no completely sincere reconciliation on the part of Lope. As for Cervantes, he continued to live, God knows how, until he had finished his book, possibly with the support of Cardinal Niño and Porras de la Cámara, though it seems strange that such a grateful man did not express his appreciation at the time.

New strokes of adverse fortune still awaited him when he thought he had the key to peace in his hand. On July 2 of 1601 his brother Ensign Rodrigo de Cervantes died heroically in the Battle of the Dunes,[7] that brother to whom Miguel had taught the profession of arms and whose career he had followed with so much delight. Miguel's loneliness was increasing.

On September 14 of 1601 the auditors of reports charged Cervantes with responsibility for 136,000 maravedis Francisco Pérez de Vitoria had paid him in Málaga, and shortly afterward they instructed Purveyor General Bernabé del Pedrosa, on post in Seville as *Residente*, to detain and imprison Miguel until he rendered accounts or produced sufficient guarantees to permit him to go to Valladolid in order to obtain final clearance there. Toward the end of 1602 Cervantes thus found himself once more in the accursed prison of Seville; it is not known whether he remained there for a few or many days or months. Gaspar Osorio de Tejeda, that treasurer from Baza whom we recognized in 1594 as one of the precursors of *caciquismo*, was the man who made a strenuous effort to force Cervantes to appear in court to settle his accounts, more from a desire to injure him than for any other reason. On January 24 of 1603 the auditors agreed that what was outstanding by Cervantes was a deficit of only 2,347 reals, probably representing bankrupt accounts which Miguel had never collected. These gentlemen also declared that they had ordered Pedroso to free Miguel from the jail in Seville without his having to appear in court when he regained his freedom. It was therefore necessary for Cervantes to go to Valladolid, where the Spanish capital had been established since January of 1601.

Miguel left Seville at the beginning of 1603, never to return. As he gazed for the last time on those towers that the sun whitewashed at dawn and gilded at nightfall he never thought that he was saying goodbye forever. He did not realize that it was then that he definitely, irremediably, had entered the autumn of life. Perhaps he did not much care. He carried his little satchel with him and in it . . . locked in it lay immortality.

CHAPTER 43

Cervantes Reads the Quixote *to Himself*

ON his journey from Seville to Valladolid, rather than brooding over the difficulties raised by the accounting gentlemen, Miguel thought deeply about his book, counting up virtues and enumerating very carefully the faults that might be found in it. During the necessary stops at inns and roadhouses he brought out the manuscript, indited with so many different papers and inks, and went over it again. He saw once more and paid close and careful attention to the places where events in his book occurred, and he may have cut out or corrected some of what he had written or made additions and insertions.

Despite the fertility of his genius it would be childish to suppose that Cervantes let his pen flow without re-reading or correcting his masterpiece, even though there is evidence that the greater part of it was already written in the first half of 1602 and that it was well known among the people of Seville. It would also show complete ignorance of the elements of literary composition to think that the *Quixote*, even if there are some purely incidental oversights, was something produced haphazardly without much thought or reflection. It is more logical and more generous to believe, as Cervantes himself declares, that everything written there was written "for a reason" and has a purpose and a meaning.

It is almost impossible to distinguish in the composition of one of those books that illuminate humanity what part corresponds to almost unconscious inspiration and what is due to deliberate thought. It is easy to identify allusions when they refer to well-known people and events. It is difficult and dangerous to hazard conjectures and hypotheses like those that have been heaped on this unique book and those that may be ventured hereafter. Even the Church cannot judge intentions and truly it is of no great importance that Cervantes, thinking like Columbus to reach the East Indies, discovered the Occident; the office of those who seek new worlds is to stumble on ones they never expected. What is important is the initiative, the faith, the courage and the constancy to get somewhere, no matter where.

Miguel was glad that he had placed Don Quixote in a village of La Mancha, and he saw clearly that his knight-errant could not be Andalusian, although for a time at the beginning he considered having him wander over the Andalusian countryside. Can one possibly conceive of a Sevillian Don Quixote? Do you believe that Andalusia could breed a gentleman capable of such a chastely Platonic love or so absolutely serious in all his words and deeds? To Miguel it seemed right that Don Quixote be a man of La Mancha, from a place where heaven and earth kiss each other at sunrise and sunset like the pure spouses of the golden legend, ignoring the tempting shadows of trees and hills and the seductive songs of voluptuously curving rivers. It was also essential that Sancho be from La Mancha. It would have been very easy for Miguel to turn the squire into a licentious buffoon or a crafty ruffian from Seville like many others he had depicted, but this contrast would have been extremely crude. No, Sancho must be another Manchegan like his serious and dignified master, incapable of cracking a joke. We note that

Sancho never says anything clever or witty; his sayings and proverbs are opportune because of their naturalness and their apparent incongruity with the occasion, but their charm lies in the figure of speech and the particular situation, as it should in real humor.

All the details relevant to Don Quixote's madness, touched upon with such sobriety, seemed to Cervantes wise and in their place. He was pleased with the first sortie, the description of the countryside of Montiel and of how the sun rose with such haste and vigor, as the sun of La Mancha always does in July. Privately Cervantes applauded the fitting and skillful manner in which he handled the arrival of Don Quixote at the inn.

All the advances Don Quixote makes are courteous and knightly. It is appropriate that he should take the mild and rotund innkeeper for an eminent Castilian and the painted prostitutes for noble damsels. The greatness of his position does not preclude his feeling hungry and declaring it without rhetoric, for the burden and weight of arms may not be borne without taking care of the belly. Just as he creates fantastic ideas of what surrounds him, so also Don Quixote has no notion of time. Shortly after he began watching over his arms they tell him four hours have gone by and he believes them. The scene where he is dubbed a knight is an obvious parody of the books of knight-errantry, but the first adventure, that of Juan Haldudo, the rich peasant from Quintanar, is reality itself, without anything high-sounding or outrageous appearing in it. Anyone who was not a knight and had never heard of Amadís would do what Don Quixote did, passing judgment and speaking with great practical wisdom. At the end of his reproof he hurls to the winds like a war cry his sonorous name: "For I am the valiant Don Quixote de la Mancha, righter of wrongs and injustices." That is Don Quixote's first clash with bitter reality, prepared with sublime art, for the worthy action fails and ends up bankrupt and counterproductive. The reappearance of the lad Andrés after many chapters and his maledictions against Don Quixote and his knight-errantries are inserted here with intuitive knowledge of the inevitable whimsicality of life.

The Toledan merchants seemed to Don Quixote like the many extraordinarily haughty people whom Cervantes had encountered in his life. The words of the mocking merchant, polished, urbane and aristocratically Toledan, which is to say the most graciously and deceitfully misleading that exist in Spain, prepare the way for the brutality of the muleteer. Don Quixote has been cudgelled for the first time, and as he considered such an insult impossible he can do no less than turn to the great Spanish resource of the golden legend, recalling the ballad of the Marquis of Mantua and delivering the consequent lamentations.

His neighbor Pedro Alonso is the first compassionate soul who does something to bring Don Quixote back to sanity. The wounded knight turns proudly on hearing his lunacies mentioned and exclaims with mystical pride, as if obeying the thought of his author: "I know who I am, and know that I can be not only what I have said, but all the Twelve Peers . . . " in which one recognizes the arrogant Castilian fanfaronade which followed the day of defeat.

In order not to bore his readers Miguel here introduces the scrutiny of Don Quixote's library in which he sets down his tastes and critical preferences, hailing those he likes and dismissing those of which he disapproves. The priest and the barber appear, the priest ingenious, subtle and crafty like so many clergymen then in a Spain not yet invaded by the wave of black melancholy which later tinged everything that had anything to do with religion. This priest, Pedro Pérez, is one of those cheerful Spanish clergymen of whom one finds small trace now in the cities, a sympathetic and kindly race, human and indulgent, worth more in souls for religion than all the friars and preachers with their gloomy ratiocinations. He never mentioned Hell to his parishioners save as a last resort; his worldly wisdom is obvious from his very first replies to Don Quixote.

Sancho is necessarily brought into the limelight to prepare for his sortie. The state of mind of this pseudo great man on sallying forth with Don Quixote on the gray ass "looking like a patriarch with his saddle bags and his leathern wine bottle" is like that of hidalgos from Estremadura and Castile on leaving for the Indies without knowing what was awaiting them, attracted by curiosity and the lure of profit. He did not know what islands, kingdoms or governments were; he may not have known the name of the King, as happens today with many peasants and shepherds in his country, but in the bottom of his soul he nourished all kinds of ambitions; he felt himself capable of being an Emperor even though he did not know what the title meant. Don Quixote, slightly deluded, slightly crafty, does not want his squire to have lowly aspirations, rather he stimulates his ambition, telling him: "Do not be so spiritless that you will be content with less than being a governor."

When Don Quixote sallied forth provided with his squire and all the trappings of knight-errantry what had his first adventure to be if not the one Cervantes had glimpsed as a lad, possibly when he first saw the windmills of the Romeral, La Mota del Cuervo or Criptana? He had to establish with epic boldness the truly intrepid valor of Don Quixote.

Is it credible that a book where events are initiated in this form, obedient to such a subtly planned artistic emphasis, was conceived and written by chance? Through the windmills Cervantes began to think about knight-errantry and through the windmills Don Quixote began resolutely to extract from his life as a poor and sensible hidalgo "the most delicate understanding there was in La Mancha." "This is a good war," he exclaimed eagerly on seeing the giants, "and a great service to God." Possibly the long blades of the oars that the galley slaves pulled on the benches of the enemy ships at Lepanto appeared to Miguel's fevered eyes much the same as the wings of the windmill. They also were giants and that was a good war and of service to God, from which honorable and profitless wounds resulted.

Don Quixote did not complain of the pain, for knights-errant are not given to complaining of any wound, even though their bowels should fall out, but he did lament his lance having failed him. Does this not recall some failures in armaments noted after the defeat of the *Invincible*?

The battle with the Biscayan comes up and again the figure of Don Quixote acquires human proportions and his true boldness is made manifest. Why does Cervantes interrupt his narration? Is it in imitation of the *Amadís* as Bowle[1] indicates? No, we do not think so. Cervantes found it absolutely necessary to introduce Cide Hameti Benengeli, the conscientious and dispassionate historian who must recount the things he believes and he himself explains that this is how history should be written.

With the defeat of the Biscayan the knightly fiction, which always tries to bring in a real event or a sanguinary happening, recovers new vigor. The balm of Fierabrás comes up again, and on that theme master and man discuss what knights-errant should eat. Taking advantage of this talk, and returning to a sphere of reason such as no vulgar intelligence can ever attain, Don Quixote describes the Golden Age to the goatherds, grows familiar with Sancho and makes him sit beside him, and treats as brothers those poor men who can barely understand him, but who just by listening come to love him. It is the saintly simplicity of the Humble Man of Assisi addressing himself to the wolf and to the timid larks and to his sister water.

From such high levels the spirit descends smoothly to the pastoral blandness of the loves and death of Grisóstomo. Here Cervantes makes use of his bucolic talent, seeking to please the courtiers and professional writers, and so that there be no doubt of the pretense the shepherd Antonio takes care to state that the admirable ballad "I know well that thou dost adore me, Olalla" (*Yo sé, Olalla, que me adoras*) was composed by his uncle, the prebendary, and Sancho falls asleep while listening to the shepherd's poem. This passage was not written for common folk, nor could ordinary people enjoy that erotic wave in which a whole district is seen quivering with desire for the loves of Marcela, or the discussions of Don Quixote as to whether a knight can exist without a lady, or the idealized description of Dulcinea, or the eulogy of Grisóstomo, in which it would not be too excessively daring to find something autobiographical. The fantasy-inspired Marcela, a figure fashioned from the same mixture that Shakespeare used to forge the volatile spirit of Ariel, expounds the Platonic concepts that Fray Luis de León vulgarized, and others he did not touch upon about love and beauty, and Miguel initiates the great subject of free will already stirring in novelists and dramatists, as it had before in philosophers and theologians.

From these ineffable heights Don Quixote suddenly tumbles to fall under the cudgels in the enraged rustic hands of the merciless Yanguesans. Don Quixote would have liked to die of rage there. "What do you want, *brother* Sancho?" he says to him, acknowledging the equality of squires and knights when in pain; and later, when he has calmed down, he discusses the quality of the affront. This tragicomic bit is preparation for the events which are to take place in the inn.

The good Maritornes opens the portal for us to penetrate this minor Iliad of humor. Real and imaginary events are mixed and jumbled here, and the author's art is such that one cannot tell where truth begins and fiction ends: or it may be that truth when it is so strictly reproduced has the appearance of fiction. He piled up events, but not in such a manner that their confusion and concatenation were not possible or even probable. The blanket-tossing of Sancho and the animosity it created in him and his intention of returning to the village, that paternal and affectionate "Sancho, my son, don't drink water, son, don't drink it," Cervantes knew well was bound to conquer and convince the reader. On leaving the inn Don Quixote loves Sancho tenderly without realizing it, and the reader loves both Sancho and Don Quixote.

Who can doubt that allusions to famous Andalusian characters are incorporated in the adventure of the two regiments of sheep in which the names and nicknames from Seville and Cádiz of Alifanfarón and Pentapolín, Micocolembo and Laurcalco, Brandabarbarán and Aleñiquen from Algarbe, Timonel de Carcajona and Pierres Papín, the hunchback card player of the Calle de Sierpes, crackle and rumble? It is not for me to throw light upon who these people were; more authoritative pens than mine must do so.

After this comes the adventure of the dead body, and for the first time the valiant Don Quixote is not so sure of himself and his hair stands on end. Possible excommunication lay across the path and Cervantes did not forget what had happened to him in Ecija, and it is to this that are due his worried, almost stammering protests: "The Church which I respect and adore as a Catholic and faithful Christian. . . ." He had already suffered many blows; already Sancho called him "Knight of the Doleful Countenance": now Sancho threw out his first proverb when the adventure of the fulling mill is initiated by Don Quixote with mystically poetic intonation. "I am he," he exclaimed, recovering all his arrogance at one blow on sniffing danger, "I am he for whom are reserved the dangers, the heroic exploits, the valiant deeds. . . ." And with this he decides to perish if need be. Is this not a true book of knight-errantry? Is not Don Quixote a real and true knight-errant, perhaps the only real and true one? Does he not confront dangers with all the courage necessary to vanquish them? And at this high point of courage and resolution Cervantes' genius interpolates Sancho's terror and evil odor with admirable skill and an extraordinary insight into the humanizing effect of contrast. Homer did not reach such heights, nor any other author of either ancient or modern times. The break of day beside the fulling mills, Sancho's laughter, the furious thrashing that Don Quixote gave him and the timely demand of the squire for his salary after his ribs had been beaten black and blue are the divine made human. It is a poem of knight-errantry that stoops and unbends until it grazes and rubs shoulders with the picaresque novel, and to show it even more clearly right after this comes the adventure of the galley slaves, in which he must be a stupid man who does not see Cervantes unbosoming himself against the whole of a society that had mistreated and underrated or ignored him upon so many occasions.

Those are not dreamed-up knight-errantries but actual palpitating calamities. With the old white-bearded bawdmonger we enter the kingdom of the paradoxical in which Spaniards love so much to wander. With Ginés de Pasamonte we see the only hero capable of facing up to the Ingenious Hidalgo. Consider the arrogant and masterful seriousness with which Ginés speaks; he is the person with the most worldly intelligence to appear in the story: mark that he has his life "written by these fingers" and pawned for two hundred reals. Who can doubt that the *Life of Ginés de Pasamonte* was one of the many books Cervantes promised himself he would write? But he did not, and he was right. His friend Alemán had already written one and later his friend Espinel would write another. The concept of Spain as the servant of many masters was made all too clear in these books. The knaves, chattering lay brothers, petty thieves and gay lads already retained naught of their ancient greatness: they were the errant villains, the grandsons of Lucius, he of the transformations.[2] This was a minor matter for Miguel; he may have intended to start something similar upon writing the first pages of *The Glass Licentiate*, but on his arriving in Italy and expanding in its splendor it drove him mad and made him say the truths which only children, lunatics and Don Quixote were to put in their right place, truths that had been wasting away within Cervantes himself for many long years. . . .[3]

The entry into the Sierra Morena is a major theme of the *Quixote* and at the same time it is a skillful retreat. The author has set down all that occurred to him regarding human justice, he has written his protest against the harshness of making men whom Nature had created free submit to being slaves, he has entrusted everything to divine law like a primitive Christian or one of today's anarchists. Always conscious of the symbolic value of his work, he understands that one must combine naturals with flats, and he plunges into the wilderness of the sierra, invents Don Quixote's penitence and makes the wild and dishevelled Cardenio appear, leaping from crag to crag. Don Quixote offers to be of service to the unfortunate gentleman, service a hundredfold greater than those rendered by ordinary humanity. The delicacy with which he presents himself to him is sublime, not now as a knight-errant who undoes wrongs and sets grievances aright, but as a man ready and apt for curing and alleviating pain by sharing it.

Cardenio, who speaks almost in verse, like an elegant poet of the pure Cordovan caste, introduces us to a world very different from what we have been through up to now. His courtly spirituality leads Don Quixote to penitence and magnifies and ennobles his action: his words, worthy of Don Diego de Mendoza[4] for the beauty and skill with which they are put together, lead Don Quixote and the reader to consort with true knights and with ladies and damsels of the loftiest rank. All the courtly adventures associated with Cardenio carry the action to such heights that Cervantes can introduce at the inn a *resumé* of the whole of contemporary society and in it depict how gentlemen and ladies of the aristocracy, grave magistrates, captive captains, tramps, and squad leaders of the Holy Brotherhood felt and acted, and how all that complex society paid attention to Don Quixote, were interested in him, and at bottom could not make up their minds whether or not he was mad.

In these chapters, as if in passing, Cervantes traced his psychology of love in depicting the types of Dorotea, Luscinda, Clara, and Zoraida, and even the confused and awkward Maritornes and the daughter of the innkeeper. He also pointed up that kind of tacit agreement which operates in society in the presence of an extraordinary man or event. All those present at the inn were as one in playing up to Don Quixote and imposing on the barber, affirming that the basin was a helmet, and later all of them, without showing it, were in agreement with the priest that Don Quixote should be caged as a madman; but it is certain that when they separated each of them went on his way thinking that only God could know for sure who was the madman and who were sane. The confusion caused by listening to Don Quixote's speech on arms and letters and seeing him in the battle with the leather winebags which was produced in the minds of the judge, the captive Pérez Viedma and the tamed Cardenio, and the uneasiness which this same doubt later roused in the spirit of the wise clergyman, are communicated to the reader, and already from the moment that the *Quixote* appeared it must have occurred to all men of good will and clear intellect who read it.

The mystical, esoterically symbolical episode of the goatherd who goes in pursuit of the pretty fugitive she-goat induces a vague disquiet today. What does it mean, that goat who, when her master tells the tale of the fickle Leandra, "looking into his face, seemed to give him to understand that she was paying heed?" Here is an incident of the highest philosophical and esthetic value that no one seems to have noticed. How often had the struggling, the unfortunate Cervantes felt himself losing his reason, his intelligence faltering, his will fainting, when he must have cried, as did the poor philosopher shepherd: "Ah, you wild one, you wild, speckled, spotted wild one. How is it that you walk with a limp these days? What wolves have frightened you . . . ?"

And the wolves, which are men pitted against one another, howl around him.

CHAPTER 44

Cervantes Ponders the Quixote—*Valladolid*

ALMOST twenty years had passed since Miguel, full of illusions, had written *Galatea*, made love to Ana Franca, and married Doña Catalina de Salazar. Whatever of youth remained in his heart could not be much. The hours of happiness had been brief; possibly all of them put together would not have filled a day. In contrast the years of affliction and misfortune had been extremely long.

The sad news of the evils that afflicted Spain as yet barely reached the placid serenity of Seville. The receptions with which the Marquesa de Denia was officially entertained were the first warning of the profound changes that were taking place in social customs and the manner of government. Once Philip II was dead the personal policy of the King was replaced by the personal policy of the favorite, and as ill luck would have it the favorite was a man of such scant intellectual and moral worth as the Duke of Lerma.[1]

Whoever has seen the portrait of Philip III by Velásquez needs no more or better description of what was not decadence but rather bankruptcy. Philip was a poor, lymphatic, chlorotic being with a drooping lip, sunken temples, expressionless blue eyes and stupidly braggart stance. He was a great horseman, not much of a reader, and so lacking in intelligence that his tutor and preceptor, the Toledan Archbishop Don García de Loaysa, could barely instil four pious concepts into his narrow cranium.

They married this poor devil of a King with a minor Austrian princess, the twelfth or twentieth daughter of one of those dukes or princes who abound in her country as hidalgos do in Spain. Doña Margarita de Austria was a worthy and completely insignificant lady who, when they went in search of her to share the throne with her husband, was found in a convent. Don Philip and Doña Margarita formed a bourgeois couple, sedate and economical, which was very well suited to the exigencies of the situation; while the sun never set on Spain's dominions the King himself now did not have a penny to spend.

Although Lerma had more of the acquisitive magpie than the eagle in his makeup, he knew very well that it was advisable to keep such people entertained, and he took them across Spain from *fiesta* to *fiesta*, arranging paid ovations for them, and made them believe in that universal felicity to the display of which stupid minds are so susceptible. A dense atmosphere of foolishness began to develop around the palace. The gentlemen of the pointed beards, sunken cheeks and dreamy eyes painted by El Greco fled from it. The seed sowed in the houses of the great by the first mystics and ascetics was being harvested by those wily clergymen who governed at their will and pleasure, absolving the frailties of the ladies and linking them skillfully with those of the gentlemen. The assurance and firmness of thought and action of the days of Philip II were replaced by an erratic restlessness and an almost gelatinous incoherence of will. Fear reigned in the royal palaces and in those of the nobility, an absurd and inexplicable fear of God alone knew what, of sin, of contamination, of heresy.

The Inquisition was vigilant but heterodoxy was nevertheless alive, and if it could not count on men as mentally illustrious as the Spanish Protestants of the Emperor's day it continued to spread inconspicuously, influencing the minds of individuals rather than the masses. The Inquisition persecuted Illuminati, relapsed heretics, scoffers and deluded folk of minor importance, at the same time overlooking concepts and ideas which swayed and molded souls from pulpit and book.

In these years when it seemed as if the whole world was dazed and bewildered there lies a whole secret chapter in the history of Spain still to be written. Misgivings, suspicions and incredible jealousies dominated the general pusillanimity of spirits. All Spaniards looked at each other askance. It would be idiotic not to realize how this restlessness, this insecurity and this ill-satisfied hunger of body and soul are mirrored in all the works of Spain's Golden Age, preventing them from taking that magnificent, severely classical stance which replaces depth of vision and human feeling in the works of the age of Louis XIV. No Spanish writer, not even Lope himself, enjoyed the peace of mind indispensable to classical perfection; they were all rebellious, nervous, excited, morbidly sensitive people and thus Spain lacks true classicism.

For Cervantes to happen upon a classical format would have meant little, however. Better than anyone else the author of the discourse on arms and letters and of the story of Cardenio and the arguments of the shepherdess Marcela could have been classical; nevertheless he was not, and it is a good thing he wasn't. What he had thought and felt in his heroic days, in the momentous years of Philip II, clashed violently with what, anticipating the general opinion, he felt and was now thinking about the grotesque times of Philip III. The brilliance of the sun of La Mancha was needed to light the earlier period; to illuminate the later one it was enough to direct the gleam of the implacable spectacles of Don Francisco Gómez de Quevedo upon it. At that critical moment when he was forging his work Spain had lost its significance, lacking that touch of madness which leads men and nations to immortal destinies. For this reason Don Quixote and the Glass Licentiate were mad, and that other fellow from Cordova, and those from Seville, spokesmen of the truth which for Cervantes seeped out from his inner consciousness.

Only a grand and epic madness, only a book of knight-errantry, Miguel thought, could lift the vulgarity and general stupidity out of the mud and floor-sweepings, and because of this he made a book of real knight-errantries. Only laughter and scorn, blows, fisticuffs and gluttony can stir this tired and dejected mob, he also thought, and because of this he created Sancho and, although not without great heart-burning, caused Don Quixote to be beaten up, outraged, ignored by the crowd, in all of which there was not a little of the autobiographical. The future is still not perceived clearly, nor can we see ahead whether we shall achieve redemption or remain as we are—he reflected later; and he permitted the First Part to end with himself and the reader greatly perplexed.

Let us not forget that this happened in 1603, when the Philip III of Velásquez did not yet exist. The knight-errant had been caged as a madman, but he was alive and he could again sally forth in search of combat, and his squire still promised himself new gains. The helmet of Mambrino was a barber's basin, whoever touched it knew indubitably, but even more deeply than this conviction the sublime concepts fallen from the lips of Don Quixote were felt in their souls. The wandering she-goat of the ill-tempered shepherd was made fast, but she could still flee from the real or imaginary wolves that pursued her.

Thus the book and Miguel's ideas remain related to the reality in which he lived, not to the very different position in which the gallant Biscayan and the valiant Don Quixote stood before the sage Cide Hamete threaded them on the point of his pen. And Cervantes, reflecting upon this, spelled out here and there and emphasized in this or that passage how, to sum it up, that proposition he had conceived depicted the whole of life and not just a particular reflection of a social condition which might continue as it was or transform itself radically, which might be a siesta or a dream. He left his readers confused and disturbed because he was confused and disturbed, but not so much so that he did not leave a door open, or at least ajar, so that a kindly hand or a subtle breeze or a hurricane could open it and give access to hope.

Cervantes was not entirely hopeless—he could not be, knowing Spain the eternally resurgent, knowing himself who had lived through so many and such arduous perils. He was confident of the future and appraised correctly the value of his work; the great world, that which existed beyond Spain and beyond the contemporary period, was sure to be his. But what he had to face up to immediately was the small world of the present.

And then something happened, something less rare than it is usually thought to be, in that the artistic vision of reality he had acquired and perfected in conceiving and writing the *Quixote* served him as a guideline along which to rearrange his own life, or at least try to. Miguel had started out with himself, with the contrasts, struggles and difficulties he had experienced in life, and from that he leaped to the books of chivalry which illuminated and broadened the horizon for him, and in this broadening and illuminating he saw how much it was possible to see of the lives of individuals and of people in general in his time, and how much of the universal and eternal life that only geniuses like him can perceive.

With renewed courage he now withdrew within himself, though he was no longer the same man as before. How could he be? If any trifle, a disappointment in love, a small matter of self-esteem, a theatrical work or a successful speech transforms us and turns us into something else, what a transformation Miguel must have gone through after having written the First Part of the *Quixote*, coinciding exactly as it did with the change that was manifestly taking place among all classes and conditions in the nation. We can scarcely imagine what had been the growth and unexpected greatness of his finally rich—more than rich, opulent—soul.

It was perhaps then that he dejectedly recognized his former error and thought how much better it would have been for him to continue writing plays and novels instead of choosing the hazards of being a commissary or tax collector; but after thinking thus he perhaps realized that he had not lost those twenty years altogether, years during which the soldier and the poet were transformed into something greater, into the only thing one can be in this miserable world, since we are sent into it for this purpose, into a *man.* In the world there was in truth nothing more to lose than life; otherwise there were no losses, or if there were losses there were ways of changing them into sure and everlasting gains. And the life presented by him in the immortal book still would not let him go and Don Quixote was also alive.

Quite aside from all this Miguel saw that the highest in the land were preoccupied with the trivialities that contaminated all the rest of society. Politicians were still politicians and literary men continued to be literary in a manner very little different from the rhetorical formalism of the past. Any attempt to make literature a true vocation was stifled, and even Lope and Góngora, although very strong individualists and geniuses of the first order, did no more than follow their trade with all its routines and pawings of the earth.

What emerged apace was an artificial society that was a reflection of the theater or that the theater reflected, for there was something of both in it, the existence of which Cervantes had already noted during his last visit to the capital. The theatricalities that usually replace heroism at the beginning of every period of decadence were breaking new ground and developing to such a point that they dominated all social classes. The prototypes of Lope and Tirso swarmed in Madrid, in Toledo, in Valladolid. Feminine sensibilities and those of the men, which after all only echoed them, became more refined, crazes and unexpected waves of excitement began to appear here and there, and an almost epileptic hysteria started to run like a black beetle over the breasts and backs of the women, who showed the way to the men then as they do now.

It was in those days that what we call neurasthenia was born, hyperaesthesia and another lot of queer names which simply indicate a lack of hardiness. Along with the lymphatic and chlorotic King and a nobility brought up by bilious and neurotic friars, candidates for madness in any climate less propitious for paradox and absurdity as a way of life, there was a restless perturbed society now incapable of great feats, eager for fictitious emotions, loving the theater.

Against this background the *Quixote* was a book of knight-errantries designed to discipline such nerves, providing a strong reaction to the jaundiced skin in the mystic cloister and to the aridity of excessively refined loves, a whiplash of a book, a hammer of a book, a torch of a book. And its full development was not yet complete, far from it, because Cervantes had not yet finished penetrating the whole of Spanish society. He was no longer in the backwater of Seville but found himself in the Court-corrupted circles of Madrid and Valladolid. It is notable that in the First Part of the *Quixote* there are madmen but there are no sick, while in the Second Part the Duchess has the ulcers that Doña Rodriguez tells us about, and the son of the Gentleman of the Green Coat suffers from another characteristic illness called poetic decadence, and Basilio, poor man, is about to commit suicide for the sake of love. . . . Thus the Second Part includes the incurable while in the First Part a broad area of doubt remains, which is one and the same thing as hope.

The Spanish Court had been transferred to Valladolid from the august grandeur of the Escorial, giving way to what suited the omnipotent Lerma.[2] This was a test the proud Duke sought to apply, first to the King, whose feeble will soon gave way, and then to the other courtiers. Lerma knew that those who would move promptly and willingly to Valladolid were his supporters, his people, the "unconditionals" as they were later called. He wanted to take an inventory of the nobles as he had made one of the moneyed class when he ordered everyone who had silver in his house to show it or suffer severe penalties.

With this Lerma initiated the most lamentable error in which all conservative politicians in Spain have persisted for many years; for them there never have been any people worthy of consideration in the country other than the nobility and the rich, never realizing that it is impossible to govern with a minority when that minority is worthless. Timidly and fearfully the silver crept out of cupboards and hiding places; fearful and timid did those who possessed anything show themselves to be. The grandees of Spain, who no longer went to war and lived on empty arrogance, were usually in debt. The burgesses who kept the precious metal in their chests, in those famous innumerable chests, became humbler and ever more paltry. It was then that the bourgeoisie was born, an example of which is the Gentleman of the Green Coat, a race of prudent, sensible, circumspect, thrifty folk, in sum, selfish people who look to someone to spur and direct them. For these also there was need for the knight-errantries of Don Quixote and the humor of Sancho. They did not laugh unless they were prodded a bit and their laughter was not noble and frank, sensual and voluptuous like that of the well-fed and clear-minded Sevillians with their elegant beards, a laughter without any double meaning. It was rather a malicious laughter provoked by tickling hearts that were a trifle scared, a trifle crafty, laughter like that induced by the *Quixote*, later sharpened and aggravated to the most acute pain by the lancet-pen of Quevedo, whose tickling drew blood.

In Valladolid, Miguel found the Court established in an outsized

Castilian village, or rather he found Lerma's courtiers, a few employees and office workers arrived from Madrid and scattered around anywhere in the available houses, and the usual retinue of poets, idlers, mischief makers and gossips that the Court raises in its train like the dust of its carriages.

On the track of the Court and of the courtiers the widowed Doña Andrea de Cervantes with her daughter Doña Constanza de Ovando had appeared as usual. Now almost in her sixties, Doña Andrea skillfully repaired the ravages of time but not those of fortune, which must have been acute since Miguel found her taking care of the clothes of the Most Excellent Señor Don Pedro de Ossorio, fifth Marquis of Villafranca, who had just returned from an expedition to Algiers. Be it by necessity or because of a desire to penetrate the houses of the great, Doña Andrea made, mended and sent out to be washed the shirts and underwear of Don Pedro and his lady, and we have a list of these clothes written by the same hand that wrote the *Quixote*.

Cervantes could observe in his own family, in the person of his ingenious and very intelligent sister, how everything was collapsing. He saw the King and Queen attending Mass at San Llorente in Valladolid with ostentatious pomp and remembered how Philip II went to Mass dressed in black with no pageantry or show of luxury, but he went to the other San Lorenzo, that of the Escorial.

It was with uncommon joy that in Valladolid Miguel came across his friend and fellow countryman the bookseller Francisco de Robles. He showed him his book, which must have already been known to Robles in view of its fame in Seville, and they discussed ways and means of presenting it to the public. Robles as an intelligent and knowledgeable man thought that the book would produce excellent results.

Miguel, encouraged by his words and by the conversations he had with friends and colleagues whom he must have found in Valladolid and who had not completely forgotten his name, wrote that gay, courtly and worldly prologue the reading of which convinces us today and will always convince us that it was written yesterday for tomorrow, because it has the freshness, the wit and the lightness of touch that some geniuses lack completely, but which those who are truly human always have. Whoever can reach that sublime level of gentle irony and amiable malice, of making fun without cracking jokes, of consummate worldliness, can call himself with reason a master of life. He deserves to be a guide and companion to all humanity, that is to say, not a herald who goes ahead playing on a huge trumpet like Victor Hugo, but rather a friend, one of those who take us through gentle and sympathetic persuasion wherever they wish and instruct us on the way, making the road both short and pleasant.

In Valladolid, Cervantes felt no nostalgia for Seville though this may seem to us impossible. He was walking in hope of glory while he trod the pavements of San Francisco, through the Royal Palace and through the patios of the Chief Accountant's Office where he went to present the receipts of his accounts, a disagreeable aftermath to his bureaucratic life. At the end of "so many years that he sleeps in the silence of oblivion," as he himself says, the Ingenious Hidalgo awakened, sure of himself and of his genius.

They had been well spent, his twenty years in Andalusia, a mother who caresses, a master who teaches, a mistress who inflames, a good soul who absolves and forgives. Now the age of sixty approached, and for the man of sixty who is not prosperous it is in Castile and its austerity that he must scratch around for a resting-place. And in Castile in what is most Castilian: Valladolid and Toledo.

CHAPTER 45

*Miguel in Esquivias—Toledo—*Don Quixote *Appears*

In the middle of July of 1604 the mother-in-law of Cervantes died in Esquivias. No man really mourns the death of his mother-in-law, and Cervantes was very much a man's man. More because of certain testamentary formalities than for any other reason it was necessary for him to go to Esquivias, and he found himself there on the twenty-first of July, legalizing with his signature the division of property between the two heirs of the deceased, namely the priest Francisco de Palacios and Doña Catalina de Salazar the younger. This is a most curious document from which can be deduced the evident contempt in which Miguel was held by his mother-in-law, his brother-in-law and his wife. After so many years of absence they doubtless considered him a lost soul, one of those vagabonds and good-for-nothings imposed by fate on many families particularly devoted to domestic order.

It has already been said that Doña Catalina de Salazar was a good lady but no heroine and just as she did not have the hardihood to risk sharing the roving life of her husband she also did not have the temperament to resist the influence of her mother and brother, those overly cautious, parsimonious and selfish hidalgos who professed the religion of Christ in order to get to Heaven and that of the maravedi for their stay on earth. In the will of her mother Doña Catalina is left more than her fair share but the cunning clergyman, her brother, managed things so that the advantage turned out to be illusory and his sister even ended up owing him money. The administrative clergyman from Toledo is in some respects a pettifogger, one who knows more civil than canon law. How he contrived the plot against Miguel and his wife's property is revealed in this dreadful paragraph to which Doña Catalina subscribed:

> And although these properties (awarded to Doña Catalina as the additional increments of a third and a fifth) according to the will may not be sold or alienated, this was on account of two considerations, one, *so that my said husband could not avail himself of them* and the other *in case I had no children*, pursuant to which the properties of the said additional increments should go to the said Francisco de Palacios, my brother.

Taking into account further that for these properties she had only the right to "usufruct and uterdominio and that Francisco de Palacios has paid sums to prevent the alienation of the said properties" and that she had no children she renounces and makes over all the properties of the additional increments in favor of her brother, and to complete this she pledges the newly planted vineyard on the road to Seseña. All this with the permission and in the presence of her husband Miguel de Cervantes, who signs the document.

Francisco de Palacios certainly aimed to punish in this way the madness committed by Doña Catalina when she gave her hand in marriage to a poor deluded poet with no patron and who to cap it all was burdened with an illegitimate child and a mass of obligations.

It is clear that Doña Catalina had abundant reason for completely losing the affection she once had for Miguel in view of his lengthy absences, and it must not be forgotten that she was sterile and that he had had fertile loves elsewhere. Year after year she had been mulling over her sterility and those other loves in the solitude of her big house in Esquivias, in the chill of her bed, in the slow and painful passage of the hours. When Miguel arrived in Esquivias from Valladolid in the summer of 1604 it was not love for his wife that brought him, as it did not bring him when he crossed half of Spain from Seville to Valladolid without stopping there. He came simply to carry out a formality. And on seeing his wife once more he realized that he had allowed the most dangerous emotional period in the life of a woman to pass. Doña Catalina was now close to forty years old, she had spent twenty of them alone, and the rebirth of passion with which she greeted her husband in 1594 upon his return from Seville was no longer in her heart.

Toledo, "massive rock, glory of Spain and inspiration of its cities," was the last lesson that Cervantes was to learn from the cities of the world. Toledo is the only capital of ancient, venerable Castile, the capital of rich females, of silent gentlemen, of secret love affairs, of massacres of Jews, of Moorish sages who could cure or poison, of builders who create new worlds and unknown kinds of vegetation on columns and friezes and riots of ornamental patterns and plaster flowers and leaves, of carpenters who join the gilded ceilings, of goldsmiths who work gold as if it were paste, of sculptor-architects who work stone as if it were gold, of image makers who paint and sculpture interminable stories and place fantastic kingdoms between a cantilever and a canopy, of sword makers who make iron into steel and steel into a ribbon which bends and does not break, of writers who refine and subtilize the language, of confessors who condone and purify the darkest corners of consciences, leaving them like shining jewels, of lean Celestinas who by their wiles inspire desire for the sweets of love, of magistral prebends like Covarrubias[1] under whose gown the whole of omniscient and doctoral Spain seems to be comprised, of theological, human, mad and sane painters, personified by the one and only, the wise El Greco, who embodies the light, the color and the life of Toledo in its most finished artistic formulary.

Those who have not lived in Toledo cannot understand one half of Miguel's spirit, just as those who have not been in Seville cannot grasp the other half. Before 1604 Cervantes had possibly been in Toledo many times and he must often have stayed at the Inn of the Sevillano, one of the most famous lodging houses for people from the villages. Do not think that because you find yourself in an inn full of muleteers and of the low-class people who frequent it you will run into the profligate and ruffianly crowd of the Compás in Seville. No. Go there this very day, for neither Toledo nor the inn has changed, and the innkeeper, the maids, the muleteers and the peasants who stay there will talk to you in the same hidalgo-like tone, grave, dignified, a trifle melancholy, or if they are gay it is the measured gaiety with which people speak in *The Illustrious Kitchen-maid*. The cult of Cervantes exists today at the inn and everyone knows that this name is an outstanding honor for the house and for the city. What a difference there is between the people depicted in that Toledan novel and the people in *Rinconete and Cortadillo* and the *Dialogue of the Dogs*! A water-carrier of Toledo may be only a water-carrier but he is a Toledan. *Civis toletanus sum*, he says with pride, and wraps himself magnificently in his cloak like a Roman in his toga.

Do not think that when the water-carriers Carriazo and Avendaño turn out to be noble gentlemen and the illustrious kitchen-maid a most noble damsel Miguel de Cervantes did this by chance, or that he ever did anything by chance. This is in the spirit of Toledo, of that treasure-house of a city where are kept the most noble relics of the slowly decaying ancient seat. See it even today. You will see those madly feverish eyes shining out from pale impassive faces like those of the Apostles of Domenico, you will glimpse those pale damsels who let their faded lives wither in the huge cold houses like ancient flowers and remember their abandonment dry-eyed, for the girl of Toledo does not weep for such griefs, out of dignity. You will see those water-carriers who talk like characters out of Lope. You will see those dignified porters, those magnificent beggars, those grave old men, those distinguished clergymen. You will harken to the silence that whispers secrets in your ear and you will feel the past taking hold of you or that past and present do not exist, because time in Toledo is a *flatus vocis*, a barren conceit.

When Cervantes passed through Toledo around August of 1604, he came across Lope de Vega, who had lived there since May, having abandoned his mistress Camila Lucinda, possibly in Seville. Lope had just married Doña Juana de Guardo, exchanging the nineteen towers of the pompous coat of arms of a hidalgo from Santander for rashers of ham, as Góngora told him, since Doña Juana was rich, the daughter of an opulent dealer in hogs. The Toledan wits scoffed to see him getting married for profit with a rich person belonging to a social class that never associated with nobles and poets. The sonnet of Góngora surely reached the hands of Lope:

> By your life, Lopillo, wipe me out
> the nineteen towers of your escutcheon . . .

This kept him in a pretty bad temper and in such circumstances coming across Cervantes in the Zocodover as he went from there on the way to his inn must have stimulated his bile, already very stirred up. It was then that he wrote in a private letter to a doctor friend of his that venomous phrase which some people have made so much of: "I do not speak of poets: what a century this is: many are ready to bloom next year: but none of them are as bad as Cervantes nor so stupid that they praise Don Quixote. . . . Will say no more lest I parrot Garcilaso when he says 'I go step by step toward satire,' something more odious to me than my little books are to Almendáres and my plays to Cervantes. . . ." This proves that Lope had already read the *Quixote* with attention and possibly re-read the famous dialogue of the canon and the priest in which Miguel initiated the criticism, later repeated so often, against the supposed unevenness of Lope's plays. It is not known how the original or copies of the *Quixote* had circulated all over Spain, and Cervantes had not yet received permission to print it, when already that shameless skirt-chasing friar Andrés Pérez[2] was writing in detestable verses with both middle and end words broken off the declaration here quoted:

> I am the Queen- of Mischie-
> better know- than the rud-
> more famous than Doña Olá-
> than Don Quixó- and Lazari-
> than Alfarach- and Celestí-

This nonsense, like Lope's well-informed unbosoming of himself against Cervantes, showed without doubt that even before it was published the *Quixote* had won the battle, since it awakened misgivings among those with great talents and small and all hastened to take cover, as has always been the case when a literary man is discovered in the background to be one of those who bring something new to the battle, or, as they say nowadays in a very expressive phrase, one of those who come "setting the Thames on fire."[3] Cervantes came "setting the Thames on fire" and the envy of the others and Lope's bad temper are the first tributes to his genius and cannot be regarded as otherwise.

On September 26 the King granted permission for the First Part of the *Quixote* to be printed. These permits were usually granted when the printing had already been done or was well on the way. December 20 was the date when its sale price was fixed. From then on no exact date can be given for its first appearance. It could have come out in January, February or afterward, but not later than May, for this would not have given time for the new editions printed in that same year of 1605. The doubt raised by Pérez Pastor as to whether it had come out before 1605 he resolved himself by a careful study of the books of the Brotherhood of Printers of Madrid.

On the other hand no one has been able to find out what the *Quixote* was worth to its author in money. It must certainly not have been much nor enough to get Cervantes out of his difficulties, for even when the literary men foretold the success of the book through their envy it cannot be taken for granted that such *a priori* reasoning could persuade Francisco de Robles to pay his friend a large sum for the privilege of selling it. At the same time it is unjust to depict Francisco de Robles as a mercenary and greedy publisher who exploited Cervantes. On the contrary, it can be clearly seen that in the conduct of their business they acted in a friendly way as old acquaintances. It is also indubitable that Cervantes did not get all the money at one time, but rather that the premature fame of his work provided him with an excuse to ask Robles for various advances on it.

But if the work did not relieve him of want it made the name of Cervantes leap at one bound into the minds of the whole world and into nothing less than a place on a level with and ahead of Lope de Vega.

A popularity as great and as sudden as that of the *Quixote* had never been known before. Five editions were printed, or up to now are known to have been printed, in the year 1605 alone. The name of Cervantes, which was not circulated through the lips or pens of other poets, as was usually the case at that time, grew enormously through the lips of the common people, of the people whose propensities had been trained in the theater and who already formed what today we call "public opinion," those thousands of ignorant men and women who build an infallible wisdom made up of thousands of easy and frivolous judgments which together form the surest and longest lasting judgment.

The *Quixote* was in everyone's hands, in the inns, in ministries, in palaces, on the desks of serious gentlemen, in the lecture halls of wild youth. The types of Don Quixote and Sancho immediately found in humanity a favorable echo to their words, an atmosphere propitious to their ideas and actions. Rarely did any book appear so opportunely.

Miguel then confirmed his feeling that the twenty years of his misadventures had not been ill-spent. During that time ideas had progressed, tastes had changed, attitudes had been revised. It was an enormous, a critical transformation, and the work that sprang from it was also enormous.

Everyone at the bottom of his soul recognized himself as somewhat of a Don Quixote, as somewhat of a Sancho Panza, and no one was offended by this. The nickname of Sancho Panza reached the Royal Palace and was soon applied to Padre Luis de Aliaga, a rustically cunning fat man who was the King's confessor. The proverbs and sayings of the squire and the lunacies of the knight became a common patrimony like the tunes and jingles which in no time reach everyone by word of mouth. At last there came to Miguel, to the tired old poet, great days of intense happiness which compared favorably with the great day of Lepanto. Arms had given way to letters. The old soldier had lost his left hand for the glory of the right. He had achieved the greatest possible renown: an entire people rejoiced in his work, some laughed, some were thoughtful. Through letters he could still expect redemption, immortality.

CHAPTER 46

Valladolid—Toros y Cañas—*Makeshifts—Ezpeleta Slain*

For a writer family peace and the respect and admiration of his own people is apt to come on the heels of fame and success, not before. So it was in the case of Cervantes. Drawn by the extraordinary hold that Miguel had over her as soon as he appeared Doña Catalina de Salazar went to Valladolid, lived with her sisters-in-law Doña Andrea and Doña Magdalena, and made the heroic sacrifice of regularizing Isabel de Saavedra, the natural daughter of Miguel, by living in the same house with her and treating her like a legitimate daughter, just as her father, her aunts and her cousin, Doña Constanza, did. It is very clear that whenever Miguel talked to Doña Catalina he could do what he wanted with her, could dissolve all suspicions or misgivings and hush all protests. Let us note this well, for there can be no real genius who does not wield a magic power over the women who surround him, who cannot convince them with a glance, dominate them with a word and soothe them with a gesture; Miguel, Lope, and Goethe had such magic.

Miguel, inspired by the fame he soon came to enjoy and the good fortune which it presaged, had now established his way of life. The family stood united, resolved to stay together. They lived in one of the new houses divided into rented apartments which were built in all haste upon the arrival of the Court in Valladolid in order to provide shelter for the surplus population which came with the King and Queen. It was in the neighborhood of the Slaughter-house near a small bridge which traversed the evil-smelling Esgueva, not far from the Puerta del Campo and therefore also close to the Hospital de la Misericordia, home of the dogs Scipio and Berganza, commonly called the dogs of Mahudes. The neighborhood was not the best in Valladolid by far, but with the growth of the Court the shortage of living space created more and more discomfort for everyone. At the same time, although glory had touched Miguel, the wealth which sometimes follows had not yet shown its face.

The family lived poorly, humbly. The women piled together as best they could in one room giving off the kitchen. Miguel had another one for all his requirements, and there was only one room with a balcony on the street. But the inhabitants of the capital were now reconciled to these straits, persuaded that the next turn on the wheel and the caprice that had brought them to Valladolid would take them away when they least expected it.

The provisional character which everything began to assume was a notable sign of the change taking place in Spain. Philip II sought to consolidate, to lay firm foundations, and his imbecile successor, or those who advised him, far from carrying on the good work, ignored the stone blocks put in place by the granitic monarch, and instead of going on with the construction they put together a makeshift dwelling of wattle. It was then that that fatally, genuinely Spanish phrase *ir tirando* [make do] must have been invented. Fraud, accommodation, adjustment began to be the public and private way of life.

Just such an adjustment, in addition to that of Doña Catalina, was made by the person one would least expect, the rigid, the stiff, the exigent clergyman of Esquivias, Francisco de Palacios, who also came to live for a time with his brother-in-law, the writer, who did not now seem so despicable since his name was famous in the whole of Spain and perhaps, perhaps there might be something to be gained from knowing him. Whether or not it was only curiosity and the obvious notoriety surrounding success that attracted the worthy priest, it is a fact that we see him serving as witness in a document supporting a ban on the clandestine editions of the *Quixote* that were being printed in Portugal. But even though his scruples had mostly vanished, the promiscuity in which the family lived could not have been greatly to his taste and the priest and his sister Doña Catalina returned to their village in the spring of 1605, possibly on the best of terms with Miguel, possibly a little put out.

If the fame of the *Quixote* caused Cervantes some troubles it also provided him an opportunity to renew several excellent old connections and acquire new ones. In Valladolid he found his friend from Seville, Señor de Higares, who had continued to live at the Court, supposedly with certain sinister designs against the Duke of Lerma. Perhaps to disguise them the noble gentleman never failed to appear at the Court ceremonies and festivities, which were then celebrated for any reason at all. Don Fernando de Toledo visited Cervantes and escorted the ladies of Miguel's family on the street, whether out of courtesy or friendship. They embroidered him a badge for when he took part in the tournaments and equestrian exercises which were celebrated either on the occasion of the Queen's happily giving birth or in connection with similar festivities in honor of the English Ambassador, Admiral Howard, who was no longer remembered as chiefly responsible for the attack on Cádiz and the destruction of our ships. Spanish memories had become so faded and slack that affronts such as the sack of Cádiz were forgotten eight or ten years after they occurred! Such was the mental confusion and absurdity that among the festivities organized in honor of the Lutheran Englishman it was by a miracle that they did not plan an *auto-de-fé* in which a few of his co-religionists could be burned.

There was nothing wrong in the visits paid to the Cervantes house by Señor de Higares and other aristocratic gentlemen, nor in their friendly relations with the Cervantes women. Doña Andrea, armed with the respectability of having been twice widowed, and Doña Magdalena in her religious coifs, now disenchanted with the world and its pomps and vanities, kept a strict eye on everything. It was only normal for young girls like Doña Constanza and her cousin Doña Isabel to have followers and suitors. There was some or perhaps a great deal of confusion in that improvised and badly organized Court; classes and qualities were not distinguished with the perception and rigidity with which they would be determined in a Court that had been long established and in which the house, the situation and the way of life of each person was known.

This confusion was very much to the advantage of frauds and intriguers of both sexes, and so in Valladolid there were clouds of parasites and spongers about whose means of support nothing was known, people of dubious character who came for the merry-making of the Court and played a role in it. It is from that time that we can date the contemptuous and irreverent acceptance of the phrase *toros y cañas*.[1] It meant that there was a salad or stew of gentlemen and of knaves disguised in the same dress whose dexterity in jousting or spearing the ring put them on the same level as gentlemen of the nobility and induced a familiarity proper to the sport or danger they shared. There has always been extraordinary indulgence in the Spanish Court for horsemen, bullfighters, actors, and mountebanks, since we have had a long series of hypochondriac monarchs whom it was necessary to amuse at all costs.

With all this tolerance and these associations there was formed that morally equivocal and confused atmosphere which would permit anything to be dared and nothing to be unforgivable. Under the protection of the Court for those who amused it, poets and literary men also began to penetrate and to be included in a position not much above that of the actors and horsemen. This was not the case in the time of Philip II, who did not like wielders of the pen near him unless it were some grave ecclesiastic or erudite friar, but now writers and poets were on the scene under pretext of entertaining or pleasing or something. Lerma was clever enough to know which of them could harm him and which not. Góngora, for example, was a dog who barked a great deal but did not bite. Why meddle with Góngora and all his slanders? Poets were needed for the production of all the arches, inscriptions, allegorical floats and theatrical displays with which the Court constantly amused itself to cover up its own misery and that of the country. And to the demand for poets, who after all cost little, was added a demand for friars to swell the ranks of the processions and feast days and for more or less authentic gentlemen to participate in the *toros y cañas*. Can one not feel a certain shade of scorn in the manner with which the people began to use the phrase? *Ir tirando* was the way of life. *Toros y cañas* was the futile appearance with which the extent of the fraud was disguised. Deceit reigned at the Court; hypocrisy was sweeping through the whole of Spain, borne on the skirts of the friars.

Somewhat disappointed by the Duke of Béjar's complete indifference to the dedication of the *Quixote*, and knowing full well how many simpletons there were among the titled gentlemen and those of the cloth, Cervantes nevertheless did not stop consorting with those he could. Besides Señor de Higares there was his friend the Count of Saldaña, son of the Duke of Lermà, who, as they used to say then, was much addicted to poetry and to helping poets and literary men. Some other gentlemen of the Court offered him protection, as did Saldaña, but it is difficult to find out under what conditions and in what form these offers were made. Cervantes knew that if even Lope needed the support of noblemen it would be a good thing for him to seek it for himself, but in this as in other things he had bad luck.

Many stories and legends have been invented to explain the coolness with which he was treated by Don Alonso Diego López de Zúñiga y Sotomayor, Duke of Béjar, Marquis of Gibraleón, etc., etc., whose name enjoyed the honor of being placed on the front page of the First Part of the *Quixote*. There is no need for any explanation save that most ordinary and natural one which history gives us to the effect that the Duke of Béjar was perhaps the silliest and most worthless of all the aristocratic young gentlemen of his period. Other talented men dedicated their works to him at the same time as Cervantes and they did not receive the slightest acknowledgement. Why would he make an exception in favor of Cervantes?

Miguel's only protectors, if charity can be called protection, given with more or less delicacy and discretion to a destitute old writer of Valladolid at a time when everyone was savoring the First Part of the *Quixote*, were the Archbishop of Toledo, the Most Illustrious Don Bernardo de Sandoval y Rojas, at whose election he thought to write some laudatory verses of which we know only a draft, and Don Pedro Fernández de Castro, first Marquis of Sarriá, who had once had Lope de Vega in his service, and later the Count of Lemos, a nephew and son-in-law of the omnipotent Duke of Lerma. At first, however, even during the heroic and triumphant sortie of Don Quixote, it is not known whether Cervantes was supported, his genius admired, or his name even known to either the recently installed Archbishop of Toledo or the powerful Count of Lemos.

Other no less interesting men of worth then began to figure in the life of Miguel and his family at the capital, and the most important of them was a certain Juan de Urbina, secretary of the Dukes of Savoy. This Urbina was the kind of man with whom Cervantes had always been delighted to associate. A man of the world and of business, he was forever involved in the most varied negotiations and the most diverse business deals. Like Cervantes he had known and enjoyed the "free life of Italy" and in it, with greater freedom and more resources than Miguel, he had bitten into all the tasty apples offered him. He was a clever, sagacious, active man with a great knowledge of humanity, the weaknesses and foibles of which he sought to exploit, and for the same reason we would have to search for a long time before we came upon anyone of his period who held Cervantes in greater esteem. What the poor actor Tomás Gutiérrez in his humble way had been for Cervantes in Seville, Juan de Urbina was for him at Court, a faithful friend, useful with advice and guidance, unselfish and truly noble. It would be senseless to try to determine in detail the favors which Archbishop Sandoval or the Count of Lemos did for Cervantes; there is no doubt that they were merely alms, temporary monetary aid, crumbs from tables where there was always a superfluity. On the other hand the good turns of Tomás Gutiérrez and Juan de Urbina, who were not high-ranking or powerful people, are indubitable and continuous, they are preserved in documents, and they had a decisive influence on Miguel's life. These were his real friends, and this is usually so with all writers; their friends are not other writers or important personages but people whom history leaves forgotten in its infinity of dark corners.

Juan de Urbina had a vast business network of his own, quite apart from his connection with the Princes of Savoy. But a businessman when he is really intelligent is not satisfied with casting his nets and counting the money his fishing has produced. He needs the company of men as talented as himself, even if they apply their talents to very different ends. Because of this the business schemes of Urbina and the literary plans of Miguel were happily discussed by the two friends and a great intimacy grew up between them. The replies that Miguel had to give to charges by the accountants regarding his tax collecting mission in Granada had not yet been concluded, and certainly Urbina was a great help to him in winding up this business satisfactorily.

As Doña Andrea said at the time, Cervantes was then in Valladolid, "a man who wrote and did business." He was not just a poet, nor did he spend much of his time with writers, since, if out of the enormous returns that the sale of the *Quixote* must have produced he could barely get enough to live on, and all his attempts to solicit the protection of some Court magnate had also until then produced nothing for him, it was natural that he seek to cope with the numerous family burdens he carried by going into business.

However, it was not only with nobles and businessmen that Miguel and his family had connections. Their home was a tenement which they shared with other families. On the ground floor there was a tavern. Above it on the first floor left Miguel lived with his daughter, sisters and niece, and a water-girl, a highland lass from the valley of Toranzo called María de Ceballos. An old friend of Cervantes, Doña Luisa de Montoya, widow of the chronicler Don Esteban de Garibay, occupied the apartment next door with her children, the clergyman Don Luis de Garibay, a young man of twenty-four who had just received his holy orders, his sister Luisa, a young unmarried girl of eighteen, and her little brother Esteban, a lad of twelve or thirteen. The Garibays were great friends of the Cervanteses, since they lived in the same house, the fortune of the rich chronicler must have shrunk considerably, and Doña Luisa was one of those ladies who have come down in life and who delight in consorting with their equals. Doña Andrea de Cervantes was also a widow who had come down in life and the two of them had marriageable daughters; it is not surprising that they liked to go to Mass together and stroll along the pavement of San Francisco, nor that at times they should return escorted by gallants.

One of these may have been a young gentleman in the habit of the Military Order of Santiago, and not just a simple hidalgo as has been said, who was called Don Gaspar de Ezpeleta, an intimate friend and dinner companion of the Marquis of Falces, Don Diego de Croy y Peulín, Captain of the King's Archers. Ezpeleta was one of the Don Juans who were then making conquest after conquest in Valladolid. Without profession or property, for the habit he wore was simple and lacked the embroidered cross, he lived a loose life, mainly under the secret protection of his friend the Marquis rather than from any resources of his own. As a result of the jousts celebrated in honor of Admiral Howard, Don Gaspar de Ezpeleta was famous, not for any great feat but for having fallen shamefully from off his horse by reason of being dead drunk, as can be gathered from the ten famous lines from Góngora:

> Let us sing of the ride
> and weep at the horsemanship

at the shameful fall
of Don Gaspar de Ezpeleta.
Oh, if I were but a poet
how much paper would I cover
and what account would I give of him!
I would at least say
that the silly fool tumbled
whereupon others tumbled to what he was. . . .

As so often happens with woman-chasing gallants who have no other occupation or way of life, Ezpeleta was not brave but a braggart, not in love but lecherous. All he sought in women was a diversion, if possible a productive one, regardless of class or condition, for he pursued damsels of virtuous appearance, God knows with what in mind, just as readily as he pinched and molested kitchen maids in the most humble dress.

In the spring and summer of 1605 he carried on illicit relations with the wife of a notary public, a lowly employee of the Tribunal of Justice called Galbán. The unfaithful creature had reached a point in her madness when she gave Don Gaspar possessions as worthy of respect and affection as the wedding rings which her husband had given her, and he carried them in his pocket with a rosary, some reliquaries, tinder, flint, cards, and love letters.

On June 7 of 1605 Don Gaspar ate with his friend the Marquis, took his siesta in the house of his patroness Juana Ruiz in the Calle de los Manteros where she lived, went out on horseback, and when night had fallen he sent his page Francisco de Camporredondo to bring him his evening short sword and a shield and to lend him his cloak, as was the habit of the hotheads who roamed the streets at night. Dressed in picaresque fashion and wrapped in his servant's cape, the brim of his hat pulled down to his eyebrows, the night-wandering gallant started toward the fountain of Agarles. Close to the Hospital de la Resurrección he came across a water-girl who, so as not to be burdened, had given her water pitcher to a loafer for him to fill and for a cuarto take to the house of her mistress Doña María de Argomedo, a neighbor of Cervantes. He must have addressed himself to the girl in the jargon of the gypsies and he even pawed her with amorous brutality, whereupon she answered him: "Go to the devil, you low-life." To this he replied by uncovering himself, and the girl recognized him as the gentleman who sometimes walked out with her neighbors. The maid then paid even less heed to the courtier's proposals, and somewhat peevishly he continued on his way toward the Puerta del Campo, closely wrapped although the weather was already warm.

On returning from the fountain the maid almost bumped into a small man dressed in black in a state of disorder, his cape dragging and his doublet awry, who was sheathing a rapier as he hastened away. This mysterious black-clad man who slipped away like a shadow, this collarless man with his dragging cape, had just exchanged sword thrusts with the noble Ezpeleta and left him mortally wounded at the corner.

The neighborhood was aroused by cries of "Help, they have killed me." The clergyman Don Luis de Garibay and the hidalgo Miguel de Cervantes rushed quickly into the street and carried the wounded man into the house of Doña Luisa de Montoya, called a surgeon and alerted the police. A Justice of the Peace named Cristóbal de Villarroel arrived and began to take the wounded man's statement. The barber-surgeon of the old mounted guards, Sebastián Macías, came very soon. Cervantes witnessed the first aid and accustomed as he was to seeing wounds he came to the same conclusion as the surgeon. Don Gaspar de Ezpeleta was in great danger. And such was the case. In less than two days he was dead and Cervantes and his family and all the neighbors of both sexes were arrested and imprisoned.

For the fourth time the Ingenious Hidalgo found himself in the hands of the police, and as in the previous times through no fault of his own, but now with the apprehension produced by experience.

CHAPTER 47

The Ezpeleta Case—The Court in Madrid—Luis de Molina

THE legal proceedings arising out of the death of Don Gaspar de Ezpeleta contain so much of the love story, the picaresque novel, and the tale of life at Court that it is quite easy to understand the interest it awakened in those who heard about it and the many absurd conjectures they dreamed up. The proceedings stemming from this incident were, like many others, improperly conducted by the public prosecutor, evidence was manipulated, the court was inept, and its verdict was contrived. Then, as it would today, it revealed the thousand miseries concealed under the roof of a domicile and the thousand villainies that the individual male or female city-dweller is ready to commit within the sacred precincts of the home by virtue of possessing the great covercle of immorality which is called a door and that great seducer which is called a key.

The confusion and promiscuity into which tenement houses force the people who live in them to mingle through the chance of a fortuitous meeting without knowing each other well, whereas other people live separated by a wall and neither mingle nor know each other at all, is without doubt one of the greatest causes of the transformation in social customs and in ethical and philosophical standards of the modern age. "My house is my castle," says the Englishman, who lives in it with his family and is the lord of it, as in the Middle Ages, and continues to follow a patriarchal way of life. Who can make this proud statement in a tenement? Who, living in an apartment house with a large family, women and servants, can be sure of not giving up some of his personality, of not losing a part of himself to the other tenants or dissipating his individuality in familiarity? A tenant is always less than a man.

In the abode where Cervantes lived in Valladolid, as described in the process, highly respectable and distinguished residents like Doña Luisa de Montoya, the wife of Garibay, and her son the clergyman, lived together with people of such low moral quality as Doña Mariana Ramírez, who was held to be the mistress of Don Diego de Miranda, and because of this and the resulting scandal she was arrested. In a single apartment on the second floor lived Doña Juana Gaitán, the widow of that *Tirsi* of the *Galatea*, that is to say of the poet Pedro Láynez, and a niece of his, Doña Catalina de Aguilera, of whom we do not know what kind of visitors she received; in another apartment was a widowed lady who called herself Doña María de Argomedo, with her sister, Doña Luisa de Ayala y Argomedo, and their servant; another housed a poor hidalgo, a miserable minor placeman called Rodrigo Montero with his wife and the maid of Doña Juana Gaitán. Finally, so that nothing would be lacking in that compendium of Spanish society of the sixteenth century, a witch wearing a religious habit, whom they called Isabel de Ayala, lived in the garret. In general the house was filled with women, while there were only two men of substance, Don Luis de Garibay, the priest, and Miguel de Cervantes, for Rodrigo de Montero appears to have been an insignificant poor devil. And with such an accumulation of women there could not fail to be gossip, lies, jealousies, slanders, and calumnies.

The process showed clearly that there was no relation between the life of that small predominantly feminine circle and the death of the noble Ezpeleta. He had frequented the house, but there was none in Valladolid in which women lived that had failed to interest him, and the one in which Cervantes lived near the Slaughter-house diffused such a strong feminine perfume that Don Gaspar was sure to penetrate it on one pretext or another. Señor de Higares as well as Don Gaspar had visited the Cervantes apartment, while the Duke of Pastrana, the Count of Cocentaina and the Duke of Maqueda, gentlemen who naturally brought some of their pages and servants with them, had called on Doña Juana Gaitán. Here a perpetual comedy of cloak and sword was being played, very worthy of being recommended to the silly asses who still maintain that the fictions of Tirso and Calderón were false. The ladies and young women of the house allowed themselves to be escorted abroad and courted, and only a few hours before the death of Ezpeleta one of the Cervantes women was on the balcony talking to Señor de Higares.

However, this never went farther than the limits set by courtly gallantry, and the proof of this is that when the perverse witch Isabel de Ayala tried to slander the daughter of Cervantes the only lie it occurred to her to invent was that she was known as Isabel de Saavedra and had been seen with Simón Méndez, a Portuguese minor civil servant or trader, probably of Jewish origin and almost certainly as old as Miguel de Cervantes.

The stupidity of this clumsy and badly conceived calumny is apparent when it might have occurred to the evil gossip to mention the name of Señor de Higares or that of Don Gaspar de Ezpeleta himself, who also had access to the house, both being young and gallant gentlemen. The calumny does not stand up, therefore, and it has needed the refined malice of a few hypocrites to believe that the publication of the legal proceedings could prejudice Cervantes in any way.

Without the slightest doubt Don Gaspar de Ezpeleta was killed by the scrivener Galbán, from whom he had stolen his honor and even the sacred relic of the wedding rings. Judge Cristóbal de Villarroell knew this from the moment he heard the statements of the page of Ezpeleta and of his patroness Juana Ruiz, who said that what a judge needed to know most was "who she is," and knowing this was enough for him to give the proceedings a calculated direction by involving all the residents of the house, both men and women, so that nothing could be found out. In the house of Juana Ruiz the judge saw the lady who had been the cause of the presumed crime, veiled and in deep mourning, and I say "presumed" because the declaration of the dying Don Gaspar de Ezpeleta that the aggressor fought like an honorable man was sufficient to exculpate him. Was anyone who killed face to face in a duel brought to justice in those days? The veiled lady, whom only a blind man would fail to recognize as the wife of Galbán, begged, implored, and importuned the judge. Leniency and something that we now call class consciousness entered into the case. Villarroell knew Galbán and saw to it that his name not be more dishonored by the death of Ezpeleta than it had been in his life. It was thus arranged that the matter be covered up and that no one be declared guilty. Juridical patching up and compromissing when there was fear of a scandal was making its appearance.

It is useless to express astonishment because Cervantes and his family were caught up in one of those entanglements with the police that were so common then, as were the quarrels, the knifings and the deaths in the street. They all came unstained out of the process instituted by Villarroell and quickly returned to their ordinary way of life. But what became obvious in this particular case and in many others was that Valladolid was in no condition to be the seat of the Court and that the insecurity of life there led to many other difficulties.

The Duke of Lerma, ever more arrogant in his position as favorite, believed that he need no longer have any fear of returning to Madrid, while no one knew what the opinion of the King might be, if in all of his dim life he ever did form an opinion. But suddenly, however much the people of Valladolid might use their influence, it was established that the Court would go back to Madrid. And so it happened in February of 1606, and with the Court departed civil servants, nobles, office-seekers, businessmen, and what today we call intellectuals, for that thing called centralization was then beginning to rule for better or for worse.

Miguel reached his sixtieth birthday at the capital, living with his family and reunited with his wife. There was little to spare but also no want in the house. Cervantes had won an enormous reputation with his books, and Francisco de Robles had no objection to advancing him money on account of promised works, the drafts of which Miguel would read to him. The secretary Juan de Urbina was his great friend and probably his advice and friendship permitted Miguel to give expression to his real or imagined aptitudes for business. The family, in which there were now two elderly ladies, was acquiring a weight, a respectability and a seriousness appropriate to well-established domiciles.

They lived in the Calle de la Magdalena, back of the palace of the Duke of Pastrana, not far from the Convent of Mercy and that of the Trinity, also close to the printing office of Juan de la Cuesta, the bookshop of Robles, and the corner where actors met.

Shortly after arriving in Madrid, Isabel became engaged to a wealthy gentleman, probably of middle age, who was called Don Diego Sanz del Aguila and who was a Knight of the Order of Alcántara. This engagement was one of the things arranged by the diligent Juan de Urbina. Sanz de Aguila married Isabel and the couple went to live in a house next to the Red de San Luis.

With his daughter married, and well married, which had been Miguel's only serious worry, he was able to enjoy for a time the peace and quiet that comes with those fair years of the sixties. Miguel loved the tranquility of his home, the gentle disposition of Doña Catalina, the wisdom and sophistication of his sister Andrea and the loving devotion of his sister Magdalena, whose unhappy human loves were being transformed into a resigned and mystical piety which sweetened her character even more. He enjoyed the friendship of a merchant as sound of judgment as Francisco de Robles, of a man of business as active and intelligent as Juan de Urbina, in whom financial sense had greatly developed a sense of reality without thereby deadening or impairing his good feeling, and of a gentleman as quiet and sensitive as Don Juan de Acedo Velázquez who, without leaving the house of the Prince of Savoy where he lived with Urbina, had entered the service of the Royal Household, discharging at the Palace the office of Outrider to the Coach of the Royal Ladies and Queen's Chamberlain, besides being a Knight of St. John. Miguel's acquaintances were those of a prudent burgess fond of his home and of his tranquility rather than those of a literary man.

That great sobriety which the Greeks called *sofrosyme* was spreading through his worn spirit, and far from intensifying his autumnal melancholy it was beginning to break it up, soften it, turn brutal shouts of laughter into smiles, wear away the rough edges of ideas, make the talent that was to astonish coming centuries ever more human, pleasing and versatile. The affection of his wife, now free from all carnal impurity, the love of his sisters, who if they had ever sinned had already been pardoned a hundred times, the relative economic ease in which he must have lived, and even his remoteness from the confused literary struggle in which some talented courtiers were engaged, created that gay serenity which shines in the *Exemplary Novels* and that supreme flexibility of thought and word to which we owe the Second Part of the *Quixote*. Cervantes on reaching sixty understood how simple and elemental is the fabric of life which the stupid consider so complex and difficult to understand; he discerned the motives of human actions with the lucidity of the philosopher, he held in his hand the passions that agitated the world, and he traced what their beginnings were and guessed what would be their ends. At the close of 1607 or beginning of 1608 his gray hairs received their consecration when he became a grandfather.

The birth of his granddaughter Isabel Sanz del Aguila must have coincided with the death of his son-in-law Don Diego Sanz, whose marriage to Isabel de Saavedra lasted only a year. A few months after becoming a widow, Isabel is known to have become engaged to a certain Luis de Molina from Cuenca, agent and secretary of the Italian bankers Carlos and Antonio María Trata. Miguel had known Luis de Molina two years before in Valladolid. He was a prudent man, active and much involved in business affairs, who had lived in Italy and had been a prisoner in Algiers, two things greatly appreciated by Miguel, who was quite pleased at the thought of having him in the family. This did in fact come to pass, but before anything else Luis de Molina was a businessman and he considered marriage to Doña Isabel de Saavedra as a business transaction.

Molina had observed that none of the necessities of life were lacking in the home of his future wife; he also knew that the deceased Don Diego left his wife very well provided with clothing and jewelry, for the inventory in the dowry agreement enumerated dresses of velvet, flowered taffeta, thin silk and satin, French and Spanish mantles of satin, damask and velvet, ruffs of Flanders lace, extravagant upper petticoats, waists and short cloaks, rings of diamonds, rubies, rock crystals and topazes, earrings, necklaces, hair nets, *agnusdéi* and crosses of gold, luxurious beds, silver services and everything that was then considered necessary for comfort. Nevertheless he considered all this inadequate or perhaps the generosity of Cervantes made him think it was wrong to marry his daughter again without a dowry, and for this reason on August 28 of 1608 he engaged himself jointly with his friend Juan de Urbina to pay Luis de Molina two thousand ducats in cash on account of the said dowry.

What is the meaning of this? It simply shows that the years have not dimmed hope in Miguel's soul, and this is an understatement; he was sure that he would shortly achieve riches although in the whole of his past life he had never managed to see as much as two thousand ducats in cash all at once.

Did he expect to get this money from his writing? It does not seem very probable, and he must rather have expected to get it from his business dealings, from the new and profitable relationships he had developed, from the friendship with Urbina and his experience in business, as also from the intelligence and sagacity of his son-in-law, in whom he recognized an enterprising man capable of raising capital, like others who at that time were beginning to build themselves up out of nothing or to emerge in certain industries, while the great properties and the funds of the noble houses were falling to pieces and being gradually wiped out.

Cervantes was too clear-sighted to think he could become rich by writing. Six editions of the *Quixote* had been printed in the first year of its publication; another one, which Miguel himself carefully corrected, was prepared in 1608 by Francisco de Robles and also printed in the shop of Juan de la Cuesta. It is the one most worthy of esteem from the point of view of correctness, and the one that should be followed as long as there is not yet a true critical edition, and even if there is one eventually. But none of this was enough to keep a family, nor could Miguel count on it for comfort and economic ease in the future.

Doubtless he put his last hopes for peace and quiet in his relationships with Urbina and Molina. Even in this he was to be a Spaniard pure and simple in believing himself endowed with great and unprecedented talents as a businessman, and all his life to hold that he was within an ace of becoming a millionaire.

He who was such a profound judge of humanity could not see that Urbina's business dealings, in which he frequently gave ear to the dictates of a generous heart, were not properly those of a man of prey, which is what a man of business should be, and that the projects and plans for making money attempted by his son-in-law suffered from the common defect of so many Spanish enterprises in that they involved a good deal of fantasy and wishful thinking. Urbina and Molina were two of those calamitous poets of business whose race has never died out in Spain.

On September 8 of 1608 Licentiate Francisco Ramos married Luis de Molina and Doña Isabel de Saavedra in the Church of San Luis. In October Molina gave a power of attorney to his wife so that she could collect some old debts due to her mother Ana Franca, and Isabel made this power of attorney over to Doña Magdalena in November. With her black weeds and her habit of the Venerable Third Order of St. Francis, Doña Magdelena was even more skillful in managing legal papers than she had been when young, and also in dealing with scriveners and clerks in search of the crumbs and scrapings that everyone gives up for lost. To this day in Madrid there are still many pious women of this type who know the nine days devoted to special worship and the forty days of Lenten fasting, and who are just as familiar with the notary's office and the courts of justice. They are quite capable of bringing forth from the folds of their cloaks what a hundred so-called students of jurisprudence could not produce from their worn and ragged togas.

Months were to go by, until December of that year, before Luis de Molina, who was so exigent in extracting from his father-in-law and Urbina the obligation to pay the two thousand ducats they had offered him, would sign Doña Isabel's articles of marriage, and it was not until April 30 of 1609 that the nuptial benediction was pronounced. Miguel was best man and Doña Catalina attended the bride, which was a great triumph for him and particularly pleasing because his wife was sponsoring the marriage of her husband's illegitimate daughter.

Meanwhile the business of the tithes of Granada and the bond of Suárez Gasco, who, along with Miguel, was required to settle up in this connection, was still pending. We do not know how this affair ended, whether Suárez Gasco paid or, what seems more probable, that it was Miguel who finally cleared up his accounts with the Exchequer. At any rate this does show that his life was not completely peaceful.

The beginning of the year 1609 brought with it another piece of bad news. Cardinal Niño de Guevara, who Miguel probably hoped would sponsor the publication of his *Exemplary Novels,* died in Seville. The desire of Miguel to take shelter with the Church was not getting anywhere, but he tried once more, recognizing how very necessary it was becoming to provide a public demonstration of one's religious sentiments.

Just then one of those terrifying readjustments of forces Spanish piety and the multiple interests entwined with it bring into action from time to time was becoming evident. In Madrid the Court and the exaggeratedly pious King, who could serve no purpose except that of being devout, had now discovered that it was the only possible use for his uselessness and the only favorable occasion for flaunting himself in public, pretending thus that he did something else besides attending profane functions and festivities. So Madrid became pious, and first the higher ranks began to deliver themselves over to beatitude and hypocrisy, then those who sought to imitate them, then the whole of the middle class, the growing number of burgesses. Here and there in churches and convents emerged new congregations, confraternities, and pious assemblies, the activities of which satisfied the vanities of the gentlemen, the great gentlemen and the young gentlemen who, like the King, were of no use for anything else. Belonging to these assemblies was considered very elegant; many half-wits and fops joined them in order to shine in the processions and nine-day ceremonies and so attract the attention of the ladies and courtesans, who are usually not averse to finding the scent of wax and incense upon their adorers. Other confraternities were the refuge of the "intellectuals" and the leading one among them was The Congregation of the Unworthy Slaves of the Most Holy Sacrament, founded on November 18 of 1608 by Fray Alonso de la Purificación, an unshod Trinitarian, and by Don Antonio Robles y Guzmán, Lord of the Bedchamber of His Majesty and in charge of his lodging when traveling, that is to say, a person of very considerable importance at the Palace, from which all this mystical commotion had come forth.

The Congregation was founded and lodged in the Convent of the Trinity in the Calle de Atocha until 1645, when it was established in the Oratorio del Olivar. On April 17 of 1609 Miguel de Cervantes was received into it as a Slave of the Most Holy Sacrament, and he declared that he would observe its holy bylaws and so signed his name. He did so by choice and possibly out of gratitude and friendship for the Trinitarian Fathers.

CHAPTER 48

The Decay of Spain—Death of Andrea—Catalina's Will

UPON reaching sixty-two years of age Miguel de Cervantes was given much more to thought than to action as his worn body lost its strength long before his spirit lost its vigor. His life in Madrid was sedentary: from his house in the Calle de Magdalena he went to attend Mass at San Sebastián or the Trinity, both of which were near, from there to chat a while at the bookshop of Francisco de Robles, which also was not far, or to the printshop of Juan de la Cuesta or the corner where the actors met to gossip in the Calle de León. At the most he carried on to the fearsome Steps of San Felipe, on the way to the Plateriás where the bookseller Villarroel dwelt. He did not want to go on to the Palace. About this he told his intimates sadly: "It is always too late for me to go to the Palace." Nevertheless these little comings and goings enabled him to observe the new social attitudes incubating in the Court.

The Court admired and encouraged men of elegant tastes whose purpose consequently was to subtilize and refine even more. In the environs of Madrid the evergreen oaks and the elms, the willows, the strawberry trees and the poplars were disappearing or had already disappeared, but as compensation there were few houses on the walls of which forests had not been painted, or poplars and elms woven into the tapestries which covered them. Nature had fled the artificialities of the Court and an art of tapestry-weaving and cabinet-work sought to imitate and replace it. Eyes deprived of natural pleasures seek them in false contrivances, and the blackness and monastic austerity of dress in the days of Philip II were replaced by variegated colors in the clothing of ladies and gentlemen—shining materials, embroidered garments, ruffs, flutings, crimpings, wide breeches, costly laces, showy petticoats and saucy little hats. Skirts began to balloon and conceits to burgeon. Very little was needed for the literature of hoopskirts and farthingales, of tight waists and crushed and withered hearts to triumph in everything and everywhere.

Because of this it never occurred to Cervantes during the period when his thinking and his productivity were at their peak to write a major work which dealt with the Court, and he never did. He also had little or nothing to do with literary people. Lope and Quevedo never forgot that they were vested gentlemen who were received at Court and were feared and envied, but Cervantes was indifferent to Lope and to his friendship or enmity, while the scent of admirations and hatreds that Don Luis de Góngora trailed behind him like a perfume from his robes did not bother Miguel even if it did Lope himself at times.

In the writing of these and others there was an atmosphere of artistic hypocrisy, of consciously artificial insincerity and of a studied scorn for Nature. The sun of the Golden Age had barely started to shine in Spain when its clarity began to be misted over by heavy clouds of theatrical texture like those which El Greco painted. Literature became courtly before the Court itself was firmly established, and as a result it lacked that marvellous harmony with society and its environment that the *grand siècle* of Louis XIV immortalized. And in this there was apparent an absolute divorce, not between the Court and the people, but rather between the Court and what was not Court.

Cervantes saw all this and knew that it was not for him; he loved Nature, the calm serenity of the fields, the singing of birds and the murmur of fountains. His world was not that of the Calle Major, not even of the steps of the courtyard of La Pacheca, but there was still a great deal left to say about the many things he had been ruminating upon in that fruitful time of early old age when fugitive impressions have come to rest and vision has cleared with the passage of the years. And Miguel saw or felt about him, in the inn and on the road, in the remote village, in the noisy port and in the solitary cloister, in the shepherd's hut and in the magnate's castle, his world, his public, the great widely dispersed mass of readers who hate artifice and fraud, that unrecognized, neglected and scattered aggregate of common sense and capacity for clear judgment that existed in Spain then as now and which no one has been able to conquer, tame or direct, for in it everyone can use with anyone who attempts to direct him that fantastic Aragonese formula addressed to the ruler in the Catalan Constitution: "Each of us is equal to you, and together all of us are greater than you."

In the state of penury in which Cervantes continued despite his reputation he observed bitterly that while he could count on thousands of people of goodwill for admiration and even love, those scattered thousands were incapable of any action in common other than a Platonic approval which was not mutually recognized or communicated. Have we not seen those fruitless efforts of the politicians who have sought to conquer the so-called *neutral mass*? It thinks soundly, feels honestly, and sees clearly, but when the moment arrives to decide to do anything the neutral mass wraps itself in its cloak and wanders off to bask in the sun, independent and happy, master of its thoughts and of its actions, great and solitary as Diogenes in his barrel.

Because of this Cervantes, though he could already count on that great number of unknown friends and admirers whose absorbed attention is the best reward of all literary work, now and again still thought that it would be very convenient to get close to some tree providing goodly shade. For this purpose, in order to obtain shelter and assistance for himself, he joined the secular Confraternity of the Most Holy Sacrament, to which the most prominent and influential people at the Court belonged, among whom he must have sought someone to shelter his graying locks. Perhaps it was then that the generosity toward him of the very illustrious Toledan Don Bernardo Sandoval y Rojas[1] had its beginnings. A cardinal so enamored of classical order, in which he saw what he considered the most finished art, could not fail to be pleased with the knowledge that the gallant soul of Don Quixote had put aside its fierce independence in order to enter a devout confraternity. That submission of Cervantes was actually a splendid victory. It was as though the conqueror of windmills had been made a knight of Santiago or of Calatrava.

If you do not know Toledo's cathedral you will not be able to understand the spirit of Don Bernardo de Sandoval y Rojas as revealed most clearly in his major work, the building of the Chapel of the Virgin and of the Octagon or Reliquary which stands behind it. Hidden in the back of the huge pile, closed off by an Escorial-type door and guarded by very strong gratings, the Chapel of the Virgin of the Reliquary tempers the daring of the Gothic naves and intrudes between them like a treatise on logic in a romantic poem. The great book of divine and human knight-errantries that the Egas and Arfes, the Villalpandos and the Copines, Master Rodrigo and Master Felipe Vigarni, carved, sculptured, fretted, worked and painted in relief, polished and made into a poem, is interrupted when one enters the Chapel of the Reliquary. In it all the lines are straight, rigid, geometrical, it is all marbles and jaspers, multicolored but cold, admirably put together but sepulchral. It is a Pantheon rather than a chapel, and the gay dark-skinned Virgin is bored to death on her golden throne under her crust of diamonds, pearls, rubies and emeralds weeping in the dark and longing for the sun's caress, which they receive only once a year when the creaking barred gates are opened, the divine image leaves its prison, and she sweeps proudly into the transept.

That is the chapel, that is the way of thinking, and that is the spirit of Don Bernardo de Sandoval and there were already many great gentlemen to whom ogival art was beginning to seem like the work of lunatics and idiots, a book of knight-errantry which should be condemned and forbidden and cut off from the admiration of zealous souls. You can see how and why the Cardinal Archbishop was a patron of Cervantes, as he was for many others, possibly without distinguishing him from the rest of the needy. He thought that the *Quixote* and the Chapel of the Reliquary, with which he was more and more pleased, complemented each other, and perhaps trusting too much to the arguments against Lope cited by the canon in the last chapters of the *Quixote*, he thought that Cervantes' talents were capable of bringing an end to the disorder, confusion and lunacy of past knight-errantries and of any that might still be attempted.

Lope also thought so and that is why he could never come to an understanding with Miguel. This was a sad mistake, as was the lamentable lack of understanding born from their having two irreconcilable characters. If Cervantes had thought only of destroying the books on knight-errantry his would have been an incidental work, as was the Chapel of the Reliquary, which no longer exists in the eyes of the artist but does not detract in any way from the enthusiasm and devotion with which the rest of the cathedral is viewed. Lope also thought that Cervantes, disappointed in attempts at playwriting, loathed his plays for what they contained of bravura and nonsense inherited from the *Romancero* and from the old Spanish legends of knight-errantry, and in this Lope was mistaken, or else he did not know Cervantes' own plays, the materials for which had likewise been worked up from epic and knightly sources.

In short the phoenix of all talents thought what many have since thought, that the spirit of Cervantes was classical, systematizing and correcting romantic fantasies in the great Spanish or rather European tradition. His Sevillian origin, his youthful Italianism, also led to this belief.

Don Bernado de Sandoval and Lope de Vega were completely mistaken, a part of posterity has also been confused, and it was necessary for romantic poets like Heine to make it clear by shouting at the top of their lungs that the *Quixote* is a romantic work, and here it is important to declare that it is not only a romantic work but that it is the greatest and finest of all the books on knight-errantry, combining the outrageous lunacy and extraordinary fantasy which characterized them with a measure of reason and humanity contained in no other book.

With such thoughts Miguel was more hopeful of going on with the work as it continued to grow in his imagination. Is it logical to think, as some have said, that Cervantes had no plan for completing the *Quixote* and that he published the Second Part only because he was incited by the publication of Avellaneda's book?

No. Ever since Miguel saw how a very large number of people had understood something, whether much or little, and some of them all, of what was included in the first part of the book, he never ceased to think of finishing it; nor can the splendid facility of language and style revealed in the second part, which recalls so distinctly the "second manner" of Velázquez, be achieved save through deep reflection.

There were not many years between the first and second parts, especially if it is taken into account that during them Cervantes worked out and finished other important works. The younger and luckier Lope wrote, quarrelled, made a lot of noise, fell in love, committed grave sins, repented of them; his was a whirlwind life. Older and less fortunate, Cervantes wrote and held his tongue, meditated, searched out flaws, tortured his imagination, all the time shut up in a room in the Calle de la Magdalena listening, as an accompaniment to his labors, to the hammers of the forge and the saws and planes of the carpenter's shop in the carriage-works of Francisco Daza, who lived opposite, or else hearing the murmured prayers of his wife and his sisters when they returned from their *novenas* and pious exercises at the Venerable Third Order of St. Francis, to which all three belonged.

Holiness had harmonized the characters and strengthened the friendships between the Cervantes women and Doña Catalina. The two ladies of the Court and the village girl were in perfect accord in all matters concerning religious zeal and in this they were also in complete accord with Doña Constanza de Ovando. On the other hand it seems that contacts with Doña Isabel de Saavedra must have been less frequent and the trouble between Miguel and his son-in-law Luis de Molina could already be seen approaching. At the same time Cervantes' days were sweetened by the love of his sisters and his daily life with them and his wife.

But as it was God's will that the Ingenious Hidalgo was never to attain complete happiness it followed that on October 8 or 9 of 1609 Doña Andrea died and was buried in the parish precinct of San Sebastián at Miguel's expense. It must have been a terrible blow to Cervantes. His sister had inherited the generosity and courage of her mother and was the head of the family. Beautiful, talented, agreeable, as confirmed by her marrying three times and pleasing three husbands, there is no doubt that she was also able to ensure tranquility and provide a pleasant life for those who lived with her. Doña Andrea was not a saint, but rather a woman of the world, and being so she was loved by her people and died surrounded by them after she had succeeded in reconciling her brother and her sister-in-law, sacrificing herself to do so, and conquering the dudgeon of Doña Catalina de Palacios by sharing devotions with her. For Miguel the death of the excellent, the helpful, the wise Doña Andrea was a great loss.

Miguel was left with his sister Doña Magdalena, his wife Doña Catalina and his niece Doña Constanza, who was also very competent and skillful. Doña Magdalena advanced daily with firmer and surer steps on the road to saintliness and on January 10 of 1610, having previously rendered an account of her life and habits, she entered the Venerable Third Order and took the veil. But her influence over Doña Catalina must not have been as great as that of Doña Andrea.

Eight months after Doña Andrea died, Doña Catalina de Salazar left the house one day, possibly after a long talk with some of her relatives from Esquivias. Her old maid María de Ugena, who had been in her service since she was a child, accompanied her and they went to the house of a fellow countryman of both of them, the notary Baltasar de Ugena. They left on some pretext without saying where they were going and without Magdalena or Miguel knowing anything about it. Doña Catalina, in full possession of all her faculties, was going to execute her will. Doubtless the clergyman Francisco de Palacios had once more managed to insinuate distrust of Miguel into Doña Catalina's mind. He perhaps told her that now at his age there was no hope of his improving in fortune or frame of mind; he may have pointed out how little his works and the fame of the *Quixote* had profited him. As far as that worthy clergyman of Esquivias was concerned Cervantes was still a poet, a man of bad principles, almost, almost an absolute madman. In short Doña Catalina, this good and faithful spouse whose love for Cervantes has been so praised and in whose tenderness and affection Miguel himself had confidence, made a will without her husband's knowledge, disinheriting him almost completely, for she left him only the usufruct for life of the little vineyard on the Seseña road, and on the other hand she bequeathed the best part of her possessions to the clergyman Francisco de Palacios Salazar who, from what can be gathered, had profited during his whole life from that property and who did not want it, in case of his sister's death, to go to his spendthrift brother-in-law.

This document has to be read slowly in order to comprehend the malice of the one who inspired it. Sooner or later Cervantes must have learned of it and this knowledge may have been one of the greatest sorrows of his life; the disappointment was all the more cruel in that it came from behind the door through which another disappointment had appeared. It is possible that Doña Catalina had a certain affection for Miguel but it is certain that she did not respect him. That will was another jab of the spur which conventional society, hypocritical society, well-ordered society, bourgeois, devout, hostile to heroisms, struck Jesuitically at the heart where a knightly spirit dwelt, attacking him craftily in his purse, stripping him in his old age, leaving him to fend for himself, never suspecting that he had the power to fashion new weapons with which to fight and already had them in the forge.

CHAPTER 49

Patronage of Lemos—The Argensolas—Magdalena's Will

DON Pedro Fernandez de Castro was thirty-three years old, married to the beautiful daughter of the Duke of Lerma, and he had a large fortune and all the most enviable honors and titles, among them the one Cervantes immortalized: Count of Lemos. He was nevertheless disillusioned with life at Court and his only desire was an appointment as Viceroy of Naples. He was being sent there after much negotiating and refusing the Viceroyalty of New Spain, returning in a rage to his properties in Galicia in order to demonstrate how much his abilities were needed in Naples.

He came to the capital at the beginning of 1610 much weakened in health and sour of temper. His unhappy mood was intensified by his distaste for a certain complicated litigation with the Count of Monterey over the estate of Viedma, and his disposition was further soured by the unexpected death of his secretary, Don Juan Ramírez de Arellano, whom he had trusted completely. The Count found himself in Madrid buried in legal business without a secretary; he was like a man who has suddenly lost his right hand. Someone pointed out to him that there was no one as fit to take care of the problems inherent in the life of a powerful nobleman and the official position of Secretary of State and War in the Viceroyalty of Naples as that suave, worldly, correct, Lupercio Leonardo de Argensola.[1]

When he was Marquis of Sarriá, the Count of Lemos had Lope de Vega as secretary, but it would seem probable that the Count was disenchanted with courtly poets, and once Lope had left the house they had never again resumed their former intimate relationship. Lupercio Leonardo, however, was a limpid and edifying poet who, when the Count wearied of business, could amuse and revive him with wise, most human and low-keyed poems decanted from the Horatian fount.

As for Lupercio Leonardo, what more or better could he expect in the way of poetic tranquility, which was the greatest of his desires, together with the bourgeois and bureaucratic placidity from which so many of his poems suffered? He lost no time, therefore, in removing to the Court accompanied by his brother Bartolomé Leonardo, the very fat cleric who was also a poet along the same lines as himself. So that the family incorporate everything that might please and satisfy the Count, to the man of the world secretary and the clergyman poet with his magnificent rotund figure, very suitable for honoring a ducal house and lending lustre to its servants' dining room, was added Lupercio's son, Gabriel Leonardo de Albión, a twenty-two-year-old youth who at fifteen was already most adept in the Latin tongue and not ignorant of the Greek, combining these merits with exemplary behavior, "worthy of better times and a better father," and especially valuable to a Court in having an extraordinary memory, for he could often hear ten *décimas* recited and reel them off without a single error.

The Leonardo family were just what the Count needed to organize a literary Court in Naples, thereby continuing the Spanish tradition. They had no sooner spoken with him than they had convinced him to take some poets with him in order to enliven the halls of the palace and attract people of good quality from among those fastidious and demanding Italians who refused to be impressed by anything but art.

A great deal of influence must have been applied and many intrigues employed to get on the list of the Viceroy's poets, which the Argensolas drew up after consulting with him. Miguel recalled his old friendship with Lupercio, who appeared to listen courteously and sympathetically, but those chosen had already been selected, including young writers of the lowest rank but good enough to divert the Count's moments of leisure without putting the Leonardos in the shade.

It requires no great discernment to understand that whether his approach was well-timed or not the two brothers would have given Cervantes little consideration. Both of them were sufficiently perceptive to appreciate and confess to their most secret selves, although possibly they did not admit it even to each other, that Cervantes was too much of a man and too much of a poet to take with them. They saw him humble and poor for the moment, in need and seeking help, but they knew very well that when he got to Naples he was bound to rise to leadership over that shiftless crowd, not only through what touched on literary matters but also through his conduct and worldly experience, even more so with respect to anything having to do with Italy.

Miguel was keenly disappointed when he saw that his modesty and dependence on them made no impression on his unresponsive friends, for he had greatly cherished his hope of once more seeing his beloved Parthenope, walking her streets and enjoying the delights of her friendly company. This disappointment embittered his old age, even though he could see in the hidden opposition of the Leonardos a tacit recognition of how superior to themselves they thought him. Cervantes and Goethe alike never were rats to take shelter in empty granaries.

It is appropriate to recall the lines in the *Parnassus* where, with his heart on his sleeve, Miguel mentions this unpleasant business:

He of the winged sandals ordered me
to get ready and land on earth
to give a message to the Lupercios. . . .
"I fear they would not give me ear,"
I answered him . . . they are
as short of good-will as they are short of sight . . .
Much I expected, aye, they promised much,
but it may be that newer occupations
force them to forget what they said. . . ."

As can be seen from these lines written in 1614, Miguel's hopes of once more walking the streets of Naples lasted four years. His claims, according to the gossip of Madrid, became a laughing stock, as did those of Góngora, Cristóbal de Mesa, and others who were rejected, but being more prudent or less desperate than the others he did not complain until much later, and then in the measured way we have seen. Góngora showed his wrath in an outspoken sonnet:

My lord the Count is going to Naples
and my lord the Duke is going to France.
Have a good trip, Princes, you who today
give weight to caracoles.
Since there is such an excess of learned Spaniards
I will offer my Muse to no one. . . .

which was not true, but genius did not give Góngora the patience it granted abundantly to Miguel for the very reason that Cervantes was more unfortunate and his troubles were genuine, not imaginary like those of Góngora. Cervantes was thus a robust and healthy writer, Góngora a neurasthenic ridden by two thousand devils.

Around May 17 of 1610 the Count of Lemos left the capital with his retinue of salaried poets. Before his departure Miguel must have told him about the *Exemplary Novels* and given him to understand that some of them were being finished and corrected in order to be dedicated to him. Who is there who does not know that the word "exemplary" and his insistence on underlining the "hidden mystery which inspires them" reflect the purpose of Cervantes, whose experience of the world made it clear to him that high-ranking gentlemen were excessively partial to including in their reading matter a touch of the didactic and of moral and political assiduousness? Some of the stories were designed for the prudent and prescient Cardinal Niño de Guevara; they must also have appealed to a man of politics in charge of as important and difficult a mission as that of governing Naples.

In *The Generous Lover, The Anglo-Spanish Lady, Lady Cornelia*, and *The Two Maidens* he limited himself to writing novels in the Italian manner, although obviously at times raising the level of the usual triviality of the *novelieri*, while in *Rinconete and Cortadillo* he offered for the Governor's consideration a study of the vices and evil ways peculiar to Seville, which were also applicable to Naples, the Seville of Italy. In *The Little Gypsy, The Power of Blood, The Illustrious Kitchen-maid, The Fraudulent Marriage*, and *The Jealous Man from Estremadura* he laid bare carefully guarded secrets of the feminine heart that are not only delightful but also useful to know for anyone who must command men, because he should understand that they are usually governed by women. Finally, in *The Dialogue of the Dogs* and in *The Glass Licentiate* a grandiose philosophical view of the world was raised, and in the second of them he propounded his "apothegms," incorporating in sententious form all the toils and frustrations his life had taught him and anticipating in the shape of the mad Licentiate the image of the superman every philosopher desirous of conquering bigger and better worlds of the spirit has always had in mind. Without the deep thought and the powerful originality of *The Glass Licentiate*, in which Cervantes, like Faust, presents himself as an eternally youthful old man, it would scarcely be possible to conceive the supreme art of the Second Part of the *Quixote*. Truths are clearly seen and clearly spoken by children and madmen. Cervantes was able to see the world more perceptively than ever when he looked at it through the eyes of the Licentiate as the necessary medium for passing from the vision of the first *Quixote* to that of the second, all the greater for being the simpler.

Cervantes was absorbed in these ideas without blinding himself on that account to minor realities. We cannot believe that the plays and interludes of the so-called second period, eventually published as *Eight Plays*, came very much before the best of the exemplary novels, but it is certain that there are at least two interludes, *The Cave of Salamanca* and *The Miraculous Reredo*, in which the philosophical perception concealed in a comic little story is that of a sixty-year old who has not only retained the good humor of his youth but has improved upon it with graces dictated by experience and the gentle irony which only a man proved by life acquires. It is the irony of the silver that is tarnished, of the eyes that fade, of the lips that sink from lack of teeth, of the mouth that laughs and does not bite, or if it bites does no hurt.

The hours and days of a monotonous and weary existence were spent by Cervantes in such meditations. He may have alternated his old established visits to the bookshops with mentally stimulating stops on the corner where actors met, since Miguel at that time lived right there, in the Calle de León across from the baker Castillo. His home must have provided little inspiration and few attractions. Doña Magdalena, more and more buried in her beatitudes, had won over Doña Catalina, who also entered the Venerable Third Order and donned its habit on June 27 of 1610. The Franciscan habits of these two good ladies intensified the ashen melancholy of the house, where only the youth of Doña Constanza, his niece, made the home a little cheerful for Miguel.

On an autumn day of that year Doña Magdalena, who was doubtless haunted by memories of her past love affairs and by the fear of death proper in one who professes the saving of her soul to be her only concern, went with her brother to the office of the notary Jerónimo Lopez with the intention of making her will. This most interesting document establishes the relationships which must have once existed between Doña Magdalena and two noble young gentlemen, Don Fernando de Ludeña and Don Enrique de Palafox. One passage of the will might be called an exemplary novel:

> Item: I declare that Don Fernando de Ludeña owes me three hundred ducats, loaned to him when he was an unmarried youth, and after his marriage with Doña Ana María de Hurbina, his wife, I went to ask for them in the presence of the said Doña Ana, and at that time in order not to distress his said wife he would not admit that he owed me them, and later, having gone again to his house because of the said debt, in the presence of the said Doña Ana María and one of her nephews, he said that if I would not make out a document he demanded of me in which I would confess that he owed me nothing, the said Don Fernando de Ludeña threatened me many times, saying that as long as he lived he would give me nothing unless I made out the said document, and when we were alone he told me that he would undertake to provide for my full support during his lifetime and that if I outlived him he would leave me the wherewithal to live on, and under the said promise I made out the document in which I declared he owed me nothing, the which I did against my will, and so I declare upon my conscience that he still owes me the said three hundred ducats. I instruct my executors to collect them, or at least tell him about them so that his conscience may be troubled, for he knows that it is true.

It is strange, but it happened so, that with the debt still outstanding, among other poems at the beginning of *The Exemplary Novels* there is a mediocre sonnet by Don Fernando de Ludeña which begins:

> Depart, Nereids from the shady shelter

and ends:

> For if it had not been destined for Apollo
> the laurel would be used today to gird
> the brow of Miguel de Cervantes. . . .

wherein one can see Don Fernando's payment in fine words but not in money.

The story that can be deduced from another provision in Doña Magdalena's will is no less interesting:

> Item: I likewise bequeath to the said Doña Constanza sixty-four ducats from two subsistence allowances given me by Don Enrique de Palafox, Knight of Calatrava, who holds them by favor of His Majesty from the subsistence allowances which are given to the said Knights, so that in my stead the said Doña Constanza receive them, for which the said Don Enrique has empowered me.

He was a nobleman from Aragón, a native of Ariza, belonging to the most ancient nobility of the Kingdom. Why did he do this favor to Doña Magdalena? Did he do it perhaps for the sake of her niece Constanza? No one knows, but according to all indications we have an exemplary novel here also.

This is a very important document, for in it one sees how disabused Miguel and his family were toward Doña Catalina de Salazar and hers. Doña Magdalena left all her present and future possessions to her niece, the only ray of sunshine in the house. On the same day and in the same document Miguel made over to Constanza his rights in the inheritance of his brother, Ensign Rodrigo de Cervantes, killed at the Dunes, to whom a large part of his pay was still due. The ties between Miguel and Magdalena and the love they bore their niece are evident. It is also clear that Miguel, now aware of the will his wife had made in secret, returned the compliment, presenting his niece and not his wife with that part of his inheritance which belonged to him and the only possessions he still hoped to have. At the same time this shows how Miguel completely ignored his daughter Isabel, from whom he was estranged because of his son-in-law Molina.

On arriving at sixty-three years of age, the horizon was closing in on Miguel. There was hardly any love left in his heart, hardly any hope. The plays and the novels and at times even the *Quixote* slumbered. Possibly whole months would pass during which dust gathered on their pages.

At the end of the year 1610 Doña Magdalena died and Miguel moved with Doña Catalina to Esquivias.

CHAPTER 50

Miguel in Esquivias—The Exemplary Novels—*The Academy of Pastrana*—*Royal Nuptials*

MIGUEL dragged his sixty-four years back and forth between the pear orchard and the newly planted vines on the road to Seseña without allowing his disappointments to undermine his eternal good humor. A few twinges in his worn-out heart warned him that old age was there to keep him company but it was certainly not accompanied by its usual drawback of a soured and uncertain temper. While he lived in Esquivias, supported by Francisco de Palacios, the worthy clergyman who now held the properties of Doña Catalina as his own, with no more conversation or society than that of the Ugenas and Quijadas, friends and relatives of the family, Cervantes' spirit still did not flag or falter. Since he had once been a whole man rather than just a literary figure, he did not experience then or ever the disease that moves many writers to live only among writers and to be interested only in poems, novels or plays while bored and disgusted with the conversation of those they deem vulgar. He did not share in the scorn of the bourgeois that nowadays usually seems to affect all those who hold either a pen or a brush in hand.

In his soul Cervantes was in rebellion against the great injustices of the world, those that seize upon and take root deep in human nature, but never against the minor inequities or small difficulties of society as it is constituted. Don Quixote battles giants, not rustic folk or those of humble stock. He rebels against the injustices, the outrages and the arrogance that oppress humanity, and in this concept he is not just revolutionary but anarchical in the best sense of the word, for he wants evil never to prevail and men to return to the gentleness and felicity of the Golden Age, which he depicted more eloquently than all the Utopias, Cities of the Sun, and Societies of the Future fabricated by ancient and modern dreamers; but with regard to the actual way of life Don Quixote is a conservative, a believer in cutting out only what is corrupt and altering or abolishing only what is misused. Because of this, though

Cervantes was a victim of the niggardliness and narrow-mindedness of his brother-in-law and those around him, he lived at peace with them, listened amiably to their ingenuous observations, and was always able to find something profitable among them.

"It is no bad thing to be a poet," he thought, putting it in the mouth of the page in *The Little Gypsy*, "but being only a poet I do not take to be very good. Poetry should be used as a very precious jewel which its owner does not wear every day, nor does he show it to everybody, nor constantly, but only when it is timely and there is a reason for showing it." Thinking thus, Miguel consoled himself during his solitary walks through the countryside, alone with his poetry because it is "a most beautiful damsel, chaste, virtuous, discreet, witty and retiring. . . . She loves solitude, fountains divert her, fields comfort her, trees soothe her and flowers cheer her," and if "she seems extremely poor and smacks of the beggar" and it is very certain that "there is no poet who knows how to guard the property he has or acquire what he does not have," as Cervantes could bear witness with his life as an example, it is also true that "there is no poet who is not rich, for they are all satisfied with their condition, a philosophy which is attained by few." Thus when Miguel found himself poorest and hardest pressed he always thought as did the graceful Preciosa: "I have a certain fantastic little spirit here inside me which leads me to great things." When some of his neighbors, men for whom the world was contained between the borders of this olive grove or that hillock, considered themselves cleverer and wiser than he was, Miguel thought about it and when alone he laughed as one who has seen much and who knows that "there is nothing better in the world than to act always in the same way, so that no one can be misled by his own ignorance," as the afflicted Ricardo said in *The Generous Lover*, and who also knows that "long peregrinations make men wise," as *The Glass Licentiate* maintained.

At the same time Miguel was sleeping long and deeply, following the advice of that same Licentiate in order to prevent or cure the disease of envy. "Go to sleep," he thought, "for all the time you are asleep you will be the equal of the one you envy," and he continued to treat himself to a plethora of reading and to devote some time to pious meditation, for he thought, as did the parents of Leocadia in *The Power of Blood*, that "thieves have no jurisdiction over knowledge and virtue nor over what is called fate." Besides, his poverty did not worry him much, for he always remembered that the greatest sum of money he ever had in his hands had not been his, and when he stupidly turned it over to Simón Freyre de Lima it had brought him more trouble, imprisonment, lawsuits and depositions than all his hard times and misfortunes. At the same time he continued to think that the worries this entailed were to be of everlasting profit to him for the rest of his days, and he therefore reflected, as did the jealous man from estremadura, that "wealth is as great a burden to one who is not used to having it or does not know how to use it as poverty is to the one who always has it. Gold brings worries and the lack of it worries, but the one is remedied by acquiring some reasonable quantity and the other is increased the more one acquires." Nor did his poverty worry him much even in moments of depression when he considered the sayings and thoughts of the poor to be useless and achieve nothing because, as the wise dog Scipio said in the *Dialogue*, "never was the advice of a poor man accepted, however good it might be," and "the wisdom of the poor is overshadowed since need and misery are shadows and clouds which darken it, and if it is ever discovered it is adjudged stupid and treated with contempt," while his interlocutor, the dog Berganza, asserts that "misfortunes seek and find the unfortunate one, though he hide himself in the farthest corners of the world." Thus he took refuge in the wise remedy of his philosophy without exaggerating or complaining, writing that "when miseries and misfortunes have wide currency and are continuous, either they end quickly in death or their continuation becomes a settled practice and habit of suffering which at its most rigorous is apt to serve as a relief." With these and other reflections inserted in the text of the *Exemplary Novels* he mitigated the dullness and insecurity of his situation if at times such things ever really did upset him.

Cervantes also accepted with singular magnanimity the situation in which he was placed by his wife's family, who treated him as if he were a somewhat insignificant outsider. There was even a demand for Doña Catalina to sign a new document at the beginning of 1612, repeating the partition of her possessions already made, and ceding to her brother, Francisco de Palacios, the additional increments of a third and a fifth of what belonged to her. And as a greater mockery, in this document there appears again, as her act of generosity, usufruct of the small vineyard on the road to Seseña (four and a half *aranzadas*, that is to say, a little more than a thousand vine-stocks and up to a hundred olive trees), the only possession which would go to Cervantes upon the death of Doña Catalina.

About this time, also, the discord between Cervantes and his son-in-law Luis de Molina had been growing considerably, and on September 17 Molina, who had quarrelled with Juan de Urbina over certain business ventures badly planned by the one and worse executed by the other, demanded before the *alcalde* Ramírez Fariñas that Cervantes and Urbina produce in cash the two thousand ducats promised in the articles of marriage of Doña Isabel de Saavedra. On November 19 the generous Juan de Urbina paid nineteen thousand reals, twenty-four hours after having been ordered to do so by the court, and Molina declared himself satisfied by that sum although short by three thousand reals. Obviously Urbina paid this out of his own pocket, for it is unthinkable that Cervantes was in a position to do it.

Miguel came to Madrid and again frequented the bookshops, seeking the company of famous writers and hoping to associate with them. Years before when he lived in the Calle de la Magdalena he had known two gentlemen, elegant poets and valiant soldiers named Don Diego and Don Francisco de Silva who belonged to the Pastrana family, thus being neighbors of his. In the *Parnassus* he said of Don Francisco:

> This great gentleman who bows
> to the teaching of the good poets
> and by their light goes to the sacred mount,
> at very least, is Don Francisco de Silva,
> what will he be at most? Oh, mellow age
> in green years full of wisdom. . . .

This gentleman established in his palace an Academy attended by the most select talents in Spain. There were other academies in the capital, centers and assemblies of poets, but none as brilliant as the one in Pastrana's house. In it, as elsewhere, the one whose voice was heard and who brooked no competition was an academician, or rather an imperious overpowering figure who dominated everyone: Lope de Vega Carpio.

It came to pass, either by chance or design, that Cervantes one day met his friend Don Francisco, who invited him to attend some of the meetings of his academy, and Miguel went along, handicapped and disillusioned as he was. Of the literary disputations at the Academy of Pastrana, which usually ended in wrangling and uproar, Lope de Vega wrote to the Duke of Sessa on March 2 of 1612: "The Academies are frenetic: in the last one two Licentiates pulled each other's hair: I read some verses with some fancies of Zervantes which resembled badly scrambled eggs. . . ." In these short phrases one does not have to be very perspicacious to see that if Lope had been reconciled to Miguel he held him in no great esteem. "Zervantes" was not in his good graces.

Lope was imperious, considered himself unique, like nearly all men of genius. He could concede that Cervantes had talent, although as a poet he was more versed in misfortunes than in verses. What he could not tolerate, what he could not abide, was the growing personality of Cervantes, whose thought, more slowly but with greater surety and depth than that of Lope in his dramatic and lyrical works, was winning over the minds of the public, and not just of one here and there, but of everyone. Lope was Nature's prodigy, and he gloried in the popularity he had won. He had agitated and made thousands of hearts to beat, and he exercised an irresistible domination over all the women of Spain. Such a privileged position cannot be shared.

Let us look at the matter dispassionately today and it will seem almost incredible that two such great men should live at the same time, like two equal suns lighting the earth, and we could even believe this and be able to see the two suns facing each other, but what is not possible in human terms is that they would not be jealous of each other.

While Cervantes was arranging with Francisco de Robles for the sale of the *Exemplary Novels* and taking care of the printing and correcting, new and great events agitated the Court, and they were known in the palace of Pastrana before anywhere else, since the head of the house, the Prince of Mélito, Duke of Pastrana and of Francavila, had been put in charge of nothing less than proceeding to Paris, there to arrange the marriage of Crown Prince Philip, later to be Philip IV, with Princess Isabel of Bourbon, eldest daughter of the deceased King of France, Henry IV, and his wife Queen María de Médici. At the same time there arrived in Madrid the Duke of Mayenne or "Umena," as the people of Madrid called him, accompanied by an illustrious retinue, likewise to arrange for the marriage of the eldest daughter of Philip III, Doña Ana de Austria, with the new King of France, Louis XIII. On August 20 the covenants of both marriages were signed simultaneously in Paris and Madrid.

There was great rejoicing in France and Spain, no small misgivings in England. The not very profitable sympathies that Spaniards have had for the French date from this time, while their lamentable hatred for England had started a considerable number of years before. It had been impossible to come to an understanding with France during the reign of their great King Henry IV, who always smelled slightly of brimstone, an odor that Escorialian nostrils could not abide; nor did Henry IV look kindly upon a king and a nation which had radically, abruptly and brutally expelled the Moriscos in the way that Spanish governing bodies like to carry out their bad ideas, for they were always better pleased with a moment of arbitrary action than by ten years of sound, small, slow, and useful reforms.

With Henry IV dead and the odor of brimstone replaced by the saintly aroma of taper and incense which the mean-spirited, devout, and uxorious Louis XIII loved to inhale, as did the uxorious, devout, and mean-spirited Philip III, there were no difficulties in Spain or France to prevent an understanding. France was beginning to copy the literature and system of government of Spain. The fictions of our novelists and dramatists were spiced and served up with a piquant French sauce to please the palates of the ladies and gentlemen of Louis XIII; that monarch also imitated the worst features of our Court. Henry IV never had a special favorite, nor had Philip III. Louis XIII had one, as did Philip III. The theory and practice of the monarchist and aristocratic regime was being transformed in France as it was in Spain.

CHAPTER 51

Visit to Alcalá—Home and the Road—Lope as Neighbor

IN the summer of 1613, how or why is not known, Miguel was in Alcalá de Henares, although he had no friends or relatives there. The city had changed considerably in appearance and way of life over the years, while the lawlessness and presumption of the students had increased and become habitual.

Read, not the solemn *History of the Universities* by the academician Lafuente, but rather Quevedo's *Life of the Rascal Don Pablos*,[1] and tell me if it was possible for fruitful work at a university to be maintained in Alcalá. As a result of the state of agitation in which the students kept the city, its families of ancient lineage emigrated one after another, going to increase further the confusion of the boiling pot of Madrid, and the escutcheons and coats of arms on the old mansions were progressively erased; only the facade of the Lizanas maintained the pomp and dignity of the nobility. The rest of the houses, turned into rooming houses for students and miserable half-starved boarding schools, became more plebeian every day. Miguel found no one who knew him or took any notice of him, but he could observe how different the savage lawlessness of the students of Alcalá was from the urbane and courtly behavior of those of Bologna.

Italy, which in times past had sent here the best, the finest and most brilliant of its luminaries, did so no longer, and there is no need to credit Miguel with extraordinary perception if he got some idea of the serious damage that was bound to follow when Spaniards turned away from the light of Italy toward France, which for them was neither a beacon nor a focus but rather a mirror that reflected their own endowments and their own blemishes, both old and new, at first life-sized, later grotesquely enlarged. What was beginning to be observed in the whole nation could already be noticed in Alcalá de Henares. There was not a single window there opening toward Italy, and recognizing this must have caused Cervantes at least as much distress as his finding hardly anyone who remembered him.

The disappointment of not seeing a continuation of what in his youth he thought had started off on the firmest foundation did not discourage him from continuing his projects. He already knew that if in his novels there was a good deal which had an Italian source there was also much that came from purely Spanish roots, and though it may have cost him a struggle he must have persuaded himself that this last was the best.

We have now arrived at the last three years of Cervantes' life and we will see that these were years of frantic literary activity, years in which, possessed of his immortality and conscious of its immense importance, he hastened to make the most of time and even wanted to stay the footsteps of death, as Joshua did those of the sun. He loved solitude when he could no longer take advantage of it, he valued and desired rest when it was impossible for him to rest, he recognized his creative genius when there was no time left for many creations to take final form.

Thus we see him, in the Prologue to the *Exemplary Novels*, obsessed by his future works, announcing to the reader "in brief, further heroic feats of Don Quixote and drolleries of Sancho Panza. After them, if life does not desert me," he says, full of a vague presentiment, "I offer you the *Trials of Persiles*, a book which dares to compete with Heliodorus . . . and later *The Weeks in the Garden*." And in case death were to arrive before he carried out these designs he did not omit to draw his portrait for posterity, the only real one we possess, since all the others that have been painted are pure fantasies absolutely devoid of versimilitude or esthetic quality:

> He whom you see here of aquiline visage, of chestnut hair, of open and untroubled brow, of cheerful eyes and hooked though well-proportioned nose, his beard silver which only twenty years ago was gold, the moustaches big, the mouth small, the teeth not important, for he has but six and they are ill-conditioned and worse placed, having no correspondence one with another, the body between two extremes, neither large nor small, the color high, rather fair than dark, somewhat bent of shoulder and not very light of foot: this I say is the face of the author of *Galatea* and of *Don Quixote de la Mancha* and of the one who wrote the *Voyage to Parnassus* . . . and other works which wander astray somewhere and perhaps without bearing the name of their owner; he is commonly called Miguel de Cervantes Saavedra.

Such projects demonstrated the obvious and perfectly logical struggle going on in the soul of Cervantes. For entertainment and moral edification he wrote and published his novels, reflections of Italy, of Seville and Toledo, but they were not what stirred and captured his fancy, nor were the plays which he no longer even offered to actors enslaved by Lope.

He began to doubt whether these ephemeral and circumstantial narratives, depicting a state of things that would not last and reflecting customs that might disappear at any moment while cities changed as Alcalá had changed in fifty years or so, would be vigorous and interesting enough to rescue his name from the obscurity of the centuries. He came to the decision that the concept of human existence he had produced was not sufficiently exact. And as a love of silence and solitude contested his inclination toward noise and crowds the two great motivations in human life, the home and the road, contended with each other. In the Second Part of the *Quixote*, which he had almost finished, the home seemed to triumph over the road, the peaceful quiet life over the life of adventure; in it appeared such pleasant images of bourgeois tranquility as the home of the prudent Gentleman of the Green Coat, such savory images of rustic feasting as the wedding of the rich Camacho, such splendid visions of aristocratic life as the castle of the Duke and Duchess, and such mellow descriptions of the well-being then available to rich people, even if they did not belong to the high nobility, as the scenes laid in Barcelona in the house of Don Antonio Moreno. Finally, though perhaps Miguel had not yet envisaged it completely, Don Quixote died in bed like a good Christian, disowning his mad adventures. Life was reason, calm, tranquility.

But Miguel was so unsure of the validity of this attitude that at the same time he was turning out in the workshop of his mind the long fable of the *Trials of Persiles and Sigismunda*, in which all is open road, all is adventure, diversity, and uncertainty. The most varied sensations disturb the characters and drag readers from here to there, following a fantastic itinerary of a kind to exhaust any creative ability but that which was the greatest in Spain.

Which of the two concepts was the true one? In his last days Cervantes seemed to think that it was the one represented by the *Persiles*, but while he was putting the two works together he leaned now toward one way of thinking, now to the other. Miguel was seemingly younger at sixty-six years of age than he was at twenty, or at least endowed with more of the liveliness and freshness of imagination, qualities usually attributed to youth, which are so very apparent in the Second Part of the *Quixote* and reach heights of morbid excitement in the *Persiles*.

Would it be too daring to speculate that those *Weeks in the Garden*, already started at this time, of which some traces remained when he was on his deathbed, was a book of repose, a book of calm and of home, and not a book of the road and of action? From the pinnacle of his sixty-six years Miguel looked back over the panorama of his life and found in it much more road than home, but might he not have been expressing his aspiration to enjoy solitude and the music of silence? Did not the human Cervantes, like the very human *Candide* of Voltaire, think that the ultimate purpose of life is the cultivation of one's own garden? Is this not perhaps one of the eternal aspirations of mankind? In the ancient books of the Sacred Scriptures is not the Paradise on earth shown as a pleasant garden, and in the Greek and Phoenician myths is there not a garden of the Hesperides ready to crown the efforts of daring mariners?

In the meantime Cervantes' fortunes were not improving. His fame, which was so great that it had crossed the frontiers of Spain, was nevertheless not really marketable, and he was poor. He could not pay for the paper or printing of his novels and Francisco de Robles had to give him credit for them. Because of this he naturally had a claim on Miguel, who was almost obliged to sell him the copyright he had proceeded to take out. This was done on September 9 of 1613, when the *Exemplary Novels* were sold for one thousand six hundred reals and twenty-four copies of the book. Whatever those who try to judge these things may say it was not a bad sale, nor did sixteen hundred reals represent a paltry sum.

A few months after that sale the heirs of Ensign Rodrigo de Cervantes began to collect the arrears of pay due him, the total of which was not finally received until 1654. The amount which the nation owed that hero, killed in the Battle of the Dunes, was his back pay for several years totalling 71,543 maravedis. Francisco de Robles gave Miguel a lump sum of 54,000 maravedis for the copyright. Were letters or arms worth more in terms of compensation? In order to get the true picture one would have to weigh the circumstances and admit frankly that the nation was already impoverished, that everything was poorly paid, letters, arms and everything else, and that just continuing to live in Spain without constant violent protest indicated an abnegation and a magnanimity worthy of commemoration in marble and bronze.

The *Exemplary Novels* were read with very great pleasure and approval. It was they that placed their author definitely in the company of what were called "geniuses of this Court." He had at last achieved by his own efforts that entry into the sacred precinct of the *literati* that he could not achieve in Seville, perhaps because he did not try hard enough. Here there was no Francisco Pacheco to portray the "intellectuals" of his time, but it can be taken for granted that their faces and manners differed little from those pampered, self-satisfied faces and those lordly airs of Pacheco's friends. Being a literary man was not yet a self-supporting way of life, however, not even for the fortunate Lope. He was a courtier like all the others, and if the King and Court moved, Lope had to follow. As for Miguel, it was in those years that he finally realized that he could earn his living ostensibly with his pen only as long as he got help from the Count of Lemos and was supported by the Very Illustrious Don Bernardo de Sandoval.

Cervantes was a neighbor of Lope de Vega, then living in the Calle de Francos, while Miguel lived at first in the Calle de las Huertas, across from the houses in which the Prince of Morocco dwelt temporarily, and later in the house where he died, in the Calle del León at the corner of the Calle de Francos, which belonged to his friend the presbyter Don Francisco Martínez Marcilla. Moreover, Miguel and Lope met frequently during services and religious observances of the Venerable Third Order, to which they both belonged.

From the second half of the year 1612 Lope was more than ever assiduous in these devotions. A great sorrow, the one he felt most deeply in all his life, had dealt him a very rude blow: the death of his son Carlos Félix, a boy seven years old endowed with natural graces and the apple of Lope's eye and heart. The wounded father sang his pain in that immortal lay: "He the sweet fruit of my soul. . . ," where paternal love is shown bleeding and weeping, for once more strongly and deeply than in any other work written in Spain. In this incomparable elegy there is a glimpse of how the pain in his soul was to lead Lope into repenting his sins and moral lapses. This sorrow was then followed as though a natural sequel by the death of his wife, Doña Juana de Guardo, who died in childbirth at the beginning of 1613. Lope thus found himself alone in his house but for his maidservant Catalina and it was then that he took in his two illegitimate children, Marcela and Lope Félix.

Misery seeks company, all the more so when it concerns a man who must necessarily externalize all his private feelings, as did Lope de Vega, who, whatever his apparently intimate poems seemed to declare, was never able to live alone with himself. He certainly thought that he came and went with his solitude, but he was never in it for more than an hour and then he had to give rein to his unmanageable genius, producing, talking, writing, in constant activity. After suffering two terrible losses in succession, however, he took shelter hastily in the asylum of the Venerable Third Order, where there was no lack of pious and compassionate brothers to remind him of how, on entering that Holy Congregation, Lope had written his very famous *Four Soliloquies on the Repentance and Conversion of a Sinner*. In this work, into which Lope put his whole soul, as he did in everything he wrote, the absolute sincerity of his feelings can be seen.

With his beloved son Carlos Félix dead, his good and infinitely patient wife Doña Juana dead, a passion for repentance grew in Lope's troubled heart. It is almost certain that he sometimes told Cervantes about this, perhaps during the pious meetings of the Tertiaries, perhaps in the printing shop of Juan de la Cuesta, where they used to meet. How long Lope's new repentance endured is part of his history, but after reading the *Soliloquies* the scant confidence he himself had in being able to persevere in his contrition can be inferred. It is probable, however, that Cervantes and Lope saw each other every day in the neighborhood, met at the V.O.T., and were reconciled, though not without mutual reservations. As a token of this reconciliation Lope mentioned the name of Cervantes in some of his plays, casually and not always with much praise, as in *Courtesy Rewarded* (*El premio del bien hablar*), when Don Juan asks: "Is not Leonarda eloquent? Is she not lovely?" and Martín replies:

> How eloquent? Not Cicero, Cervantes,
> Juan de Mena, nor any before or since
> were as eloquent and as learned. . . .

Another of its consequences was that in the *Parnassus*, when many poets, some good, some mediocre and some bad, had been named as defenders of Parnassus:

> Another cloud rained down great Lope de Vega,
> a notable poet whose poetry and prose
> none can surpass, nor even reach. . . .

In all of these and many other expressions exchanged between the two great men there were moments of sincerity and frankness and others of artificiality and social conventionality. They accepted each other now, but they still did not hold each other completely in esteem, nor perhaps understand each other either artistically or on a private and friendly basis. It cannot be definitely stated that there were hatreds, though the springs of hate had not dried up in the soul of Cervantes, who even in this showed his youthful vigor, nor can it be stated that at any moment they reached a complete and frank understanding. They were neighbors, they saw each other, sorrow had brought them together for an instant, and the moves of the Court served to separate them again. In any case Cervantes was now a genius of the Court, he was well and favorably known to all, and the wisdom and morality of his exemplary novels got a pleasing reception by the most circumspect standards.

If Miguel was seeking to win the confidence and gratitude of other

Court poets when he drafted the tercets of the *Parnassus* in the moments when he put aside the *Quixote* and the *Persiles*, it is not likely that it served such a purpose completely. In view of his many preoccupations and the gigantic effort he was making, which would send him to his grave, he could scarcely maintain social relations with all those people, and it is probable that he saw less and less of them as he wrote more and more every day. With the two prodigious tales of the *Quixote* and the *Persiles* in his head he must have lived in a world of fantasy, oblivious to everything, becoming a thinking and writing being quite distinct from his normal self.

CHAPTER 52

The Journey to Parnassus

MIDWAY in life, with a chain on his ankle and an iron collar around his neck, Miguel wrote his immortal letter to Mateo Vázquez, a work of blood and pain, of living misery. The tercets of that letter are as good as the best that have been written in Castilian, including those of the famous Captain Andrada.[1] As for those prattling critics for whom there is not the slightest doubt that Cervantes wrote hastily and carelessly, without reflecting or without polishing, has it never occurred to them that the best poetical works from his pen are sonnets and tercets? If he ever wanted to unbosom himself and give reign to his intimate feelings he did it in sonnets like the one, "I swear to God this grandeur doth astound me. . . ." or like the one, "In July we witnessed another Holy Week. . . ." Besides the sonnets he wrote some admirable tercets in the epistle to Mateo Vázquez when he was in the last extreme of anguish there in Algiers, and he composed admirable tercets in the *Parnassus* when he was in the last extreme of life.

Miguel undertook the *Parnassus*, therefore, at the highest and most memorable point in existence, that in which man, scenting the proximity of death, seeks to tell the future what he has been and in the telling to interlard sincerity and simplicity with some touches of genuine modesty, but naturally combining it with the honest pride of one who is sure that he has produced a solid piece of work. Let us follow Miguel's thought in this invaluable biographical document and we will see what he believed of himself, though not what he necessarily thought of others, since in this work, as in the *Song of Calliope* in the *Galatea* and in Lope's *Laurel Wreath of Apollo*, too many poets were praised for all of them to be worthy, any more than was César Caporali,[2] whom he imitated, and by imitation cast him into oblivion,

> when the poet returned to his country alone
> and without a cent, he told what on the wing
> carried this one's fame to the other pole.

Miguel, who had tasted the bitterness of the poet who returns to his country alone and penniless, and who had recently savored it again when he returned in the same condition to Alcalá de Henares, started by boasting of his modesty by saying

> I read my ill attained hopes. . . . ,
> to seem like a poet who has
> the grace which Heaven denies me. . . .

These lines have been fatal for him, since hundreds of imbeciles have seized upon them and without anything more to go on proclaim Cervantes' poetic incapacity, "which he himself recognized," and have condemned him outright. But let us follow him in his thoughts and feelings.

The poet goes his weary way,

> For in the weight upon my shoulders
> with which Fate has burdened me
> I read my ill attained hopes. . . .,
> But as one always starts off wrong,
> with faith in my desire I let the road
> lead my feet, gave my head to the winds.
> Finally, upon the crupper of destiny,
> taking the choice that sat in the saddle. . . .

he sets out with his eyes fixed on the future. He knows well what poets are on the journey of life.

> Weeping over wars or singing of loves,
> life passes them by as in a dream
> or as time is like to do for gamblers.
> Poets are fashioned from a dough,
> gentle, smooth, flexible and soft
> and fond of the hearth in another's house. . . .

But he knows himself and says:

> Let readers then go on with their reading,
> of which the rude unpolished masses say
> that I am a poet fashioned thus:
> A swan by my white hair and by my voice a hoarse
> black raven, while time is unable
> to smooth the knotty trunk of my genius.
> And to the top of the turning wheel
> never for an instant could I reach,
> for when I try to ride it, it is still.

Therefore he flees from the falsity of the Court of Madrid, he bids farewell to the Prado and to the Steps of San Felipe, as well as to the playhouses and the hungry times in Madrid.

> Farewell, public theaters, applauded
> for the ignorance which I see exalted,
> recited in a hundred thousand absurdities,

in which it is beyond doubt that he alludes to Lope. . . .

> Farewell, slow starvation of a hidalgo
> who, not to see myself dead before your door,
> today leaves behind my country and my own self. . . .

He already knew what the "slow starvation" of the hidalgos was and what the Court made of it. Fortunately he lived at times with old memories, and the thought of the sea recalled to his mind the images of glorious days. These memories revive the weary traveller and lift his heart. Since none of his contemporaries has done him justice save the masses who quote the *Quixote* and the *Exemplary Novels*, he, Miguel himself, will do himself justice through the mouth of the god Mercury who says to him:

> "Oh, Adam of the poets! Oh, Cervantes!
> What is this knapsack and this garb, my friend,
> which seems to indicate aimless ramblings?"
> Replying to his question I say:
> "Señor, I journey to Parnassus and as a poor man
> in this dress I continue my journey."
> And he said to me: "Higher than human and higher
> than the spirit of Cyllenius[3] hast thou risen, for you
> all honors and all riches are superfluous,
> For you have answered as would a soldier,
> old and valiant, attested
> by the injured hand you bear.

I know well that in the stubborn naval battle
you lost all movement of the left hand
for the greater glory of the right.
And I know that the superhuman instinct
of the rare contriver that your breast contains
was not given you in vain by father Apollo.
Your works discover the corners of the earth,
borne on the crupper of Rocinante,
inspiring envy to attack.
Press on, rare contriver, press on
with your subtle mind and lend your help
to Apollo, for whom yours is important."

Was it not right for Cervantes to leave to posterity his claim to supremacy, to immortality, as all the great creators have done? He understood this and felt that he was leaving the world an imperishable work, and he wished to convey this to his own century which had repaid him so poorly. He felt death approaching and wanted to prolong the exhilaration of being alive, the joy of living he had never ceased to feel in his soul. He looked about him, saw friendly and hostile poets, all beneath his praise, and there he left them, each inserted in a tercet like the dead in a graveyard . . . but no, not all of them. Cervantes knew how to anticipate the judgment of posterity in the case of others as well as himself, and having dealt with Góngora in one tercet, Espinel in another, Salas Barbadillo, Suárez de Figueroa, Balbuena and Cabrera de Córdoba in still others, when it comes to speaking of Quevedo it needed at least four:

"For Don Francisco de Quevedo it will be
hard to come," I then said. And he said to me:
"Then I cannot go from here without him.
He is the son of Apollo and he is the son
of the Muse Calliope. We cannot leave
here without him, on this I will stand firm.
He is the scourge of foolish poets,
and will kick out of Parnassus
the bad ones we have and those we can expect."
"Oh, Señor," I replied, "his stride is short[4]
and he will not get there in a whole century."
"To that," said Mercury, "I pay no heed. . . ."

Only one tercet, already quoted, shows us the great Lope de Vega dropped from the sky,

a notable poet whose poetry or prose
no one can surpass or even equal,

and though the praise may come a trifle late and be a bit misleading it should nonetheless be acknowledged. Following this the poet sings of his disappointment over the promises made him by the "Lupercios," as he calls them, seeing from a distance the beauty of Naples stretched out before him, its white houses reflected in the waters of its lovely gulf.

All the poets, whether starving or well-fed, come to the garden of Apollo and sit in the shade of its hundred laurel trees. Only Cervantes got there late, as always in his wretched existence, and he remains standing:

> Finally, first were occupied
> the tree trunks of that wide circle,
> in honor of the delicate poets.
> Before me an infinite number
> found seats, and thus I remained standing,
> indignant, angered and exhausted.
> To myself I said: "Is it possible that I am so
> obstinately persecuted by an angry fate
> which injures many while it fears none?"
> And turning to Apollo with troubled speech,
> I told him what anyone who cares can hear. . . .

"Exhausted," yes, but also "indignant" and "angered." Here are three most eloquent adjectives, definitive, inimitable in describing a state of mind. The man who at sixty-six years of age is in such a temper is a man who is eternally young, whom the blows of an infamous fate will not bring down even at the foot of the sepulcher. Let us see how Miguel takes advantage of the opportunity to offer Apollo and the world an account of his merits and services; and though the quotation may seem long, never mind, for it would be silly to set forth in clumsy prose what he himself wrote in incomparable verse about himself and the ventures and misadventures of his life.

> And I spoke thus to Delius[5]: "One cannot estimate,
> Señor, the inane crowd which follows you,
> and approaches the sacred laurel tree.
> Ignorance and envy pursue him,
> and thus ever envied and persecuted,
> the good he hopes for is never attained.
> With my genius I shaped the dress
> in which the lovely *Galatea* appeared
> before the world, and so was saved from oblivion.
> Because of me the *Confusa*, far from disordered,
> appeared admirable in the theaters,
> if it is right to believe this from her fame.

I, in a style thought reasonably good,
have written plays which in their day
had something of the serious and of the mirthful.
In *Don Quixote* I have provided entertainment
for the melancholy and fretting heart,
at whatever season and for all times.
In my *Novelas* I have opened up a path
whereby the Castilian tongue can
with propriety show some extravagance.
I am he who in invention doth exceed
the many, and he who fails in this respect
is bound to be left with a false reputation.
From my most tender years I loved
the sweet art of gracious poetry, and
by it did always seek to please you.
Never did my humble pen ply
in the region of satire, a lowliness
which leads to infamous requitals and enmities.
Essentially in honor of my writings
I composed the sonnet which begins:
'I swear to God this grandeur doth astound me!'
I have written an infinite number of ballads
and that of *Celos* is the one that I esteem
among others which I hold as damnable.
Because of this I am distressed and wounded
seeing myself the only one to stand, with no tree
designated to lend me support.
I am, as is often said, on the point of
delivering to the press the great *Persiles*
by which my fame and works increase.
I, in chaste and subtle thoughts
arranged in sonnets by the dozen
have honored three kitchen-maids as subjects.
Also, the equal of *Filis*, my *Filena*
echoed through the forests which heard
more than one and another cheerful chorus.
And in the varied sweet rhymes the gentle breezes
bore away my hopes which were strewn
in the forests and in the sand.
I had, I have and I shall have thoughts,
by Heaven's grace, which happily keep me
safe and free of all flattery.
I never set my feet upon the road
where lies, frauds and deceits lead
to the total ruin of holy virtue.
I do not rage against my lack of fortune,
though to find myself standing, as I do,

and in such a place, makes me weigh my hurt.
  I am content with little, though I desire
much." To which unhappy thoughts Thymbraeus[6]
replied with these soothing words:
  "Ill fortune comes much delayed
and takes a course from so far away
that it is feared but never avoided.
  Good comes to some all of a sudden,
to others little by little and unaware,
and evil keeps no different style.
  The good which is acquired, conserve
with skill, diligence and prudence, for
this is no less a virtue than its winning.
  You yourself have made your fortune
and sometimes I have seen you hold it,
but in the imprudent it does not last.
  But if from your complaint you wish to come
not confused but cheerful and consoled,
fold up your cape and seat yourself upon it.
  For a happy state is perhaps apt to come
when fate denies it without reason,
there is more merit in deserving than achieving."
  "It would appear, Señor, it is not noticed
that I have no cape," I answered him.
He said: "Even so I am glad to see you,
  Virtue is a cloak with which to hide
and cover the indecency of poverty
which is immune and free to escape envy."
  I bowed my head before the wise advice
and remained standing, for there is no good seat
if favor or wealth do not provide it.
  Some of them murmured, seeing me deprived
of the honor that I thought was due me,
from the planet with light and virtue replete.
  Whereupon the day seemed to acquire
a new splendor. . . .

Do you know of any poet capable of speaking about himself, his misfortunes and his disappointments with greater dignity and nobility? Apollo, having heard of Miguel and recognizing his merits, speaks to him in the language which was perhaps that of the trees near which he wished to live in the shade. Apollo advises him to sit down and wait. It would seem that the home is going to triumph over the road. But this is not what happens. The poet, sure of himself, goes forward. He has now sung his own praises with a sublime and honest lack of modesty. As he himself declares:

Never was I content or satisfied
with hypocritical niceness. I simply
wanted praise for what I had done well. . . .

He still has to explain his Esthetic, the principles he usually obeys in thought and composition. And to do so he begins by distinguishing between two classes of poetry.

"This, which is the real poetry,
the serious, the witty and the elegant,"
said Mercury, "the lofty and the sincere,
Always splendidly apparelled,
shows itself wherever it may be
when doing so is important to its vocation.
It never serves or bows to the rabble,
writing parodies, mischievous and crass,
least silent when most ignorant.
There is another false one, greedy, dull and aging,
great lover of the tambourine and liver fricassee,
which never leaves the eating stall or tavern.
It cannot rise two, nay one, handbreadths from the floor,
it is fond of weddings and christenings,
generous of hand, short of cerebellum.
At times it is seized by paroxysms.
It cannot quite pronounce and if it does
it makes absurdities and commits solecisms. . . .
But this one that you see is all in order,
the gala dress of the heavens and the earth,
with which the Muses entertain themselves. . . .
There lives with it in the same mansion
divine and moral Philosophy,
of purer style and of true elegance.
In the middle of the day it can depict
night, and in the darkest night
the lovely dawn which pearls create.
It hastens the flow of rivers
and checks it, incites fury in the heart
and then seduces it to gentleness.
It flings itself vehemently into the midst
of gleaming arms in contention locked,
confers victories and victories takes away.
You will see how rural forests lend
their shade and shepherds their songs,
how it mourns evil and rejoices in pleasure. . . ."

And having set forth this definition of poetry as he conceives it he later confesses to the principles of his particular and personal esthetic:

Plainly I saw but know not whether to write it
that toward things held to be impossible
my pen has ever shown itself reserved.
Those that have glimmerings of possibility,
of sweetness, softness and of being true
are expounded in my quiet scribblings.
My small talent never opens the gates
to disparity and always holds them
wide open to harmony.
How can an extravagance please
unless it does so on purpose,
a witty saying showing the way?
For then a lie is satisfying
when it seems true and is written
with grace to please both wise and simple. . . .

This is what today we would describe as a profession of naturalistic, realistic or what is called veristic faith. For Cervantes truth and reason are the only basis of art. Paradox and absurdity are only elements deliberately used in satire. There is no more significant and valuable declaration by the author of the *Quixote* than this. Let it be understood once and for all, he says, that he is not seeking disparity but harmony. He warns posterity not to see eternal antagonisms in the contrast between Don Quixote and Sancho, but merely adventitious differences, and in a superior harmony they are finally resolved. Perhaps for this very reason and because his conscience was not entirely at ease regarding the realization of this project of his, Cervantes appreciated the *Persiles* more than the *Quixote* for the qualities of consistency and harmony that are made completely obvious in it.

His soundness of mind is such that he does not accept the present that Apollo offers to feeble poets: the remedy for their weakness is the excrement of Pegasus, a horse fed on amber and musk packed in cotton wool[7] who drinks the dew of the meadows. This remedy, Apollo says

"cures giddiness and heals the hurt. . . ."
"So be it," I answered him, "congratulations.
My mind stands for the moment firm
nor does any giddiness trouble me."

With this the poet returns home. Those who have not been included in the *Parnassus* greet him with mocking laughter:

I, the cunning one, I a poetaster already old,
returned their greetings amiably
without showing ill humor or frowning. . . .

Various young men, high-collared and starched, tell him his genius is already worn out. The poet pays no attention to them and returns wearily to his obscure old dwelling.

He still thinks it advisable to illuminate certain points in the *Addendum to the Parnassus*, in which he cannot help mentioning with new praises "the famous Vicente Espinel" and Don Francisco de Quevedo, nor does he resist the urge to mention his own unfortunate plays once again.

"Why are they not acted?" he is asked by the lad sent by Apollo, Pancracio de Roncesvalles, in depicting whom Miguel shows what he would have done if he had set out to portray the dandies of Madrid.

"Because managers do not seek me out nor do I go in search of them."

"They must not know that Your Honor has them," Pancracio argues.

"Yes, they know," Miguel replies, "but as they have their bread-and-butter poets and all goes well with them they do not seek bread made from the best quality of wheat; but I intend to give the plays to the printer so that they can see at leisure what happens quickly and is overlooked and not understood when they are acted; and plays like songs have their times and seasons. . . ."

In the *Parnassus*, finished twenty-one months before Cervantes died, it is hard to find a line which is not full of freshness, exuberance and youthful elegance. He dedicated it to a young lad, barely fifteen years old. The young gentleman was called Don Rodrigo de Tapia and he was a Knight of Santiago, the son of the powerful and generally esteemed courtier Don Pedro de Tapia, Judge of the Royal Council and Consultant of the Holy Office of the Supreme Inquisition. It is very probable that Miguel did not even know Don Rodrigo de Tapia, and it is certain that the dedication was of no practical use whatever to him. Forseeing this and prepared for it, he had written the last of the ordinances and counsels of Apollo to Spanish poets:

> Item, be warned that if any poet were to be favored by some prince, let him not visit him frequently, nor ask him for anything, but rather take things as they come, for if divine Providence must sustain the disgusting reptiles of the earth and worms of the water it will also have to support a poet, however disgusting he may be.

CHAPTER 53

Saint Teresa Poetry Contest—The Quixote *of Avellaneda—What Marqués de Torres Heard*

Now that Cervantes was well known and listed among the Court poets, of whom he was the oldest, he did not overlook the first opportunity he had of showing himself in public with the dignity his eminence and years deserved, and in due course he entered with youthful enthusiasm the first literary competition which offered.

It was a poetry contest which took place at the Court on the occasion of the beatification of the Venerable Religious Teresa de Jésus by Pope Paul V after repeated representations by King Philip III and all the luminaries and dignitaries of the Spanish Church as well as consultative and secular bodies, the universities, the Duke of Lerma and whatever gentlemen were important or counted for something.

The Roman Court was not as liberal then as it is now in the matter of beatifications. To obtain them it was necessary for saints, besides being saintly, to have strong advocates, and it was only when they were energetically recommended by eminent and illustrious people that they could succeed in being placed on the altar. On the other hand it is well known that in life and in death the divine Woman of Avila made ferocious enemies who persisted savagely in presenting the crystal clear life of the saint as confused and turbulent. Even after the beatification, in order to obtain the canonization eight years later, it was necessary for the King of France, Louis XIII, and the Most Christian Queen María de Médici to write imploring letters to Paul V and to send him as ambassador the Marquis of Treynel, who also failed to soften the resistance of the Pontiff. Saint Teresa was not canonized until the twelfth of March of 1622, by decree of His Holiness Gregory IV. In the same decree another four of the greatest saints of the Universal Church were raised to the altar: Philip Neri, Francis Xavier, Isidore the Farmer, and Ignatius Loyola. Saints of this quality do not turn up every day.

The joy of the Carmelites upon seeing their founder and Mother beatified must have been immense. Nevertheless it does not seem that they were the only or possibly even the chief organizers of the Madrid poetry contest. The competition was an elegant, refined festivity attended by people of the highest society. The jury was made up of three aristocratic young gentlemen of the Court, to wit: Don Rodrigo de Castro, son of the Count of Lemos; Don Melchor de Moscoso, son of the Count of Altamira; and Don Francisco Chacón, son of the Count of Casarrubios. Who should act as adviser to the tribunal thus formed but Lope de Vega Carpio, the ubiquitous, the indispensable, the inevitable? It is obvious that the three young gentlemen were there only as decorative figures of the kind who usually take part in such festivities to give themselves lustre. They placed themselves, as bejeweled as possible, behind a richly decorated, tapestry-covered table, ready to be the target of feminine glances, at the same time posing as important literary people, a thing which embellished one's image much more in those days than it does now. Lope announced the subjects for the competition, and one of them read: "To him who with the greatest charm, erudition and elegant style, maintaining lyric strictness, makes a Castilian song of not more than seven stanzas in honor of the divine ecstasy of our Holy Mother in the manner of Garcilaso's 'Gentle Lament of Two Shepherds' (*El dulce lamentar de dos pastores*) will be given a silver pitcher, the second eight yards of camelot, and to the third a pair of silk hose."

Miguel, for whom it would be very advantageous, in order to promote the publication of his new works, to win a prize at such a famous festivity, must have visited the son of his patron, the Count of Lemos, and perhaps due to his influence and also because Lope in those days of repentance and friendly cordiality wanted to show Cervantes that his ill-will had vanished, Miguel was lucky enough to win one of the prizes, we do not know which, and to have his song read by Lope himself at the solemn function celebrated on October 12 of 1614, attended by the flower of the Court of Spain.

For Miguel's vanity, and some of it was still left, as we have seen revealed in his own words, there could not have been a more glorious triumph than to be read before the most accomplished men of the Court and hear his verses issuing from the lips of a Lope who before had praised him with cautious civility. He wanted to prove that his poetical talent was still fresh and if he did not do it through the verses, which were rather mediocre, he deserved something for his initiative and daring in making the attempt. Autumns had always been favorable to him and without any doubt that one was to be very much so, for it at last put things in their right place and left Miguel famous, extolled by one who had always been his enemy and applauded by the Court that had been indifferent or hostile to him for so many years.

On the other hand an old poet is pleased above all other honor or esteem by the respect and company of the young, which is honor for today, glory for the morrow, and at that moment Miguel saw himself applauded by young men like the scions of Lemos, Altamira and Casarrubios and by Don Fernando de Lodeña, Don Rodrigo de Tapia. Knowing humanity as few men do, Miguel understood that there is no greater error than that of old men who ignore the young, do not value their appreciation, are not grateful for their admiration, and do not seek their company or talk to them. This is compelling evidence that a man has no faith in his work or confidence that it will outlive him. When one believes in tomorrow one begins to appreciate those who find themselves nearest that tomorrow. For that very reason many young poets figure in the *Parnassus*, which must have been published around that time.

Cervantes was gay and happy with this new longed-for glory when one day he entered the shop of one or the other of his two bookseller friends, Robles or Villarroel, and was shown a book on the frontispiece of which there appeared: "SECOND VOLUME OF THE INGENIOUS HIDALGO DON QUIXOTE DE LA MANCHA, *which contains his third sortie: and is the fifth part of his adventures, Composed by the Licentiate Alonso Fernandez de Avellaneda, native of the Town of Tordesillas. To the Mayor, Aldermen and hidalgos of the noble town of Argamesilla, happy birthplace of the hidalgo Knight Don Quixote de la Mancha. Licensed. In Tarragona, in the house of Felipe Roberto. Year 1614.*"

With feverish eyes behind hastily donned spectacles, his hands trembling with rage and dismay, Cervantes ran through the first pages of that gigantic fraud, the approval signed by Doctor Rafael Ortoneda, the licence of the Vicar-General of the Archbishopric of Tarragona, Doctor Francisco de Torres y Liori, the insolent, insulting, tasteless, and pedantic prologue:

> less boastful and aggressive toward his readers than that which Miguel de Cervantes Saavedra put in his First Part and humbler than the one that followed in his *Novels*, which are more satirical than exemplary though not without merit. He will not understand the rationale for this history, which carries on with the ostentation that he started and the abundance of true stories that came to his hand; and I say hand, for he himself confesses that he has but one: and speaking in a way for everyone, we must say of him that like a soldier old in years but young in spirit he has more tongue than hands; but he may complain of my work because of the profit I take from him for his Second Part; yet at least he must confess that we both have an end in view, which is to banish the pernicious reading of inane books of knight-errantries, so

> common among untutored and lazy people: although we use different media he then took umbrage at me for the same things and more specially at one who is so justly hailed in most foreign countries and to whom our nation owes so much for having most creditably and fruitfully entertained the theaters of Spain for many years with innumerable wonderful plays with the artistic power the world demands and with the moral authority to be expected from a minister of the Holy Office. Let no one be shocked that the *Second Part* comes from a different author, for it is nothing new for different people to continue a tale. How many have told of the loves of Angélica[1] and her adventures? The *Arcadias* have been the work of various writers; *Diana* is not all by the same hand. And then Miguel de Cervantes is now as old as the castle of San Cervantes and through the years so discontented that everything and everyone enrages him, and on that account he is so lacking in friends that when he wanted to adorn his books with high-sounding sonnets he had to attribute them, as he himself says, to Prester John of the Indies or to the Emperor of Trapisonda,[2] because there is no titled person to be found in Spain who would not be offended at having his name used at the beginning of books by the author of whom it is rumored that at last, please God, he has now been admitted into the shelter of the Church! Let him content himself with his *Galatea* and prose plays, which is what most of his novels are; let him not fatigue us. . . .

Cervantes was accustomed to falling from gloriously happy days into those of the greatest misery, but the artful and hypocritical mischief hidden behind such insults to his honorable old age and his most honorable scars unhinged him, drove him beside himself and uprooted all the prudence, conformity and resignation which the years and his many troubles had instilled in his heart.

With the odious book in his hand he consulted friends, investigated, and undertook to discover who was the malicious person who wanted to cause him such deep mortification. It was no easy task. The book had been printed in Tarragona, but the author indubitably hid behind a pseudonym and no one in Tordesillas knew of the so-called Licentiate Alonso Fernández de Avellaneda. There was no doubt about two things: first, that the author was from Aragón, since his work was full of Aragonese expressions; and second, that he was a great admirer of Lope de Vega and probably a clergyman or someone confusedly erudite in theological and classical studies.

As time went on Cervantes was able to confirm that the fictitious Avellaneda was from Aragón, but he knew nothing more according to all indications, nor have any of the many great minds dedicated to such researches been able to discover anything of value. Up to the present time, despite the various hypotheses expounded by learned men, nobody has proved indubitably who Alonso Fernández Avellaneda could have been.

Reading the wretched book, Miguel found it hard to believe that such wickedness as was distilled in the Prologue could find room in such a poor and unoriginal mind as the work itself revealed. Those who have spoken well of it either belong to the sad company of the envious, the impotent, the "left behind," or they lack all literary sensibility. The *Quixote* of Avellaneda is worse than bad and resembles the real one no more than a two-peseta brilliant resembles a diamond worth twenty thousand. Only those who confuse glass brilliants with diamonds can be taken in by it, and they not only confuse them but go into society adorned with splinters of broken glass like Indian savages with glass beads. Everything in this book is false, awkward, vile.

It was only a provincial mind, not yet very well informed as to the affairs of the Court or the new values and latest judgments regarding such things that would let loose an abortion like the *Quixote* of Avellaneda and speak of the *Arcadia* and *Diana* in the same breath. All the writers of the time had already realized the enormous difference there was between the *Quixote* and all other works of fiction, and no one had laid hands on a book considered untouchable from the very beginning. Only Vicente Espinel was secretly meditating something that was more or less a compromise, a cross between *Guzmán de Alfarache* and *Quixote* which would not tarnish the reputation of either, and it is to such sophistry that we owe *Squire Marcus of Obregon.*[3]

The indignation that reading the false *Quixote* aroused in Cervantes was responsible for the haste with which here and there he larded into the text of his Second Part as many allusions as he could against the false Avellaneda, without, however, falling so low as to resort to personal insults or abuse, most probably because he had not been able to find out with certainty from whom the violent attack had come.

The whole of the winter of 1614 and the first months of 1615 he spent at home or in the printing shop of Juan de la Cuesta, correcting here, retouching there, fattening up this bit, trimming that one. In February of 1615 his work was finished. Upon presenting it for approval he found an excellent friend in Licentiate Márques de Torres, who was to examine it by mandate of Doctor Gutierre de Cetina, Vicar-General of the City of Madrid. Let us console ourselves for the shamelessness of Miguel's detractor by reproducing the fine and rare words in which Márques de Torres expressed his approval:

> Quite different has been the effect of the writings of Miguel de Cervantes on our own nation as well as on foreign peoples, inasmuch as they long to behold as something miraculous the author of those books which, by reason of their decency and decorum as well as their

urbanity and the pleasing qualities of their discourse, Spain, France, Italy, Germany and Flanders have received with general applause.

I certify as true that on the twenty-fifth of February of this year 1615 the most illustrious Señor Don Bernardo de Sandoval y Rojas, Cardinal Archbishop of Toledo, having gone to return the visit paid by the French Ambassador who had come to deal with matters regarding marriages between the royal house of his country and that of Spain, many French knights among those who accompanied the Ambassador and who were as courteous as they were intelligent and fond of *belles-lettres* came to me and the other Chaplains of My Lord the Cardinal to inquire regarding the most highly regarded books of quality, and coming by chance on this one which I was at the time engaged in reviewing they no sooner heard the name of Miguel de Cervantes than they began to give tongue, speaking highly of the esteem in which his works were held not only in France but in neighboring kingdoms, in particular the *Novels* and the *Galatea*, the first part of which some of them knew almost by heart. They were so enthusiastic that I offered to take them to see the author of those works, an invitation they accepted with a thousand signs of intense desire. They went on to question me in great detail regarding his age, his profession, his rank and condition, and I was obliged to state that he was old, a soldier, a hidalgo and poor; whereupon one of them responded gravely: "How then that Spain does not see to it that such a man is maintained in luxury out of the public treasury?"

One of the other gentlemen made this astute observation, saying: "If it is necessity that obliges him to write, please God he never has abundance, in order that being poor he may continue to enrich all the world with his works."

For Cervantes these words were as balsam upon the wound dealt him by the false Avellaneda. Universal glory now touched with invisible wings the brow of the old soldier, hidalgo and poor.

CHAPTER 54

The Plays

THE hidalgo with the silver beard which had been gold twenty years before came out into the Calle de Atocha with slow and halting steps. He stooped slightly as he walked, like one who feels the time is near for rooting around before lying down, and the knitted brows of his usually jovial and good-tempered face marked the disquiet that stirred within.

That very day his friend the bookseller Juan de Villarroel had made this disconcerting disclosure: "From Your Honor's prose much may be expected, from your verse nothing,"[1] which the good Villarroel did not say contemptuously or as his own personal opinion, rather as citing the judgment of a famous and well-qualified author, but not without a certain compassionate note of which the hidalgo was well aware, being accustomed to suffer the pity of others.

Chewing his cud of bitterness, he went his way wrapped in his cloak, shiny from the brush rather than from the tailor's iron, and wishing he could stop thinking about poetic and theatrical ventures, he turned toward the friendly house of the Trinity which appeared on the left and dominated the street, at that point extremely narrow. He entered the portal as if it were his own home and proceeded to the chapel where he had already often found relief from the griefs and heartaches of his life by lifting his spirit to higher things. The postern in the great door of the cloister revealed the stone arches up which jasmine climbed and in the garden three meek acacias and a robust and proud laurel. Suddenly all the light through the postern was completely blocked out by the very image of success in the theater in the person of Doctor Alonso Ramón, who was leaving the convent in haste. The author of *Three Women in One* (*Las tres mujeres en una*) and of *The Unborn Saint and Deathless Martyr* (*El santo sin nacer y mártir sin morir*) is already about to trade the festive pen of the playwright for the serious one of the historian.[2] He looked upon the poor poet from the depths of his habit and greeted him briefly with a smile that seemed to the hidalgo one of justified scorn, which is the sourest kind of smile there can be.

This encounter deprived Cervantes of any inclincation to take refuge in the tranquility of the church; he turned quickly about and again sallied into the Calle de Atocha, thinking the most lugubrious thoughts, turning over in his mind the words of Villarroel and what seemed to him the pitying smile of the friar Doctor Ramón.

Who had told the bookseller what so distressed the old poet? Had it perhaps been Doctor Ramón himself? Could it be those young courtiers who applauded him with such apparent goodwill at the Santa Teresa literary competition? Who could tell if, as he had sometimes suspected, those spruce and witty young gentlemen were making fun of his gray locks, perhaps at the malignant instigation of. . . . ? But no; even to himself the hidalgo did not want to name Nature's prodigy, lord of the theatrical kingdom. Lope overshadowed him with a radiant and luminous aura that filled the world with plays, appropriate, felicitous and well reasoned, he held all the actors enslaved and he had "written more than ten thousand pages: and every one of them, which is one of the greatest things that can be said, he had seen acted or at least heard that they had been acted: and if some, and there are many, have tried to share the glory of his works, all of them together cannot attain in writing even half of what he has done alone."[3]

On thinking he would write this, the hidalgo recalled the words which Villarroel had parroted, having heard them from a titled author, and he reflected: "Either I have been changed into someone else or the times are getting much better, with everything turned topsy-turvy, for times past have always been the ones to be praised."

As he turned over such sophistries his feet bore him unconsciously to the corner where the actors gathered in the Calle del León. Some of the players who were arguing about professional matters called to him hoping to hear the opinions of such an elegant genius or perchance to laugh at his witty sayings. The hidalgo knew them all, including the amusing actor and dancer Pablo Sarmiento, old María, Gabriela and her daughter, young Francisca María, and several others, among whom the authoritative voice of Andrés de Claremonte, author of famous plays, tangled in histrionic polemics with the rumble of Pedro Cerezo de Guevara, his collaborator.

They were of course talking about Lope, and one actor, Alonso de Heredia, maintained that the sun of the stage was beginning to decline toward its setting. It was said of a certain Friar of Mercy named Gabriel Téllez[4] that he had brought from the fruit orchards around Toledo where he lived an unusual and admirable play, *Saint Joan* (*Santa Juana*), compared with which the tumult and hurly-burly of Lope, the sententious edifications of Doctor Ramón, the meekness of that other Doctor, Mira de Amescua, and the artifice of Licentiate Miguel Sánchez were left far behind.

"And of Your Honor, Señor Cervantes," added Alonso de Heredia, "it is also said that you have a cofferful." The actors laughed at the mention of a coffer, with laughter the hidalgo took to be a sneer. He turned his back on them and muttering to himself, sad with a mortal sadness, he turned the first corner and entered his house.

The room where he was wont to work was on the ground floor with a large grated window giving on the street. Through its greenish panes, never touched by the sun save possibly at the height of summer, since it faced the north, it was not uncommon to see the old poet seated in an armchair of worn Russian leather before a bare table without drawers working on his imaginative schemes for novels and theatrical works.

Night was falling when he arrived. He unbuckled his sword, hung his cape and hat on a nail, and went out for a moment, returning with a lighted oil lamp he put on the floor by the corner where the coffer stood that was the occasion for the laughter. From it he took out one after another the manuscripts of plays of his which had never been staged or even read. There were many big sheets of demy paper, frayed and yellowed from waiting so long, covered with a bold Spanish type of writing with showy and vigorous strokes in its *esses* and *tees*. In them, thought the hidalgo, not so long ago lay what was the best of his thinking, in them lay the glory of future centuries in which his praises would be heard throughout the known world. And, bent down as he was, huddled over the black mouth of the open chest, the light from the lamp which struck him from below formed a kind of aureole of strange sparks from the old man's hair, no longer golden, and heightened his pensive brow, making of the aquiline face something like the profile of a majestic and noble bird wresting a coveted prize from a deep flaming crater.

He had put everything he held dear in life into those unread and unwanted plays. To give up the glory of seeing them in the theater caused him infinitely more pain than the insults and absurdities of the false Avellaneda. To put them away or publish them without their being seen by the public was like making his will, saying farewell to the world, bequeathing to posterity something that his contemporaries had been unable to appreciate. Just by turning the pages of the plays he could review his whole life.

Three of them, *The Prisons of Algiers, The Great Sultana* and *The Gallant Spaniard*, summarized completely the period of his captivity. Going over them, Cervantes recognized the excellence of design and style, such as this from *The Gallant Spaniard*:

> I do not doubt that you will conquer,
> for the coward is naked
> though he be clothed in steel. . . .

and the types so admirably alive, like the soldier Buitrago in this same work, who ranks well above the comic actors in Lope and Tirso, and that marvellous ballad of the captives and galley slaves, equal to the best of the great Cordovan, Góngora, whom Cervantes honored by imitating him:

> A galliot struck bottom
> in a creek of Algiers,
> almost five miles from Orán,
> a place full of Turks. . . .

The scenes of *The Prisons of Algiers* were bits torn from his heart and it is the most poetic of all the many dramas written upon this subject: In it one reads the ballad:

On the shores of the sea
that with its tongue and its tide. . . .

and in it are presented the tragic, innocent, arch-Spanish figures of the two Christian children, Janico and Francisquito, who die as martyrs for their faith in a moving scene, possibly evoking the memory of the saintly children Justo and Pastor, patron saints of Alcalá de Henares, all the more deserving of notice because in our theater or our novels there are not as many interesting or attractive children as there are bold, mischievous and intractable youngsters. It is the great geniuses of poetic invention (Dickens, Balzac, Galdós) who appreciate and use childhood and madness as touchstones of maturity and reason.

Finally, in *The Great Sultana*, life in Constantinople is depicted with a perceptiveness and realism in no way inferior to the real life descriptions of the clever scoundrel and excellent writer Cristóbal de Villalón,[5] and this play includes a sonnet which must be one of those Miguel showed Doctor Sosa in the prison in Algiers but which has escaped attention:

To you I turn, great Lord, who annulled
at the cost of your life and blood
the disaster of Adam's first fall
and where he cast us down you raised us up.
To you, blessed Lord, who sought
of the hundred ewe-lambs the one that was lost
and finding her pursued by a wolf
upon your holy shoulders raised her.
To you I turn in my bitter sorrow
and it is you, Lord, who must succor me
for I am a lamb now missing from the fold,
and I fear that sooner or later
should you not come to my rescue
this hellish serpent will overtake me.

The feelings that filled his soul during his great tribulations in Algiers were not too different from those he now experienced when his self-respect was wounded by the opinion of an author whose name he did not know or even dared to suspect. "From Your Honor's poetry nothing can be expected. . . ." He could only entrust himself to divine justice and to the judgment of centuries to come! And perhaps with the foresight of a man of genius he may also have divined that the centuries to come would consider him a second-class poet. He may perhaps have foreseen the contempt of many and many a ridiculous poetaster and many a prattling critic who were later to assert, without having read them, that Cervantes' poems were bad and his plays unfortunate.

His thoughts wandered from recollections of Algiers and Turkish life to those drawn from an Italianate subject or his Italian reading, as expressed in *The Labyrinth of Love*, a work of his youth, of the days when fugitive loves lightly caressed the heart of a soldier-poet, and to those drawn from the books of knight-errantry. Hence *The House of Jealousy and Forest of Arden*, in which the Emperor Charlemagne appears and speaks, as well as Reynaldos de Montalbán, Roldán, Bernardo del Carpio, the traitor Galalón, the magician Malgesi, the beautiful Angélica, in short all the principal characters of the chivalrous legend of the Carlovingian cycle. It is a book of knight-errantry brought to the stage, and it has a bucolic and pastoral side very similar in its tone and atmosphere to that which the Titan, William Shakespeare, delighted to intercalate in some of his own plays of knight-errantry, like the one entitled *As You Like It*. And so that there be nothing lacking even in such a complicated legendary mixture the gay and realistic note which the author always carried in his soul includes in the *House of Jealousy* an amusing character from Biscay similar to those the author as a child in Seville saw acted by the great Lope de Rueda, whose wit when recalled by an old man exhilarated and refreshed him among the vexations and weariness of old age.

In such a varied repertory as the eight plays in the coffer there could not fail to be one that was exemplary and holy, presenting the purely Spanish figure of the libertine who repents and becomes a saint, Mañara before Mañara existed, and this Mañara was much like the real one,[6] being his fellow countryman, drinking the waters and breathing the air of the Guadalquivir. In his early life this Mañara is a bully, a braggart, an *hombre* like those in the jail in Seville. We see him portrayed in the House of Charity which he founded, with a face amazingly like that of Velázquez' buffoon Pablillos from Valladolid, that is to say, exactly as he was before being converted, and later we see him emaciated, ennobled, beautified by penitence and contemplation in the deathmask preserved in that same House of Charity. He is none other than Cristóbal de Lugo, *The Fortunate Procurer*.

Those who stupidly repeat the opinion the bookseller Villarroel heard and persist in the belief that Cervantes was not a dramatic author and that his plays have no merit, do not recognize how Cervantes had a faculty of insight into the future and how he smelled out and presented the great romantic figures of the Spanish stage and the great drama of spiritual life. They have overlooked a most extraordinary work, the source from which so many others have derived. What could be more Spanish, more daring, more dramatic than the scene of temptation in this marvellous drama which neither Calderón nor Tirso in similar situations has been able to surpass? Did Cervantes understand clearly what his *Fortunate Procurer* was, as we can appreciate it today in the knowledge that it was written a good many years before the conversion of Mañara, and that in it are included all the feelings and nearly all the events which concluded in such dramatic action? It is not often that an author can sink his hand in the entrails of society and draw from it the living sentiments which govern it and will engender events that have not yet taken place. Are there many playwrights either before or since to whom Heaven has granted this gift of anticipating the truth, seeking it out in what is most deeply buried in contemporary consciousness?

The old man turned from the plays to the interludes, and first of all to one he called a play, since it had three acts, a witty farce about *Pedro de Urdemales* in which masterly scenes of Andalusian gypsies are presented, drawn with the precision of a Goya. Another comic trifle, also in three acts, was *The Link*, in which his only intention was to make his public laugh, and he would have done so, and he would do so today, if such a merry contrivance were to be staged.

He was groping in the dark and scarcely saw the injustice with which the actors and, as far as he could see and hear, the poets were treating such excellent works. It cost him immense trouble to sell them for a paltry sum when as a last resort he offered them to Juan de Villarroel, including with them eight interludes, eight masterly works, eight jewels in which Michelangelo became Benvenuto Cellini. Wholly convinced that in them he had reached the ultimate in artistic perfection, he finally decided to give them to the printer.

In spite of everything, having resolved to sell such a rich part of his youth, he collected the manuscripts, placed them lovingly on the table, and from a small cupboard he brought out some newer sheets of paper covered with blots and scratchings out. They constituted the manuscript of the masterwork with which he would shut the mouths of the backbiters, filling the envious with bile and those who would see it acted with joy. The title of the still unfinished play was *More Than Meets the Eye*, and its author gazed at it as sixty-year-old fathers gaze upon their newborn children. Once this unique work was published there could be no doubt that its author would be talked about, as Doctor Ramón and the divine Miguel Sánchez and that other Father of Mercy in Toledo were talked about, and the rapier tongue of Góngora would be sheathed forever.

As for Lope. . . . Oh! at the thought of Lope the hidalgo felt a knot in his throat. What was he, of what was that man made for whom the theater had no difficulties or secrets and who could fling himself over unfathomable precipices and always land safe and sound at the bottom? Lope, who had devoted himself all his life to "constant vigorous activity," flattered by princes, sought after by the ladies, acclaimed by the populace, admired by the learned and fêted by the ignorant. As an author he wrote, wrote and wrote, he produced and produced, he distilled tragic and comic fables tirelessly. Was it easy, was it possible, to compete with such a prodigy? Were eight old plays and a ninth, even though it be the eighth wonder of the world, weapons for such a competition?

And thinking thus, with a clear appreciation of his own value and that of the other, which is unusual among writers, the old poet leaned on his two hands, his elbows on the table, his high forehead shining, and he allowed two deep furrows to cleave the long face, down which ran one knows not what bitter moisture.

For a long hour he stayed so, until Lope himself came to draw him out of his self-absorbed misery, a Lope still gallant and good-looking, dressed as a clergyman, his eyes gay and provocative, his moustache martial. Passing by on the street he had seen his neighbor and wanted to have a talk with him, and upon entering and seeing him in such extraordinary anguish that he had not even noticed the presence of his visitor, he looked closely at the disconsolate poet, put both hands affectionately on his shoulders, and in a kind voice asked him: "What is this? Dost thou weep, Señor Miguel de Cervantes?"

CHAPTER 55

The Second Part of the Quixote

"DON Quixote de la Mancha," Cervantes stated when he sent his plays to the Count of Lemos, "has won his spurs in his Second Part in order to go and kiss the feet of Your Excellency. I believe that he will arrive complaining that they have persecuted and maltreated him in Tarragona, although for better or worse he has learned that he is not the subject of that history but it is supposed to be another who tried to be him and did not succeed."

The fifth of November of 1615 is the date of the approbation in which Doctor Gutierre de Cetina simply certifies that "it is a book of much licit entertainment combined with much moral philosophy." The fact that as many months as there are between March and November transpired between the approbation signed by Licentiate Márquez de Torres, who was appointed by Doctor Gutierre de Cetina as Vicar-

General, and the one by Padre Josef de Valdivielso, who was commissioned to examine the work by order of the gentlemen of the Council, leads one to suppose that the whole summer was spent on the typesetting and correction of the seventy-three pages[1] of manuscript. The correcting having been finished on October 21 and the licence issued on November 5, the Second Part of the *Quixote* must have appeared in the first days of the Month of the Saints [November] of 1615.

Miguel breathed a sigh of satisfaction when he saw it in the bookshops. He had been under pressure from many quarters and he wanted even more to publish it "so as to be quit of the loathing and nausea" that the false Quixote of Avellaneda had caused, as he said in his dedication to the Count of Lemos at the end of October.

That autumn of 1615 was Cervantes' last and, as luck would have it, being the last it was also the most glorious of his life. Infirm and sickly as he was, but not surrendering to the enormous burden of work his aged shoulders supported, his illness, far from impairing his faculties, so sharpened them that he could delight in his work, find pleasure in it, and anticipate in his bones the glory to come. He loved the story of Don Quixote as a faithful legitimate spouse and the story of Persiles and Sigismunda as a passionate lover like those who sometimes cheer the autumns of old men.

The affair of the false *Quixote* continued to infuriate him and make him smart, like prickly heat or an attack of smallpox in old age, but he was unable to discover who its author was or what its compass and consequences might be. At times he would generously forgive and then he would forget and attack the invisible trickster who had embittered his last days and destroyed his beatific equanimity. A young man who has been robbed of any garment or jewel of value will soon lose the feeling of loss, but an old man robbed, though he be as great as Goethe or Cervantes, cannot forgive completely.

The other loves and passions of the earth had faded away for him and as happens to many old men his eyes had become lighter in shade, turning from blue to the color of ashes, and his vision had lengthened greatly, changing from myopic to presbyotic. Now he could see only large and distant things; he could sense small and nearby things but he could not see them.

In general Miguel by this time was a cheerful, good-natured old man, scarcely aware of the small things of life, those that touched him closely, as we have just said. His wife, his sister, his niece, his daughter now had become part of this category of things too small to be perceived. For him life no longer presented the difficulties of the past. He shows clearly by his expressions of gratitude that neither the Count of Lemos from Naples nor Don Bernardo de Sandoval from Toledo had forgotten him and that both continued to make their small contributions. His old friend and fellow countryman, the bookseller Francisco de Robles, would also never have let him return to his former straits, for he fully realized how much it suited him to be on good terms with such a productive author, besides which we have no reason to believe that booksellers have any harder hearts than the rest of humanity.

Miguel must have had little to do with literary men and would leave his house only when absolutely necessary. Illness was working silently on the natural robustness of the old man. What did he suffer from? He was thirsty. How easy it is to find most eloquent symbolisms in natural things! It could be said here that the thirst of Cervantes was not only physical and that his Knight-Errant is only a symbolical incarnation of the thirst for goodness, reason and justice which afflicted the world then and continues to do so today. It would also not be an overstatement to assert that if Cervantes prized the *Persiles* above all his other works this is because it is a fountain-book, a source-book, which flows smoothly and refreshingly like the water of a clear shallow stream, and for this reason it was such a delight to its author, who could continue work on it without tiring himself, with greater facility, freedom and fluency than ever before, simply by giving reign to his fancy and with the aid of a fertile imagination letting it speak of the old, far-off things he could see so well with his impaired vision.

Upon finishing the Second Part of the *Quixote* and proceeding to complete, burnish, and polish the resplendent *Persiles,* Cervantes found himself in that situation where all great artists arrive when they are old and which most of them happily do not realize. The mastery, dexterity and airy lightness of conception and expression are so great in them and their imaginative facility is so enormous that they lose their stirrups, forget that what is omitted is as important as what is said, and fail to appreciate that there is greater and more distinct skill in remaining silent than in speaking. The facility of some young chatterboxes is lamentable; even worse is the unrestrained garrulity of those old men for whom there are no impediments to thought and speech. Cervantes had reached the highest peak which any writer could attain; from it there was no other way to go than down. The old like going downhill; the old like to deceive themselves into thinking it is uphill and on the way down they maintain the illusion that old age and exhaustion have not yet caught up with them and even that their stumblings are daring leaps and their falls the result of superabundant youthful vigor.

It was because of this that Cervantes preferred the *Persiles* to the *Quixote*, not, as stupidly insinuated by some, because he was not fully aware of the enormous and immortal value of a work devised "for the universal entertainment of the people," of a work, according to Samson

Carrasco, the popularity of which was such that "the children fingered it, the young read it, the men understood it and the old praised it . . . some pick it up if others put it down, these demand it importunately while those beg for it," of a work regarding which Don Quixote himself said that "thirty thousand volumes of my history have been printed and thirty thousand thousands are on the way to being published if Heaven does not intervene."[2] The love of Cervantes for the *Persiles,* his last child, fruit of his fertile old age, did not blind him to the value of the *Quixote*. In all the texts quoted and in many others in the *Quixote* Miguel testifies to the immortality and universality of his book, while he praised the *Persiles* only to the Count of Lemos, who in fact probably liked it better than the *Quixote*. "With this"—they are Miguel's words—"I take my leave, offering Your Excellency the trials of Persilis [*sic*] and Sigismunda, a book which I will finish within four months, *Deo volente*, which will be either the worst or the best which has been written in our tongue, I mean of those for entertainment, and I add that I regret having said the worst, for according to the opinion of my friends it approaches the greatest possible excellence."

The greatest possible excellence! Does this not sound like the praise of an old father for his last-born without forgetting in the depths of his soul his love for the first-born, a fine, strong young man who is a credit to the family? Cervantes did not write one single line on the immortality of the *Persiles*; he was always wholly persuaded of that of the *Quixote*. The poet loved the mistress who cheered his old age, but he knew she was not the one to make him immortal. This is the right way to look at Cervantes' psychology in this matter, as so many writers have obviously decided to do. No one believes in unconscious geniuses; this romantic theory has been definitely abandoned. And if there is any work in which the most absolute consciousness of what the author is doing shines through it is in the Second Part of the *Quixote*.

The Second Part of the *Quixote* marks in its thinking and style what might be called the "second manner" of Cervantes. In it the author catches a glimpse of people and things, gets a clear idea about them and presents them in precisely synthesized lines and strokes. He sees all the things that we see without reacting to them, but he responds to what he sees, forcing our inattentive glibness to do likewise. For him there is no insignificant detail and if once he is careless or appears to have forgotten something you can be sure that he has done it on purpose because it deserved to be ignored. He says what he wants to say, keeps silent when silence matters to him, he has no use at all for rhetorical frills, he dresses and adorns the phrase with the thought and not the thought with the phrase. He is not one of the *literati* of his time nor of any other time.

For Cervantes there is no such thing as this vain and empty fiction that has been deluding mankind for many centuries under the name of Literature. For Spain before any other country has been reserved the glory no one has wanted to recognize, thanks to the stupidity of her sons, of writing with complete sincerity, with human naturalness. The greatest and most gifted of all her writers had in him nothing of the "classical" in the academic, showy and artificial meaning of that awful word. Try to fit Cervantes into any *grand siècle* as comfortably as that of Louis XIV accommodates those noble gentlemen of the embroidered coats and powdered wigs whose names are Racine, Fénelon, Labruyére, saints whom the vaulted niche fits perfectly, and you will see how the shoulders of the wrestler, the legs of the walker, the arms of the soldier and the noble head with hair powdered only by the dust of the road comes out of the frame, breaks it, smashes it. Once and for all let us affirm resolutely that Cervantes is not a *literato*, as Valásquez is not an ordinary painter. The Second Part of the *Quixote* is not *literature* just as *The Ladies in Waiting* (*Las Meninas*)[3] is not *painting* in the usual sense. At times Nature chooses such men to write or paint, as it chooses another who can lift weights of five hundred pounds and still another like the fish Nicolás[4] who swims twenty leagues without tiring and lives at ease under the water.

Pictorial comparisons applied to literature tend to be shopworn but apt. The Cervantes of the First Part of the *Quixote* is like Velásquez before the *Ladies in Waiting* and the portrait of the *Sculptor*. Little by little Nature, for she does not improvise, was elaborating, working over, perfecting the eyes and brains of the painter and of the poet so that they would be able to see light as she herself does and darkness when she makes it, handling light and shade at will, for she paints with the sun and the moon on her palette. Velásquez cared not a fig for painters and painting nor Cervantes for *literati* and literature when the one painted the *Ladies in Waiting* and the other wrote the second *Quixote*. Cervantes put his book in the hands of the whole world, those of children, young people, old people, innkeepers, travelers, but not in the hands of professional writers.

Miguel now went over his work carefully and it pleased him greatly. He understood very well how the action and the characters which produced it had been developed and embellished until they attained an immortal symmetry, but not because the action was more intricate, since, unlike Lope, Cervantes was less and less interested in action and he had less need of it to obtain an artistic result. In this Second Part there are eleven introductory chapters in which hardly anything happens. Don Quixote becomes more discursive in his madness, which is like saying that his viewpoint is broader, his purposes greater, his behavior more human.

In order to give him greater stature Cervantes creates the only new figure in the fable, central and essential to his beginning and his end, that is to say, the common sense, logic, method, prudence, dry reason, cold deduction incarnate in Bachelor Samson Carrasco. Have you noticed how the Bachelor laughs? If you have observed it you will have seen how that same cold, insincere, sly laughter of one who is sure of himself, who thinks he is always right, comes at you instantly in apparent mockery or affectionate contempt or as an exulting "knowledge of the world" on the lips of the rationalists, the self-seekers and the discreet, judicious established folk who are always consistent and assured whenever you undertake any generous lunacy. Carrasco will not make you seem ridiculous with a loud peal of laughter in public, but he will undermine you with a smooth smile, behind your back. He is not bad, nor does anyone think he is bad; he is moved by the purest intentions (those with which hell is paved) and the most rational objectives. He appears to be completely convinced of only one thing, and to that most lamentable conviction of his we owe the debasement of the character and idealism of Spain. This conviction has been formulated millions of times by orators and those who govern, by newspapermen, pseudophilosophers and pseudopoliticians, and it has already encrusted millions of brains: that *theory* is one thing and *practice* something very different.

From the beginning could you not see clearly how neither the common and simple feeling of Master Nicolás, the barber, nor the kindly and superior philosophy of the priest Pedro Pérez (one of the forerunners of our modern peaceful friend Abbé Coignard) sufficed to keep Don Quixote from renewing his lunacy, and how the devastating, egalitarian, managing, down-to-earth common sense of Samson Carrasco, moving spirit of this Second Part, made Don Quixote die in bed, leaving dreams of glory behind without a backward glance. Do you realize how, as the supreme contrast in his work, Cervantes understood that the honest simplicity of Sancho was not enough, and why in the Second Part Sancho is no less mad than his master, while conscious of his master's madness, and that on becoming mad Sancho is better, more humane, gentler in his manners, pleasanter in his speech, less obstinate, and even braver and bolder? Why is this? Because in the course of his weary life Cervantes had seen that even the Sanchos are possessed of natural goodness and honest instincts and much can be made of them. "All our lunacies"—says the mad graduate in canonical law from Osuna who insisted to the chaplain from Seville that he was the god Neptune[5]—"come from having empty stomachs and heads full of air." Miguel already knew the lunatics with empty stomachs and heads full of air and he understood that the hungry Sanchos and the raving Neptunes were not those that caused the greatest harm but rather the

Samsons, well fed and reasonable, who digest and discourse with perfect regularity at the cost of the hunger and madness of others.

Knight and squire, the priest thinks with great perspicacity, are cast from the same mold. The two are mad, one because of the emptiness of his stomach, the other because of the emptiness of his head, and the madder they are the more tenderly are they loved, until in the end we love the Knight of the Ideal, as we do the simple and innocent squire, who, ever since the confrontation with the actors' cart, is called "good Sancho, prudent Sancho, Christian Sancho and sincere Sancho." Rocinante's friendship with the gray donkey is also touching. Even in this detail one can see Cervantes' desire to tone down the notion of sharp contrast, which he had now abandoned, for master and man, without their knowing it, were now being guided by the hidden hand of their "rational" friend Samson. Samson is the name of a mediocrity, after the heroes of the days of Don Juan de Austria were dead and the mediocre like the Duke of Lerma, in the shadow of the insignificant like Philip III, came to life and prevailed.

Is there anything more characteristic, anything clearer, than the delight with which Miguel depicts that rustic Socrates called the Gentleman of the Green Coat in his bourgeois felicity, reasonable, settled in his corner and wise in his retirement, just as Lope had depicted him in his Horatian verses in the pattern of Fray Luis de León? Don Diego is the incarnation of that society of Philip III which by then wanted no heroes and did not believe in them, of that society which no longer maintained falcon or greyhound trained for hawking or coursing but instead hunted partridges with a decoy or sent a ferret to drive rabbits into the nets, with no need for anyone to work at pursuing them through the thickets but rather to sit quietly by the warren.

The Gentleman of the Green Coat, with his temperate and well-ordered way of life, his prudent and sensible reasoning, is the image of a comfortable world, calm and peaceful. Don Quixote listens to his arguments with docile courtesy but the adventure of the lions comes up and it is there that the hero shows that he is in truth a hero. The spirit of Lepanto is concealed under the armor of Don Quixote and he intrepidly attacks the lions, but before doing so, confident in himself, he flings at the prudent gentleman and his bourgeois society these magnificently depreciative words: "Señor hidalgo, let Your Honor go with your tame partridge and your bold ferret and let each man attend to his own business: this is mine and I know whether these gentlemen the lions will come at me or not. . . ." When Don Diego answered him Don Quixote pushes the jest even farther and says to him: "Now, Señor, if Your Honor does not wish to witness what you believe will be a tragedy spur the dappled mare and place yourself in safety. . . ."

Is it credible that a man who thinks and feels like that, with the sincere enthusiasm reflected in narrating this major adventure he presents so eloquently, proposes to banish the world's knight-errantries or despise knights-errant? The high point of the work and the greatest display of courage and determination on the part of the hero, the true knight-errant, is the adventure of the lions, seriously undertaken by Don Quixote and recounted seriously by the poet in words that Homer himself could not rival. Homer would have made the lions come out of the cage and would have described the bloody battle in masterly fashion. Cervantes, more human and truthful, fills the breast of his hero with precisely the spirit required to complete the exploit and at the culminating point of his madness he makes him return to reason, not to the reason of Samson Carrasco but to the divine *nous* which governs worlds and dictates these sublime words to him: "Close the door, friend, and bear witness to what you have seen me do: how you did open for the lion, how I awaited him, how he did not come out and how he lay down again. That ends my obligation . . . and may God come to support reason and truth and genuine knight-errantry."

Is it possible to speak more clearly or declare more patently what Don Quixote stands for? Reason and truth are the real knight-errantry: reason and truth which wander helpless through the world, beaten here, stoned there, unrecognized by the foolish, persecuted by the mediocre, poorly rewarded and treated ungratefully by all the world and ready to die on the road or in the street, in a fight or at the inn. That is Don Quixote and with epic Homeric seriousness his creator gives him a most honorable nickname, the "Knight of the Lions." What may come later is of little import. Come what may, Don Quixote has confronted the lion, has provoked it, has been ready to subdue it. The intent is more important than the deed. The idea has had sufficient validity to make a deep impression on the spirit of whoever considers the exploit carefully. After being the Knight of the Lions one can be everything else without dishonor.

From this climactic scene the fable goes down hill. Don Quixote is already as much as one can be in life. All that he now lacks, as does his author, is that sublime spiritualization that the proximity of death will bring.

CHAPTER 56

The Second Part of the Quixote

To construct a book with a protagonist who has the strength and importance of Don Quixote becomes something of a struggle, as in love or in a war between equals, where one does not know who will master whom. In the First Part, Don Quixote mastered his author, left him with his spirit subdued, in suspense. The lively tempo with which the adventures succeed each other, and even more the fear that its author had of boring his readers, inhibits Cervantes somewhat, and Don Quixote dominates his author as well as his readers. He returns to his village vanquished but not willing to acknowledge it. In the Second Part, Don Quixote has aged a great deal. Many more years have passed over him than those that elapsed between the publication of the first and second books.

The little we know of our sojourn in the world and the best ways of making it tolerable, in other words what is usually called philosophy, we have not learned through our youthful disappointments but through the disillusionments and despairs of a few oldsters who have had the grace to write of them so that the benefits of experience might be passed on. There is nothing more admirable than an old man with illusions, which is as much as saying a young old man, a light-hearted old man, a bold, sagacious, sympathetic old man. Illusions and hopes were Cervantes' only riches, but he was so opulent in them that he carried them with him to death and beyond.

The first *Quixote* is no better than the first *Faust*, but compare the second parts of both poems and while the thinking is essentially the same you will notice immediately the sureness with which Cervantes solved all difficulties and ended his work in a manner to comfort all men of all times, while Goethe's strength and confidence in his genius failed him at the precise moment when it was most needed, and he threw everything away, thinking to dazzle his readers with a parade of epic scenography he had learned in Italy. Compare the chill that remains in the heart after the end of the second *Faust* and the warm, human sadness with which you read the last chapter of the *Quixote*.

The reason for this is abundantly clear and was provided by that French gentleman who spoke of Cervantes with Licentiate Márques de Torres and said: "If it is necessity that obliges him to write, please God that he never has abundance." A happy, rich, lucky, loved man like Goethe, a classically insensitive old pagan like him, could not have written the Second Part of the *Quixote*. Goethe did not possess the art which his life had taught Cervantes of converting a tear and a grimace of pain into a smile and a smile into a peal of laughter. The Great Pagan did not possess the supreme *quid* of humor, the highest expression of human genius.

Furthermore Goethe was not a Catholic and Cervantes was. In his last hour, after having suffered every sort of misadventure, the aged hidalgo sadly realized that he still had to solve the greatest problem of all, the problem of how he would be judged, and at the last moment he took refuge in the sacred and put his hope in the unknowable, since he could not trust the known. In the last stages of his life he clung to this last illusion, to this final hope. He died happy, for he died hoping. Do you perceive the difference? Goethe would have disenchanted Dulcinea and would have taken Aldonza Lorenzo to the foot of Don Quixote's deathbed, sure of what he himself had said:

> The girl who, dressed in a rag,
> sweeps best on Saturdays,
> is the one who will caress you
> most lovingly on Sunday.

In spite of the refinements and paganisms he had collected in Italy, Goethe is a German who in village roadhouse or inn perhaps would not have been put off by the stench of Maritones, while Cervantes. . . . Ah! Cervantes, the Spanish hidalgo, is the most perfect example of human refinement, and his knight, as an English author says, is the prototype of the "gentleman" sensitive to the slightest indelicacy.

See him thus in the house of the Gentleman of the Green Coat. Don Quixote is not in sympathy with either the patriarchal regimen which exists there or with the stilted arguments and courtly verses of the poet son whom the worthy Don Diego had begotten, but he knows how to please both father and son, to act with the most noble courtesy, to be superior to the best, finer and more delicate. The Gentleman of the Green Coat is astounded at seeing how a man as mad as he must be to undertake the adventure of the lions can speak and act with such refined courtesy; he does not understand that the lips speak from the fullness of the heart. Don Quixote leaves, and that orderly, peaceful and calmest of bourgeois families is left in deep perplexity. What Don

Diego de Miranda and his wife Doña Cristina and his son Don Lorenzo felt and thought after their visitor departed the author does not tell, leaving as many amusing gifts for his readers as there are loose ends in his work, but each can imagine for himself how Don Quixote's passage through the decent secluded home of the discreet gentleman carried with it the illusion of heroic gaiety.

Cervantes was not suited to the kind of happy middle-class life represented by Don Diego and by the Horatian image of his ancestral home, but he leaves it to us to decide for ourselves. One would have to be very dull to think that after the truly heroic feat with the lions he pictured the selfish and comfortable repose of Don Diego as something desirable and presented it as a perfect way of life. Cervantes loved Horace, but it is actually a vision out of Petronius or of Rabelais that follows with the nuptials of Camacho.

It is thought that Cervantes devised this episode especially for Sancho, so that Sancho could drink wine, gorge himself, and let loose three or four jokes between four or five belches. An indubitable error! At Camacho's wedding Don Quixote speaks little and does less. The spectacle of gross abundance and material felicity does not stir his senses or make him utter a single word, but in the midst of a carnal display which calls to mind luscious memories of the Arch-priest of Hita and his Pantagruelesque battle with meats and fishes, an unhappy love affair presents itself with the incident of poor Basilio. Then everything is spiritualized, Don Quixote speaks, and the author sings of the love of Basilio and the generosity of Camacho with equal sympathy, as if to show that at the end of his life Cervantes is persuaded that a tender lover, ready to kill himself or to die for love, is just as worthy of esteem as a very rich man who enjoys being generous.

By then Cervantes was not thinking like Don Quixote or like Sancho but like both of them together. The contrast is disappearing, the radical difference is fading, the author is beginning to realize that all human nature is one, all its contradictions are explicable and its antagonisms reconcilable.

Before Kant and with greater clarity than he, the author of the *Quixote* has seen and described in human terms the difference between common sense, universal consensus, and the lower level of consciousness, known as *practical reason*, as against *pure reason*, the supreme reason which stands above all events and is common to them and to ideas. And before Kant and better than he did, he has broken down and revised the notion of opposition in human terms, arriving at the congruity of opposites and at the overriding harmony and synthesis of human nature, because pure reason under the influence of Don Quixote ends by ennobling and educating humble practical reason, the ordinary common sense of Sancho, and every reader who is not insensitive perceives how the feelings and ideas of master and man are harmonizing, the latter rising somewhat, the former descending a trifle, until the two spirits are one. Take note in this how the absurdities of Sancho in his grossness and the sublime inaccessibility of Don Quixote are becoming converted into reasonable discourse, human and harmonious. Here we glimpse a system of social organization and education of the squire by the knight and of the knight by the squire which already had roots in many medieval books such as those of Don Juan Manuel.[1] Cervantes believes in supermen like Don Quixote and the Glass Licentiate, but being more rational and better disposed than Nietzsche, he does not set them apart from the crowd, nor do they despise or find fault with it but draw near to it and in this way provide a lofty example of philosophy. Miguel knew nothing of the petulant and hateful words which later came to be used to disparage humble people. For him there were no "bourgeois" or "Philistines," no "masses" in the bad sense of the word.

But the book of knight-errantries continues and after the deep draughts of prosaic reality that the two heroes have just absorbed it is necessary for something as crazy, incredible and fantastic as the tale of the cave of Montesinos to follow. Here is a new secret bond between Don Quixote and Sancho, already united irrevocably by the enchantment of Dulcinea. Possibly inspired by the scepticism of the Licentiate's cousin, that student who accompanies the knight and the squire on the excursion to the cave and whose talk upsets the two of them, unaccustomed as they are to having anyone participate in their discussions and adventures, Sancho does not believe a word of what Don Quixote says he has seen in the cave of Montesinos. For his part Don Quixote is also not very sure that the whole thing was not a nightmare. This admirable, this superb doubt, of such clinical value, puts Don Quixote in the case of a master who in a way is inferior to his squire and must to some extent be at his mercy and dependent on his generosity. Thus sometimes in life our best intentions are thwarted through a trifle which binds our existence to that of an inferior being who throws cold water on our pleasures and dampens our enthusiasms. How often did Cervantes not find himself in this same situation?

A few passages later the mysterious, the epic, the formidable figure of Master Pedro appears, the man whom Cervantes loved as one of his finest creations, and to make it even more interesting Master Pedro has with him his enigmatic monkey, whose leaps and grimaces produce in us as intensely disquieting an impression as do the leaps and howls of the dog Montiel in the *Dialogue of Scipio and Berganza*. No one better than Cervantes has been able to titillate his readers by producing from the depths of reality these animals endowed with intelligence who leave us with fantastic ideas. The creator of the beautifully drawn figure of Master Pedro regretfully bids him farewell, promising himself that he will continue his activities at greater leisure. After this comes the adventure of the enchanted boat and when the bemused reader is ready to believe that the course of events is going to drag for Don Quixote, as for so many characters of the written novel and in real life, the encounter of the wandering hidalgo with the Duchess introduces master and man to a new and unknown world.

The twenty-seven chapters which deal with the adventures of Don Quixote in the palace of the Duke and Duchess are considered by many to be the best of the fable by far. In them Cervantes used the most amusing adventures, the most varied incidents, everything he could possibly do to enliven the story.

The language becomes more lofty, the dialogue more lively than ever, the descriptions briefer and better organized. There is nothing that could not have happened either in the castle of Pedrola, seat of the Dukes of Villahermosa, Counts of Ribagorza, gentlemen of the royal house of Aragón, or in any other lordly mansion such as that which the favorite of Philip III owned in Lerma and other great and noble gentlemen in various places. It could all have happened exactly as it is told and it all could create in the mind of Don Quixote new illusions to renew and aggravate his firm faith in his knight-errantries. The events are put together in such a way that master and man find themselves wrapped up in the fiction and accepting it, and with them the reader, who also is unable to distinguish where the play-acting ends and where reality begins, as so often happens in real life.

In these chapters there is an uneasy equilibrium between reason and madness, logic and disorder, which without a doubt is the great secret of human life and which only Cervantes and a few other philosophers like him have mastered. Little by little the beneficent idealism of Don Quixote was infiltrating the most obstinate spirits, that of the simple good-hearted Sancho to begin with, later that of the artless villagers. Only in the ducal palace where people of the highest rank in Spanish society reside, even when at moments the Duke and Duchess seem to be taking him seriously, the truth is that from beginning to end he is considered a madman with whom they can amuse themselves. It is only in these Court-bred souls that there is no touch of compassion for the Knight of the Ideal. It is only there that they make fun of him and fail to understand him. Cervantes knew only too well what the gentlemen of the Court were like, the Duke of Béjar, the Count of Saldaña and possibly some others whom he had approached to seek favor. Perhaps it is not too venturesome to see a direct relationship between the feasts and games which the Duke and Duchess celebrated in their castle, taking Don Quixote as a pretext, and those other festivities in which the Count of Lemos with his courtiers and followers amused themselves in the palace of the Viceroy of Naples, making fun of the enormous buttocks of the clergyman Bartomé Leonardo. Miguel, whose thoughts were ever turning toward Naples and who constantly nursed in his soul an illusory hope of returning to that scene of his youthful delights, was not unmindful of the Count of Lemos and his palace when he described the events in the ducal castle.

Perhaps Cervantes imagined the noble and refined words and the chivalrous actions of the Ingenious Hidalgo from La Mancha as being his own in case he found himself amid such opulence and elegance, and perhaps, disappointed and finally convinced that he could expect nothing from the haughty, inconsiderate, frivolous, ignorant and mocking aristocracy of his day, or maybe letting his pen fly with no particular intentions, he made Don Quixote leave the castle after all the adventures and misadventures he had experienced there, as he made Sancho quit the island of Barataria, without leaving in the fickle and irresponsible souls of the Duke and Duchess and their servants any gentle memory of the lunatic wisdom of the knight-errant or of the human simplicity of the squire. There were many, before and after the Duke and Duchess, who had to do with Don Quixote and when taking leave of him loved him or admired him or at least felt compassion for his extravagances, recalling his reasonable discourse and commending his praiseworthy intentions, his sincere and honest feelings. No one, not even Ginés de Pasamonte, having once injured, teased or maligned the good knight, felt himself capable of repeating his perverse actions a second time. Only the prestigious dukes were to be so inhuman that when the poor gentleman returned defeated from Barcelona they could still prepare a vicious and ridiculous masquerade bereft of art or good taste, namely the death of Altisidora, like a stale joke warmed over from those they had formerly invented.

It does not seem possible that there have been those who categorize the Duke and Duchess as very witty and refined and who do not observe that they are precisely the ones who are unrefined, gross and clumsy, as against the Knight whose words have been enough to civilize shepherds and villagers and make them mannerly, as well as to raise the base rustic character of Sancho Panza to his own level. In the ducal palace the real Duke, the great gentleman, the one worthy of being respected and served, is Don Quixote. Is it not something to think about that the goatherds understood and appreciated Don Quixote and that the lordly gentlemen from high society could neither appreciate nor understand him? In these twenty-seven chapters Don Quixote proves that it is vain to drag an ideal through regal halls seeking favors from those who had never seen the ugly face of want. Ideals are not preached nor golden ages promised under vaulted ceilings, at rich tables, upon embroidered tablecloths, nor did the effective preacher ever sit in soft armchairs of emblazoned velvet. Great ideas must be launched with the skies overhead, with a stone for a pulpit, with a tree for a backrest, before an audience of men and women with sun-tanned faces and candid hearts. What could the Duke and Duchess know or understand of such things? More or less what the Count of Lemos, still in Naples, could understand or know, preferring as he did the brittle and stereotyped poetry of the brothers Bartolemé and Lupercio.

More than happily his author brought Don Quixote out of the castle of the Duke and once more set him on the road. In the perennial struggle the road had won over the home once again. The Knight returned to his adventures and as if all that went before were not obvious enough, he came across the valiant, wise and generous bandit Roque Guinart, or Pedro de la Roca Guinardo, the great-grandfather of the generous robbers of Schiller and the whole swarm and numerous family of the great adjusters of an unjust and prejudiced society. After Don Quixote there is no character in the whole book more sympathetic, more human, with a clearer concept of life than this good bandit Roque Guinart in whom Cervantes sees, as all perceptive thinkers have always seen in men of his quality, nothing less than a man determined to correct injustices in his own way and repair by brutal outrage the nefarious deficiencies and crimes of society.

Roque Guinart is the opposite and the counterpoise to the Duke of Lerma: Roque would not have existed without the Duke. In history there are at times outbursts like this in which banditry on high is echoed by another kind of widespread banditry which inspires hatred and is loathed only by those directly injured by it. No one loathed Roque Guinart just as no one hated José María or the seven sons of Ecija. People have always felt or suspected that there is a justice higher than the corrupted and prostituted justice in the hands of venal judges and thieving scriveners. It was such a feeling that inspired the pages in which Cervantes speaks of Roque Guinart with as much admiration as affection. Memories of his youth and of the free life of Italy awakened and exhilarated the mind of the aged writer when he depicted an enviable life like that of Roque Guinart: to risk freedom with greatness and daring was the most worthwhile thing in the world. Note how sensitively, how deeply the author of the *Quixote*, the soldier of Lepanto, was conscious of how Spanish heroism has had to take refuge in mountain crags and nest in the hearts of bandits, since for some time it had been banished from the Court. Roque Guinart is the first of all the robber captains who replace the old soldier captains both in reality and in popular epic poetry: he is a descendant of Don Juan and Don Álvaro, of Don Lope de Figueroa and of Don Manuel de León. Take him to America and he would not be called Roque Guinart but Francisco Pizarro. The adventurous life of Roque delights the author buried in the plebeian confines of his "ancient and gloomy lodging" on the ground floor in the Calle de León. He dreams of such a life and not of the comfortable mediocrity of Don Diego de Miranda.

Unfortunately the time for heroism is past. It is necessary for the Knight of the Lions to be defeated and that his defeat come on an important occasion in such a way that he may never again raise his proud head. For this purpose Cervantes chooses Barcelona, the beautiful, the illustrious, the powerful, the rich. The gaiety reigning there is the best background for "the adventure that distressed Don Quixote more than any that so far had befallen him."[2] Let us read and re-read this adventure and we cannot but realize that nowadays we have missed the profound symbolism which pervades all his roles, and especially the sad, painful, dispirited and feeble words of the swooning vanquished knight. Cervantes put all his heart into this, here he brought out the gift of tears which he had mastered as few of our writers have. Who can fail to be stirred by the crumbling of the inner castle, the dreamlike citadel of Don Quixote's illusions, and is not moved to pity him and his poor horse, whose weakness is almost human! Who has not wept on reading of the adventure with the pigs which befell Don Quixote as the culmination of his humiliation and abasement? And who will not be lifted for the last time out of the depression induced by such happenings when he sees how Don Quixote, like his author, could produce new illusions and new hopes from the ashes of those that had just overwhelmed and destroyed him? Before he had recovered from the bitterness of his defeat he was dreaming of devoting himself to a comfortable pastoral life and to cultivation of the serene poetry of the countryside, as one who now knew from cruel experience that in the country truth can be found by one who seeks it, or the pious lie by one who has lost faith in truth.

Don Quixote and Sancho finally reach their village, dejected, vanquished, but happy with the bucolic resolve they have taken. A hare crosses the road, dogs chase it: that is a bad augury. Some lads carelessly pronounce certain words that can have mysterious meanings. A shudder of terror runs through Don Quixote.

Don Quixote enters his house, falls ill, regains his reason, dies. An unutterable sorrow floods our spirits. We mourn the death of Don Quixote and the rebirth of the worthy Alonso Quijano. We are distressed not so much because Don Quixote died as because he died convinced that once he had been mad. To us this undeceiving seems a new deception, the loss of all his illusions a new illusion. And seeing him die, hearing his words, unequalled in simplicity and grandeur unless by those of the Gospel, we all think of our own deaths and review our own lives, recognizing our self-deceptions and fearing that some sprouts of illusion still remain in our souls which will have to be rooted out and destroyed with cruel pain to ourselves.

No other known writer has achieved the intimate uprooting of our whole being produced by the death of Don Quixote. Here Homer yields, Dante is silent, Goethe is abashed and takes refuge in his classic egoism. Only Shakespeare can look serenely on this, for only he, like Cervantes, could convert a tear into a smile, a smile into a peal of laughter, and finally change the laughter to a smile and make that smile turn once again into a sob.

CHAPTER 57

The Trials of Persiles and Sigismunda

PROUD and pleased with himself over having written the ultimate book of knight-errantry, and having given birth to what he thought were the first exemplary novels on the model of the Italian *novelieri*, Cervantes wanted to construct the first long novel of modern times according to an original pattern of his own, and to that end he wrote in the moments of leisure left him from the plays and *Don Quixote* the "septentrional tale" of *The Trials of Persiles and Sigismunda*.

In writing it Cervantes succumbed to the inclination of all elderly men to boast that they retain their imaginative powers alive, fresh and exuberant. At the risk of tiresome repetition we recall the second part of *Faust*, the superabundance of fantasy its author put into it and the confusion in which the reader finds himself among such varied and disparate images. Here—Cervantes thought, as Goethe was to think, as other illustrious old men thought and think—I am going to put in from my harvest everything I know and can imagine, so that those to come will think that I could still have been able to live two hundred years composing masterpieces. And without his intending it the work turned out to be even more a book of knight-errantry than the *Quixote* itself, not in the sense that it embodied any unattainable ideal but in that it was a book of the road, a book in which there is no repose, in which the home, peace and calm are forever being destroyed.

But let us not speak now of how he carried out his intent but rather of what he intended to do. When Cervantes undertook what he regarded as the heroic and immortal enterprise of the *Persiles* he had already half persuaded himself that since Lope had reached the top of the playwriting kingdom it was impossible through the theater to attract and influence the public, ends to which of course every author aspires, whether consciously or not. In any case a great man never tries to cut the ground out from another great man or take over a spot he already occupies.

Reluctantly and with many mental reservations Cervantes conceded to Lope the empire of the theater in all its aspects while within himself he was sure that *More Than Meets the Eye* and a few more of his unpublished plays were better than any of Lope's. It must have cost him a great deal to put aside this old man's illusion, but he did it, leaving the always vulgar mob of the theater to amuse itself with nonsense. The frantic activity, the scant intelligence and the awkwardness of the actors, the riotous impatience and inattention of the public, so often observed by Cervantes, made it necessary to debase art in the theater and reduce it to a craft for which he had no aptitude. Great geniuses, indulgent and benevolent, practical painters of life, as Saint-Beuve calls Cervantes, were never good at making cardboard figures out of reality and even less at distorting it to present only its angles and corners in perpetual conflict.

Cervantes knew that his nature did not lead him, like Lope, by the road of rage and violence which is necessary to produce extravagant action, dealing in blows and speaking in shouts with the object of forcing the inattentive minds of spectators bound up in their own affairs, their own little passions or their own absorbing conversation to turn toward the stage in shock, or at least with interest.

Miguel realized that it was useless to put in writing for the stage more of human nature than what a crowd jammed together in a playhouse can tolerate. When we are alone we are all humane, patient and anxious to please, just as we are uncomfortable, intolerant and offensive when we are part of a crowd. That unregarded mass which includes the humdrum homeloving gentleman, the damsel or lady who never goes to the theater, the godly man who knows the world, and the mature and thoughtful man, these constituted Cervantes' public, as they always did the public of novelists, and it is rare when it ever coincides with the theatergoing public of excitable, street-gadding, thoughtless loiterers and homeless people, young ladies and gentlemen wanting to show off, lovers and their lady-loves, bored and weary people suffering from an enormous *ennui* and the curiosity to see action typical of those who are incapable of taking action themselves. The two publics are very different and always were. In case anyone were to overlook this Cervantes is careful to note, in the Second Part of the *Quixote*, the quality and condition of the people who had read the First.

While he recognized this, Cervantes himself perhaps felt that there was a certain dearth of action in the Second Part. Except in the chapters regarding the ducal castle it is essentially ideas rather than material things that predominate, and each adventure seems to be a reflection, a consequence or a distinct facet of the one idea which logically pervades the book. Perhaps Cervantes reached the point of doubting that his work would produce the effect he wanted due to a lack of great and varied activity. He may also have decided to woo the very numerous public that Lope had already seduced and carried away by the magic and fecundity of the ant-hill restlessness in his works. It was clearly necessary to make a great book of the road, of fantastic and nonsensical adventure which, beyond all reason and custom, would stir and enrapture this public already habituated to believing the most incredible tales and seeing the most extraordinary events follow each other in three hours.

For this purpose he looked for a model in *Teágenes and Caricles*, the Greek novel of the decadent Heliodorus,[1] from which so many other extravagant fictions had come, and he started by imagining his heroes as completely exotic and unreal, making Persiles a son of the King of Iceland and the lovesick Sigismunda the daughter of the King of Friesland. The imagination of Cervantes, brought up on reading books of knight-errantry and a vision of the most incredible exploits and the rarest perils, as set forth in the first two books of the *Persiles*, cannot be represented better than by recalling the very curious geographical maps which were drawn by order of the Emperor Charles V and published in Cologne by the famous Dutch geographer Gerard Mercator[2] between 1560 and 1595. Examine these interesting maps, compare them with modern ones, and you will see what a distorted and strange notion they had of reality as we conceive it today, while men risked themselves on seas and coasts without knowing anything with certainty nor with the exactness indispensable for navigation. All the continents seemed to Mercator very much wider and shorter than they really are. Africa is almost round, America looks like one of those heavy shapeless summer clouds, the Scandinavian peninsula has an infinity of promontories which existed only in the imagination of the good Mercator or of the terrified navigators who furnished him with data and in whom the memory of dangers overcome magnified things, mixed up descriptions and altered distances and proportions. They look like maps from the country of the Chimera, charts of the Kingdom of the Absurd, and we are amazed that mariners could navigate with such feeble aids, that generals could command armies and monarchs dictate laws and govern countries of which so little was known.

Many times when examining these misleading maps I have thought what it would have been like if Philip II, when the sun never set upon Spanish dominions, had been able to study a handsome planisphere instead of that little impostor of a terraqueous metal globe which he had in his cell at the Escorial. What it would have meant to Cervantes himself, ready to write the "septentrional tales," if he really understood the great poetic mystery of the North, imbibed its marvellous legends, incorporated them into our esthetic treasure, translated them into our language! When he undertook the *Persiles* he already knew that in the North extraordinary lights could be found, unheard of ideas and novel sensations, but all these names of Iceland, Friesland, Lithuania, the Barbarous Isle, the Island of Snow and the Island of the Hermits represented only misty visions, while the names of Periandro and Auristela, of Rutilio and Transila, of Arnaldo and Sinforosa, of Policarpo and Zenobia do not correspond to human beings but to vague creatures of fiction and fantasy.

To those who, tired of reality or satiated with it, which is more often the case, and unaware of the inexhaustible beauties of the world, take pleasure in those nightmare books in which the march of thought and action is not subject to any logical standard or human reasoning, the first two books of the *Persiles* can be recommended as among the great purely imaginative works, like the literary fancies of Thomas de Quincey or the pictorial fantasies of Arnold Böcklin. Examine the famous picture *The Island of Mystery* by that most original artist, a picture which seems to depict the islands our immortal author imagined in the first two books of the *Persiles*, and this will confirm how there is no modern or ancient manifestation of creative fancy or delicate art unknown to him or toward which at one time or another he did not turn his attention. Those first two books, then, were aimed at a part of the public that Cervantes imagined to be longing for sensations never before experienced, hungry for unprecedented happenings. In imagining them he put all of what was most artfully contrived in his soul.

But having finished them, the author was struck by this simple, this human consideration with which he starts the third: "Since our souls are always in continuous movement and they cannot stop or rest unless they are reconciled to their fate . . . is it not a miracle that our thoughts follow upon each other, that this one is taken, that one left, one is pursued and another forgotten, and the one which is most tranquil, that will be the best, on condition that it is not involved in any error of judgment." Thus to Cervantes' weary mind came new ideas that were already old to him when he brought the principal characters of his story out of the regions of the North, where they had been entangled in intricately involved adventures, and having got them on the sea where would the old poet take them but to Lisbon, to the beloved city of his best years?

Happy and excited as one who touches land after an extremely long voyage, Miguel delivers through the lips of Antonio that magnificent panegyric of Lisbon, graceful and pleasing to the ear as the language of love from an old man in love:

> You will now know, my beloved barbarian, how God is served. You will now see the rich temples in which He is worshiped, you will see at the same time the Catholic rites with which He is served and you will observe Christian charity at its loftiest. Here in this city you will see how many hospitals are the executioners of illness and destroy it and one who loses his life in them, wrapped in the efficacy of innumerable indulgences, wins a life in Heaven. Here love and purity hold hands and walk together; courtesy does not permit arrogance to approach; and bravery does not allow cowardice to come near. All its inhabitants are civil, courteous, generous and loving, because they are considerate. The city is the greatest in Europe and the one with the greatest trade; the treasures of the Orient are unloaded in it and from it they are distributed throughout the universe; its port is capacious, with not only ships that can be counted, but movable forests of masts created by the ships. The beauty of the women stirs admiration and love, the gallantry of the men is a marvel, so they say. Finally, this is the land that gives Heaven holy and most abundant tribute. . . .

Memories of Lisbon bring Cervantes out of the fantastic regions through which he had been flying. They make him relive his youth, they draw him once more to well-known beaten paths, they put the book into the area of reality and make his characters follow a clear itinerary through places like Badajoz, Guadalupe, Trujillo, Talavera, Toledo, La Sagra, Aranjuez, Ocaña, Quintanar de la Orden and others similarly well known and commonplace. Here pure and misleading fancy loses its privileges, truth is imposed and it dominates the fable to the point of introducing in Trujillo "two gentlemen who are known both in it and in the whole world; one of them is Don Francisco Pizarro and the other Don Juan de Orellana, both young, both unmarried, both rich, and both extremely generous in all things," as if by this evocation of two such illustrious and heroic-sounding names Cervantes wished to show the world that it was not necessary to go up to Northern regions in order to encounter great paladins of the unknown, valiant searchers for the mysterious, and inhabitants of obscure untrodden regions.

In this part of the narrative real and possible episodes follow one after another, such as that of Feliciana of the Voice, that of the flat-nosed old woman in whom the image of death may be conjectured, that of the mysterious pilgrim who always appears unexpectedly, and that of Martín Benedre, the Pole, which is without doubt an account of an actual incident witnessed by Miguel himself. The travelers arrive at the Tagus river, they see the towers and walls of Toledo in the distance, and Miguel cannot repress the memories of olden times nor fail to hear the pleasant murmur of the noble river whose waters repeat to the heedless ages "the gentle lament of two shepherds."[3] He exclaims full of poetic ardor:

> The fame of the river Tagus is not something that can be kept within limits or be ignored by the most remote people of the world, for it reaches out to all and is manifest to all and it awakens in everyone a desire to know it . . . and thus because of this and because of having sometimes revealed to the world the famous works of the never praised as he deserves poet Garcilaso de la Vega, and he having discovered, read, looked upon and admired them, as soon as he saw the clear river he (Periandro) said: We will not say here Salicio brought his singing to an end but rather here Salicio made a beginning in his singing; here in his pastoral poems he surpassed himself; here his bagpipes echoed; at the sound the waters of the river paused, the leaves of the trees were motionless and the winds were stilled; as a result admiration for his song spread from mouth to mouth and people to people over the whole earth. Oh blessed crystal clear waters, gilded sands—do I say gilded?—rather are they born of pure gold, receive this poor pilgrim who adores you from afar and thinks to worship you when near. And gazing upon the great city of Toledo this is what he said: Oh, solid rock, glory of Spain and light of its cities, in whose breast the relics of the valiant Goths have been preserved for uncounted centuries in order to restore once more its vanished glory and to be the bright mirror and guardian of Catholic rites! God bless you, therefore, oh holy city!

The itinerary the characters in the *Persiles* follow on their way to Rome is the one we have already seen Miguel follow when young as servant to Monsignor Julio Aquaviva. In his old age a splendid vision of Italy, from which he considered himself exiled, appeared again before the eyes of the poet. Thus he scatters happy memories of his youth throughout these last two books of the *Persiles*. He is not the ordinary old man for whom any bygone day was better; Miguel is sure that in all reason and with complete justice it can be affirmed that former times were better, and it is not simple happenchance that he mentions Pizarro, Orellana, and Garcilaso de la Vega, but because he is convinced that those men were more manly than those of the present day, braver in action and more mature in speech. Already close to death, Miguel is making a kind of recapitulation or inventory of the great loves of his life and by this biographers may trace by external appearances and known facts a little of the inner truth that dwelt in his heart. They should not despise this pilgrim's tale but rather should study and analyse it word by word and line by line with as much care and attention as the *Parnassus*.

Miguel wrote the first two books of the *Persiles* to please his readers and particularly to entertain the leisure hours of the Count of Lemos and his aristocratic friends. In them he showed how his imagination was still lively and fertile and how when the opportunity offered he could envision unknown worlds and undiscovered regions and provoke in the mind of whoever read him those new stimuli whose springs are mastered only by great geniuses. But after rounding the summit of the first two books, ancient Castilian realism takes possession of his pen, the characters of the imaginary narrative come to life, the incidents and episodes are more realistic, the places represent actual landscapes, cities, rivers and woods and even the language acquires a precision and clarity which has never been surpassed even by its author himself in any other work of his. Cervantes did not create the "long Spanish novel," as some authors have declared, though imitations of the *Persiles* were written at the same time and appeared soon after it. Some of them were excellent, but after the public's attention had been diverted from the books of knight-errantry, in which the *Quixote* was no small influence, though not as much as has been said, the need for poetic action always sought by the masses was satisfied in the theater, which was all action and intrigue in the hands of Lope, Tirso, and Vélez de Guevara. Actually *The Trials of Persiles and Sigismunda* goes only part way in that direction, for its author wanted it to be a reflection of life.

To this day it is extraordinary, examining it carefully, that one who has shown in the Second Part of the *Quixote* the broadest and most universal concept of life, expounding it in such a well-organized way, could still have enough vigor left to present at the same time a gallery of such varied pictures and stories, some real, others as artificial as those with which the *Persiles* begins.

Cervantes did not get to see his last work printed, but he did see it finished, corrected, revised, and polished by himself with as much care as any of his other books. Here, in this unjustly forgotten book, is where he realized that promise of his in the *Parnassus* when he offered

> to sing with a voice so tuneful and persuasive
> that they will think I am a swan and that I am dying.

CHAPTER 58

The Last Illness—The Heart and the Brain

IN the early months of the year 1616 the old hidalgo returned to Esquivias where his wife Doña Catalina was living. At times his illness distressed him grievously, but not so much as to exhaust his heroic patience. From early youth he had never been daunted by pain nor did he ever abandon hope, although sometimes now, when the intolerable and insatiable thirst[1] of the dropsical assailed him, he had to fall back on all the resignation he had built up over many and many a year not to give way to complete despair.

Miguel's sound constitution is attested by his ability to bear hardships cheerfully, by the absence of any previous pathology and by the age he reached—sixty-eight years lived to the full. His hero Don Quixote also testifies by his own hardihood to that of his author.

His body could not escape old age, however, and this made inroads, not on the splendid solid texture of the brain but rather on the blood vessels and the heart. Arteriosclerosis is the technical term for this aging of the circulatory system. At first masked, insidious, multiform and chronic, arteriosclerosis as such was an illness unknown in Cervantes' time. Dropsy, which the doctors of those days considered an illness in itself, was nothing more than a symptom.

The difference between heart and brain as compared with the other organs is that they are nourished by rest, by an equilibrium between what they give and what they receive. The tireless activity of Cervantes' brain was fed by the natural self-satisfaction, the certainty which he shows a hundred times over, that his works would be passed on to posterity amid universal acclaim. Among the many bad things about the profession of writer the saving grace is that he finds his reward in his own work even if he gets nothing else out of it, and he goes peacefully to another world for having accomplished something he thinks memorable, a comforting self-deception that makes him drag life's burdens like the blinkered mules of the irrigation wheel who know not whether they are working for immortality or in order to water some beds of cabbage.

In the case of Cervantes his widespread popularity and the enormous response to the *Quixote* helped to keep his mind active. Disappointments and disillusions had been forgotten, although it cost him trouble to eradicate from his mind some illusions, such as that of writing for the theater. His tacit and never-confessed battle with Lope had ended in mutual esteem and acceptance. At the same time his brain rested, as only the brain can rest, through a change of direction and type of activity by planning new and different works.

The brain of Cervantes was therefore unimpaired, healthy, fresh and youthful until the last days of his life, just as his pen was eloquent and moving until the final moment. But if the brain was nourished adequately this was not so with the heart, which found no rest and no nourishment in love and happiness. The things that Miguel most enjoyed in life were intellectual. He did not despise the flesh, as did the mystics and ascetics of his day, but all his works make it plain that he was much more a man of feeling than of the senses.

In no other writer do we find as in Cervantes the supreme human art of reconciling the attraction of pleasure with the fascination of purity in matters of love. Not even Lope, a doctor of amorous science, has equalled Cervantes in this sublime perceptiveness which has enthroned him in the hearts of women capable of understanding Epicurus and loving Plato, of whom there are many more than a few unfortunates think. At the same time, if we analyse carefully the reasons for Miguel's brushes with Lope, we may find that it is not a purely literary matter. No, the whole world knew that Lope was loved by women of all sorts and conditions and that Lope could not have created such an immense variety of unfettered passions as gave life to his theater if he had not found himself in that feverish whirlwind which sweeps the world and in which we are involved willy-nilly, some enjoying it as Lope did, others suffering as Cervantes did, without ever reaching the satisfaction we all seek.

You can be sure of it, you can believe it: in the bottom of his soul Cervantes envied Lope his loves and flirtations, his domination of women, more by his personality than by his writings. This was a kind of fruition that always seemed enviable to Miguel and because he never had it the Ingenious Hidalgo was to be unhappy in love all his life. Is it not strange that Don Quixote had seen Dulcinea only once or twice and had never had a single word with her? It would seem that Cervantes had reached the stage of Plato without passing through that of Epicurus.

His love affairs in Naples and Portugal and his passion for Ana Franca were wretched fare for a mighty yearning for love, all the stronger for not being carnal, and it was not to fade or disappear with the flight of youth. And examining the matter closely it is not difficult to recognize, however sad this may make us feel, that no one really loved Cervantes as deeply and tenderly as he deserved. Only his sister Andrea, generous in love, was capable of providing him with that deep and lasting affection that genius needs to live happily, as pearls need the touch of feminine flesh or the softness of velvet, but Doña Andrea was busy all her life with the most diverse activities, she had three husbands, and she could not give her brother the constant attention he needed.

And what of Doña Catalina de Salazar? Let us face the facts and not blame her entirely. An unknown poet arrives in a village and love whispers in the ear of a shy girl of the place. The girl listens, marries the poet and comes to love him, but after love there is life to be faced and harsh, inexorable life forces the lovers into a necessary but unhappy separation during which the youth of both of them is wasted. Love can still be rekindled but a woman who has spent twenty years alone in a great empty house in a melancholy village is of no use for this.

Wandering through the shabby rooms or sitting on a bench at the door, the old hidalgo considers this situation, which has saddened and shortened his life, and in it he recognizes, not any error, for he has not been at fault nor has his wife, but rather his unlucky star. His mind is healthy, strong, ready for action, prepared for fruitful work. But the heart is sick, enfeebled, like those men, many and many of them, who are to be seen in all the villages of Spain who reach old age with the body turned into a sickle from so much bending over the plough-handle and stamping the first furrow and who have never known plenty, nor even the food they need for such a hard and continuous struggle with the earth and who have but one desire, to make a hollow, lie down and surfeit themselves eternally with that same earth.

At times the old man, strolling in the outskirts of Esquivias with some friend or kinsman, would reach the fountain of Ombidales near one of his wife's properties. He would sit down on a rock and now and again wet his throat once more with the running water. Nearby the larks hopped about, gracefully bobbing their heads crowned by little pointed tufts; their song was also pointed: *to-to-vi-i*! Further off among the vines the partridges that had been mating since February made a pattern, the hens cooing in a strong dark contralto as the fierce males replied, challenging each other from hillock to hillock: *ssi-ssi-sssi*. The croaking jackdaws had fled in swift flocks from the stripped olive trees and the cuckoo had sought refuge in them and on a sunny afternoon it sent forth its first summons to the joys of spring, still late in coming.

His sick heart feared spring, which had never been as kind to him as autumn. In order not to face springtime in the depths of the country he returned to Madrid to bury himself in his gloomy old lodging, and on the way, he tells in golden words:[2]

> Thus it came to pass, beloved reader, that two friends and I coming from the famous town of Esquivias, famous for many reasons, one for its illustrious lineages and another for its very illustrious wines, I felt as if behind me there came pricking in great haste someone who appeared to wish to overtake us, and he further showed this by crying out that we spur not so. We awaited him and a rustic student mounted on a she-ass and clad all in gray came up. He wore gaiters, roundtoed shoes and a sword in a metal-tipped scabbard, a starched walloon and flat braids. It is true that he had no more than two whereby at times the walloon tipped to the side and he had great difficulty in keeping it straight; coming up to us he said: Are Your Honors going to the Court to obtain some office or benefice, for His Most Illustrious of Toledo is there and nothing less than His Majesty, to judge by the haste with which you journey for in truth my ass has been hailed as champion traveller more than once? To which one of my companions replied: The hack of Señor Miguel de Cervantes is to blame for this, for he is somewhat long of stride. Barely had the student heard the name of Cervantes than, alighting from his mount with the saddle pad falling in one direction and the portmanteau in the other, for he traveled with all this high style, he headed for me and managing to seize my left hand he said: Yes, yes, this is the hale and hearty cripple, the all-famous, the sprightly writer and consummately the delight of the Muses. I who encountered this great tribute of praises for me in such a short time felt it would be discourteous not to respond to them and embracing him around the neck, thereby nearly ruining the walloon for good, I said to him: That is an error into which many ignorant admirers have fallen. I, Sir, am Cervantes, but not the delight of the Muses, nor any of the other bits of nonsense Your Honor has uttered. Take up your ass and mount, and let us travel in goodly converse what little remains of the journey. The courteous student did so, we reined in somewhat, and at a leisurely pace we continued on our way, in the course of which my illness was discussed and the worthy student declared me past recovery, immediately saying: This illness is the dropsy, which all the water of the ocean sea could not relieve, even if it were not salt. Your Honor, Señor Cervantes, must regulate your drinking, not forgetting to eat, for in this way you will recover without any other physic. Many have told me so, I replied, but however I try I cannot leave off drinking as though I had been born for that purpose only. My life is coming to an end and by the calendar of my pulse, which at the latest will complete its course this Sunday, I will end that of my life. Your Honor has got to know me at a grave moment in my life, certainly I have no time to show myself grateful for the good will Your Honor has shown me. Whereupon we reached the bridge of Toledo and I entered by it and he turned to do so by that

of Segovia. . . . He embraced me once more and I returned the compliment. He spurred his ass and left me in such a sorry case as he was a sorry horseman on his ass. This might have provided a great occasion for me to write with much wit, but one cannot always choose. A time will perhaps come when I can pick up the broken thread and say what I have failed to say here and what I know I should be saying. Farewell to graceful speeches, farewell to witty sayings, farewell to fun-loving friends. I am dying and longing to see you soon making merry in the other world.

CHAPTER 59

The Last Patron—Death of Cervantes

THE Archbishop of Toledo, Don Bernardo II de Sandoval y Rojas, was rusticating at Buenavista in early March, fleeing the forlorn discomfort of the huge cold walls of the Archiepiscopal Palace. Buenavista, a handsome countryhouse on a slope of the right bank of the Tagus is, as its name indicates, a place of quietly beautiful perspectives. From there the sun shines across the dark-hued hills of San Bernardo where the olives lean awry; to the left are the famous orchards of apricot and almond trees, the wild grape vines and an intruding prickly pear which lives in the corner of a wall. Farther to the left the noble city, glory of Spain, shines like a jewel perched on its pedestal of living rock, and toward its center the air is boldly pierced by the pointed tower of the Cathedral and the square Morisco belfry of San Román, famous in history and in Spanish epic poetry.

Don Bernardo had known all the greatness and all the pettiness of the world and no spiritual or material matters held any secrets for him. As Inquisitor General he understood perfectly the pangs of conscience and as State Councillor the cunning pilferings of politics; as Head of the Spanish Church he exercised discreetly but firmly the formidable power entrusted to him. As an eminent grandee of the highest rank, on several occasions he had had to advance funds to King Philip III and recently he had provided him with fifty thousand ducats. He could do so easily, since his own revenues from the Archbishopric were never below some six million reals, based on such a strong foundation as the moral power of the Archbishop, which was invincible and the most solid and positive in the nation.

During his siestas and moments of repose at Buenavista he amused himself chiefly by reading books which transcended the weaknesses of humanity. He hated Gothic art and therefore all idealistic and romantic exaltation, all knight-errantries, whether human or divine. At bottom he possibly loathed roving women like Saint Teresa, the restless knights of Loyola and every spirit nourished on books of knight-errantry. His was a neoclassical spirit, calm and steady, fond of detail, a lover of sober richness, of clear and simple lines, of precise and clean-cut diction.

For all these reasons he was highly gratified when one of his attendants, perhaps the enthusiastic Licentiate Márques de Torres, read the Second Part of the *Quixote* to him or gave it to him to read. Don Bernardo had seen Cervantes once and he thought he could remember having helped him occasionally as being a poor poet, hidalgo and old soldier. Nevertheless he was not particularly pleased by the First Part of *Don Quixote*, by the suspense in which the mind was left, not knowing whether the madness of the Knight of La Mancha would or would not persist. But when he read the Second Part and saw Don Quixote die in bed as a Catholic Christian, restored to sanity and abjuring his madness in sublime words as if he were persuading the whole world by his lofty example to abandon the extravagances and absurdities into which their insane unreason had led them and seeking to keep them within the classical, orderly and rectilinear bounds of life, the illustrious prelate approved with all his soul, recognizing at last that Cervantes was the man with the clearest mind of his day.

Naturally Don Bernardo drew from the book conclusions that suited his own standards. Oh! Yes—thought the wise and politically minded old man, who was well aware of the main reasons for the "lunacies of Europe," as Quevedo put it, and for the stupidities of Spain—this is the positive, the real: the unhappy and lamentable period of the neo-Gothic fantasies, of the strife of knights-errant and the heroic deaths of paladins on the field of battle has ended; the age of peace and reason has arrived if the hidalgo can die tranquilly in his familiar bed, forgiving all and forgiven by all. And following upon the death of Don Quixote the good Archbishop foresaw an era of classic discipline and harmonious magnificence which came, not in Spain but rather in France, and it was for that future age of peace and harmony that anxious hopes were expressed by the sonorous murmur of the Tagus flowing grave and solemn at his feet and by the song of the wind in the poplars that served as counterpoint and created the fugue in the deep canonical song of the river.

Pleased by the reading, which had power to stir him even in his old age, the Archbishop of Toledo asked if Cervantes had been given any favors recently. Somebody informed him that the old poet was ill and as short of money as usual. Don Bernardo then gave explicit orders that the author of the *Quixote* must never be forgotten.

Back in his house in Madrid, Cervantes had lost almost all hope of being cured, but he was encouraged and comforted by the help that came to him from on high, even if it was so late. Not only did Archbishop Don Bernardo send him material assistance but also a letter he had written or dictated, consoling him in his latest tribulation. One good thing about classical minds is that they recognize the desires and needs of humanity and know when and where and to whom to give what is due. Cervantes replied to the gift and the letter with the last thing he was to write before he took to his bed. It is the famous old document which presides over the solemn sessions of the Spanish Royal Academy and which reads:

> A few days ago, Very Illustrious Sir, I received the letter of Your Most Illustrious Lordship, and with it further favors. If there could be a remedy for the illness that afflicts me the repeated signs of favor and assistance your illustrious person has dispensed to me would suffice; but finally it has so intensified that I think it will be the end of me, though not of my gratitude. May God keep you as one who carries out so many holy works so that you may enjoy their fruits there in your holy glory, as is the wish for you of your humble servant who kisses your magnificent hands. In Madrid, 26 of March of the year 1616.
>
> Very Illustrious Sir.
> Miguel de Cervantes Saavedra

He wrote this letter with so much care and attention that two copies of it, with slight variations, are still in existence. The perceptiveness of the last days of his life, which at times approached the superhuman, told him that the recognition of his genius by a man such as Don Bernardo de Sandoval y Rojas was a sure advance notice, or to put it better, it was the first congratulatory message regarding immortality sent him by future centuries. The portals of the eternal were opened for him by the hand of the man who, after the pontiff of Rome, was invested with the highest spiritual power. A great peace was flooding Miguel's soul, an overwhelming humility pervaded his ailing heart.

Brought to bed by the severe pains he suffered, he did not want to die without embracing the ultimate ideal of his life, religious faith. At the last he wished to resolve that great doubt which had confronted Sancho Panza when Don Quixote explained to him in Chapter 8 of the

Second Part, "our deeds must not go farther than the bounds set us by the Christian religion we profess," and describing what the giants and other concepts of knight-errantry meant he added, "when we combat giants we are slaying arrogance, we overcome envy by generosity and good-heartedness, choler by a quiet bearing and calm spirit, gluttony and somnolence by our fasting and the vigils we keep, lust and lasciviousness by the loyalty we hold to those we have made the ladies of our thoughts, laziness by going to all parts of the world searching for opportunities that can and will make us famous knights among Christians." To which Sancho, after putting to his master the difficult question of whether it was greater to resuscitate a dead person or to kill a giant, responds by suggesting to Don Quixote that the two of them become saints in order to become famous more quickly, "and mind you, Sir," he says, "that yesterday or the day before they canonized or beatified two little barefoot friars whose iron chains with which they girdled and tormented their bodies it is now considered extremely lucky to touch and kiss and they are held in greater veneration, they say, than the sword of Roland in the armory of the King our lord, whom God keep. Thus, my master, it is better to be a humble little friar of any order than a valiant knight-errant. . . ."

The worried Miguel discussed this last problem with his good friend, the owner of his house, the priest Don Francisco Martínez Marcilla, who felt that it would be very advisable for Miguel to take his solemn vows in the Venerable Third Order of St. Francis, a ceremony which took place on April 2 of 1616, in that same gloomy old room of the aged poet, who could not even get out of bed. Once he had professed, Miguel realized that this was another kind of knight-errantry, that of humility, as the previous ones had been those of arrogance and vainglory, and if it eased his mind to die a Christian it delighted and sweetened his last hours that he died as a knight of an order founded by the holy Don Quixote of Assisi.

After all, he thought, now rejecting all bitterness and all rancor against the world, he had never been anything else than a poor supplicant wedded for life to poverty. In order to suffer extremes of need it had scarcely been necessary for him to profess it or to be fond of want and privation, as other brethren of the Venerable Third Order boasted of being, brethren as little humble and as little poverty-stricken as the Lord High Constable of Castile, Don Juan Fernández de Velasco, and Lope de Vega himself, who were also professed Tertiaries. When he took his vows Cervantes drew closer to Sancho Panza in his recognition of the vanity and emptiness of life. Who knows if in his secret soul he did not sometimes answer himself with Don Quixote's own words?

For it is certain that occasionally he could feel strength being reborn in his breast and he even opened a small window to hope. In one of those moments of relative happiness his imagination turned toward his beloved Naples and the figure of the Count of Lemos came to mind, for he knew that disillusionments had started to dismay and overwhelm him also, and then the almost moribund old man, sitting up in bed with the greatest effort, mastering all his pain and distress, dictated or wrote the golden page that sets forth his last thoughts so well. It is the dedication of the *Persiles* and in it Cervantes put all that was most noble in his grateful soul, repaying with unprecedented usury the favors he owed the Count of Lemos.

Those ancient couplets which were famous in their day, that begin "with my foot already in the stirrup," I would have wished were not so opportune in this letter of mine, for I can begin it with almost the identical words, saying:

With my foot already in the stirrup,
with the anguish of death upon me,
noble lord, I write this to you.

Yesterday I received extreme unction and I write this today. Time is short, anguish increases, hopes dwindle, and in spite of all this I cling to life because of the desire I have to live and I would like my life prolonged until I could kiss the feet of Your Excellency, and it might be that such would be the joy of seeing Your Excellency safely back in Spain that it would give me new life. But if it is decreed that I must lose it, may the will of Heaven be done, and at least Your Excellency may know of this my desire and know that in me you have a servant so dedicated to your service that he would wish to go even further than death to show his devotion. With all this, even if it lies in the realm of prophecy, I would be delighted by the arrival of Your Excellency, I would rejoice to see you pointed out and further rejoice that my hopes turned out to be true and even enhanced by report of the generosities of Your Excellency. There still remain in my mind certain vestiges and tokens of the *Weeks in the Garden* and of the famous *Bernardo*. If by chance, by my good luck, which would not be luck but a miracle, Heaven were to give me life, you shall see them, and with them the end of the *Galatea* which I know Your Excellency likes, and I want to carry on with those works. God keep Your Excellency, as he may. From Madrid, on the nineteenth of April of one thousand and six hundred and sixteen years.

Your Excellency's servant,
Miguel de Cervantes.

Miguel wrote those lines four days before his death. In them he provided a synthesis of his thinking about life, of which he, like all the great geniuses who lead humanity, had been a faithful and obedient lover. Those words written face to face with death incorporate the supreme philosophy Miguel inherited with the Cordovan blood, half Seneca, half Muslim, of his grandfather Licentiate Juan de Cervantes. "I cling to life because of the desire I have to live," he says, in a moment of quixotic hope . . . and a second later he says as Arabs would, "but if it is decreed that I must lose it . . ." and he adds as they and Seneca would, "may the will of Heaven be done." In the last days of his life these two opposite tendencies mark the fundamental equilibrium of his superhuman spirit. With reason the movement of the spirit has been compared with that of a well-balanced pendulum, but there are few souls who, close to the very end of life and struggling against the agonizing transition to death, can maintain the marvellous flexibility found in Miguel's last words.

His last four days must have been torment. The difficult and stertorous breathing characteristic of cardiac patients wracked that aged breast. The poor dying man sat up in bed supported by four or five bolsters and pillows. The wide forehead which had always been a mirror of light was fading, turning dull; his pale aquiline nose became more hooked, prehensile, seeking the mouth; the martial moustaches drooped dispiritedly in the final abandonment of the whole struggle. One last shudder, one last *pneuma* or mysterious exhalation from the mouth and nose, a gentle, slow inclining of the head upon the chest signalled the end. The Ingenious Hidalgo was dead. It was the twenty-third of April, 1616.

At the foot of the bed Doña Constanza de Figueroa, Doña Isabel de Saavedra and Doña Catalina de Salazar were sobbing and the good clergyman Don Francisco Martínez Marcilla was praying. The news soon spread through the neighborhood. Many people entered to look at the corpse and from the meeting place of the actors all the players came to see the sprightly writer and delight of the Muses lying dead. Lope de Vega, his neighbor from across the street, also entered, looked at the corpse and prayed a while before he went out, pensively shaking his head.

Later the Tertiary Brothers of St. Francis came, clothed their brother in religion in the habit of the V.O.T. and placed him in the coffin. Since the route of the funeral was to be short, only a few steps from Cervantes' house to the Convent of the Trinitarians, the people of the neighborhood and the actors filled the narrow street completely. The Tertiary Brothers then took the coffin up on their shoulders, the face of the corpse uncovered as the rules of the V.O.T. require.

Behind the coffin walked some rich folk, grandees of Spain and men of title in the Kingdom whom it pleased to attend humble burials and thus display their stainless piety in public. Among them, between marquises and counts, perhaps in the company of his new patron, the Duke of Sessa, the clergyman Lope de Vega Carpio showed off his beautiful sacerdotal habit, the cross of St. John on his breast. Two modest poets of whom little was known save that they admired the dead man followed the funeral procession: Luis Francisco Calderón and Don Francisco de Urbina, a kinsman of the secretary Juan.

The interment at the Convent of the Trinitarians was poor and unceremonious. Earth covered the body of the Ingenious Hidalgo; red bricks covered the grave. No tombstone or inscription of any kind was placed on it, not even a humble glazed tile. We do not know where the body of Cervantes lies, or if anything remains of it.

We also do not know what happened to the manuscripts of *Bernardo* and *The Weeks in the Garden*, of the play *More Than Meets the Eye* or the Second Part of *La Galatea*. The small respect the wife of Cervantes deserves from us is further diminished when we consider the lack of care she showed in collecting her husband's manuscripts, for doubtless after he was dead she held to the narrow standards of a village family and regarded all these things as libidinous and lunatic. A year after the death of her husband, however, Doña Catalina sold the copyright of the *Persiles* to Villarroel. The sum that he gave the widow was the first and probably the only money that Doña Catalina received from the literary works of her husband.

And having arrived at this point nothing important remains for the biographer to relate. Let the philosopher and the critic speak now, for they have more than enough material to discuss. The narrator, parodying thereby the ancient colophons of many books, can now only write at the end of this one the sacramental words:

FINITO LIBRO, SIT LAUS ET GLORIA
MICHAELI CERVANTES
FINIS

Madrid, January/February of 1905.

APPENDIX 1

Works of Miguel de Cervantes

Title		*Published*
Galatea (*La Galatea*)		1585
Early Plays		
Life in Algiers (*El trato de Argel*)	(printed in 1784)	
Numantia (*La Numancia*)	(printed in 1784)	
Battle of Lepanto (*La batalla naval*)		1584
The Perplexed Lady (*La confusa*)		1587
The High-spirited Arsinda (*La bizarra Arsinda*)		
Don Quixote (*El ingenioso hidalgo Don Quixote de la Mancha*)		
Part One		1605
Part Two		1615
Exemplary Novels (*Novelas ejemplares*)		1613
The Little Gypsy (*La gitanilla*)		
The Generous Lover (*El amante liberal*)		
Rinconete and Cortadillo (*Rinconete y Cortadillo*)		
The Anglo-Spanish Lady (*La española inglese*)		
The Glass Licentiate (*El licenciado Vidriera*)		
The Power of Blood (*La fuerza de la sangre*)		
The Jealous Estremaduran (*El celoso extremeño*)		
The Illustrious Kitchen-maid (*La ilustre fregona*)		
The Two Maidens (*Las dos doncellas*)		
Lady Cornelia (*La señora Cornelia*)		
The Fraudulent Marriage (*El casamiento engañoso*)		
Dialogue Between Scipio and Berganza (*Coloquio que pasó entre Cipión y Berganza*) sometimes rendered as *The Dialogue of the Dogs* (*El coloquio de los perros*)		
The Pretended Aunt (*La tia fingida*) not established		
Journey to Parnassus (*Viaje del Parnaso*)		1614
Addendum to the Parnassus (*Adjunta al Parnaso*)		

Title	*Published*
Eight Plays and Eight New Interludes (*Ocho comedias y ocho entremeses nuevos*)	1615
Plays (*comedias*)	
The Prisons of Algiers (*Los baños de Argel*)	
The Great Sultana (*La gran sultana Doña Catalina de Oviedo*)	
The Gallant Spaniard (*El gallardo español*)	
The Labyrinth of Love (*El laberinto de amor*)	
The House of Jealousy and Forest of Arden (*La casa de los celos y selvas de Ardenia*)	
The Fortunate Procurer (*El rufián dichoso*)	
Pedro de Urdemalas (*Pedro de Urdemalas*)	
The Link (*La entretenida*)	
Interludes (*entremeses*)	
The Election of the Magistrates of Daganzo (*La elección de los alcaldes de Daganzo*)	
The Widowed Procurer (*El rufián viudo*)	
The Divorce Judge (*El juez de los divorcios*)	
The Miraculous Reredo (*El retablo de las maravillas*)	
The Cave of Salamanca (*La cueva de Salamanca*)	
The Counterfeit Biscayan (*El vizcaino fingido*)	
The Vigilant Guardian (*La guarda cuidadosa*)	
The Jealous Old Man (*El viejo celoso*)	
The Trials of Persiles and Sigismunda (*Los trabajos de Persiles y Sigismunda*)	1617

Unpublished and probably uncompleted works:

More Than Meets the Eye (*El engaño á los ojos*)
The Weeks in the Garden (*Las semanas del jardín*)
Bernardo
Galatea, Part Two

APPENDIX 2

Spanish Currency and Taxation in the Sixteenth Century

Currency

The Spanish monetary system of the sixteenth century was organized by Ferdinand and Isabella in a pragmatic of 1497 which reduced the chaotic Castilian coinage to a semblance of order, but it was still somewhat complicated and unstable in terms of both real values and the relationships between different units of value. An important factor in this was the inflow of gold and silver from America, particularly the flood of silver toward the end of the century. Another was the deficit financing of heavy expenditures by Charles V and Philip II on their diplomatic and military adventures abroad. The result of these and other developments was a disastrous inflation that raised price-levels four-fold during the century, leading to progressive debasement of the currency and a sharp rise in the cost of living. This was accompanied by increasingly confiscatory taxation and strenuous efforts to extract the last maravedi from the unfortunate taxpayer. In this biography all of these developments are referred to from time to time.

Maravedis are often mentioned by Cervantes and his biographer. These started out as small copper coins but later became a money of account.

Reals were widely circulated small silver coins roughly akin to the English sixpence of the same period in the way they were used. They were eventually debased to copper *reales de vellón* containing a small fraction of silver. The real was equivalent to 34 maravedis in the internal monetary system.

Ducats were originally gold coins taken over by the Catholic Kings as the basis of the currency system, but after 1534 the ducat became a money of account valued at 11 reals or 375 maravedis. (Cervantes' contract with Osorio in Chapter 35 called for payment at the rate of 50 ducats "which are" 550 reals.)

Escudos were coined from 1534 to replace gold ducats and were worth 8s.6d. at par of exchange. Originally equivalent to 330 maravedis in the internal system, after 1566 they were calculated at 400 and after 1609 at 440 maravedis. The Spanish doubloons of the seventeenth century were gold coins representing various multiples of the escudo, the most famous being the *doblones de a ocho* or "pieces of eight" in pirate lore. They represented eight escudos and weighed one ounce Troy weight.

Crowns were gold coins equivalent in value to escudos which circulated from ancient times to the end of the seventeenth century.

The *dobla*, known in the Middle Ages as *peso de oro* or *castellano*, was another circulating gold coin worth 12s.6d. at par of exchange. Under the Catholic Kings it was reckoned at 490 maravedis or 14 reals and 14 maravedis, but it rose in relative value over the century to 544 and again to 576 maravedis.

Besides these there was a heavy *vellón* coinage of progressively debased copper-silver alloy in varying proportions circulating in various units of value, of which the biography mentions only the *cuarto*. This coin, calculated as equivalent to 4 maravedis, circulated for a time and eventually disappeared. The manner of its use in daily life made it the Spanish cousin of the English penny, as the *ochavo* of 2 maravedis was a ha'penny.

The ransom of Cervantes negotiated by Fray Juan Gil in Chapter 24 is difficult to calculate in view of the multiplicity of currencies involved, some confusion in terminology as between ducats and escudos, and the unstable monetary relationships of the period. However, taking the ducat of 375 maravedis as our money of account, we can start with the 1,077 reals or nearly 100 ducats that Doña Leonor had collected in Chapter 22, and we can assume that Doña Andrea contributed another 200 ducats. (The King's contribution of two years before had gone to ransom Cervantes' brother Rodrigo.) The 100 doblas provided by the Order of Trinity represented perhaps 130 ducats and Miguel's banker friends are said to have loaned him 220 ducats. The total sum available to Fray Juan Gil in various currencies therefore came to 650 ducats, but we can speculate that a heavy premium had to be paid to get together 500 Castilian escudos in gold from various sources in Algiers. The Order paid for the homeward passages of Cervantes and his friends, but if there was any money left over it is not mentioned.

As for the ransom itself, if we take 500 gold escudos at a par of exchange of 8s.6d., it would appear that this sum was equivalent to over $1,000, which in those days was a great deal of money in any currency.

Taxation

In this biography there are only a few indirect references to the burden of taxation borne by the Spanish people under Charles V and Philip II. A multiplicity of levies (*servicios*) legislated by the Cortes was progressively supplemented by sales of privileges, arbitrary confiscations, and eventual resort to bankers for loans (*juros*) at high rates of interest. Throughout the period, however, the Crown could count on two forms of taxation inherited from the past and requiring no legislative approval. Early in the century they accounted for perhaps 80 percent of the royal revenues, although at the end they became less important relatively as other sources of income were tapped. These were the taxes which Cervantes sought to collect in Granada in Chapter 38.

1. The *tercias reales* (royal thirds) represented one-third of the tithes paid to the Church; a papal bull of 1494 vested them perpetually in the Crown as a form of Vatican support for the Catholic Kings.

2. The *alcabala* was a 10 percent sales tax of the value-added variety, borrowed from the Moors and introduced in 1342. Its great virtue was that it was levied on all classes, including the high nobility, the clergy, and the hidalgos, groups often exempted from other forms of taxation, while it took the needs of the poor into account by exempting bread, wheat imported by sea, and a brief list of other necessities. This tax was very productive, and generations of Castilian rulers clung to it for that reason. It was difficult to collect, however, and Ferdinand permitted towns and tax districts to "compound" the tax by assessed lump-sum payments (*encabezamiento*), leaving their collection from individuals to local administrations, where the right to extort them was usually auctioned off to tax contractors. The assessments established by Ferdinand were raised periodically, to four-fold by the time of Philip II, who found it necessary to reduce them by 25 percent when Medina del Campo and other trade centers were being put out of business.

APPENDIX 3

Bibliographical Notes

His contemporaries saw little reason to write about Cervantes, and the few clues to his life history that survived him, other than those contained in his own works, were the dry stuff of official records, payrolls, court cases, wills and the like, but they were immured in Spanish archives until a few inquisitive spirits began to turn over those bundles of yellowing paper. As it was, more than two hundred years elapsed after the death of Cervantes before Navarrete was able to publish in 1819 a biography which included for the first time a documented account of Miguel's military service and captivity derived from the Archives of the Indies in Seville.

During the rest of the nineteenth century Spanish and British "Cervantists" unearthed further details which they published in literary journals or monographs, and were turning with some success to the writings of Cervantes himself. In addition to clearly autobiographical matter, close analysis suggests that many passages in his works were actually drawn from his life experience. All of this was incorporated into progressively expanded histories based on a growing number of established facts, although many gaps remained. The search for additional documents regarding Cervantes and his family was continued in the twentieth century by Rodriguez Marín (1947) and Astrana Marín (1948–57), who appear to have exhausted the field.

At best, therefore, every biographer of Cervantes has been limited to assembling and interpreting such facts as were available at the time of writing, facts establishing little more than that "Cervantes was here." These have stood like checkpoints in a cross-country auto rally between which travelers find their way as best they can. As each writer endeavored to introduce something new into his work his speculations often differed considerably from those of others, leading to many a literary squabble.

The attached tabulation lists most of the full-length biographies of Cervantes and the more important collections of documents concerning him and his family. More of these works are in Spanish than other languages, naturally—about twice as many as in English. The Spanish, British, and American scholars who have translated or annotated the *Quixote* and other writings, it appears, were often moved to give some account of their author, while every strictly biographical approach to

Cervantes is inevitably combined in greater or less degree with discussion of his works.

Literary interest in Spain's premier writer and one of the world's greatest has continued unabated into the twentieth century, during which twice as many biographies of Cervantes have already been published as in the two previous centuries combined. While a few of these are the work of scholars there has been a definite trend toward what might be termed "popular" biography, with novelists now taking over from the savants.

Navarro Ledesma's work stands somewhere between the two extremes. It is too imaginative and too indifferent to scholarly apparatus to be wholly acceptable to the pedestrian biographers of the past; it is too faithful to Cervantes and his sixteenth-century Spanish background to be dismissed as no more than a romantic tale. In the body of literature about Cervantes, taken as a whole, this book represents a turning point at which the preoccupations of the pedants were left behind and new life was infused into the story.

Biographies of Cervantes

This list was made up from a variety of sources, including the catalogues of the New York Public Library and the New York Society Library, the bibliographies attached to various biographies of Cervantes, the 1964 edition of *Diccionario de Literatura Española*, Revista de Occidente, Madrid, and other miscellaneous records. It does not claim to be exhaustive but it surely includes every work of any importance.

Spanish Language

Eighteenth Century

1737 Mayans y Siscar, Gregorio (1699–1781), *Vida de Miguel de Cervantes, natural de Madrid*, Briga-Real, Madrid, 1737, 104 pp. Reprinted in Madrid, 1750. This was the first biography of Cervantes, completely superseded by later scholarship.

1778 Pellicer, Juan Antonio (1738–1806), *Noticias literarias para la vida de Cervantes,* Madrid, 1778. Pellicer followed up clues provided by Martin Sarmiento (1691–1770) in his MS. *Noticia de la verdadera patria de Cervantes* to report for the first time on the records of Cervantes' baptism and marriage, uncovered in Alcalá in 1752, and on some details of his early life.

1800 Pellicer, Juan Antonio (1738–1806), *Vida de Miguel de Cervantes Saavedra*, Madrid, 1800, 264 pp. This was originally prefaced to Pellicer's 1797–98 edition of the *Quixote* and was the first to hint at the rivalry between Cervantes and Lope de Vega.

Nineteenth Century

1819 Navarrete, Martín Fernández de (1765–1844), *Vida de Miguel de Cervantes Saavedra*, Imprenta Real, Madrid, 1819, 643 pp. This gave for the first time details of Cervantes' military service and captivity based on documents discovered in 1808 in the archives in Seville. Navarrete was the original author to send Cervantes to Rome in the train of Monsignor Aquaviva. Republished in Barcelona, 1834, 494 pp., and in Madrid, 1866.

1863 Morán, Jerónimo, *Vida de Miguel de Cervantes Saavedra*, Imprenta Nacional, Madrid, 1863, 223 pp. This biography broke the story of Cervantes' alleged flight to Rome as a fugitive from justice.

1876 Máinez, Ramón León, *Vida de Cervantes,* Cádiz, 1876, 400 pp.

1878 Díaz de Benjumes, Nicolás (1829–84), *La verdad sobre el Quixote. Novísima historia critica de la vida de Cervantes*, Madrid, 1878, 343 pp.

1892 Lizcano y Ataminos, Francisco, *Historia de la verdadera cuna de Miguel de Cervantes Saavedra*, Madrid, 1892, 464 pp.

1897 Pérez Pastor, Cristóbal (1833–1908), *Documentos cervantinos hasta ahora inéditos*, Madrid, 1897 and 1901, 2 vols.

Twentieth Century

1902 Asensio y Toledo, José María, *Cervantes y sus obras*, Barcelona, 1902. Republished, Barcelona, 1946, 563 pp.

1905 Navarro Ledesma, Francisco (1869–1905), *El ingenioso hidalgo Miguel de Cervantes Saavedra*, Madrid, 1905, 608 pp. Prepared to mark the tercentenary of the first edition of the *Quixote*. Second edition, Madrid, 1915. Republished in Madrid in 1944 and in Buenos Aires in 1947.

1915 Montoliú, Manuel, *Vida de Cervantes*, Barcelona, 1915.

1916 Oliver, Miguel de los Santos, *Vida y semblaza de Cervantes*, Barcelona, 1916, 367 pp. Republished in Barcelona, 1947, 282 pp.

1916 Bonilla y San Martín, Adolfo (1875–1926), *Cervantes y su obra*, Madrid, 1916, 262 pp. The author collaborated with Rudolph Schevill to edit the complete works of Cervantes.

1917 Savj-López, Paolo, *Cervantes*, translated from the Italian by Antonio G. Solalinde, Madrid, 1917, 247 pp.

1933 Tomás, Mariano (1891–1957), *Vida y desventuras de Miguel de Cervantes*, Barcelona, 1933.

1939 Cassou, Jean (1897–), *Cervantes*, translated from the French and published in Mexico, 1939, 244 pp.

1943 Espina García, Antonio, *Cervantes*, Madrid, 1943, 158 pp.

1945 Arbó, Sebastián Juan (1902–), *Cervantes*, Barcelona, 1945, 600 pp. This work by a novelist has gone to a third revised edition in Spanish (438 pp.) and has been abridged and translated into Italian, German, French and English (London and New York).

1947 Rodriguez Marín, Francisco (1855–1943), *Estudios cervantinos*, Madrid, 1947, 656 pp. This culminated and summarized his work over the years since 1905.

1948 Herrero García, Miguel (1885–1962), *Vida de Cervantes*, Madrid, 1948, 649 pp.

1957 Astrana Marín, Luis (1889–1960), *Vida ejemplar y heroica de Miguel de Cervantes*, Madrid, 7 vols. 1948–57. This monumental work undertook to exhaust the field of Cervantes documentation.

1965 Motta Salas, Julián, *Vida del principe de los ingenios, Miguel de Cervantes Saavedra*, Mexico, 1965, 430 pp.

1967 Cabezas, Juan Antonio (1900–), *Cervantes del mito al hombre*, Madrid, 1967, 456 pp. Novelist-journalist-biographer Cabezas draws on Rodriguez Marín and Astrana Marín for material regarding the Cervantes grandfather in Cordova and Miguel's childhood, the history of Ana Franca, and similar details. Cabezas has an affectionate regard for Navarro Ledesma, referring some twenty times to his work.

English Language

Eighteenth Century

1738 Mayans y Siscar, Gregorio (1699–1781), *The Life of Miguel de Cervantes Saavedra*, translated from the Spanish by Mr. Azell, London, 1738, 103 pp. This was included in Jarvis' 1742 translation of the *Quixote*.

1781 Bowle, John (1725–88), author of an annotated English translation of the *Quixote*, published a biography of Cervantes in *The Gentleman's Magazine*, London, 1781.

Nineteenth Century

1839 Roscoe, Thomas, *The Life and Writings of Miguel de Cervantes Saavedra*, London, 1839.

1863 Edwards, Amelia Blandford (1831–92), *The Story of Cervantes*, London, 1863, 240 pp.

1888 Watts, Henry Edward (1826–1904), *Life of Cervantes*, in his English translation of the *Quixote*, London, 1888, pp. 31-255. Published as *The Life of Miguel de Cervantes*, London, 1891, 291 pp. Republished in a revised edition as *Miguel de Cervantes, his Life and Works*, London, 1895, 240 pp.

1892 Fitzmaurice-Kelly, James (1858–1923), *The Life of Miguel Cervantes Saavedra*, London, 1892, 396 pp.

Twentieth Century

1908 Smith, Robinson, *The Life of Cervantes*, London, 1908, 121 pp. A fifth edition was published by the Hispanic Society of New York in 1932.

1919 Schevill, Rudolph (1874–1946), *Cervantes,* University of California, 1919, 330 pp. Published in New York, 1919, 388 pp. and republished in 1966. The author edited the complete works of Cervantes in collaboration with Bonilla y San Martin.

1927 Ner, Jacques Élie Henri Amboise (1861–1938) used the pseudonym Hans Ryner. His biography of Cervantes was translated from the French by J. H. Lewis as *The Ingenious Hidalgo: Miguel Cervantes*, New York, 1927, 243 pp.

1931 Ybarra, T. R., *Cervantes*, New York, 1931, 260 pp.

1934 Tomás, Mariano (1891–1957), translated from the Spanish by Warre B. Wells as *The Life and Misadventures of Miguel de Cervantes*, Boston, 1934, 255 pp.

1935 Frank, Bruno (1887–1945), translated from the German by H. F. Lowe-Porter as *A Man Called Cervantes*, New York, 1935, 301 pp.

1940 Entwhistle, William J. (1895–), *Cervantes*, Oxford: Clarendon Press, 1940, 192 pp.

1947 Bell, Aubrey F. G. (1881–1950), *Cervantes*, University of Oklahoma, 1947, 256 pp.

1955 Arbó, Sebastián Juan (1902–), translated from the Spanish and abridged by Else Barea as *Cervantes, the Man and his Time*, New York, 1955, 261 pp.

Other Languages

French

1930 Lyonnet, Henry, *Cervantes*, Paris, 1930.

1936 Cassou, Jean, *Cervantes*, Paris, 1936, 244 pp.

German

1934 Frank, Bruno, *Cervantes, Ein Roman*, Amsterdam, 1934, 367 pp.

1947 Schörr, Friedrich, *Cervantes, Leben und Werk des Grossen Humoristen*, Berne, 1947. Republished, 1963.

1949 Ruegg, August, *Miguel de Cervantes und sein Don Quixote*, Berne, 1949, 487 pp.

1966 Krauss, Werner, *Miguel de Cervantes: Leben und Werk*, Berlin, 1966, 253 pp.

Italian

1913 Savj-López, Paolo, *Cervantes*, Naples, 1913, 247 pp.

Notes

Chapter 1

1. An important university town about twenty miles from Madrid, to which the University was eventually removed. Cardinal Cisneros founded this institution in 1508 and its faculty included some of the greatest scholars in Europe, while its student body approached five thousand in the sixteenth century.

2. Francisco Ximénez de Cisneros (1436–1517), Cardinal Archbishop of Toledo (1495–1517), rose to prominence under Ferdinand and Isabella and served as regent after the death of Ferdinand in 1516 until Emperor Charles V came to the throne of Spain in 1517.

3. This drinking song in macaronic Latin translates roughly as: "Hail, the clear color of wine, / Hail, its unequalled flavor / you get us drunk / your famous potency."

4. The *gaudeamus* recommends having a good time while still young.

5. This was a revolt (1519–20) against the new Emperor by a number of the cities of Castile because of his Flemish affiliations and his threat to their ancient privileges.

6. Juan Martínez Silíceo (1486–1557), Cardinal Archbishop of Toledo (1546–57), great scholar and tutor to Prince Philip, taught his royal pupil Latin, French and Italian, making him notably proficient in Latin.

7. This was the *Biblia Políglota Complutense* (Complutum was the Roman name for Alcalá), commissioned by Cardinal Cisneros, who recruited for this purpose a cadre of eminent scholars who also served as members of the University faculty. Work started in 1502 and the six volumes were printed by Brocar between 1514 and 1517. The Old Testament was presented in parallel Greek, Latin, Hebrew, and Aramaic texts in four volumes; the New Testament was in Greek and Latin; the sixth volume contained an index, a Hebrew-Aramaic vocabulary, and a Hebrew grammar. The Greek text of the New Testament was the first to be printed in Europe and the Old Testament was the standard Hebrew text for two centuries.

8. Benito Arias Montano (1527–98), confessor to Philip II, renowned Orientalist and theologian on the faculty at Alcalá, was a great linguist and profound student of the Scriptures.

9. Charles V defeated the German Protestant princes of the Smalkadelic League in the battle of Mühlberg (April 24, 1547). His victory led in 1548 to the Diet of Augsburg, in the course of which the "Augsburg Interim" in the struggle between Protestant and Catholic powers was negotiated.

10. This was a plot against Andrea Doria, the Emperor's vassal in Genoa, engineered by Giovanni Luigi Fiesco, a Genoese nobleman, in the course of a factional feud. Fiesco was supported by Pier Luigi Farnese, Duke of Parma, who was assassinated on September 10, 1547, possibly with the knowledge and consent of the Emperor.

11. Spanish universities of the sixteenth century granted degrees of Bachelor, Licentiate, and Doctor. A Bachelor had to study for six years, a Licentiate

("licensed" to teach) for four years more, and a Doctor had to prepare and defend a thesis. The title "Licentiate" was popularly applied to any University scholar and to all lawyers.

12. This house has been identified as No. 2 Calle de Imagen, but only traces of the original structure remain.

13. The Latin phrase *Deo gratias* (thanks to God) was an expression used in those days upon entering a house.

14. The real (pronounced *re-al*) was a widely circulated silver coin. See Appendix 2 for this and other Spanish coins of the time—maravedi, cuarto, escudo, etc.

15. Navarro Ledesma has little to say about Miguel's Cordovan grandfather, a lawyer by profession, who pursued a controversial career in politics as an Assistant Corregidor in half a dozen cities of Castile, including five years in Alcalá where his congenitally deaf son Rodrigo was born.

Chapter 2

1. In other words, "It's all Greek to me."

2. Orán was captured in 1531 by Spanish troops led by Cardinal Cisneros and Don Álvaro de Bazán. It was held as a Spanish outpost in North Africa until the eighteenth century.

3. Cervantes mentions in one of his novels that the student body at Alcalá included two thousand medical students, more than could hope to find employment as physicians.

4. The nation was patched together when Aragón and Castile were united in 1475 under Ferdinand and Isabella, dubbed "the Catholic Kings" by the Pope.

5. This was a crossroads town between Valladolid and Segovia, the site of so-called "fairs" to which merchants and bankers came from all over Europe; it was a mercantile and financial center of European importance in the sixteenth century.

6. This term applies to the thousands of lyrico-narrative poems, of which the older ones were sung by minstrels in the fourteenth and fifteenth centuries or circulated in manuscript copies. Many of them were collected and printed at various times during the early sixteenth century in anthologies devoted to legendary heroes.

7. The names listed are those of sixteenth century military leaders as against heroes in Spanish epics and the annals of knight-errantry.

8. The ailing and bankrupt Emperor Charles V abdicated the Imperial throne to his brother Ferdinand and bequeathed the rest of his realm, including Spain, the Netherlands, Milan, Naples, and Sicily, to his son Philip. The Emperor departed Brussels in 1556 for the Hieronymite Convent of Yuste and spent the rest of his life in a nearby dwelling.

9. In those days the term "leprosy" was often applied to the irritating mange or itch from which nearly everyone suffered.

10. This discussion of Latin tags and "whoever it was that said it" comes from the Prologue to Part I of the *Quixote*. The quotations have no particular significance, since Ovid is speaking of the pleasure of having many friends, while Aesop disapproved of selling freedom for money.

11. *Amadís de Gaula* was a chivalresque novel by Garcia Ordóñez de Montalvo, published about 1508, often reprinted and avidly read in Spain. It was probably derived from a lost Portuguese original.

12. Traditionally Saints Ignatius and Teresa both read books on knight-errantry

when young, and Teresa confesses in her autobiography that she contemplated writing one.

13. The Squire of the Sea was an epithet for Amadís.

Chapter 3

1. The Escorial is part mausoleum for the Emperor and his descendants, part royal residence reflecting Philip's interest in his books and his pictures, and part the church and monastery of San Lorenzo (Saint Lawrence) that the King had vowed to build in memory of the saint on whose name-day (August 10, 1557) Spanish troops had wiped out a French army at St. Quentin. The ground-plan of this complex is reminiscent of the gridiron on which the saint was martyred.

2. In Chapter 14 of Part Two of the *Quixote* Cervantes mentions "that famous giantess of Seville known as La Giralda," presumably referring to the four-meter bronze statute of a woman bearing a palmleaf placed on top of the belfry of Seville Cathedral in 1568. Cervantes implies that the statue is a weathervane and the word *giralda* in Spanish means a weathervane in the form of a statue.

3. The Company or Society of Jesus, i.e., the Jesuit Order, was founded in 1534 by Saint Ignatius of Loyola, a soldier turned priest, as an expression of militant Christianity and one aspect of the Counterreformation. It was recognized by the Pope in 1540 and during the sixteenth century the Jesuits were active as preachers, teachers, philosophers, historians and men of letters.

4. Francis Borgia (d. 1572), Marquis of Lombay and Duke of Gandia, was a Catalan nobleman who became a Jesuit in 1548. In 1565 he was elected General of the Order and served for seven years while it was expanding rapidly. He was canonized in 1671.

5. Doctor Constantino Pérez de la Fuente, a member of the cosmopolitan humanist circle around the Emperor Charles V, was a victim of the Inquisition's "discovery" in 1557 of Protestant communities in Seville and Valladolid, a discovery to which there was a horrified reaction.

6. This is one of twelve short "novels" by Cervantes listed in Appendix 1 as *Exemplary Novels*, so called because each of them was supposed to point a moral. They were written at various times over the years but remained in manuscript until they were assembled and printed in 1613. Many quotations from them appear in this work, as do references to the plays also listed in the Appendix.

7. The "teacher Nebrija" refers to Antonio Martínez de Cala (1444–1522), who was called Antonio de Lebrija or Nebrija from his birthplace. Humanist and Latinist, he studied at Bologna and as a Professor at Salamanca he is credited with reforming the teaching of Latin in Spain through his often reprinted *Introducciones latinas* (1481) and his *Vocabulario latinoespañol* (1492). He also wrote the first Spanish grammar in 1492.

8. The *Colegio-Universidad de Santa María de Jésus* was founded in the latter half of the fifteenth century by Rodrigo Fernández de Santaella, author of a Latin lexicon. It was an educational institution of somewhat lower rank than a full-scale university.

9. Garcilaso de la Vega (1503–36) was a young nobleman who attended the Emperor's Court where he shone as a musician and became an outstanding lyric poet who altered the whole style of Spanish poetry by bringing in Italian influences. He served in the Imperial armies before Vienna and in Tunis, but was killed in a minor skirmish in Provence during an unsuccessful Spanish invasion of France.

10. Fernando de Herrera (1534–97), a cleric of Seville, was a great lyric poet,

particularly famous for his love poems inspired by the hopeless passion described in the text.

11. Quoted from a sonnet written by Cervantes on the death of Herrera.

Chapter 4

1. *Compás* here refers to a district or area assigned to a monastery or convent, more or less analogous to a cathedral close in England. In other usages it is an urban district of any kind.

2. The *Audience* was a court of justice administered in the name of the local feudal lord, who appointed its judges and maintained its own prison for the punishment of wrongdoers, all quite independently of the municipal government. Hence the enmity.

3. The *sambenito*, a yellow robe decorated with scarlet flames, was worn in religious processions by confessed heretics convicted by the Inquisition.

4. Lope de Rueda (1505–65), a gold-beater by trade, became a famous playwright and actor-manager, as described in the text. The quotations about him in this chapter come from Cervantes' Prologue to his *Eight Plays*.

5. Cervantes quoted this verse in his play *The Prisons of Algiers*.

6. *Paso* was the term used by Lope de Rueda to describe his farces in which comic episodes were introduced in dramatic situations.

7. The *entremés*, or interlude, of which many were written by the authors of the time, was a short comic piece presented between the acts of a play. It was so designated to distinguish it from Lope de Rueda's *paso*.

Chapter 5

1. Saint Teresa de Jesús (1515–82) became a Carmelite nun in Avila in 1534 and in 1562 founded her first reformed convent. Her plans for reorganizing the Carmelites were opposed by civil and religious authority, including that of the Inquisition, but she persisted in establishing new convents, traveling widely in Spain for that purpose. She was an outstanding writer of several famous mystical works, and of a less important guide for the behavior of the nuns of her Order.

2. The Carmelite Order was originally a sect of hermits established in 1156 on the slopes of Mount Carmel (near present-day Haifa). Their Rule was written 1206–14 by their leader Brocardo. After the fall of Jerusalem in 1244 they moved to Europe and became a mendicant Order which expanded rapidly, incorporating nuns from 1452, and was reorganized into Calced (shod) and Discalced (unshod) Carmelites. Saint Teresa broke away to bring nuns and eventually friars under a strict Primitive Rule of Poverty.

3. Pedro Calderón de la Barca (1600–81), Jesuit priest and Chaplain of the Court, belongs to a generation later than Cervantes. He was the leading playwright of his time in Spain, a prolific writer of religious, historical, mythological, and philosophical plays. He was associated particularly with the drama of "cape and sword" and was also famous for the *autos sacramentales* described in Note 3, Chapter 36.

4. Father Aliaga was the King's confessor at the time.

5. The *Retiro* was and is to Madrid what Central Park is to New York.

Chapter 6

1. *Diana* was the principal work of Jorge de Montemayor (1520–1561) which established the pastoral novel in Castilian literature.

2. *Betis* was the ancient name for the Guadalquivir River, derived from *Bética*, the traditional father of Andalusia.

3. Don Carlos was spending some time in Alcalá, reputedly for his health, and studying at the university with Alexander Farnese and Don Juan de Austria, his uncle, when he suffered the fall described in the text, pitching down the "staircase of Tenorio." This expression presumably refers to *Don Juan Tenorio*, the immensely popular play by José Zorilla which first appeared in 1844 and has been shown repeatedly on the Spanish stage. It presents the whole repertory of duels and seductions associated with the ancient theme of Don Juan and this allusion to it implies that Don Carlos was following in the footsteps of Don Juan.

4. The *Theatin* monks formed a religious order founded in 1525 by the Archbishop of Chieti (later Pope Paul IV), the ancient name of Chieti being Teate. It was organized to combine the contemplative life of monks with the active duties of the secular clergy in preaching, teaching and visiting the sick.

5. Juan López de Hoyos (?–1583) was a parish priest and teacher of humanities in the Latin School of Madrid. His 1569 volume on the death of the Queen included six short poems by Cervantes, accompanied by the affectionate words of his teacher.

Chapter 7

1. The Italian epic poem *Orlando furioso* by Luis Ariosto (1474–1533) was translated by several Spanish writers and widely read in Spain.

2. Lucan, or Marcus Annaeus Lucanus (A.D. 39–65), wrote the *Bellum Civile*, better known as the *Pharsalia*, a rhetorical epic poem about the struggle between Caesar and Pompey.

3. Many writers, including some biographers of Cervantes, have written extensively about the fate of Don Carlos, allegedly imprisoned in the Palace and harshly treated by his father, if not actually poisoned or murdered.

4. Fray Luis de León (1527–91), Augustinian friar, scholar and humanist, was one of the great mystics, along with Saint Teresa and Saint John of the Cross, and also one of Spain's most distinguished lyric poets.

Chapter 8

1. Cardinal Espinosa (1502–70) used his great influence with the King to moderate the initial severities of the Inquisition and oppose the ruthless policies of the Duke of Alba in Flanders.

2. The poetry of Luis de León was not printed until 1631, when Quevedo published a collection.

3. Luis de León was jailed by the Inquisition for his attitude toward the Old Testament and for translating the Song of Solomon into Castilian verses. He was imprisoned for nearly five years before being brought to trial, cleared and released. While in prison he wrote his greatest mystical work, *The Names of Christ* (*Les nombres de Cristo*), first published in 1583.

4. Arms versus letters as paths to glory are mentioned several times in this biography as well as in Part One of the *Quixote*, Chapter 38.

5. *Persiles* is used here and elsewhere as an abridgement of *The Trials of Persiles and Sigismunda*, the long novel by Cervantes discussed in Chapter 57. The quotations and the incidents referred to in this chapter come from Book III of the *Persiles*.

6. The story of Miguel's journey to Rome in the train of Monsignor Aquaviva

was first put out by Navarrete in 1819 (see Appendix 3), on the ground that in 1569 Cervantes was writing home from there for the certificate of *limpieza de sangre* (i.e., "purity of blood," free of Jewish or Moorish taint) required at that time of any aspirant to a career in the Church and presumably to employment by Aquaviva. In 1840, however, an official document was found in the archives at Siamancas which indicted "one Miguel de Cervantes" *in absentia* for inflicting "certain wounds" on Don Antonio de Sigura, a resident of Madrid, and condemned him to the loss of his right hand and banishment for ten years. This was reported in Morán's 1863 biography on the assumption that this was the young Cervantes of the Latin School and that he had in fact fled to Rome as a fugitive from justice. Some biographers have shrugged this story off as unproved (Miguel de Cervantes being a common name), while others insist that it is fully corroborated by certain passages in Cervantes' works. There is no dispute over the assumption that Cervantes made the journey to Rome by land through Barcelona, Provence and the Piedmont, as recounted in the *Persiles*.

Chapter 9

1. The fractured Italian spoken here by Spanish soldiers translates as: "Get ready, landlord; come here, you rascal; bring the meatballs, the chicken, and the macaroni." This and other quotations in the chapter come from Cervantes' novel *The Glass Licentiate*.

2. Marie Henri Beyle (1783–1842), the French novelist who wrote under the name of Stendhal, spent a number of years in Milan and his love of Italy was reflected in his novel *La Chartreuse de Parme*.

3. The passage about Lucca is from Chapter 19, Book III of the *Persiles*.

4. Torquato Tasso (1544–1595) was the greatest Italian poet of the late Renaissance and author of the epic *Jerusalem Liberated* (*Gerusalemme liberata*) published in 1575. He was a son of the poet Bernardo Tasso mentioned in Chapter 10, Note 7.

5. Juan Ruiz, Archpriest of Hita, was probably born in Alcalá near the end of the thirteenth century and he died in prison about the middle of the fourteenth. He is remembered for his satirical poem *Book of Good Love* (*Libro de buen amor*), published in 1330 and compared to Chaucer's work for the gaiety and lustiness displayed in those of his verses which have survived.

Chapter 10

1. The formidable Spanish *tercio* was a military formation originated by the Great Captain, Gonzalo Fernández de Córdoba (1453–1515), and perfected during his successful military campaigns in Granada and Italy. A *tercio* comprised about 3,000 men organized in a dozen or more companies incorporating pikemen for defense against cavalry and arquebusiers for unprecedented firepower, all protected by more armor than that of the archers of the past, although not so much as to hamper mobility. As a result Spanish infantry dominated European battlefields for a hundred years.

2. The *Maestre de Campo* commanded the *tercio* with the help of company captains and ensigns. This title was used for field commanders until after the Thirty Years War of the seventeenth century, when the *tercio* was replaced in Europe by the infantry regiment commanded by a colonel.

3. In 1557 Spanish forces besieged St. Quentin and won a great victory over the French army which sought to lift the siege. The Escorial (Note 1, Chapter 3) was built to commemorate the victory.

4. The Alpujarras are the mountains of Granada to which rebellious Moriscos (converted Moors) retreated defiantly.

5. This refers to the second revolt of the Moriscos (1568–70).

6. A native of the district of Alcarria, in which both Guadalajara and Alcalá de Henares are situated. The quotation is from the *Quixote*, Part One, Chapter 39.

7. Bernardo Tasso (1493–1569), father of Torquato Tasso (see Note 4, Chapter 9), was the author of a heroic poem *L'Amidgi* based on the *Amadís de Gaula*, the Spanish novel of knight-errantry.

8. Luigi Pulci (1431–87), poet and companion of Lorenzo de Medici, wrote the heroic-comic poem *Morgante Maggiori* as his major work.

9. Giovanni Boccaccio (1313–1375), writer and humanist, one of the great figures in European literature, is best known for the hundred stories of the *Decameron* (1349–51). One of his successors in that field was Masuccio Salernitano (Masuccio from Salerno), who wrote and recited notably licentious *novellas* printed in 1476.

10. Marcantonio Colonna, an Italian general of the famous Colonna family, was given command of the Pope's twelve galleys in 1570.

11. Juan Andrea Doria (1466–1560), soldier of fortune and the greatest admiral of his time, was appointed in his early forties to command the Genoese galleys which served under various Italian princes, the Pope, Francis I of France, and finally the Emperor Charles V. In 1528 Doria established the republic of Genoa under the protection of the Emperor.

12. Don Juan de Austria (1545–78), natural son of Charles V by a German lady, Barbara Blumberg, was brought into the Palace by his half-brother, Philip II, made a soldier, and given command in Granada. When the League was organized the Italian Colonna, the Genoese Doria, and the Venetian Zeno all claimed the supreme command and none would serve under any of the others. Philip II resolved the difficulty by appointing Don Juan, who outranked them all.

Chapter 11

1. The Sieur de Brantôme was the French Ambassador in Madrid and the author of famous memoirs.

2. The *Mandrache* at Genoa was an artificial harbor.

3. Don García de Toledo (1514–78) commanded the Spanish and allied naval forces which took the North African fortress of Peñon de Vélez in September, 1564. He was replaced as the Spanish Captain-General of the Sea by Don Juan and was living in retirement in Italy, forced out by the League politics described in Note 12 of Chapter 10.

Chapter 12

1. Not to be taken literally. Homer's Phaeacians lived under King Alcinous on the fabulous island of Scheria, at the extreme western limit of the earth. The ancient name of Corfu was Corcyra.

2. The speech here attributed to Cervantes was so reported by Castañeda in his deposition of March 17, 1578 supporting a petition for aid in ransoming Miguel. (See Chapter 18.)

3. There is some ambiguity about Cervantes' post *en el lugar del esquife* (in the place or area of the skiff or longboat). Some translators have put him on the quarterdeck, others in the longboat in the water, where such boats sometimes functioned in a sea fight. The most reasonable assumption is that the boat was

carried on deck and that a squad of soldiers was stationed in that area, whether or not the boat had been off-loaded into the water in preparation for battle.

4. Naval battles at the time of Lepanto were conducted mostly by ramming, grappling and boarding operations and were usually decided by soldiers fighting hand-to-hand on the decks after preliminary exchanges of gunfire between ships' batteries.

5. Don Juan had the ram on his galley cut short to improve the field of fire of his bow guns and in particular to facilitate plunging fire directed at the hulls of the Turkish vessels. Presumably other captains did likewise and we can envisage soldiers advancing along the stump of the ram as a boarding party stormed an enemy vessel. The reference to "archery" may be a reminder that Turkish troops of the time were still using bows and arrows.

6. This quotation is part of Don Quixote's famous discourse on arms versus letters. (See Note 4 to Chapter 8.)

7. These verses are quoted from the letter in tercets which Cervantes addressed to Mateo Vázquez from Algiers. (See Note 2, Chapter 21.)

Chapter 13

1. Saint Teresa's *Heavenly Mansions or the Inner Castle* (*Las moradas o castillo interior*), published in Salamanca in 1588, is regarded as one of the greatest Spanish mystical works. (For Teresa see Chapter 5, Note 1; for Ignatius, Chapter 3, Note 3.)

2. Don Álvaro de Bazán, Marquis of Santa Cruz (1526–88) was the "never defeated" Spanish admiral who won a number of victories in the Mediterranean, as indicated in the text.

Chapter 14

1. Don Manuel Ponce de León was mentioned in Part Two of the *Quixote*, Chapter 17, in connection with the adventure of the lions. The story comes from an old ballad and was used by several later poets, including Robert Browning in *The Glove*.

2. A Spanish fleet captured the island of Djerba (Los Gelves) in October 1559 as a preliminary to an attack on Tripoli, but the fleet and garrison were surprised by the Turks in March 1560, when the second Duke of Alba was killed and some 10,000 Christians taken prisoner.

3. The "captive" tells his story in Part One of the *Quixote*, Chapter 39.

4. Alexander Farnese, Duke of Parma (1545–92), was a grandson of Charles V and son of Margaret of Parma (1522–86), the Emperor's natural daughter, who governed the Netherlands as his regent (1559–66).

5. Cervantes' pastoral novel *La Galatea* is discussed in Chapter 26.

6. The treaty establishing the Christian League stipulated that the Captain-General (Don Juan) would not fly any personal banner but only that of the League.

Chapter 15

1. The Duke of Sessa (1585–1635), former Governor of Milan, was attached to Don Juan as indicated in the text, and later commanded the Spanish forces in Naples and Sicily. For his grandfather, the Great Captain, see Note 1 of Chapter 10.

2. The *agnusdéi*, derived from the Latin for "Lamb of God" (*Agnus Déi*), was a reliquary worn around the neck, especially by women.

3. Lorenzo van der Hámen, a Spanish writer of Flemish origin, wrote a book about Don Juan published in Madrid in 1627.

4. Charles V captured La Goleta and Tunis in 1535.

5. Lofraso's book, on which the curate commented in Chapter 6 of Part One of the *Quixote*, was published in Barcelona in 1573.

6. Jacobo Sannazaro (1458–1530), a Neapolitan of Spanish origin, wrote *La Arcadia*, first of the pastoral novels combining prose and verse. It was published in Naples in 1504, and a Spanish translation appeared in Toledo in 1549.

Chapter 16

1. An ancient place called *Parthenope* after the Siren of that name was the site of *Neapolis* (Naples), founded in pre-Roman times.

2. The verses in this chapter are quoted from Cervantes' long poem *Journey to Parnassus*, discussed in Chapter 52. Its title is often abbreviated to *Parnassus*.

Chapter 17

1. This marks the first major step in the career of Antonio Pérez as confidential secretary to Philip II. He appeared in Chapter 8 when his father left the impudent lad in the Royal Secretariat.

2. Mateo Vázquez (1542–91) played the role of loyal secretary to Philip II from 1573, when he left the service of Cardinal Espinosa for that of the King, after several years as page and secretary to the Cardinal. He was Miguel's boyhood friend in Chapter 3.

Chapter 18

1. The *pie de amigo* was an iron collar around the neck, fitted with a sharp point that forced the wearer to keep his head up, used on prisoners when being whipped or publicly humiliated.

2. Taken from Act III of Cervantes' play *Life in Algiers*.

Chapter 19

1. Quoted from Act III of Cervantes' play *The Prisoners of Algiers*.

2. Padre Diego de Haedo published his *History and Topography of Algiers* (*Historia y topografía de Argel*) in Valladolid in 1612.

3. Cristóbal de Villalón is thought to have written *Turkish Journey* (*Viaje de Turquía*), incorporating an account of his long captivity among the Turks, which was not printed until 1905.

4. The *Cruzada*, or Crusade Fund, was instituted by Ferdinand and Isabella to help finance the expulsion of the Moors from Spain, after which it was extended in theory to North Africa, and in the sixteenth century it became a source of royal revenue. Funds were raised for this purpose by the sale to the population at large of "bulls" or indulgences peddled all over the country by clerics and minor officials.

5. The cave is supposed to have been located about six miles east of the city.

Chapter 20

1. The Duke of Alba (1507–82), Grandee of Spain and third Duke of the powerful house of Alvarez de Toledo, was one of the famous generals of Charles

V in the wars with France and at Mühlberg. Under Philip II he served for a time as Viceroy of the Netherlands and was noted for the ruthlessness of his policies and for harsh discipline.

2. These verses are quoted from Act II of Cervantes' play *The Prisons of Algiers* and referred to in Chapter 54.

Chapter 21

1. The storm about to break upon Antonio Pérez in 1578 was the discovery by Philip II that his trusted confidential secretary had been plotting with the Princess of Eboli over the Portuguese succession and against Don Juan and the Duke of Alba over policy in the Netherlands. He was also accused of selling state secrets and conspiring to murder Don Juan's secretary Escobedo. Cardinal Granvelle and Juan de Idiáquez were summoned by the King and the Princess and Pérez immediately taken into custody, the Princess in the Pastrana Palace and Pérez in jail, where he was held for some years. Under torture Pérez finally confessed to the murder plot but he escaped and fled to Aragón, eventually to England and France, where he spent the rest of his life (d. 1611) maligning King Philip and reputedly selling state secrets to the British and French.

2. The rhymed letter to Mateo Vázquez was discovered in 1863 in the archives of the Altamira family.

Chapter 22

1. The expedition to Mostagán in 1541 was an attempt by Charles V to capture Algiers. It ended in disaster due to a terrific gale.

2. *The Gallant Spaniard* was the title of one of Cervantes' plays.

Chapter 23

1. These were the books the Glass Licentiate carried with him into Italy as recounted in Cervantes' novel of that name. *Hours of Our Lady*, also known as *The Little Office of the Blessed Virgin*, was composed in the ninth century and during the Middle Ages, with various additions, it became the *Book of Hours* (the eight hours of the liturgical day). This breviary for the laity lent itself to private devotions and was in use throughout Europe, originally in Latin, later in other languages.

Chapter 24

1. As recounted in Book VI, lines 466–486, of Homer's *Iliad*.

2. Reported by Haedo in his *History*. (See Chapter 19, Note 2.)

3. The currencies in which Cervantes' ransom was raised are discussed in Appendix 2.

4. The *aspero* was a small silver coin in general circulation throughout the Middle East.

5. Some of the "many paragraphs" are to be found in Part Two of the *Quixote*, Chapter 58.

Chapter 25

1. Cristóbal de Moura (1538–1613) was a Portuguese nobleman who served Philip II during the annexation of Portugal and throughout the last years of the

reign. He reputedly blocked the claim of the Duchess of Braganza to the Portuguese throne by "burying her husband in gold."

2. Luis Gálvez de Montalvo (1546–91) produced *Phillida's Shepherd* (*El pastor de Fílida*), a pastoral novel which appeared in Madrid in 1582. Both Lope de Vega and Cervantes praised him fulsomely, Cervantes in a sonnet and via the curate in Chapter 6 of Part One of the *Quixote*.

3. The *quintilla*, as its name implies, is a strophe of five verses, usually of eight syllables, sometimes of eleven (endecasyllables), in various rhyming patterns.

4. Juan Rufo Gutiérrez (1547–1620) served under Don Juan in Granada and at Lepanto. His *Austriada* was published in 1584.

5. The endecasyllable is a verse of eleven syllables in various combinations of accents, most commonly on the second, sixth and tenth syllables.

Chapter 26

1. Betis is the ancient name for the Guadalquivir River; the Ebro and the Pisuerga are also Spanish rivers. The Sebeto, named for the nymph Sebetis, is the present-day Formello River in Italy. The "daring boy" was Phaeton, who undertook to drive the chariot of the sun god Helios, failed to control the horses, and fell into the River Po when Zeus hurled a thunderbolt at him.

2. He recalled it by repeating it in the *Parnassus*, Chapter 4.

3. For more about Góngora see Note 1 to Chapter 39.

4. Terceira, the largest island of the Azores, was the scene of a resounding Spanish naval victory over the French in 1582. Cervantes was not involved in any way, but his brother Rodrigo participated as a soldier in Figueroa's *tercio* and was rewarded for bravery. Lope de Vega was also with the fleet, young as he was, but in what capacity is not indicated.

5. Lope de Vega Carpio (1562–1635), whose rivalry with Cervantes is a major theme of this biography, was of humble origin, his father having been an embroiderer by trade. He was born in Madrid, educated by the Theatin monks, and sent to Alcalá for further study under the protection of the Bishop of Avila. The biography is full of references to him and his activities, all part of his history. (Navarro Ledesma contemplated writing a biography of Lope de Vega.)

6. Pedro de Padilla's poems were much admired by Lope de Vega and Cervantes but are no longer regarded as outstanding. They were published in various collections of poetry between 1580 and 1585, after which Padilla disappeared into a Carmelite convent.

7. Ana Franca, or Ana Villafranca, has been identified as the beautiful but illiterate daughter of a wool merchant, brought up as half-relative half-servant by her uncle, a minor law officer in Madrid. In 1580 she was married off at the age of seventeen to another small-time wool merchant, said to be a rough-mannered Asturian. She bore him a daughter and three years later (1584) her love affair with Cervantes produced another daughter. The child was christened Isabel Rodriguez de Villafranca and was thus accepted initially as legitimate offspring of the marriage. She was later known as Isabel de Saavedra.

Chapter 27

1. The *Universal Chronicle* (*Crónica General*) of King Alfonso "the Learned" (*el Sabio*) of Castile (1221–84) was an early history of Spain reduced to prose from the even earlier epic poems. It was followed by many other Chronicles.

2. Numantia, a city on the Douro River near present-day Soria, was the

stronghold of one of the Spanish tribes battling the Romans. After a protracted siege it fell to Scipio Africanus in 133 B.C.

3. This quotation and others in the chapter are from the Prologue to *Eight Plays*.

4. Pedro Láynez (1538/42?–1584) is less well known for his lyric poetry than he is for the praises of Lope de Vega and Cervantes. He was one of Cervantes' great friends and his widow is mentioned in Chapter 47 as living in the same apartment house as the Cervantes family.

5. Vicente Espinel (1550–1644) got his benefice in Ronda and became musical director for the Bishop of Madrid. His picaresque novel about Squire Marcus was published in 1618. (See Chapter 53, Note 3.)

6. Zoilus, a Greek writer of about the fourth century B.C., was celebrated for his asperity toward Homer and thus became the prototype of a captious and malignant critic.

Chapter 28

1. Quoted from the Prologue to the *Persiles*.

2. *Mais* are maravedis in vulgar parlance now obsolete. The *aranzada* is a land measure which in Castile equals 44.7 square meters or 53.46 square yards.

Chapter 29

1. The Ateneo Club was organized in Madrid in 1820 by a group of young writers and intellectuals. It still exists after an interval during the Civil War. Navarro Ledesma was a member.

2. The phrase about the foot in the stirrup was used by Cervantes in the Prologue to the *Persiles*, where he attributed it to an old ballad.

3. Quoted from the Prologue to Cervantes' *Eight Plays*.

4. The *Santa Hermandad* (Holy Brotherhood) was established in 1476 as a militia organized to enforce law and order on the highways and in the countryside, but by the sixteenth century it had degenerated into a rather corrupt local constabulary, as is made clear in various references to its personnel in the *Quixote*.

Chapter 30

1. The *tarasca* was originally the figure of a serpent or dragon representing the Devil, borne in religious processions on Corpus Christi Day to symbolize the triumph of Christ over evil. In the course of time it was accompanied by other symbols, such as the *Nabolena*.

2. Don Quixote visited the Gentleman of the Green Coat in Chapter 18 of Part Two of the *Quixote*.

3. Lupercio Leonardo de Argensola (1559–1613) served the Count of Lemos in Madrid and Naples, as recounted in the text. He translated some Odes of Horace and his own poetry was influenced by Horace, Virgil, and the Italian poets.

4. Esteban de Garibay y Zamallos (1525–99) was librarian to Philip II as well as author of the *Chronicle* described in the text, which was published in Antwerp in 1571.

5. For Benito Arias Montano see Chapter 1, Note 8. He was commissioned by Philip II to supervise publication of the *Biblia Políglota de Amberes*, the magnificent Royal Antwerp edition of the Polyglot Bible printed by Plantin in eight

volumes between 1569 and 1573. It was based on the *Complutense* (Chapter 1, Note 7) with some revisions and additions.

Chapter 31

1. The *arroba* as a liquid measure equalled 4.263 gallons.

2. The exploits of the seven sons of Ecija were recorded in ballads, folklore and the extensive romantic literature about Spanish banditry in the early nineteenth century. In fact the "sons" constituted a large band of outlaws, 400 or 500 strong, recruited from guerillas and army deserters during the post-Napoleonic era. They terrorized the countryside of Andalusia and created havoc in the small towns until they were finally rounded up and their leaders hanged in Seville when the *Guarda Civil* was organized in 1844.

3. Fernán Gonzalez was a tenth-century Castilian knight mentioned in Part One of the *Quixote*, Chapter 49. Epic poems sung by troubadours recorded exploits of the heroes of the time in a cycle culminating in the *Cantar de mio Cid*, written in 1140. The Cid, personification of Castilian martial spirit, was Rodrigo Diaz de Vivar, who died in Valencia in 1109. His surname *mio Cid* was an Arabic term for "my lord."

Chapter 32

1. The noblemen who served in the fleet were expected to meet their own expenses and support their retainers.

2. The "knight on the wall" refers to the legend of Guzmán el Bueno, an ancestor of Medina-Sidonia. He was besieged in Tarifa in the thirteenth century by rebel forces who held his son captive and when they threatened to kill the boy unless he surrendered Guzmán threw his dagger down from the battlements in a gesture of defiance.

3. The "blood of Austria" is that of the Duke of Parma, grandson of the Emperor Charles V of the House of Austria. The Duke had succeeded Don Juan as Regent in Flanders. (See Chapter 14, Note 4.)

4. The *Batrachomyomachy* was an ancient Greek mock-heroic poem recounting battles between frogs and mice.

Chapter 33

1. The *seguidilla* is a verse form of seven lines used for lively Spanish songs and dances, extended to mean the accompanying dances.

2. The "father of the poetry of saints" was Gonzalo de Berceo (1195–1264), the first known Castilian poet, who wrote lives of several saints of the Rioja area.

3. The Master of Avila was St. John of the Cross (1542–91), who studied with the Jesuits and entered the Carmelite Order in 1563. Saint Teresa recruited him to help reform the Order and he founded a number of monasteries of the Discalced Carmelites. He is regarded as the great passionate mystic poet of Spain whose works include the famous *Dark Night of the Soul* (*Noche oscura*).

4. For Herrera see Chapter 3, Note 10. As indicated in the text he wrote in fields other than lyric poetry.

5. Juan de Mal Lara (1524–71) was a writer of no great distinction whose life was devoted to study and teaching. He settled in Seville and opened the School of Humanities and Grammar (*Escuela de Humanidades y Gramática*) in which many writers of the "Seville school" were enrolled.

6. At that time all trade between Spain and America was channeled through Seville, where the Guadalquivir River provided a port for oceangoing vessels.

7. In Cervantes' novel *Rinconete and Cortadillo*, which deals with the adventures of two country lads in the Sevillian underworld, this patio serves as headquarters for the criminals recruited, controlled and protected by Monipodio.

8. This ballad is one of those in lighter vein attributed to Cervantes in Chapter 40.

9. *Celestina* was the title commonly given to *The Tragicomedy of Calixto and Melibea,* a play written in 1498 by Fernando de Rojas (1476–1541) while studying law in Salamanca. The first of some thirty editions of this famous work was printed in Burgos in 1499. Its relevance here lies in the central character of Celestina, who became accepted in Spain as the prototype of a procuress, more or less as Boccaccio's Pandarus became her male counterpart.

10. These were two bravos who served Monipodio in the manner of "enforcers" in a present-day criminal organization.

Chapter 34

1. The Contract House (*Casa de Contratación*) was founded in 1503 to regulate trade relations with America, of which Seville had a monopoly. It was a combination Bureau of Foreign Commerce, Bureau of Navigation and Court of Maritime Law. Its banking functions and archives were eventually taken over by the Bank of the Indies in Seville.

2. The *arroba* here is a dry weight of a little over twenty-five pounds.

3. To go through the hills of Úbeda, where in fact there are no hills, is a figure of speech denoting something incongruous or wide of the mark.

4. These are references to the mystical writings of St. John of the Cross.

Chapter 35

1. Corregidors were established by the Catholic Kings to bring the municipalities under central control. They were appointed by the Crown, had judicial functions, and headed municipal administrations otherwise staffed by locally elected officials—mayors, aldermen, etc.

2. *El Tempranillo* (Early Bird) José María (1805–33) was an Andalusian bandit chief operating against travelers in the Sierra Morena whose deeds were romanticized in ballad and folklore and by English and French travelers to Spain in the post-Napoleonic period. He was captured in 1831 and pardoned by the King on condition he join the fight against bandits.

Chapter 36

1. The canon was addressing the meeting of the Chapter of Seville held in the courtyard of Los Olmos on July 8, 1401 to consider the state of the old mosque consecrated as a Christian church after the reconquest of Seville in 1248; it is now the Cathedral.

2. The Knight was of course Saint Ignatius Loyola, the Man was Juan de Avila, the Apostle of Andalusia, while the Woman was Saint Teresa. The giant Caraculiambro is mentioned in Chapter 1 of the *Quixote*.

3. The term *auto* was applied from the thirteenth century to theatrical performances, religious or profane, staged in churches, by strolling players, or in the processions of Corpus Christi. In the Middle Ages they began to be called "mysteries" or "moralities", and from the second half of the sixteenth century

those with religious themes were termed *autos sacramentales.* The outstanding characteristic of the sixteenth-century *auto* was its use of allegory, presenting ideas or symbols such as Lust or Lechery. Many were anonymous and many were written by the dramatists of the day.

4. In Cervantes' exemplary novel *The Illustrious Kitchen-maid* the tuna fisheries of Zahara are described as the ultimate in roguery and the school through which a master rogue must pass to deserve that title. The fisheries of Zahara are also mentioned in Chapter 39 as notably profitable for the Duke of Medina-Sidonia.

5. These are some of the names Don Quixote applied to the imaginary leaders of the armies of sheep he encountered in Chapter 18 of Part One of the *Quixote.*

Chapter 37

1. For a description of the royal tithes and sales taxes see Appendix 2.

2. The Nasrid dynasty of Moorish rulers of Granada expired with the final surrender of that Kingdom to Spanish forces in 1492.

Chapter 38

1. *Caciquismo* is the exercise of political influence in a town or district by a *cacique.* This Carib word for an Indian chief, borrowed by the Spanish and still current, denotes a man who wields excessive political and administrative power over a constituency; in other words, a party or political boss.

2. For the "compounding" of sales taxes see Appendix 2.

3. This applies to the tithes, of which one-third went to the Crown, the rest to the Church. See Appendix 2.

Chapter 39

1. Luis de Góngora y Argote (1561–1627) enjoyed a benefice from the Cathedral of Cordova, became Royal Chaplain to Philip III, and spent much time at Court. He was one of the leading poets of his day, ranking with Lope de Vega, Quevedo and Cervantes, and he inaugurated a baroque lyric style labelled "Gongorism." He never published his works, which circulated in manuscript and were printed in various collections with or without his permission, until *Poetical Works of the Spanish Homer* were put together the year he died. For the purposes of this biography he is mentioned most often in connection with his acid wit in satirical verses, particularly those in which he pursued a feud with Lope de Vega.

2. The sack of Rome occurred in 1527 when the Emperor sent his troops to counter the Holy League of Cognac (1526) in which Pope Clement united France and some of the Italian principalities. The unpaid, starving and mutinous German and Spanish soldiers under the Constable of Bourbon got out of hand, marched on Rome and sacked the Eternal City, committing unimaginable atrocities.

Chapter 40

1. The *Account* is a sketch thought to have been written by Cristóbal de Chaves. An interlude on the subject, dubiously attributed to Cervantes, is also in existence. "Gallardo" was Bartolemé José Gallardo y Blanco (1776–1852), erudite author of a bibliography of "rare and curious" books published after his death.

2. Mateo Alemán (1547–?) was educated at Salamanca and Alcalá and is best known for his *Adventures and Life of the Rogue Guzmán de Alfarache,* commonly referred to as the *Pícaro* (*Rogue*). The first part of this work was published in Madrid in 1599 and went through several editions. After a spurious Second Part appeared the genuine one was published in Lisbon in 1604 with the addition of *Panorama of Human Life* (*Atalaya de la vida humana*) to the title. The *Pícaro* was an important addition to the wave of picaresque literature inaugurated in *Lazarillo de Tormes* by an unknown author, published in 1554 to introduce an element of reality into a literature dominated by the extravagances of knight-errantry and the pious rhetoric of the mystics.

Chapter 41

1. The *Libro de descripción de veraderos retratos de ilustres y memorables varones* was published in Seville in 1599 by Francisco Pacheco (1571–1654) and republished in Madrid in 1870 as *Book of Portraits* (*Libro de retratos*).

2. Francisco Gómez de Quevedo y Villegas (1580–1645) came of a good family and was educated by the Jesuits and at Alcalá (1596–1600). Courtier, politician, poet, prose writer, and first-class satirist, he was one of Spain's greatest literary figures, already famous in Cervantes' time. He was the first prominent Spaniard to introduce round instead of rectangular spectacles and was painted by Valásquez in a pair of them. This gave rise to the punning term for this type of spectacles, known as *quevedos*, i.e., *que vedo* or "what I see". The family motto also contained a pun: "I am he who stopped—*el que vedó*—the Moors."

3. Juan de la Cueva (1550–1610), mentioned in Chapter 39 as one of the Sevillian poets who satirized the Duke of Medina, turned out nostalgic verses during a stay in Mexico and returned to Seville to write epic, romantic and satirical poems, but was most famous as a dramatist, notable author of *The Defamer* (*El infamador*), legendary antecedent of *Don Juan.*

4. *Lazarillo de Tormes* was mentioned in Chapter 40, Note 2 as the original picaresque figure in Spanish literature of the period.

5. A slightly different version has it that the widowed Ana Franca turned tavernkeeper to support herself and two daughters. Cervantes' pious sister Magdalena, who had kept an eye on them, regarded this as no situation in which to bring up her brother's child. Magdalena took her over, therefore, more or less as household help, while Cervantes undertook to acknowledge paternity and give his name (Saavedra) to the girl after the death of her mother.

6. In Seville and a few other cities an *Asistente* was appointed to carry out the functions for which Corregidors were responsible in other communities. For Corregidors, see Chapter 35, Note 1.

7. The term *polaquería* derives from the Polaco Party that governed Spain for a time (1850–54) in a despotic, arbitrary, and undemocratic fashion.

8. Lyceus was a surname for Apollo, traced to the Greek word for "light" but popularly connected with the word for "wolf".

9. The query as to "who is this female who comes from nowhere?" is answered by a graduate "in military law." She will repay with a "peace be with you" and the King "will pray for us."

Chapter 42

1. Fernando Niño de Guevara (1541–1609), son of a noble family, studied at Salamanca and advanced rapidly through the hierarchy. He was named Cardinal in 1596 and Philip III appointed him Inquisitor General in 1599. In 1600 he

arranged a famous *auto-de-fé* attended by royalty and soon after became Archbishop of Seville.

2. Archer Milton Huntington (1870–1955) of New York devoted his life to Hispanic studies and founded the Hispanic Society of America in 1904. He left many treasures to the Society's museum in New York.

3. Two of these titles eventually appeared among Cervantes' *Exemplary Novels*, but the authorship of *The Pretended Aunt* has not been established beyond dispute.

4. Juan de Arguijo (1560–1623) was a wealthy nobleman who wrote exquisite sonnets and played Maecenas in Seville. He was the Alderman who impoverished himself to entertain the Marquesa de Denia in Chapter 41.

5. The *décima*, sometimes called an *espinel* because Vicente Espinel (Chapter 27, Note 5) is credited with inventing it, is a strophe of ten lines of octosyllables in a special rhyming pattern. It is also sometimes referred to as double *quintillas*.

6. Lope de Vega's *Dragontea* was a topical poem about the life and death of Sir Francis Drake.

7. The Battle of the Dunes on the Belgian coast was won by Count Maurice of Nassau and a force of Huguenots in the course of recapturing Rheinburg, which the Spanish had taken in 1598 and lost in 1601.

Chapter 43

1. John Bowle (1725–88) was an erudite English Hispanophile who published an English translation of the *Quixote* and a biography of Cervantes in 1781.

2. Lucius was the young Roman hero of the *Metamorphosis* by Lucius Apuleius (125–?), a rambling episodic novel also known as *The Golden Ass*. The hero was transformed by magic into an ass and in one episode (Book III) he was captured by bandits.

3. The reference here is to the sententious "apothegms" which appear in Cervantes' exemplary novel *The Glass Licentiate*.

4. Diego Hurtado de Mendoza (1504–73), a nobleman from Granada, had a distinguished career under Charles V and Philip II as ambassador, soldier and writer.

Chapter 44

1. Francisco Gómez de Sandoval y Rojas (1550–1625) was a grandson of St. Francis Borgia (Chapter 3, Note 4). As Marquis of Denia he had gained great ascendancy over the mind of the heir apparent and as soon as Philip II died his son dismissed his father's advisers and placed the whole of his government in the hands of the Marquis, soon named Duke of Lerma. He immediately appointed relatives and friends to high office, isolated Philip III, and for over twenty years was the real ruler of Spain. He has been condemned by historians for private avarice and public extravagance.

2. The Duke of Lerma owned a good deal of property in and around Valladolid.

Chapter 45

1. Sebastián Covarrubias y Orozco (1539–1613) was a Toledan cleric famous for his *Thesaurus of the Castilian or Spanish Language* (1611), a classical dictionary often resorted to and quoted by students of sixteenth-century Spain.

2. Fray Andrés Pérez is believed to have written under the pen-name of López

de Ubeda the picaresque novel commonly known as *The Naughty Justina* (*La Pícara Justina*) which appeared in Medina in 1605.

3. "Setting the Thames on fire" is a less than literal but nevertheless accurate translation of the Spanish *venir pegando* (making an impression).

Chapter 46

1. The phrase *toros y cañas* translates literally as "bulls and reeds", referring to various forms of bullfighting as practiced in Spain and to a form of jousting or spearing the ring from horseback in which reeds or canes replaced the spears of former times.

Chapter 48

1. Cardinal Bernardo Sandoval y Rojas was an uncle of the Duke of Lerma, who appointed him Cardinal Archbishop of Toledo, a see said at the time to be worth 300,000 ducats a year.

Chapter 49

1. For Lupercio Argensola see Chapter 30, Note 3.

Chapter 51

1. Quevedo's *History of the life of the Rascal Called Don Pablos, Example for Vagabonds and Mirror for Scoundrels*, also known by the short title *History of the Great Scoundrel* (*Historia del Gran Tacaño*), was published in Zaragoza in 1626, although probably written earlier. It is clever, cruel and coarse in its account of the adventures of Pablos, including some at Alcalá.

Chapter 52

1. Authorship of the *Moral Letter to Fabius* (*Epístola moral a Fabio*), one of Spain's finest poems, has been attributed in the past to various sixteenth-century writers and is regarded by some critics as anonymous. In 1875, however, the erudite bibliophile Adolfo de Castro y Rossi argued on the basis of a manuscript in the Columbus Library of the Cathedral of Seville that it was the work of one Captain Andrés Fernández de Andrada, about whom little is known.

2. The *Parnassus* of Cervantes is believed to have been modelled on the *Viaggio di Parnaso* published in 1582 by Cesare Caporali from Perugia, who was otherwise undistinguished.

3. Cyllenius was a surname for Hermes, who was born in a cave on Mount Cyllene in Arcadia. Among his attributes Hermes was the god of eloquence.

4. Quevedo was club-footed.

5. Delius was one of the surnames of Apollo; he and his sister Artemis were born on the island of Delos.

6. Thymbraeus was another surname of Apollo, derived from his celebrated temple at Thymbra in the Troad area where Troy stood.

7. Vials of perfume were packed in cotton wool for shipment.

Chapter 53

1. Angélica, who rejected Orlando for Medoro, was the heroine of Ariosto's *Orlando furioso*. (See Chapter 7, Note 1.)

2. Prester John and the Emperor of Trapisonda were named in the Prologue to Part One of the *Quixote*.

3. For Espinel and his book see Chapter 27, Note 5.

Chapter 54

1. The phrase about Cervantes' shortcomings as a poet is from his Prologue to *Eight Plays*.

2. Alonso Ramón (Remón) (1565–1632) wrote more than two hundred plays, was praised in the *Parnassus* and mentioned in the Prologue to *Eight Plays*. He was also chronicler of the Order of Mercy but his history of the Order was criticized and rewritten by Tirso de Molina.

3. This passage about Lope de Vega is from Cervantes' Prologue to *Eight Plays*.

4. Fray Gabriel Téllez (1571–1648), who used the pen-name of Tirso de Molina, studied at Alcalá and lived in Toledo for a time. He was much involved in the literary life of the period and among his many works were a number of plays on religious subjects.

5. For Villalón and his book about Turkey see Chapter 19, Note 3.

6. The "real" Mañara was Miguel de Mañara Vicentele de Leca (1626–79), a Sevillian nobleman who spent a dissolute life in his youth until, according to legend, a voice warned him of death while he was on his way to an assignation. He turned respectable and married, but after the premature death of his wife he retired to a convent of unshod Carmelites. Returning to Seville, he joined the Brotherhood of Charity, became its Superior in 1662, and among many good works founded a House of Charity for the poor.

Chapter 55

1. Cervantes was presumably writing on demy sheets of paper (15 × 20 inches in size), and they wrote small in those days. Paper was expensive.

2. The phrase about "thirty thousand volumes" comes from Part Two of the *Quixote*, Chapter 16.

3. This famous picture by Velásquez is now in the Prado in Madrid.

4. The "fish Nicolás," referred to in Chapter 52 of Part Two of the *Quixote*, was a legendary swimmer of sixteenth-century Sicily. An account of his feats was published in Barcelona in 1608.

5. This lunatic appeared in Chapter 1 of Part Two of the *Quixote*.

Chapter 56

1. Don Juan Manuel (1282–1349?) was a nephew of King Alfonso "the Learned." He fought in the wars of the time but devoted most of his life to letters. One of his philosophical works was the *Book of the Knight and the Squire* (*Libro del caballero y del escudero*), which is probably what Navarro Ledesma had in mind.

2. "The adventure that distressed Don Quixote," etc., is actually the title of Chapter 44 of Part Two of the *Quixote*.

Chapter 57

1. Heliodorus was a Greek writer of extravagant romances in the third century A.D. His *Aethiopica* about an Ethiopian princess was translated into Castilian

Spanish as *Teágenes y Caricles* by Francisco de Vergara, Professor of Greek at Alcalá, whose version has been lost but was probably available to Cervantes, who drew from it inspiration for his *Persiles.*

2. Gerardus Mercator was the Latin name of the Flemish geographer Gerhard Kramer, who devised the "Mercator projection." This maps the earth with parallels of longitude equidistant through their length. One consequence is that land areas are distorted, more enlarged on the map the greater their distance from the equator, so that on a map of the world Greenland, for example, appears equal in area to all of South America.

3. Garcilaso de la Vega's sonnet *The Gentle Lament of Two Shepherds*, on which the poetry contest in Chapter 53 was based, is paraphrased here and in the following paragraph.

Chapter 58

1. The symptom of thirst suggests that Cervantes was suffering from diabetes in addition to his cardiac insufficiency and consequent dropsy.

2. This famous passage is from the Prologue to the *Persiles.*

Index

ABOUT THE AUTHOR

Francisco Navarro Ledesma was born in 1869, son of wealthy parents who managed to lose all their money before they died. His father was from Toledo and his mother was born in Madrid. The son studied in Madrid, where he earned his Doctorate in Philosophy and Literature. After the university he started working as an archivist and librarian in Alcalá and was head of the Toledo Museum. As the family fortunes deteriorated he was forced to find employment as a journalist and he also taught school, first in Toledo and then in Madrid. He labored tirelessly to keep afloat a debt-ridden household which insisted on maintaining an apartment in Madrid, a house in Toledo, another in a neighboring village and a country house on one of their farm properties. At the age of thirty-six, on a tour of Old Castile to work up material for a series of articles on ancient Spanish cities, he injured his leg in a fall. By then a well-known writer, he was provided with a special train to take him to Madrid, where he died in 1905 of a blood clot occasioned by his injury.

Working under great pressure he wrote innumerable newspaper and magazine articles and editorials on every conceivable subject—politics, literature, art criticism, poetry, or anything else required. He edited school books on both foreign and Spanish literature, wrote speeches for the Prime Minister, and finally was just able to finish his one major work, a biography of Cervantes entitled *El ingenioso hidalgo Miguel de Cervantes Saavedra*. This was a fantastic success when published in 1905 on the tercentenary of the first appearance of *Don Quixote*, and it is still in print.

As a talented and prolific writer who never had time to prune or polish his work, Navarro Ledesma possessed qualities which might have developed into something important had he not died just when he was achieving sufficient renown and financial independence to dedicate himself at last to serious writing. He had several other biographies planned, including one on Lope de Vega and others on Quevedo and the Archpriest of Hita.